Johnson & Johnson

Child Development Publications

The First Wondrous Year

Your Toddler

The Preschooler (forthcoming)

Editorial Advisory Board

Kathryn Barnard, R.N., Ph.D.
Professor of Nursing, Department of Maternal Child Nursing, School of Nursing, University of Washington.

Bettye M. Caldwell, Ph.D.
Professor of Education, Director, Center for Child Development and Education, College of Education, University of Arkansas at Little Rock.

Michael Lewis, Ph.D.
Senior Scientist and Director, The Infant Laboratory, Educational Testing Service, and Clinical Professor of Pediatric Psychology at Babies Hospital, Columbia University Medical Center.

Sally Provence, M.D.
Professor of Pediatrics and Director, Child Development Unit of Child Study Center, Yale University School of Medicine.

Brian Sutton-Smith, Ph.D.
Professor of Education and Folklore, University of Pennsylvania.

Staff

Editorial

General Editors
Richard A. Chase, M.D.
Richard R. Rubin, Ph.D.

Text Editor
Nancy McGrath

Photo Editors
Bill Parsons
Henrietta Brackman

Photography
Bill Parsons

Photo Coordinator
Donna Rae Moore

Prints by
Image Photo Labs
New York City

Design

Concepts
D. Michael Williams

Graphics
Ronan Kearney

Illustrations
Mary Ellen Crowley
Irene Trivas

Project Coordinator
Mary I. Flaherty

Parent-Child Network
Donna Rae Moore, Director
Susan G. Doering, Ph.D.
John J. Fisher III, M.A.
Doris Welcher, Ph.D.

Ages One and Two

Your Toddler

Ages One and Two

Your Toddler

Text by

Richard R. Rubin, Ph.D.

John J. Fisher III, M.A.

Susan G. Doering, Ph.D.

Photographs by

Bill Parsons

Johnson & Johnson

Child Development Publications

MACMILLAN PUBLISHING CO., INC.
NEW YORK

COLLIER MACMILLAN PUBLISHERS
LONDON

Macmillan Publishing Co., Inc.
866 Third Avenue, New York, N.Y. 10022
Collier Macmillan Canada, Ltd.

Library of Congress Cataloging in Publication Data
Rubin, Richard R
  Your toddler.
  At head of title: Ages One and Two.
  Bibliography: p.
  Includes index.
   1. Child development. 2. Children—Management.
I. Fisher, John J., joint author. II. Doering, Susan
G., joint author. III. Parsons, Bill. IV. Johnson
and Johnson, inc.   Child Development Publications.
V. Title.
HQ767.9.R8   1980   649′.122   80-152
ISBN 0-02-559550-4

10 9 8 7 6 5 4 3 2 1

Printed in the United States of America

Contents

Foreword

During the past ten years we have witnessed a sudden, enormous growth in scientific knowledge about early childhood. And this growing body of information has led to a tremendous rise in the amount of child-rearing information available to parents. Books, training classes, newspaper columns, pamphlets, magazines, and even television shows for parents are appearing in ever increasing numbers.

Not only is child-care information for parents increasingly available, but more and more parents are actively seeking out such information. The most popular child-rearing book, Dr. Benjamin Spock's *Baby and Child Care,* is now the best-selling nonfiction book of all time except for the Bible. Thirty million copies of Dr. Spock's book have been sold, and it has been translated into twenty-six languages. Other books about child care have also achieved a wide readership. A recent survey shows that almost every parent reads at least one such book, and that nearly half of all parents read three or more.

Parents read books on child rearing in part because they lack other reliable sources of practical advice about babies and children. Young parents are more alone today than ever before. Grandmothers and other relatives, who used to be our foremost child-care authorities, often live too far away to be available with advice or help or support when it is needed. Besides, attitudes toward child rearing are changing so fast— partly as a result of our new understanding of the capacities of young children—that our parents' notions often don't sit well with us anyway.

Increasingly, parents today are turning to books on child rearing not just for advice on practical issues of child care but also for information about how children develop and how parents can contribute to this development. In fact, these issues have become the *main* interest of many readers.

There Are No Simple Formulas

The parents who consult child-rearing manuals today are hoping to answer their questions, to calm their doubts, and, above all, to learn how they can realize their hopes for their children. With such a weight of need and expectation, in the face of a mounting tide of sometimes contradictory advice, it's natural that many parents wish they could find somewhere a "Ten Commandments of Child Rearing" to see them through the trials of daily life with their toddler, and to help them stimulate his or her intellectual, social, and psychological development at the same time. But of course *nobody* has the final answer. As the well-known child-development authority Eda LeShan has said, "We parents are lucky to have so many people spend so much time studying childhood. But we need to understand that there will never be simple rules for anything as complex and exciting as raising children."

Our Aim in Creating This Child Development Guide

There is no single, simple approach that will provide quick relief for the doubts or solid support for the dreams we all have about our children. When you live with a child you know him or her better than anyone else possibly could, and you're in a better position than any "expert" to discover what works and what doesn't, for the child and for you.

Our aim in creating this guide is twofold. First, we want to build your confidence as a parent. We want to help you see that it's better to make your child-rearing decision "by the baby" than "by the book." When you decide what to do by carefully observing the behavior of *your* child, you can feel secure that you are making the soundest possible decisions. Then you can relax and trust your instincts.

Of course, confidence and competence go hand in hand. So our second aim is to provide you with the information you need to do your job well. We will be telling you how very young children develop, and how you can work with the normal growth processes to help your child develop happily to his or her fullest potential. Our advice and information don't come in the form of formulas and final answers, however. Instead, this guide is intended to equip you to develop a child-rearing style all your own that's tailored to the needs of your individual child.

How We Created This Guide

This guide represents the joint efforts of a team of specialists in early childhood. This group includes behavioral scientists, physicians, writers, graphic designers, and photographers, as well as an extensive network of parents. Together we have created a resource that we believe is unique. The guide contains

the very best and latest information on development during toddlerhood, gleaned both from a study of scientific reports, books, and articles and from research carried out specifically for this guide.

The graphic format of the guide is designed to make the information it contains as attractive, easy to find, and easy to read as possible. The large number of illustrations is intended to show the many changes toddlers go through, and the enormous variety that's possible even among children who are all about the same age. Pictures are often more effective than words in communicating just how different from each other toddlers really are in their appearance, in their skills, in their interests, and in their overall style of development.

The contribution that our network of parents has made to this guide is truly invaluable. By talking with us about the issues that interested and concerned them most, these parents helped us decide in the first place what topics we should write about. When the project got underway they provided insights and examples to enrich our discussion of each topic we took up. They welcomed us into their homes so we could photograph them and their children. And they commented upon and criticized our positions and helped us improve our writing.

This guide is organized into three main sections. In the first section we discuss the process of growth and development during toddlerhood, taking up the new skills a child acquires during this period, and considering important areas of practical concern such as sleeping, eating, learning to talk, and toilet training.

In the second section of the guide we discuss a toddler's behavior and personality. We concentrate on issues of discipline, pointing out that it's essential to understand the capacities, needs, and limitations of a child in a particular stage of development in order to discipline him or her effectively and lovingly. In this section we also discuss the toddler's special relationship with his or her father, and how he or she relates to other children, including brothers, sisters, and friends. And we talk about how toddlers relate to other adults who may care for them, as well. In this section of the guide we also discuss special situations with which many parents of toddlers must deal. These special situations include being a single parent, moving to a new home, taking a toddler to the hospital, and adjusting to a toddler's handicap.

The third section of our guide is called "Play and Playthings." The attention we devote to this topic reflects our fundamental belief that play is a major avenue for learning—and for loving—during early childhood. This section is full of ideas that will help you encourage your toddler's learning in a warm and loving way.

This guide is addressed to both mothers and fathers. The *you* that we use throughout refers to both parents, or to either one. In referring to the toddler we have made a point of alternating between *she* and *he,* trying to make shifts between these pronouns in a way that

will not be too jarring to you as you read. It has become almost standard in recent books on child rearing to lament the exclusive use of the masculine pronoun in other books about children, and then to go ahead and continue the practice, explaining that there is no single word in the English language that means "he or she." This policy seems to us to beg the question. We hope you will find our solution to the dilemma at least as appealing. After all, toddlers do come in both sexes.

It's clear that this guide is not a medical handbook for parents. We think books such as Dr. Spock's *Baby and Child Care* adequately meet that need. What we have tried to provide instead is the best, most recent information about what toddlers are capable of and what they like, together with suggestions for putting this information to work in a natural, relaxed, enjoyable way. Our goal is your toddler's happy growth and development.

Richard R. Rubin, Ph.D.
John J. Fisher III, M.A.
Susan G. Doering, Ph.D.

PART ONE
Growth and Development

1
Introduction

The span of about eighteen months after a child's first birthday is often referred to as toddlerhood. It is a period of tremendous growth. During this relatively short period your child will acquire an impressive array of new abilities. Some of these are basically physical skills: beginning to walk and to run, to climb, to stand up and sit down, to jump, and to turn around in a circle. He will also learn to throw a ball and to pick up even very small objects quickly and easily. In fact, he will develop enough skill with his hands to begin feeding himself—even if he's pretty messy at first—and to help dress himself, at least with items of clothing that are easy to get on.

Other new abilities of toddlerhood are primarily cognitive, or intellectual. Children begin talking during

this year, and before long they are able to carry on real conversations. Talking is a powerful tool for broadening their experience in numerous ways. It enables them to begin to understand their own moods, by naming them, and it markedly broadens and increases the pleasure of play. You'll notice that once your toddler can use words, he'll begin to play imaginatively, enjoying make-believe or "let's pretend" games.

During the second year toddlers start to acquire a sense of themselves as individuals, too, and to have special feelings about their own possessions. That's why "Me do it" and "Mine" may become your toddler's watchwords when he learns to talk.

At the same time, your child's love for you is growing, too. Now that he can walk and say a few words, he's likely to rush to the door when you arrive home from work, calling your name and holding out his arms so that you'll pick him up and hug him. He also takes great pride in sharing his discoveries and his successes with you. When the two of you are out for a walk together, he'll bring you the dandelion he's just picked as if it were a matchless gift. And when he manages to build a tower of blocks by himself for the first time, he'll shout for you to come see what he's accomplished. Your toddler also shows how special you are to him when he begins to imitate the things he sees you do. When you clean, he may follow you from room to room, dragging a dingy cloth and earnestly "dusting" everything he can reach. When you get dressed in the morning, he may drape one of your old ties (or scarves) about his neck and parade around beaming.

Toddlerhood Is a Transitional Stage of Development
Taken together, the expanded awareness and emerging skills of toddlerhood make your child seem like much more of a real person. And he *is* considerably more capable and independent than he was as a baby. Despite the tremendous growth of this period, however, toddlerhood is in many ways a transitional stage of development. The toddler has left behind forever the total dependency of babyhood, but it will be many months before he'll be able to do much for himself without the guidance of a caring adult. In a way, toddlerhood has a lot in common with adolescence, which stands between childhood and adulthood. And like

a teenager, a toddler often shows the frustration he feels with being "in-between."

During toddlerhood your child's reactions may often swing from one extreme to the other. Sometimes he may be determined to assert his independence, fighting against your control and help at every turn with shouts of "No!" or "Me do it!" But other times he'll collapse into a state of total dependence, clinging to you, panicking when you leave him for even a moment, and whining for you to do things for him that in his securer moods he's been able to do by himself for several months.

So, as important as it is for you to enjoy and encourage the signs of your toddler's growing independence, you can't escape the fact that his skills, his understanding, and his experience are still very limited. And these limitations are of a kind that will make him in some ways even more demanding of you now than he was as a baby. His memory is so short that he'll probably make the same mistakes and get himself into the same jams day after day—and cry for you to rescue him every time. Because he can't think ahead—can't conceive of the future, in fact—he's often unable to wait patiently even for the thirty seconds it takes you to pour him some apple juice; he may fuss at you all the while you're trying to get something ready to please him. In fact, some days his behavior may drive you up a wall. Children are probably more thoroughly exasperating (as well as more vivid, spontaneous, affectionate, unselfconscious, and utterly charming) during toddlerhood than at any other age.

Obviously, it won't do to treat such ambitious and spirited creatures the way we treat helpless, docile babies. And just as obviously, it won't do to expect them to measure up to the standards we've set for the behavior of, say, five-year-olds, who have at least a basic understanding of such concepts as *right* and *wrong* and *yours* and *mine,* and who can remember from one day to the next what's been forbidden.

For toddlers we have to come up with an approach that's in between: flexible enough and at the same time definite enough, indulgent enough and at the same time firm enough to suit the very specific needs, abilities, and limitations of these very special, but complicated and contradictory small people. This is not by any means an easy job.

What Do Successful Parents Do?

Research scientists have lately been trying to find out why some parents deal with toddlerhood better than others. Burton White and colleagues of his at Harvard University recently studied the families of thirty-nine young children in an intensive way, to see if mothers who seemed to be doing a particularly good job with their toddlers had any traits in common. And Dr. White found that these mothers did share a number of important characteristics.

They created an environment that was safe and stimulating for their children, rather than forcing their

Research shows that essential ingredients of successful parenting during toddlerhood include providing the child with protection, security, and love.

toddlers to live in a completely adult-oriented home.

They were able to live with the inconsistencies that toddlers normally show.

They were generally accepting of their toddlers' behavior, letting them try most things they wanted. But they were willing to set limits calmly and firmly when this was necessary.

They acted as learning consultants to their toddlers, offering suggestions, answering questions, and providing assistance "on the fly" when it was needed. They did not spend long periods of time in formal efforts to teach their children.

Clearly these mothers had found an approach to their toddlers that suited the children's transitional state of development. They managed to encourage their toddlers' independence while also providing their children with protection, security, and love. As a result, the children of these mothers appeared to be unusually

*The most successful parents
also manage to encourage
their toddler's independence
—letting him try most
things he wants to do.*

competent and well adjusted. Dr. White found that when these children were three years old, they showed a wide range of abilities in greater or more impressive ways than an average three-year-old. Their language was advanced, and they showed a remarkable ability to anticipate consequences, to deal with abstractions, to make interesting associations, and to plan and carry out complicated tasks. They were unusually competent in the way they related to other people, as well. They could use adults as a resource after first determining that a job was too difficult to manage on their own. They showed pride in their personal accomplishments. And

they could effectively express both affection and mild annoyance with adults and with other children.

In the broadest possible terms, this is what all parents of toddlers should aim for—and what this guide is intended to help you do in your own family. In the following pages we will try to give you specific information about the developing needs and capacities of toddlers, and along the way we will also suggest some specific steps you can take to make this difficult, but also wonderful and extremely important time as rewarding as possible, not only for your child but also for yourself.

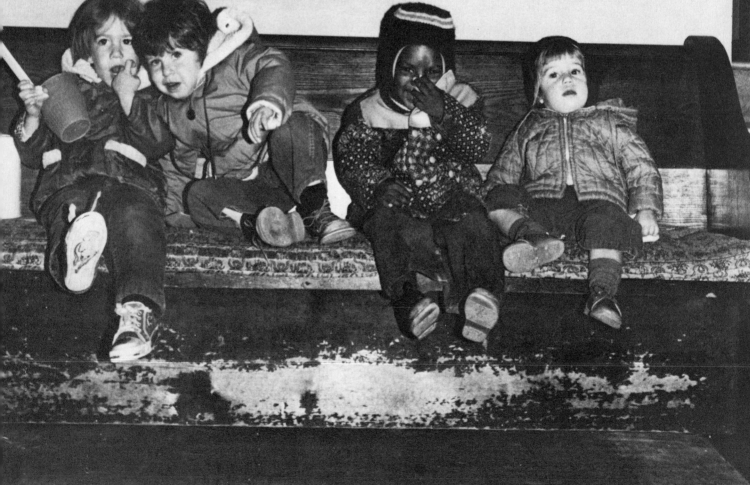

2
What Is a Toddler?

Indeed, just what *is* a toddler?

We can say that a toddler (at least as presented in this book) is a person between the ages of twelve and approximately thirty months. But beyond that, we can't say anything that will hold true for all toddlers always. So here we'd like to present a pictorial overview of the wonderful variety represented by toddlerhood, to suggest a few of the many different delights and conflicts and comedies of this most splendid time of life.

What is a toddler?

> *I am part of the sun as my eye is part*
> *of me. That I am part of the earth my*
> *feet know perfectly, and my blood is part*
> *of the sea. My soul knows that I am*
> *part of the human race, my soul is an*
> *organic part of the great human race, as*
> *my spirit is part of my nation. In my*
> *very own self, I am part of my family.*
> > —D. H. Lawrence

> *Will you, won't you, will you, won't you,*
> *Will you join the dance?*
> > —Lewis Carroll

Now that this growth and expansion has started I am unable to stop it. I feel so strangely released. I feel no boundaries within myself, no walls, no fears. Nothing holds me back from adventure.

　　　　　　　　　　　　—Anais Nin

Life is a long discovery, isn't it?
You only get your wisdom bit by bit.
—Hilaire Belloc

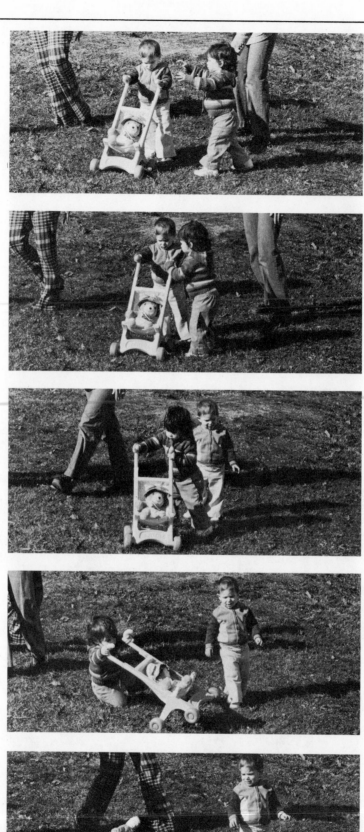

There's nobody else in the world, and the world was made for me.

—A. A. Milne

Ignobly vain, and impotently great.
        —Alexander Pope

*I dote on myself, there is a lot of me and all
so luscious.*
                                        —Walt Whitman

I will be the gladdest thing under the sun!
I will touch a hundred flowers and not pick one.
                    —Edna St. Vincent Millay

I am a parcel of vain strivings tied
By a chance bond together
—Henry David Thoreau

Can I see another's woe
And not be in sorrow too?
Can I see another's grief
And not seek for kind relief?
—William Blake

I live not in myself,
but become portion of
that around me.
  —Lord Byron

I run, I run, I am gather'd to thy heart.
                    —Alice Meynell

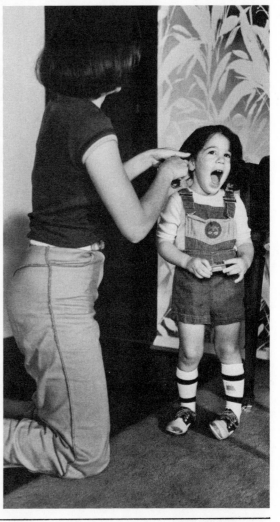

And I have loved you so long,
Delighting in your company.
                    —Anonymous

The face is the mirror of the mind.
        —St. Jerome

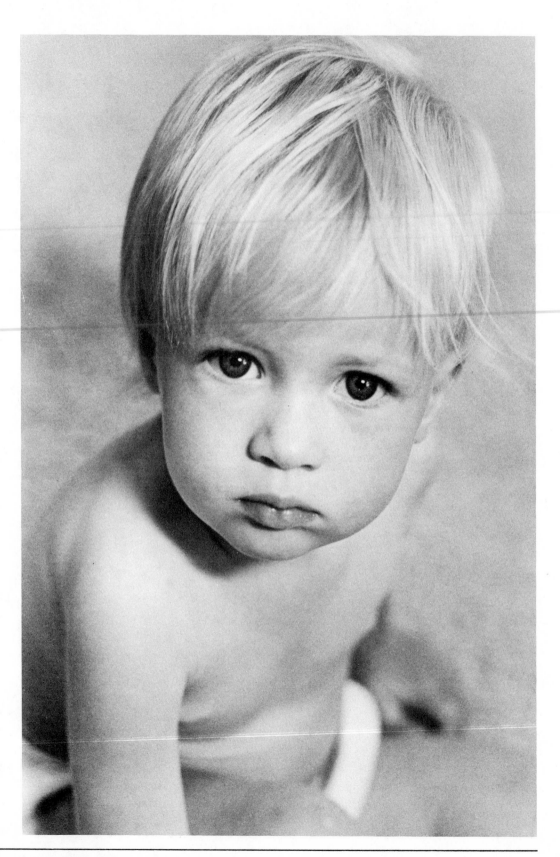

i spill my bright incalculable soul.
                    —e. e. cummings

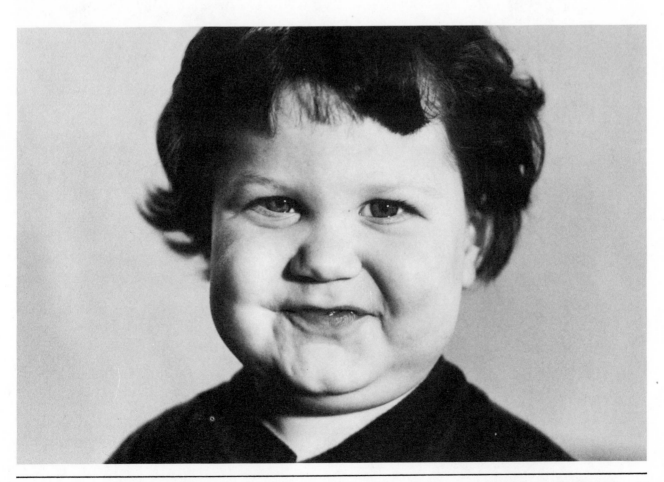

Child of pure, unclouded brow
  And dreaming eyes of wonder!
    —Lewis Carroll

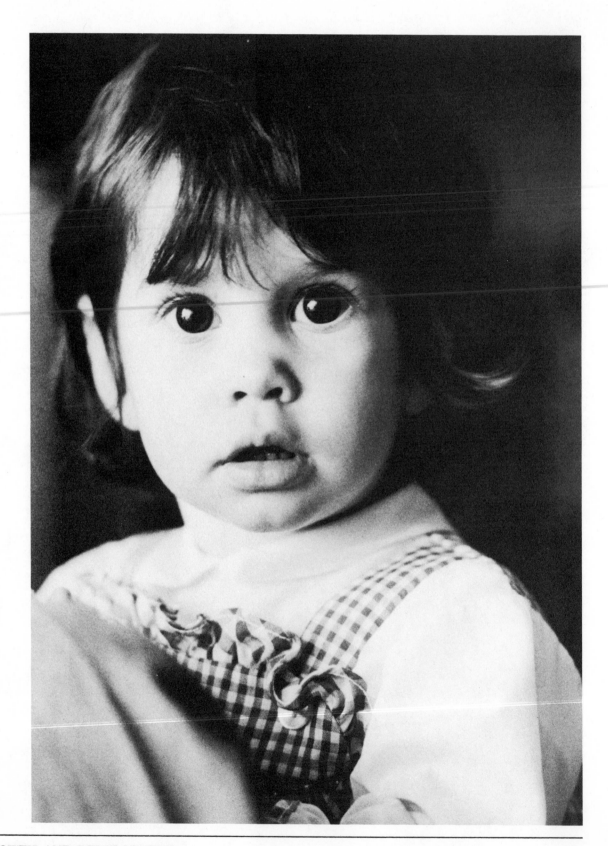

*Sometimes, looking deep into the eyes of a
child, you are conscious of meeting a glance
full of wisdom. The child has known nothing
yet but love and beauty. . . . And yet you meet
this wonderful look that tells you in a
moment more than all the years of experience
have seemed to teach.*
                                        —Hildegarde Hawthorne

...and parents talk about their toddlers.

"Over the past year my child has grown into her own person. I guess that's why our friendship has blossomed so."

*"Having him near gives me this feeling of peace and
warmth way down inside."*

*"My daughter's an amazing bundle of renewable energy—
always exploring something. And always learning. She
inspires me to grow."*

"She's both my reason and my excuse to be playful."

"Sometimes she stops whatever she's doing and looks as if something inside is making her almost burst with happiness."

"My daughter makes me aware of my own strengths; and, I hate to admit it, my shortcomings. She makes me look at myself more closely."

"I find myself staring at his face, loving its openness and softness. He reflects such purity."

"My kid reminds me not to take myself so seriously."

"I find myself rediscovering the world as my toddler discovers it the first time."

"She's always bringing me things she finds, and says, 'Mommy, see, mommy, see.' She draws my attention to lovely details."

"It feels wonderful to have a family. I feel this connection
with the future, this marriage with so much of life."

3
Your Toddler Is an Individual

When we're introduced to a child for the first time, one of the first questions we're likely to ask is "How old is she?" We tend to think of behavior in terms of age, so how old a child is tells us a lot about what to expect of her. Throughout this guide we will refer to the age at which particular developments tend to occur in the life of a toddler. But we will point out time and again that different children reach important milestones at different times, and that no two children experience a particular developmental stage in exactly the same way. So you don't need to worry if your toddler differs somewhat from the descriptions we provide; variation will be the rule rather than the exception.

Differences in Personality Among Toddlers

There are countless examples of ways in which toddlers the same age differ from each other. But there's one area of difference which is especially important: personality. "Personality" describes the basic style of an individual's behavior. We're all familiar with the fact that adults differ in personality. We know some adults who are sunny, cheerful, and optimistic under almost all circumstances, and others who are exactly the opposite, individuals who see the negative side of nearly every situation. We know adults who are very outgoing and others who are very shy; adults who are highly emotional and others who are extremely reserved. We simply take it for granted that each adult has a distinctive personality; that's obvious. But recently evidence has been accumulating that suggests something that's not so obvious: important differences in basic behavioral style are present at birth.

One group of scientists, including two psychiatrists, Drs. Stella Chess and Alexander Thomas, and a pediatrician, Dr. Herbert Birch, studied a large group of children from birth until they were ten years old. They asked the parents of these children about the children's typical reactions to routine caretaking activities such as sleeping, eating, dressing, eliminating, and moving about. And after tabulating all of this information, they discovered that the children differed a great deal from their very first hours of life. Even more important, they found that, in a basic way, the differences that were observable between babies in the early weeks tended to persist as the children grew up.

From the very beginning there were substantial differences among the children Dr. Chess and her colleagues studied in general *mood,* in *activity level,* and in *adaptability* to changes in routine. The scientists also found that there were large differences among the children in the *intensity* of their responses, in their *tendency to approach or withdraw* from new experiences, in their *persistence,* and in their *distractibility.* The children also varied in the *regularity* of their natural sleeping and eating cycles, and in their *sensitivity.* A child's characteristic behavior in all of these nine categories is what Dr. Chess and her colleagues call *temperament.* We might think of temperament as the inborn factor in a child's developing personality.

Dr. Chess found that a surprisingly large number of the young children she studied showed a consistent overall pattern in their basic style of behavior. Most of them were what is often called "easy." These youngsters took things pretty much as they came and were comfortable most of the time. They were regular, accepted new experiences easily, had mild reactions to hunger and to other discomforts, and adjusted smoothly to changes in day-to-day routines.

Dr. Chess and her colleagues identified another group of children who could be described as "slow to warm up." These youngsters shared many of the characteristics of easy children, but they needed more time to get comfortable in new situations. When handled sensitively, these children soon overcame their initial shyness.

A third group of children Dr. Chess and her colleagues studied was distinguished by the trouble they seemed to have getting comfortable and staying comfortable. The children who fell into this category could be called "difficult," because life often seemed so hard for them—and for their parents. These children expressed their likes (and much more often their dislikes) in no uncertain terms; they generally reacted forcefully and negatively to new experiences and to even minor changes in routine; and they seemed to get hungry and sleepy without warning, and at completely irregular times during the day.

The Practical Importance of Personality Differences

The work of Dr. Chess and her colleagues seems to hold two important practical messages for parents. First, since your child brings a basic style of reacting

to life into the world with her, *you are not responsible for every aspect of your child's behavior*. For example, if her basic style is "difficult," she's bound to cry more than an "easy" child, no matter how much you do to make her comfortable. Second, *it's important to recognize your child's basic style,* and to take it into account when you deal with her. "Difficult" children, "slow to warm up" children, highly active children, persistent children, and even "easy" children all have special needs and sensitivities. When their basic style is recognized, respected, and taken into account, all children can develop happily and to their fullest potential.

Unfortunately, the issue isn't always as simple as this, in part, at least, because parents have their styles, too. When a toddler's style conflicts with the style of one or both of her parents, it's that much more difficult for all of them to get through this trying stage. It's hard for the parents to meet their toddler's needs without feeling they are making sacrifices. Still, hard or easy, doing your best to respect your toddler's basic style is really a practical necessity. If you don't, you'll probably find that you are fighting against the current throughout her entire childhood.

Of course, these messages have a special importance for the parents of a toddler whose basic style is "difficult." Every child has difficult days. And during certain stages of development—the period of toddlerhood when contrariness is especially common, for example— many children are uncomfortable a good bit of the time. But as we've said, some children seem to have a lot more than their share of difficulties and discomforts at nearly every age and stage of development. If your child is one of these, you probably know it. And if you're like the parents of many difficult children, you probably take more blame for your toddler's difficulties than you should. In fact, parents have a tendency to feel they've failed when nothing they try makes their child comfortable. Besides, a difficult child can drive even the sturdiest parents to distraction and to frustration. And frustration turns to anger, which almost inevitably gets turned against the child, at least occasionally. This only makes the parents feel worse about themselves. Sometimes it's hard to keep this in mind, but you should try: *if your child's basic style is difficult, it's not your fault; and it's not your toddler's fault, either.*

Parents of difficult children often say that the worst part is feeling that nothing they do makes a difference. Their toddler rarely gives much sign of responding to their efforts. The fact is, though, that parents *do* help by maintaining their patience with a difficult toddler, by being flexible in the way they respond to her needs, and by keeping the stress she feels to the lowest levels possible. They are helping her adjust to life at a pace that is not overwhelming to her. And by treating her with restraint and consideration, they are helping her learn how to handle frustration. If they can react to her this way consistently, she will gradually become more comfortable with both herself and the world she lives in, and will learn to respond to other people more easily, except at times of unusual stress.

You should respect and work with your toddler's basic behavioral style, but you can't change it, even though from time to time you may wish you could. It's important to love and enjoy your child for what she is. Difficult children are often also unusually active and lusty. They sometimes turn out to be especially perceptive and capable of unusual ranges and depths of feeling. So don't waste time trying to "correct" a difficult child's personal style. Concentrate on the things you can do something about: love, play, toys, talk, space for your toddler to try herself out in, and discipline; all of the things we discuss in this guide.

Differences Between Boys and Girls Appear Early in Life

Every child is an individual. But as most of us have noticed, girl toddlers seem to differ from boys the same age in some consistent ways. Scientists have taken a special interest in these differences, and they have devoted considerable effort to documenting some of them. They have found that, on the average, girls develop faster than boys. Girls walk, talk, and begin using the toilet or potty, for instance, a month or two before boys do.

By the time children are a year old or so, their toy preferences and play interests also tend to differ depending on their sex. In one study of thirteen-month-old toddlers, the girls tended to choose toys that involve fine-muscle coordination, such as a pegboard. They would usually sit on the floor and play quietly with some such small toy. The boys, on the other hand, would run around the room with their toys, banging them and using them vigorously. They would often take a toy lawn mower and roll it over the other toys. In addition, the little boys spent a lot of time examining doorknobs, lights, and covered electrical outlets.

Other studies show that as early as two years of age boys are more interested than girls are in wheeled toys, especially cars, while girls prefer dolls. By the time girls are two years old, these studies say, they are more sociable, more talkative, more compliant with adult demands, and more dependent upon adult approval than boys the same age, while there is strong evidence that boys this age are more aggressive.

These differences between girls and boys are striking because they correspond so closely with widely held beliefs about basic differences between males and females. But of course, no one would suggest that *all* boy toddlers are more aggressive than *all* girls the same age, or that any of the other frequently noticed differences we've mentioned apply to all children. In fact, there are many scientists who question the whole idea of widespread differences between the sexes. They claim that few, if any, differences exist, and that many popular beliefs about the psychological characteristics of the two sexes have little or no basis in fact. So the debate over whether boys and girls really tend to behave differently, and when the differences, if they exist, first appear, rages on, fueled by reports such as those of Dr. Berry Brazelton, the noted pediatrician, who says that he has observed differences in the behavior of boys and girls even when they are infants. (He has found that newborn boys are more likely to be vigorous and physically active, while newborn girls are more likely to be quietly observant of the sights and sounds around them.)

Differences in the Way Parents Relate to Boys and Girls

Do the differences between girls and boys that parents and scientists such as Dr. Brazelton have documented mean that there are inborn and even necessary differences in behavior between the sexes? The character of the differences and the fact that they appear so early in life might make us think so. But as Dr. Brazelton and others have pointed out, the parents' knowledge of the sex of their baby influences their treatment of the child from birth. So the differences that become increasingly clear from the first months of life may not really be inborn at all. As soon as a baby is born, our response to it is conditioned by the child's sex. We may get a blue blanket for a baby boy and a pink one for a baby girl. And we almost always choose a name that will clearly identify the child as a girl or a boy.

Other important differences in the way parents behave with girl babies and boy babies are less conscious, and less obvious, but they are no less important. Even in a hospital nursery, a skilled observer can tell from the way a mother handles her child whether it is a girl or a boy: girls are treated as if they are fragile, while boys are treated as if they are sturdy. This may be hard to believe, but studies have shown that mothers respond more quickly to the cries of their newborn daughters than they do to the cries of their newborn sons. And mothers touch their baby daughters more often than they do their infant sons, and talk to them more, as well.

After the first few months, there are even clearer differences between the way parents behave toward sons and the way they behave toward daughters, and inevitably these different parental attitudes have an influence on a child's behavior. Parents are constantly letting a child know whether he or she is acting appropriately, and their ideas about what's appropriate differ considerably according to the child's sex. Boys are generally granted the freedom to be assertive, to explore, to roughhouse, and to get dirty to a greater degree than girls. And they are discouraged from acting in ways that are considered unmasculine. A boy toddler may be admonished for his tears with a statement such as "Boys don't cry." And his interest in trying on his mother's shoes or putting on her lipstick or makeup is much less likely to be viewed as "cute" than the similar interests of girls his age.

Of course, young girls also receive messages about how they should behave. There is some evidence that parents restrict their daughters more than they do their sons when the children try to explore objects and learn about the physical world. And studies show that parents are likely to respond positively when a girl toddler asks for help, while a boy toddler is more likely to get a negative response or to be ignored, forcing him to solve the problem himself if he can. In addition, parents provide a different physical environment and different play materials for their daughters than for their sons.

A recent survey revealed how the parents of ninety-six children under the age of six furnished the rooms of their sons and daughters, including the toys they supplied. The boys' rooms contained a wide range of toys, representative of various adult occupations, while the girls' rooms almost invariably contained only dolls, dollhouses, and domestic objects. Toys such as wagons, boats, and buses were almost completely absent from the girls' rooms. Equally striking was the absence of baby dolls and toy domestic equipment from the boys' rooms.

Children's rooms represent a substantial part of their environment. And the content of their rooms determines the things boys and girls involve themselves with for amusement and instruction. The findings of this study make clear the extent to which boys are typically provided with objects that encourage activities directed away from the home—toward sports, cars, animals, and the military—while girls are given objects that encourage activities directed toward the home—keeping house and caring for children.

Helping Our Toddlers to Be Themselves

We can't eliminate *all* of the conscious and unconscious differences we create in the early environments of girls and boys, and few of us would even want to try. But many parents today want to reduce the pressure created by *rigid* sex-role stereotypes, such as those which dictate that males should *never* be gentle or females strong and aggressive. They want to give children of both sexes greater freedom than they themselves had as children to develop interests and ways of behaving that match their personalities. Increasingly, concerned parents are trying to make sure that their little girls are given an opportunity to be active—to climb and get dirty and take risks—and to play with cars and trucks if they want to. And they are trying to make sure that their little boys have a chance to express their nurturant feelings—by having dolls to hug and care for, for instance, if they choose to.

The books we read to our children can influence their development as powerfully as the toys and play opportunities we provide for them. Today, many children's books restrict girl characters to more passive and less exciting roles than boys and show mothers only in such activities as housekeeping and child care. But fortunately, this situation is changing. In response to a growing demand for materials that support the fullest possible development of an individual child's potential, there are many more books being published in which the girl characters are as brave, active, and clever as the boys, and where fathers are shown participating in the same domestic tasks as mothers.

Your toddler is different from every other toddler in the world. She doesn't look the same as anyone else, and she doesn't have exactly the same needs or interests or special strengths, either. When you learn to recognize and respect your toddler's own unique style, your job as a parent is easier and more rewarding. And your toddler's development is enhanced as well, because you are giving her the most effective support any child can receive: the freedom to be herself.

4
Feeding and Weaning

You will probably notice a big change in what goes on at mealtimes right around your toddler's first birthday. You become aware that his appetite seems a lot smaller than it was a few months ago, and you may begin to worry about whether he's eating enough. As a baby, he was always eager for the breast or bottle, and his mouth opened like a hungry bird's when you fed him his solids. Now he sometimes turns away, closing his mouth tightly as the spoon approaches, or disdainfully sweeps his finger foods off the high chair tray and squirms to get down. Your toddler's mealtimes are affected by two major changes during this period: smaller appetite and growing independence.

APPETITE AND NUTRITION

Smaller Appetite
Luckily, as your child grows, his appetite doesn't keep growing too. (If it did, he'd weigh 105 pounds by the time he went off to kindergarten.)

The size of a toddler's appetite doesn't depend on how big he is but on how *fast* he's growing—his growth rate. The charts on these pages show growth rates for average girls and boys in the first two and a half years of life. As you can see, the growth rate from birth to the first birthday is tremendous: babies double their birth weight by four or five months, and triple it in the next seven or eight months (by one year). So it's no wonder that at first infants seem to do nothing but eat.

But in the next year and a half, the growth rate slows way down; a toddler gains only six to eight pounds in the course of the next eighteen months. It stands to reason that his appetite should become smaller too. Some toddlers appear hardly to care about eating at all anymore; they're so busy practicing their new abilities to walk and explore. Others seem to want no more than a mouthful of each food they're offered. As one pediatrician put it: "The toddler's not indifferent to food, but to *too much* food." The amounts you try to serve him may be more than he wants or needs.

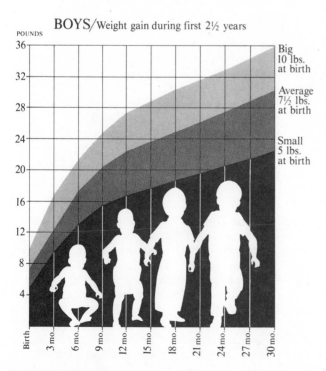

BOYS/Weight gain during first 2½ years

POUNDS

Big 10 lbs. at birth

Average 7½ lbs. at birth

Small 5 lbs. at birth

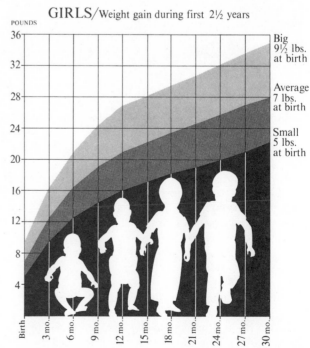

GIRLS/Weight gain during first 2½ years

POUNDS

Big 9½ lbs. at birth

Average 7 lbs. at birth

Small 5 lbs. at birth

habits are formed in the first few years and these habits are very hard to change later on. Take an adult, hooked on sugar-coated doughnuts for breakfast, and try to get him to switch completely to more nutritious whole-grain products. It's very difficult. But if you start your toddler off with whole-grain breads, he'll eat them happily. (Later, when he tries doughnuts for the first time, he'll probably wonder why people like them so much.)

What Is Good Nutrition?
A balanced diet, containing sufficient amounts of protein, vitamins, minerals, carbohydrates, and fats, is easy to provide if you know just a few basic facts about nutrition.

1. Proteins build the body. They build new tissues and cells and repair worn-out or injured tissues. Protein is particularly plentiful in milks, cheese, eggs, lean meat, beans, and nuts.
2. Vitamins help the body work right. Different vitamins occur in different foods, but most vitamins are found in milk, eggs, whole-grain cereals, breads, fresh vegetables, and fruits. If you eat a variety of foods, you should not need to use a vitamin supplement.
3. Minerals, such as iron and phosphorus, help build the body and keep it working right. Minerals are found in all unrefined foods—fruits, vegetables, meats, whole grains, eggs, milk—but some minerals are destroyed when grains are refined or bleached and when vegetables are cooked in water. So it's important to include raw and unrefined foods in your diet.
4. Carbohydrates (sugars and starches) give us energy. Carbohydrates are found in just about every food you can think of, but are especially concentrated in cakes, cookies, crackers, and other typical snack foods. Since the body converts excess carbohydrates into fat, it's best to limit sweet and starchy foods.
5. Fats are an energy store. Foods particularly high in fats are butter, margarine, cream, salad dressing, and desserts made with these ingredients. Since excess fat leads to overweight, even in babies and toddlers, it's important to limit these foods too.

How can you tell how much he needs? He'll let you know. No toddler yet has deliberately starved himself to death when nutritious food was available! Take a look at your toddler. Are his eyes bright? Is his flesh solid, his color good? Is he animated and usually happy? Is he on the go from dawn till bedtime? Then he's not starving. If he has the energy to exhaust *you* day after day, you can be sure that he's getting enough food.

Why Good Nutrition?
Eating nutritious food during the toddler years is doubly important. It's important because you want your child to be healthy and strong right now. But it's important in the long run, too, because our lifelong eating

Getting Your Toddler to Eat Nutritious Foods
How do you go about getting nutritious, well-balanced meals into your toddler? An interesting experiment, done many years ago by Dr. Clara Davis, showed that young children, if given the chance, will choose to eat a healthful diet. Dr. Davis offered a wide variety of nutritious foods to a group of babies between eight and ten months old and let them decide completely what and how much they wanted to eat. She found that, over time, these babies chose a combination of foods that

any nutritionist would call a well-balanced diet. Each *meal* wasn't balanced, and often several meals in a row were not, but over several days each baby's choices added up to excellent nutrition.

This means that if you serve your toddler a variety of nutritious foods, several times a day, and then let him decide what he wants and how much, in the long run he will feed himself a well-balanced diet. This doesn't mean that you don't need to know about nutrition. You do, because "toddler's choice" only works if a variety of nutritious foods are made available, and you have to choose, prepare, and present these foods.

Further, it doesn't work if *non*nutritious foods (junk foods) are available to your child. A child who can fill up on pretzels or doughnuts at 10:00 A.M. isn't likely to pay much attention to his trayful of nutritious choices at lunchtime.

It is also important to make nutritious food available more often than three times per day. Busy, active toddlers can't fill all their energy needs on only three meals in twenty-four hours. They need refueling more often than adults, and that means minimeals, or snacks.

Many mothers object to snacks because they think that snacks are junk food. It's true that when adults snack, they often grab convenience foods, such as potato chips, cookies, doughnuts, or a piece of coffee cake. But snacks can just as well consist of nutritious foods, though having these handy may take a little more planning. Pieces of fruit, a celery stalk or a carrot, a few spoonfuls of yogurt, whole-grain crackers, slices of hard-boiled egg or a chunk of cheese—all are very healthful and would be handy for snacks. Combine two and add a cup of fruit juice (*not* fruit drink or soda pop), and you have a nutritious minimeal for your busy toddler.

Another surefire way to get a variety of healthful foods into your toddler is very simple: *you* eat them. What are your eating habits? Your toddler admires you and copies everything else you do. Naturally he'll copy the way you eat as well. When you sit down for that midmorning cup of coffee, have one of his snacks instead of the slice of pie left over from dinner. (If you keep this up you'll find that you look better and feel better, though we can't promise that your energy level will reach that of your toddler!)

At both mealtimes and snack times, serve your toddler very small amounts of each food. That way he won't feel stuffed (and rebellious) in advance, as he might faced with a heaping bowlful. He'll let you know when he wants seconds, by pointing and reaching before he's very verbal, and with a loud and definite "Moah!" later on in his second year.

Don't urge a toddler to clean his plate or to eat "just a little bit more for Mommy." Remember: he knows best how much he needs, and any pressure to eat beyond that point could make him rebel and possibly eat even *less* in the long run. Forcing extra food can also lead to obesity, which we will discuss more fully later.

Keep meals pleasant and your toddler's attitude toward food will be positive. If you introduce punishments, anger, and rigid rules at mealtimes, your toddler will lose his appetite completely. Wouldn't you?

Rewards shouldn't be part of meals either. Saying, "You can't have your cake until you eat all that broccoli," teaches a child to prize junk food above all other foods and to see nutritious foods as unpleasant. Actually you want your toddler to learn just the opposite.

We're not suggesting that you insist, "Eat up all your cake or you can't have any broccoli." We're simply suggesting that food shouldn't be connected with punishment *or* reward. It should just be presented several times a day, without pressures, and your hungry toddler left to eat what he needs.

Substitutions

There is no one food or type of food that your child must have to remain healthy. Variety is what's important, and substitutes are always available. It is the common experience of many parents that small children and vegetables don't seem to get along too well. But luckily, vegetables and fruits have roughly the same nutritional contents. So if your toddler detests vegetables, just offer him more fruits. If he's not pushed, he'll acquire a taste for most vegetables eventually.

But don't forget to try raw vegetables. Many small children are happy to crunch on a sliver of green pepper or will eat a slice of a carrot with delight, while they won't go near the mushy cooked versions. Since raw vegetables are more nutritious anyway, you've come out ahead. And have you tried vegetable juice? How about vegetable soups?

A few children of this age turn against milk and won't touch the stuff for a while. Don't worry if this happens. Although milk is a convenient way to meet several nutritional needs at once, there are others. Try cubes of cheddar cheese or spoonfuls of yogurt or cottage cheese. Slip milk into your toddler's soups, scrambled eggs, mashed potatoes or mashed bananas, and he won't even notice.

Too Much of a Good Thing

He doesn't need as much milk as he did during his first year anyway. A pint (sixteen ounces) of milk per day is enough for the average toddler. If your child drinks a lot more than this, he is getting too many calories from milk and probably failing to eat enough of the other foods he needs to stay healthy. This eating habit could lead to obesity as well as poor health. So help him cut down. Does he take most of his milk from

bottles? Maybe he just needs lots of sucking. Give him fruit juice or water in his bottles and offer milk only in his cup. This is a good time for him to learn to like skim milk, too, but change over slowly, by adding skim to whole milk in gradually increasing proportions.

Everybody used to think that a fat baby was a healthy baby and that a chubby toddler was cute. Not anymore. Doctors tell us that fat babies and toddlers are a lot less healthy than normal children. Furthermore, we now know that overweight toddlers are very unlikely to lose their "baby fat" as they grow up. Instead they are destined to be the fat adolescents and adults of the future. Scientists have discovered that when a young child eats too much and becomes overweight, there are actual changes in his physiology and metabolism that will make him have a problem with weight for the rest of his life.

It's easier to prevent obesity than to treat it after it occurs, as anybody who has been miserable on a diet knows. So if you suspect that your toddler is becoming overweight for his size, check with your pediatrician. The following rules will help prevent obesity, or if your child is already overweight, will reduce his gain:

1. Make a wide variety of nutritious foods available.
2. Make junk foods (especially sweets) unavailable. (Don't even keep them in the house. You know how tempting they are.)
3. If you serve desserts, make them nutritious: custards, fruits.
4. Help him to learn to enjoy skim milk instead of whole milk.
5. Set a good example in your own eating habits.
6. Serve small amounts and let your toddler request more.
7. Don't require a clean plate.
8. Don't coax, "Just one more mouthful!" Let your child feed himself. He'll never force himself to eat one more mouthful than he really wants.
9. Never use food as a reward or pacifier.

Sweets are doubly dangerous. They not only fill your child with empty calories, preventing him from eating nutritious food and making him fat, but they also damage his teeth. It's hard for mothers of toddlers to keep this in mind, because the damage won't show up for a few years, but sugar consumption is directly related to tooth decay. If your child gets hit in the mouth with a baseball bat and loses a tooth, it's easy to recognize cause and effect. But keep in mind that if you let him have sweets regularly, you're destroying his teeth just as effectively (and more of them).

People aren't born with a sweet tooth; they *learn* to crave sweet things if they're given lots of them in the first few years of life, especially when sweets are used as rewards. Do your child a big favor and don't give him a "sweet tooth"! If you don't let him sample cakes, cookies, candies, jams and jellies, popsicles, soft drinks, and imitation fruit drinks, he won't know the difference. He'll find out about sweets later, of course, but by then his tastes will be formed and he'll be able to take them or leave them.

Avoiding Dangerous Foods

There are a few types of food that are actually unsafe for toddlers. Popcorn, nuts, and other small hard foods can be sucked into a child's windpipe rather than going down his throat, and could thus choke him. (Older children and adults have larger windpipes, less easily blocked off, and better cough reflexes.)

If your child does start to choke on something, try these steps—fast.

1. Stick your finger down his throat and try to hook the food particle out.
2. If that doesn't work, support his chest with one hand, and with the heel of the other hand, give four rapid, forceful blows between his shoulder blades.

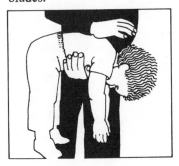

3. If that doesn't work, stand behind the child. Put your arms around him as if to hug him. Be sure the thumb side of your fist is just under his rib cage, right above his navel. Grasp your fist with your other hand and make four quick, hard upward thrusts, as shown in the drawing below. Repeat if necessary.

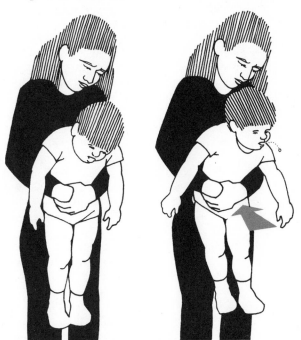

INDEPENDENCE IN EATING

Your toddler is taking steps toward greater independence in many areas, and you can expect this to show up at the dinner table, too.

Feeding Himself

He will want to feed himself. Now is the time to build most of his meals around what is called finger food and let him go to it. Feeding himself will give him a lot of satisfaction as well as needed practice, and it will save you time and energy, too. While he's gnawing on cucumber slices or chasing a pea around his feeding tray, you can throw together the salad for the family dinner, or eat your own meal in peace.

We've already suggested several foods that toddlers can handle themselves, and you can probably come up with many more, but here is a partial list.

> *vegetables:* cucumber, carrot, or celery stick; slice of green pepper; chunk of tomato; broccoli floweret; mild pickle slice; pitted olives; string or lima beans
> *fruits:* half a banana; slice of apple; chunks of peach or pineapple; dried apricots; orange or grapefruit sections
> *eggs:* slices of hard-boiled; bits of scrambled
> *soft meat:* bite-size pieces of ham, chicken, hamburger, stew beef, tuna fish, or any other boned fish
> *dry cereals:* Read labels and steer away from cereals that are sugar-coated or artificially flavored
> *starches:* whole-grain muffin or slice of bread; chunks of boiled or baked potato; cooked noodles, macaroni or rice; whole-grain cracker; crusts (good for teething on)
> *cheese:* hunks or slices of cheddar, Swiss, Muenster, or any other mild, unprocessed cheese

Your toddler will also make it clear that he wants to start learning how to use a spoon to feed himself now. Chances are he'll show you by grabbing the spoon you're using. Let him have it (while you continue feeding him with another spoon), and observe his attempts to fill the spoon and convey its contents to his mouth. That's a complicated maneuver, isn't it? He's bound to spill the food at first, but even so, it's a good idea to let him practice when he's so eager. If you discourage him now, worrying about the mess, one of two things may happen. If he's the determined sort, a battle of wills may develop between the two of you which could make mealtimes miserable. Or if he's more placid by nature, he may just give up—after all, he values your opinion and you've let him know that you want to do the feeding. And then when he's around two, and you decide it's about time he learned to feed himself, you may find that he's lost interest.

Of course, there are times when you feel that you *must* feed your toddler—when you want to get soups or mushy cereal down him, for instance. If you've given

him lots of finger-food freedom and spoon practice at other meals, he'll probably let you take over now and then. If there's some resistance, you can give him a spoon of his own to hold or some finger foods on the side. If there's *lots* of resistance, though, it's better to skip soups for a while. Your toddler certainly doesn't need them. Look back at the list of suggested finger foods and you'll see that everything a toddler needs (except liquids) is included among those foods. He could feed himself entirely and still be getting excellent nutrition.

Let your toddler try sloppy foods occasionally. Give him a small spoon and some mushy casserole, and let him dig in. He may make less of a mess than you thought he would, but even if he is a gooey disaster at the end, he will have benefited from the practice. (In the next section we suggest some ways to deal with the inevitable mess.)

Likes and Dislikes
As you offer your toddler a wider variety of foods, you'll notice that he begins to develop strong likes and dislikes. Respect them. You do want him to be a discriminating adult, don't you? It has to start sometime. You should know in advance, though, that a discriminating toddler isn't quite the same as a discriminating adult. With an adult, at least you can count on his love for artichokes lasting from one month to the next. On the other hand, when you prepare a nice cheese omelet for your toddler—who practically *lived* on omelets last

week—he may turn up his nose and refuse to touch it. A toddler's tastes change fast. (Under the circumstances, you may certainly be forgiven for feeling annoyed. Omelets don't keep.)

This is a good argument for keeping a toddler's menu simple. The easier a food was to prepare, the less upset you'll feel when your toddler refuses it. It's also a good argument for serving a variety of foods. If your toddler ignores your cheese chunks but eats peaches, chicken, and bread, you shouldn't be bothered at all.

When given a choice in foods, many toddlers seem to go on food binges. Suddenly they want nothing but peas and beans for several meals in a row, spurning your offers of cheese, eggs, and meat. Don't let this worry you. Remember Dr. Davis's experiment, and rest assured that his diet will come out balanced by the end of the week.

Giving your toddler his choice in feeding means that you respect your child's wishes concerning amounts of food as well as types of food. Don't push for just a little more. Your child knows best what his needs are. He may even choose not to eat at all for a meal or two. Probably he's got a good reason for not being hungry: his teeth hurt, he's very tired, he's interested in doing something else. Accept his decision, and offer a healthful snack in a few hours.

Exploring Food
Small children who are experimenting with every other object in reach will naturally explore the properties of

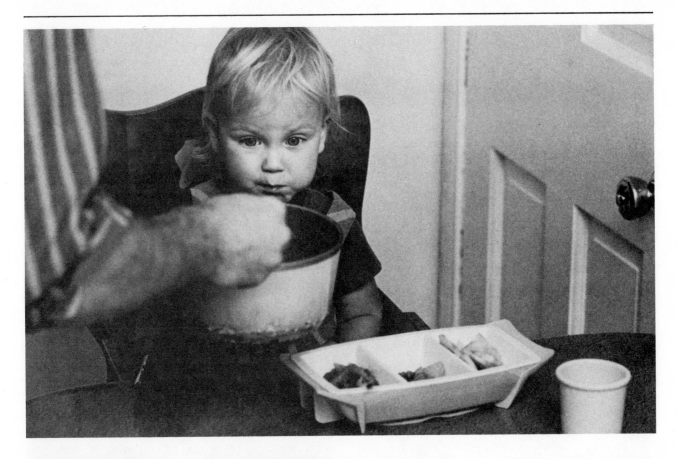

their food and drink, too. Fingerpainting with oatmeal, patting soup, squishing lima beans into green mush, and seeing how gravity affects a piece of banana pushed over the edge of the feeding tray: these are all learning exercises and fun for a toddler, if hard on civilized adult observers.

Your toddler isn't being bad when he turns his cup upside down. He's fascinated by the puddle forming on his high-chair tray and loves sliding his finger around in it. He has no idea why this activity bothers you.

He'll mix up concoctions such as yogurt, raisins, and sliced liver that make you lose your appetite—and then eat them up with relish. He'll play interesting mouth games with his food and drink, experimenting with dribbling, bubbling, and spitting.

He'll bang and poke and spin his spoon and his bowl or plate, rather than using these utensils for the purpose you had in mind. Your household pets will begin gathering under his feeding chair in happy expectation of something better than dog chow, and your toddler will oblige.

What About the Mess?

Parents differ greatly in their tolerance for mess. Some let their children explore even bowls of soup to their hearts' content. Others feel upset when a little egg gets slightly smeared in the normal course of a meal. Every parent draws the line somewhere, and it's up to you to decide how much you can take. But wherever you decide to draw the line, do it calmly and firmly, not in explosions of anger. Remember that your toddler is exploring, not being bad.

Here are some suggestions to help you prevent some messes, and cope with what can't be prevented.

1. Put only small amounts of food within your toddler's reach. This includes the amount of milk or juice in the cup. Smaller portions make smaller messes.

2. Use the helpful items now available for toddlers: cups with tops, spouts, and weighted bottoms; bowls and plates with suction cups underneath.
3. Allow self-feeding and exploring only with the less messy foods. Unless you can handle the results, don't even give your toddler a bowl of applesauce or oatmeal.
4. Don't leave food too long. You'll notice that your toddler will eat fairly efficiently at the beginning of the meal, when he's hungry. He begins experimenting later, as his appetite wanes.
5. Use prevention rather than punishment. Either take the food away or lift your toddler down *before* your boiling point is reached. It's much better to stop the progression of events early on than to wait till disaster strikes and then be unable to control your anger.
6. Be firm, but not punitive, about things that really bother you. Many parents, for instance, draw the line at throwing food. If food throwing bothers you, stop it as *soon* as it happens, always. Tell your toddler clearly, "*No* throwing food," as you remove him from further temptation. Then quietly clean up the mess.
7. Provide alternatives. If you just cannot stand to see your child playing with food, offer similar experiences in other forms. Let him splash with water in the bathtub or out in the yard, and get his fingers messy with squishy clay or dough or fingerpaint.
8. Take steps to messproof:
   Dress your child in a coverall bib or in clothes that are about to be washed anyway. Feed him in a chair with a large, wraparound tray.
   Feed him in the kitchen, where the floor is easy to clean.
   Keep a damp washcloth handy so you'll be able to wipe off his hands *before* he runs them through his hair.

Manners at Mealtime
By adult standards, toddlers have absolutely horrendous table manners. That's because toddlers have to explore their food and because they haven't developed much skill with spoons or cups yet. Even if he wanted to, your toddler couldn't conform to the standards of neatness and politeness that adults find easy and natural. So it's important to adjust your expectations to his capabilities.

Keep in mind that sitting still for any length of time is hard for a newly mobile explorer. Any child of this age is likely to start wiggling and then progress to noisy fussiness if you force him to sit at the table through a whole adult-length meal. If your toddler is itching to be on the move again, you know he won't eat much more anyway, so you might as well just put him down and let him return to exploring. As he matures, especially when he becomes verbal and can join in dinnertime conversations, he'll gradually learn to sit at the table for longer and longer periods.

Eventually, of course, you want your child to master enough of the rules to be able to go out and eat in polite society. How will he learn? There are two steps that you can take right now to insure that your toddler will eventually develop passable table manners. The first is patient understanding of his limited abilities, combined with lots of opportunities to practice the skills of self-feeding. The second is your own good manners.

Most of this chapter has been concerned with helping you understand your toddler's developmental level and capabilities. It should be clear now that if you're patient with his first fumbling attempts at using a spoon, within a few months he'll have mastered spoon use and no longer be dumping food down his chest. As he gets more efficient with spoon or fork, he'll automatically eat less with his fingers. If you've encouraged him to use his cup with a spout, by two years he'll have stopped dribbling milk all over. If you've allowed him to eat what he needs and to refuse foods he doesn't want, he won't make an unpleasant scene about disliked foods when you eat at a friend's home in a year or two. Neatness will develop slowly as your child's skills develop.

But the very best way to teach good mealtime manners is to practice them yourself and to let your toddler see you doing so. Some parents exclude their toddler from their evening meal "because he's too sloppy." But this can become a self-fufilling prophecy. A child who's always fed by himself never gets to learn to be neat and polite the natural way, by watching other people eat neatly and politely. Since your toddler spends a good deal of time and energy trying to imitate you, you might as well make use of this by giving him lots of opportunities to eat with the rest of the family. Then he'll get a chance to learn firsthand what you consider suitable mealtime behavior. He'll note that you say, "Please pass the salad," instead of just grabbing some, that you don't talk with your mouth full, and that you use your napkin when the food misses your mouth. Soon he'll be trying to do these things, too; they will make him feel very grown-up and proud. And you'll have good reason to feel proud, too.

SUCKING NEEDS AND WEANING

The Toddler's Need for Sucking
Because sucking from a bottle or breast is the only way that young babies can get their food, people tend to associate sucking with babyishness. As your child passes his first birthday and changes from a passive, immobile baby to a fast-moving, busy toddler, he suddenly seems grown-up. Many parents wonder if it's time to wean their toddlers from the bottle or breast now. But your toddler is still a baby in many ways, and his need for sucking may remain strong through his second year or even longer.

For a one-year-old, sucking is no longer just a way of getting milk; it has come to mean love and warmth and security, too. For this reason your child may need to continue to suck for comfort even though he can drink from a cup fairly well and eat a wide variety of solid foods now. Actually, sucking needs are sometimes even greater during parts of the toddler years than they were during the first year, because this period is particularly full of stresses and big adjustments. Your toddler often has to find some way to comfort and calm himself, and sucking may frequently be his choice. (You can read more about how toddlers find comfort in the chapter called "Loving and Comforting Your Toddler.")

What Is Weaning?
Weaning your child from breast or bottle is a gradual, step-by-step process that is probably already well underway. The first step in weaning took place the day you gave your infant his first spoonful of baby food, probably sometime before he was six months old. The second step took place when he began to eat table foods or finger foods, probably when he was between six and twelve months of age. The third step, around the same time, was when you introduced your baby to the cup, teaching him that sucking is not the only way to drink liquids. So there remains only that last step—no more sucking from breast or bottle—for weaning to be complete. And there's no hurry. If neighbors or in-laws seem to pressure you by asking, "When are you going to wean that child?" just say, "Oh, I have been since he was five months old."

There is no "right" age for completing the last step of the weaning process. Researchers in child development have concluded that what matters is not so much *when* a child is weaned as *how* he is weaned. Abrupt weaning, no matter when it occurs, often causes problems. In contrast, gradual weaning, timed by the child's readiness, seems hardly to be noticed by most toddlers.

So plan to continue weaning your child slowly. There will be lots of overlap: your toddler may learn to drink well from a cup at mealtime, but still insist on sucking early in the morning and just before bedtime at night. And there will be periods of regression, usually in response to stress: if your toddler has an ear infection or you've just moved to a new house, he may suddenly need the bottle or breast five times a day even though he had been down to only two. Such ups and downs are to be expected in the self-weaning process; when your toddler feels ready, he'll take that last step.

Weaning the Breast-Fed Toddler
Some breast-fed children give up the breast before twelve months, but many continue to find comfort in breast-feeding well into the second year. You will begin to notice changes, though. Feedings will become shorter and less interesting to your toddler, because there is so much else for him to do. In fact, his feedings may resemble snacks more than meals except perhaps at sleepy times: early morning and before bedtime. Your toddler will also welcome a swig or two when he needs comfort, such as after a fall or a fright. As overall sucking time decreases, your breasts respond by manufacturing less and less milk, so the final step in weaning will be easy and comfortable for you whenever it occurs.

One of the many conveniences of breast-feeding is that weaning from the breast is naturally synchronized with your child's growing independence. Whenever your busy toddler wants the breast, he has to come to you and lie or sit on your lap for his snack. In other words, he's forced to be dependent on you. As the months go by, his growing desire for independence will automatically make him show less and less interest in the breast. A bottle-fed toddler, on the other hand, usually feeds himself. His drive for increasing independence is fulfilled by holding his own bottle and taking care of his own sucking and comfort needs, so he is likely to become *more* attached to his bottle during the second year of life.

Remember that sucking has come to symbolize love and comfort to your child now that he's a toddler. If you want to encourage him to move along in the weaning process, be especially sure that he's getting lots of love and cuddling from you outside of the nursing situation. So comfort him more and more by holding, hugging, and rocking, and less and less by automatically popping the nipple into his mouth.

Weaning a Bottle-Fed Toddler

The weaning of a bottle-fed toddler will differ depending on whether he is always fed in his parent's lap, with the parent in charge of the bottle, or whether he is used to feeding himself. If you have continued to hold and bottle-feed your toddler, weaning him will be similar to weaning a breast-fed baby, as described in the previous section. His increasing desire for independence will make him less and less willing to lie in your lap and suck on the bottle, and he will gradually and naturally wean himself.

If your toddler is used to controlling his own bottle, on the other hand, his increasing independence will make the bottle seem more attractive and interesting for a while. In fact, if he has only recently started holding his own bottle, and you're eager to wean him, you may want to go back to feeding him the old way, in your lap. But if he has been controlling his own bottle for many months, you will probably find it difficult or impossible to persuade him to return to the dependent way. You should just go along with his habits. Most children who have become independent bottle-feeders need to keep their bottles throughout the stressful toddler period, so you can expect a bottle-fed toddler to wean himself sometime during the third or fourth year.

There is one type of self-feeding in which it is necessary to intervene, however. Physicians and dentists have found that toddlers who are allowed to take a bottle of milk to bed with them, and who fall asleep sucking, show a high incidence of severe tooth decay. The condition is even called "nursing-bottle caries," and doctors are now firmly recommending that *no* baby or toddler be permitted to take a bottle to bed. If your child nurses himself to sleep in your arms, on the bottle or the breast, that will not cause problems, because as soon as he's asleep, you slip the nipple out of his mouth and there is no more milk available. Toddlers who take their bottles to bed, however, often fall asleep with a pool of milk, which has natural sugar in it, surrounding their new little teeth. Severe tooth decay can take place very rapidly under these conditions.

If your toddler is already in the habit of soothing himself to sleep with a bottle of milk, you will have to help him change his bedtime ritual. Try rocking him and holding the bottle; even if he won't accept such passivity during the day, he may be willing to as he drifts to sleep. Or give him his bottle with only water in it. (Do not use fruit juices: they contain natural sugars, too.) Be patient with your toddler during this period; it isn't easy for him to change his favorite bedtime comfort rituals, and the shift may take weeks.

Another step to take if you want to help your toddler move toward eventual weaning is to check to see if you have gotten into the habit of giving him a bottle to comfort him or keep him quiet. This practice often seems like a good idea at the time, but in the long run, it only increases a child's attachment to his bottle. So you might try substituting other methods of comfort when your toddler hurts himself, or is frightened, and other methods of entertainment when he's bored or whiny.

Between his first birthday and the end of toddlerhood, your child will make giant strides in feeding behavior. He will go from being fed to feeding himself, and he will progress from eating with his fingers to handling a spoon or fork with a fair degree of success and accuracy. Whereas at twelve months he had to be served foods that were soft, by thirty months he'll be able to enjoy almost everything you eat, including crisp and chewy food. He will also have learned to drink competently from a cup, having outgrown his one-year-old dependence on the breast or bottle.

If he's not quite ready yet to dine at the White House, he'll be at least halfway there, and if you've been careful about offering him only nutritious foods all along, he'll also be well on the way to establishing an eating pattern that will serve him well for life.

5
Sleep Problems Are Common

Sleep problems of one sort or another are practically universal during the second year of life. A recent survey of seven hundred parents of one-year-olds showed that 50 percent of these toddlers *regularly* made a major fuss about some aspect of sleeping. Your toddler may go through a phase of not wanting to go to bed or not staying in bed once she's there. She may start waking at night again, although she's slept through for months now. She may resist naptime all of a sudden. Sleep problems are so common during toddlerhood that we probably shouldn't even call them problems—though they certainly seem problematic to the frustrated parent who is trying to deal with them night after night.

From this perspective, your child's infancy may seem like a golden age: a tired baby just pops off to sleep no matter where she is, even on someone's lap amid the commotion of a large family reunion. Tired toddlers, however, often resist sleep even when they're clearly exhausted and miserable.

Of course, toddlers need less sleep than infants do, just as adults need less sleep than children do, so it's no wonder that their sleeping habits start changing at this age. Several recent studies have agreed that one-year-olds sleep an average of only thirteen hours out of twenty-four—about twelve hours at night and the rest at naptime. Remember, however, that this is just an average and that the range is great. Researchers found a few live-wire toddlers who needed as little as nine hours sleep, and, at the other extreme, a small number who slept as much as eighteen hours. Whether your child was a wide-awake baby or a sleepier one during her first year, she'll probably continue to sleep more or less than the average in a similar way during her next few years. So if you know you're the parent of a live wire, you might as well accept later bedtimes and earlier awakenings. It's better not to waste emotional energy settling and resettling a toddler in bed for sleep that she doesn't need. You can't force extra sleep.

Going to Bed

Though reconciling toddlers to bedtime is often difficult, some approaches are definitely more successful than others. The biggest single step you can take to make things easier for both yourself and your child is to establish a regular routine. It's a good idea to start, every evening, by giving your toddler a warning that bedtime is coming up. If you just swoop down unpredictably and carry her off to her bedroom, right in the middle of some important game, she will naturally become outraged and resist going. But if you start by preparing her verbally—"It's going to be bedtime soon, so you'd better start to park your cars now"—you'll ease her into the idea and meet less protest.

It helps to have a regular bedtime (as long as it's based realistically on your toddler's actual sleep needs), too. Your toddler will then become accustomed to getting ready for bed at about the same hour every evening, and so will be less likely to rebel. Needless to say, some flexibility is in order. On the Fourth of July, or the night Grandpa and Grandma arrive from Cleveland, or any night when the afternoon nap was extra long or late, you may decide to put bedtime off till later. If bedtime falls at a predictable time on *most* nights, your child will soon understand that these are special occasions and enjoy them accordingly.

Once the toys have been put away and the pajamas are on, how can you help your toddler go to bed peacefully? Many parents find themselves using age-old soothing rituals—lullabies, nursery rhymes, a quiet time together in the rocking chair, sucking on breast or bottle—without ever having made a conscious decision to do so. These ritual ways of giving comfort seem almost instinctive, and at the end of an active day they really work. By slowing your toddler down and relaxing her, the traditional rituals ease the transition from

fully awake activity to sound sleep. (Adults have such rituals too. We often use a warm bath, a drink, or a quiet half-hour with a book or favorite TV show to help ourselves unwind before going to sleep at night.)

Well-chosen rituals can also make your toddler feel especially secure and loved. Particularly if they involve the child's regressing to more "babyish" ways—sucking on something or stroking a familiar blanket while being cuddled in your arms—they summon up the feeling of complete security she had as an infant and so make it easier for her to relax and fall asleep.

All successful bedtime rituals involve two important components: (1) they're relaxing, and (2) they give the child the intense and uninterrupted attention of one or both of her parents for a short while. It's easy to see how the relaxation helps nudge your toddler toward sleep. But so does the extra attention. Around one year, many children begin to feel some anxiety about separating from their beloved parents, and sleep (at least in our society, where separate bedrooms are common) is a type of separation that can seem quite frightening. Studies have shown that a small child who gets a lot of love and attention throughout the day has an easier

time letting go of her parents at night. Toddlers who have had less attention during the day have more reason to cling. But every child, no matter how secure, appreciates a period of concentrated attention from her parents at the very end of the day.

Each toddler's parents will have a different set of bedtime rituals, but following are some of the more common ones. Remember that what is soothing for one toddler may turn out to be stimulating for another. You will want to see what works best for your child, as well as what suits your own temperament and interests.

The most common bedtime ritual for toddlers is some form of sucking. A child may suck on a bottle or the breast, pacifier or fingers, blanket corner or teddy bear's ear. (Remember, it is important not to let your toddler take a bottle of anything but unsweetened water to bed with her. See the "Feeding and Weaning" chapter for reasons.) Often the child sucks while being held, cuddled, or rocked by one of her parents. Sometimes sucking is simply the last step in the bedtime ritual, introduced just before the toddler drifts off to sleep. Common rituals that may be used to lead up to this moment include warm baths, a small snack or drink if

it's been a while since dinner, a song or two (that's what lullabies were invented for, but your special song can as easily be a pop tune or a golden oldie from your childhood), a story or a chat about the pictures in a favorite book, or just a quiet talk about what happened during the day or what tommorow will bring. Some toddlers like to tuck a few dolls or animals in and tell *them*, "Now go to sleep!" before they're willing to do the same themselves. And many, of course, like to have some soft animal or doll or special blanket in bed with them. (See the "Loving and Comforting Your Toddler" chapter for more on "loveys," or transitional objects.)

A pre-bedtime roughhouse match with Daddy or Mommy is not a good idea for most toddlers. Children generally have trouble moving from the heightened excitement and tension of such games to the relaxed sleep state. Roughhousing is a great sport, and worth finding time for in every week's crowded schedule, but it's not appropriate at bedtime.

Be warned that whatever your ritual is, your toddler will probably insist that it be the same every night for long periods. Sameness is what rituals are all about; they make your child feel secure precisely because they can be counted on not to change. But your toddler's inflexibility about her bedtime ritual can lead you into trouble if you let the ritual get out of hand. Make sure your routine doesn't become too long and complicated. Bring your toddler one glass of water or read one story, if that's your custom, and then stand firm about seconds: "You had your drink. Now it's time to go to sleep. Good night," and leave the room.

When other events in a toddler's life suddenly change radically, bedtime rituals will be particularly helpful to both toddler and parent. For instance, if you're visiting relatives and your toddler is sleeping in a strange bed and bedroom, or if Mommy has just gone to the hospital to have a baby, then the familiar bath followed by the poems recited in the rocking chair, the cup of water, and then bed with the pink panda, just as always, will help your toddler feel secure and able to go to sleep.

It is particularly important to make sure that any baby-sitter who will be putting your toddler to bed, or comforting her if she wakes in the night, knows exactly what rituals your child is used to. The sitter may not sing the same folk song you do, but she can at least rock and give water and make sure the pink panda hasn't fallen out of the crib. When Daddy and Mommy aren't there, it's *especially* important to keep everything else as familiar as possible.

Going to Sleep

Most of the time, after all these nice rituals, a sleepy toddler will cooperate and go to sleep. But sometimes she will talk to herself for a while or sing a tuneless song, or even give a few complaining cries (clearly not serious) before drifting off. As long as she's not really upset, let her take the time she needs to fall asleep.

At one time or another, though, most toddlers will start some serious crying at bedtime—a desperate and unrelenting cry that requires a response from you. At this age the most common cause of such bedtime crying is separation anxiety. You have become so important to your toddler that she becomes anxious when she can't actually see or touch you. At twelve or thirteen months, she's not yet able to understand that although you are out of her sight, you still exist and will return. This is a

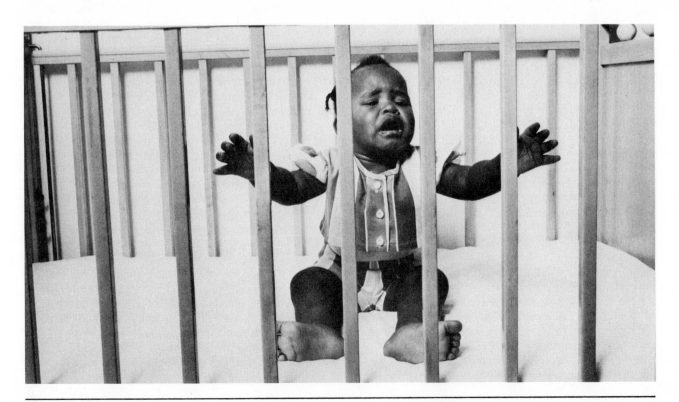

difficult concept, and one that she won't begin to understand until she nears her second birthday. So it's important not to ignore or punish your toddler's cries for help at bedtime. If separation anxiety is the problem, your refusal to come will only make things worse: she'll conclude that she *has* been abandoned, just as she feared.

The first thing to try is simple verbal assurance. A soft call from outside her door—"It's okay, honey. Mommy and Daddy are right here. Now go to sleep"—may do the trick. Leaving her door partway open so that she can hear familiar family sounds may be helpful too.

If this doesn't work, then try a few comforting techniques that keep her quiet and in bed. Don't suddenly turn on bright lights and bustle noisily into her room, and don't immediately take her back out to where the action is. Instead, keep the room dim and pat or rub her back as she lies in her crib, talking soothingly or repeating her favorite song until she has calmed down. Then tell her firmly that it's time to go to sleep and leave the room. This may be enough reassurance.

If your toddler gets upset all over again, it's worth repeating whichever rituals got her to bed in the first place. If that means more rocking, or another round with the breast or the bottle, then provide this. It's best to do these things in the quiet, darkened bedroom, however, to convey the message that although you're available for comfort, it *is* bedtime and you're not going to let your child start the day all over again. This is the best compromise between leaving a young child alone and desperately upset, and giving in to her by getting her up again.

Although separation anxiety is the most common cause of bedtime difficulties, there are other possibilities to think about. The first reason to consider is whether your toddler is really sleepy yet. If there's some good reason why she might not be, such as a late nap, why continue the struggle? Get her up and try again in another hour. Or maybe you've been sticking to her infant schedule without giving it enough thought, and it's time for a later bedtime every night.

Another possibility to consider is whether your child has been seeing enough of Daddy (or Mommy, if she works outside the home). Some parents automatically put a toddler to bed at a set hour, say 6:30, every night. If Daddy leaves early in the morning and doesn't arrive home again till 6:00 P.M., your toddler may be letting you know that she and Daddy just don't get enough of each other. Why not make 7:30 the regular bedtime instead, and encourage Dad to take over a large part of the bedtime ritual, if he hasn't already? You may have to make naptime later, but you'll probably gain an extra hour of sleep in the morning in return.

Toddlers hate to leave the action, so make sure that the pre-bedtime activities surrounding your child are not too exciting and noisy. If there are older brothers and sisters, you may have to ask them to go outside with their fun, or to tone it down for a while.

Although this sounds paradoxical, toddlers can sometimes have trouble going to sleep because they are *too*

tired. Overtiredness—which is indicated when a child begins whining, rubbing her eyes, pulling at her hair, or acting unusually clumsy—can make a toddler just too wrought up to relax into sleep. If your toddler has begun to go to pieces like this, you'll probably have to spend some extra time with your relaxing and comforting rituals before you try putting her to bed. But a child this age shouldn't have to disintegrate completely before her parents intervene. She needs to be removed from all the excitement before she gets to this point. If your child often seems to go to pieces at the end of the day, consider moving her bedtime to an earlier hour.

What about a toddler who learns to climb out of her crib and so can return to the family when she doesn't feel like sleeping? This can be a real problem, not only annoying to adults who want some peace, but downright dangerous for the unsupervised toddler. It's much easier to *prevent* nighttime wandering than to cure it once it's a habit, so do everything you can to keep this from getting started. The best prevention is to go to your toddler when she needs you, consistently, as we have already suggested. Then it won't even occur to her to try to go to *you*. (Nighttime wandering is found most frequently in families where the parents make a point of never responding to calls from a child once she's been put to bed.) Another preventive measure is to keep dressing your child in sleeping bags (nightwear with arms but a bag instead of legs) as you did when she was an infant. Obviously a sleeping bag will considerably impede her ability to climb out of the crib. And of course it's always a good idea to make sure that adjustable crib sides are pulled all the way up each night.

But suppose it's too late for these measures, and you already have an agile crib-climber who arrives back in the living room, smiling and ready for play, ten minutes after you put her to bed? *Never* reward her for her feat—even mildly—with smiles or indications of how cute she is and how clever to negotiate the stairs so quietly. Deal with the matter quickly and firmly, though not angrily, carrying your toddler *straight* back to her bed. Tell her definitely, but lovingly, "It's time to sleep now. So you stay in bed and go to sleep." If you act angry, she'll get upset and then you'll have two problems to deal with. She isn't getting up to be bad; she just wants to be with you and she can't understand why all of a sudden you don't want her around.

If your child climbs out of bed regularly, make absolutely certain that her room has been toddlerproofed. Make her bed safe. If you're going to keep her in the crib for a while longer, keep the side *down* (so that she has less far to climb—or to fall) and lower the legs, if they're adjustable. Or consider switching your toddler to a regular bed now. Some parents solve the problem by simply giving their child a mattress on the floor for a few years; then she certainly can't fall out of bed and hurt herself.

Many families with a night-wandering toddler have wondered if locking the bedroom door might be an acceptable solution. But if you remember that the reason a toddler climbs out of bed and comes for you in the first place is that she's anxious about being left alone, you'll have no trouble understanding that locking her in her bedroom is definitely not the answer. All her worst fears would be realized if she found herself locked in. A better solution would be to put a gate across her doorway, thus keeping her from harm without making her feel imprisoned. But if you do this, be sure to respond promptly if your toddler stands at the gate, rattling it and calling for you.

A toddler needs a regular bedtime so that she'll get enough rest, but her bedtime may be even more important to her parents than it is to her. Parents need privacy and time to themselves, and above and beyond this, the parent who has been keeping up with the toddler all day wants simple relief. To recover your sense of humor and enjoyment of yourself as an independent adult—not to mention your ability to relate to your spouse as an equal, a partner, and a lover—you *need* to be free of your toddler at night. Don't feel guilty about wanting your child out of the way by a certain hour, or about feeling annoyed when she has trouble settling down; these are natural reactions. But when your child is having trouble going to sleep, try not to communicate your impatience to her. She'll settle into sleep sooner if you respond helpfully, but matter-of-factly, to her needs. Assure yourself that there are easier times ahead. Before too long, if you're understanding and supportive of your toddler now, you'll find that she's going to bed more and more often without incident, and you and your spouse will be able to count on having uninterrupted time to yourselves in the evening.

Staying Asleep

Studies have shown that the average toddler wakes up two or three times a night, but usually gets herself back to sleep so that her parents never even know she woke. Parents who say, "My eighteen-month-old sleeps through," simply mean that their child doesn't need to *summon* them when she wakes each night. Not all toddlers drift back to sleep so easily, however. In the survey of seven hundred parents mentioned earlier, one-third of the parents reported having had to go to their one-year-olds during the night preceding the interview.

Toddlers wake and cry for you to come for several reasons. Separation anxiety or loneliness in the middle of the night are common causes. Teething pains or symptoms of some mild illness are possibilities too. Stressful or new situations—visiting relatives, a move to a new bedroom, or the arrival of a new baby—may cause your toddler to wake for reassurance for several nights, until she gets used to the change. Tensions or arguments with her care giver during the day can also cause frightened nighttime waking. And toddlers often have vivid and scary nightmares, even before they are verbal enough to describe them to you.

Again, you should not ignore or punish your toddler when she needs you during the night. She doesn't wake herself on purpose, so it doesn't make sense to regard her calls as a bad habit to be broken. If you leave her crying in fear or pain or loneliness, she'll only get more upset. If the child is crying because she's afraid of being abandoned by you, her worst fears will be realized when you don't respond to her cries. If she's feeling frightened because she just wakened from a nightmare, she'll become hysterical alone. In the long run, it will take much longer to calm and comfort your toddler if you leave her panicked and crying for a while before you finally go to her.

What can a parent do about nighttime waking and crying? First, wait a moment. Listen to the type of cry. Needless to say, if it's a desperate, terrified cry, you'll go to your child immediately. But if it's just a mild, complaining cry, your toddler may be able to go back to sleep on her own. If she's still complaining after several minutes, or if she begins to sound more upset, then it's time to get up and let her know that she can depend on you for help when she needs it.

Use the comfort techniques that worked earlier in the evening: hold your toddler while you walk or rock her and murmur soft reassurances. If you're still nursing your child, you'll probably find that a few minutes on the breast will enable her to drift back to sleep very quickly. If you're not nursing, a few sips of water from a cup or bottle may help. Keep the room dim and quiet to give your child the message that this is sleep time, not get-up-and-play time.

If your child has been really terrified by a nightmare, you may need to use more drastic measures to pull her back to reality. Children this young are not able to distinguish fact from fantasy. If your toddler has just had a nightmare about being eaten by a bear, she'll think that the bear is still lurking in her bedroom, even if you live in midtown Manhattan. In this case, if holding and loving don't quickly calm her, you may have to turn on the lights to show her that she's in her familiar bedroom and that everything is in its place. Never laugh or poke fun at your toddler's nightmares when she's older and can describe them to you. They're real to *her*. Respect her tale while calmly assuring her that everything is all right, that there are no bears here at all and never could be. Show her, if necessary.

Many parents find that the easiest way to quiet a toddler and get her back to sleep quickly is to take her into their bed with them. There are good reasons why this comfort measure works so well. Throughout history, babies and young children have slept with some other warm body—usually parents or brothers and sisters—and in most parts of the world they still do. Young animals of every species cuddle against their mothers or litter mates to sleep. Actually, the frequent isolation of Western babies and toddlers at bedtime is a rather unusual custom. Reports have shown that babies and children who sleep with others are far less likely to cry at bedtime or during the night than children who lack this comfort. With someone else always nearby, a small child simply has no reason to feel separated or lonely. In fact, parents who provide separate bedrooms for their children are often surprised to find that, if they are allowed to, the young children in the family will usually migrate to the same room or even the same bed come nighttime.

Many books warn parents against taking their children into bed with them, but the authors don't seem to give any sound reasons for being against this practice, except to say that it might form a habit. Naturally any good comfort measure (rocking, being patted, sucking) will turn into a habit for a time if it fulfills a real need in the child. You might even say the "habit" is a proof of the measure's effectiveness. So if taking your toddler into your warm bed occasionally seems like a good solution to you, don't be afraid to do it. If the idea bothers you, then use other comfort techniques.

When you have a nighttime baby-sitter for your toddler, remember how important it is during the age of separation anxiety to spend some time letting your toddler get to know the sitter before you leave. Be sure to teach the sitter your toddler's comfort rituals. *Never* sneak out without telling your child, hoping she won't wake up and find out. Nothing could be more terrifying to a child this age than to wake up, cry for Mommy in a panic, and suddenly have a stranger walk into her bedroom! It would take your toddler a long time to learn to trust you again after an experience like that. Even if your toddler almost never wakes at night, it's not worth taking this chance. Let her know you're leaving.

Although most nighttime waking in toddlers can be handled fairly quickly and easily, having a child who wakes up regularly can be exhausting. Interrupted sleep can make the most even-tempered adult nasty and impatient. If your toddler is waking up too often at night for everybody's comfort, check out some of the possible reasons and see how many you can eliminate. Is she warm and cozy enough in bed? Has she had enough food and drink before bedtime? Are her days as calm and cheerful as possible, or are they full of upsets and arguments? (Living with a toddler means that some upsets are inevitable, but if big fights between toddler and parent are occurring daily, that's just too much conflict for anybody to handle. The chapters on discipline may give you some suggestions on how to handle these difficulties.)

Try a few simple measures that might make your toddler feel more secure. If she's often afraid, would a night-light help? Or leaving her door partially open with the hall light on? Could a sibling sleep with her? Or would you mind taking her into your bed, just till the fearful phase is over? If you don't want to do this, Daddy or Mommy might try sleeping in the toddler's room for several nights, just to break the cycle of waking and crying. As soon as your child stirs and begins to whimper, the half-awake parent can mutter, "It's okay, Sarah. I'm right here." This tactic often works very well, and within a week you can move back into your own room.

If your toddler requires a lot of comforting each night, be sure that Mom and Dad share the task. Then each of you will be only half tired and half grumpy the next day; neither of you will be *completely* unable to meet the demands of your job, whether it's outside work or another day full of toddler care. It isn't easy to live with a night-waker, but take heart. The phase will pass as the child matures, and she'll feel safer and more secure because of her parents' willingness to help her through the night.

Early-Morning Waking
A toddler who rises with the sun and crowing roosters is usually cheerful and charming. Her parent, who wants to sleep for another hour, isn't. There's not much you can do to prevent early waking, except for experimenting with a later bedtime, if that's agreeable. But there are several methods you can use to buy a little extra sleep even after your toddler's awake.

If you put toys in the crib the night before, your toddler may be kind enough to play and talk and sing for a while alone and happy. (On dark winter mornings, a night-light may be necessary: who can be expected to amuse herself in the dark?) A brother or sister in the same room can be a real help in this situation also. Siblings seem to enjoy each other more before breakfast than at any other time of day, maybe because, as long as Mom and Dad are in bed, they can't compete for their parents' attention.

Some mothers find that they can get up and give their toddler a bottle or a cup of dry cereal in the crib, and then stagger back to bed to sleep a while longer. Breast-feeding mothers often find it convenient to take the toddler into their bed at this point, drifting back to sleep as the toddler nurses quietly. Or if Dad is getting up for work at this hour anyway, he can take his toddler into the bathroom and then to the kitchen with him, thus giving Mom another precious hour of sleep.

Naptimes
Most children make the change from two naps a day to only one sometime during their second year. The transition period, when two naps are too many but one isn't enough, can be a difficult time for both you and your toddler. You'll have to be prepared to go back and forth between one nap and two for a while. And you'll have to be flexible in other ways too. If your child won't take a morning nap but gets frantically overtired by her usual lunchtime, for example, you'll do well to move lunchtime up to 11:30 or even 11:00 for a while. You should make an effort to avoid particularly exciting or tiring activities in the morning, too. Your child will eat and sleep much better when she goes down for her nap at noon if she isn't exhausted and cranky.

Right after lunch is the most common time for the daily nap, and for good reason: most of us feel a little slowed down and drowsy after a meal. And a child is often more willing to go off to her bed at this point because she hasn't yet had a chance to get involved in some new and fascinating activity.

If your toddler wakes happily from her nap and will play contentedly in her bed for a while, by all means let her. But don't confine her to the crib if she's asking to

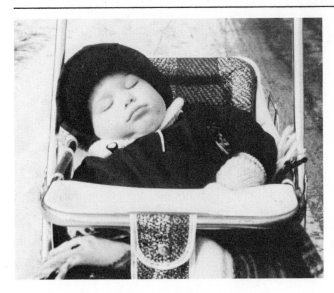

get out and rejoin the family. Having her out of the way a little while longer may seem convenient to you at the moment, but in the long run this custom could lead her to see her bed as a prison.

If you wake a toddler up from a nap, she's likely to be disoriented and unhappy; it's best to let her wake up naturally. But of course there will be times when you *have* to wake her. When there's no avoiding it, plan to wake her slowly and gradually and give her a lot of loving and holding time. Don't wake her abruptly and rush off somewhere in the car, or you'll find yourself with a very grumpy traveling companion.

Sleep problems are so common during toddlerhood that every parent can expect to experience at least one or two. But, fortunately, the period doesn't last long. And if you use these suggestions to help your toddler deal with sleeping, you can look forward to much more peaceful times soon.

6
How Your Toddler Learns to Talk

The way a child learns to talk is miraculous. The skill involved is tremendously complex, yet a toddler picks it up at a speed that is nothing short of astounding. In just one year, between his first birthday and his second, a child goes from saying no words at all to a point where he is able to carry on fairly complete (though simple) conversations with his parents. During the second year of life, the average toddler learns to say about 200 words. Even though these 200 words make up only a tiny fraction of all English words—there are 400,000 altogether—they amount to almost half of the 500 that are used most frequently in typical adult conversations. Studies show that these 500 words make up *90 percent* of those used when adults talk to each other. After his second birthday, the toddler's language skills continue to grow by leaps and bounds. Before he is three, the typical toddler has a vocabulary of about 1,000 words.

When a child learns to talk, he acquires an enormously powerful tool. Language will make it much easier for him to relate to other people, to learn from them, and to ask for help, than it was when his only ways of communicating were crying and gesturing. And words also open up whole new realms of experience for a child. In his first year, the world was only what he could see, hear, and touch in the moment. But words change all of that; they enable a child to think, and later to talk about things that *have* happened or *will* happen or *may* happen, as well as about things that *are* happening. Language also allows a child to learn from the experiences of others, as those experiences are described in words. And words provide a toddler with the tools he needs to make believe.

All in all, learning to talk is a major milestone in your toddler's development. That's why his first words are such a thrilling accomplishment. They signal the beginning of talking, just as his first steps were a sign that he'd soon be getting around on his own.

Children Are Learning to Talk
Before They Can Say a Word

Your toddler will probably say his first words sometime around his first birthday. But he actually began learning to talk many months before. During the last ten years, scientists have applied increasingly sophisticated techniques to studying the development of language. One effect of this research has been to make us aware of just how early in life the process of learning to talk begins. All during babyhood, in fact from his very first day of life, your child was laying the groundwork for his new skill. He was learning to identify speech sounds, and he was working hard to produce these sounds himself.

Recognizing different speech sounds is the beginning of understanding a language and learning to use it. Studies show that almost from the moment of birth a baby pays special attention to the sounds of speech. Just a few minutes after he's born, he will turn his head toward the sound of someone talking much more often than to any other sound. And in no time at all, he begins to make fine discriminations among the speech sounds he hears. Research shows that even one-month-old babies can hear the small but important differences between such similar speech sounds as *pa* and *ba*.

The way scientists discovered that babies can hear these sound differences is interesting in its own right. Several years ago, researchers observed that babies who are sucking from a bottle will suck more rapidly when they hear a new sound, especially if it's a speech sound. When babies hear a new speech sound—*pa*, for example—on a tape recorder, they suck very rapidly. If the sound is played repeatedly, their sucking rate goes down to a steady level: they're losing interest. But if a different sound—*ba*, for instance—is introduced, the babies' sucking rate immediately shoots up again, and stays there for a while until the new sound has been repeated a number of times. Recently, other scientists have confirmed these findings using a different technique. They designed a toy that would light up for a baby only if he turned to it just as the speech sounds he was hearing changed. Babies enjoy interesting sights, and infants as young as five months old quickly learned to play this game—proving in the process that they could distinguish between different speech sounds. In fact, in this study the babies also showed they were able to recognize particular speech sounds even when the syllables were spoken by different people.

These findings suggest that one of two things must be going on. Either a baby is born with the ability to recognize the subtle differences in speech sounds, or he acquires this skill very rapidly in the first few weeks after he's born. In either case, this skill, which is basic to learning to talk, is working very early in life.

It's much easier for a child to *hear* different speech

All babies babble. In fact, babbling has been called the universal language of infancy. Babies around the world babble nearly identical varieties of simple sounds.

sounds than it is for him to *make* these sounds himself. That's because the muscle coordination involved in speaking can be very difficult. It takes about a year before a child can make sounds that are recognizable as words. But it doesn't take that long for him to use sounds to communicate.

The first sound a baby makes is a cry. And within a few weeks, if not sooner, his cries begin to form a kind of language. Each type of cry has its own special sound and meaning, which a baby's parents learn after a time to recognize. That's why when you listened carefully to your baby's cries, you could often tell whether he was in pain or hungry or lonely or just feeling fussy.

By the time a baby is six or seven months old, he begins to actively practice making the sounds we use when we talk. He produces sequences of simple syllables, such as *bababa* or *gagaga*. This is called babbling. Babbling gives a baby practice in coordinating the muscles of the throat, tongue, and lips to make speech sounds. All babies babble. And Japanese babies babble nearly the same sounds as American babies. In fact, babbling has been called the universal language of infancy. Regardless of culture, country, or native tongue, babies around the world babble nearly identical varieties of simple sounds.

The Emergence of First Words

No one knows for sure how words grow out of babbling. Sometimes it seems as if the first words appear overnight, though the process is actually a continuous one. One thing we *do* know is that first words incorporate the various speech sounds a baby has been practicing while babbling. In fact, the resemblance between babbling and early talking is so close that it's not unusual for parents to mistake babbling sounds for real words before the child has actually attached any meaning to

them. Typical first words often consist of single sounds —*ba, da,* and *ma,* for instance—which then become pairs of simple sounds: *baby, dada,* and *mama.* Because of their rhythm and intonation, these utterances often sound like one-word songs or rhymes. In fact, though, they are parts of the strings of sounds that a baby made while babbling.

A baby's first words are almost always names for the things that are most important or interesting to him: people (*mommy, daddy, baby*); animals (*dog, kitty*); and objects (*ball, cup, juice, cracker*). Other common first words, like *hi, bye-bye,* and *more,* grow out of the most important activities in a baby's day. Action is extremely important to young children—they love to see things happen and to make things happen—and their early language reflects this fascination, too. Part of the reason toddlers learn the words *dog* and *ball* so early is probably that these objects move in interesting ways.

Of course the most common first words are also ones a toddler frequently hears his parents say. How often do you say something like: "Here comes *daddy!* Let's go to the door and meet *daddy!*" or "Is my *baby* hungry? Want a *cracker?* Here's a nice crunchy *cracker.*" Or "Do you want to play *ball?* Go find your *ball.* Where's your *ball,* Carol?" Or "Look at that *dog* go!" When a toddler hears a word frequently, and the word is always used in the same context and given a special emphasis, he's on his way to learning to say the word himself. And, of course, the ecstatic reaction that greets his early efforts to say *certain* words gives him a special incentive to learn those words. The first time a child utters sounds that even faintly resemble *Mommy* or *Daddy,* he's likely to be absolutely deluged with appreciative praise: "He said *Da-da!* He said it! He knows me!" Excitement like this lets a child know that he's done something pretty special, and it encourages him to repeat his performance. He says the word again, and his parents echo it, perhaps adding a new inflection, or pronouncing the word more correctly. In this way, the toddler and his parents work together to improve his new skill in using words—especially certain words.

Occasionally an unusually sensitive toddler may be inhibited by his parents' enthusiastic responses to his early efforts to talk. He may interpret their attention as a form of pressure rather than as encouragement. So if your toddler seems a bit dazed by your excitement at his first words, you may find that toning down your reaction actually helps his language learning.

How a Toddler Learns New Words

It's no simple matter for a toddler to learn new words. In fact, it's an incredibly complicated task, and he must work hard at it. When you point out an object to your toddler—a ball, for instance—and name it for him, he must figure out which of the features he sees mean "ball." Studies show that as young children learn to recognize familiar objects and then to name them, they also start building general concepts and grouping things in categories. Eventually your toddler will learn that balls can be big or small, hard or rubbery, red or blue or striped, but that they are all round and all bounce or roll. But before he gets this concept down pat he's bound to say "ball" to more than a few oranges and light bulbs and bathtub drains (all of which are just round objects to him). And when you think about what complicated thinking is involved, it's no wonder.

Toddlers often refer to a variety of objects, actions, people, or events by the same name if they have one or more important features in common. Scientists who study early language development describe words used this way as "overextended." A toddler's tendency to overextend word meanings can be amusing or upsetting or both, depending on the situation. How do you feel when your toddler cheerfully greets every man he meets as *daddy?*

Since your toddler's overextended use of words lets you see how he makes connections in his mind, it can be fun to try to figure out what features he is paying attention to when he overextends the meaning of a particular word. Toddlers often use a single word to refer to—

several things that are part of the same whole. *Tree* may be used for leaves or bushes or a forest.

several things that have the same shape. Round stones and balls and radishes may all be called *moon*.

several things that are the same size. *Fly* might mean insects and specks of dirt and dust and bread crumbs and even polka dots.

several things that make similar sounds. Horns, whistles, sirens, and bird songs may all be called *beep*.

several things that move in the same way. A toddler may say *choo-choo* whether he's talking about a train or a bus or a truck or a bicycle.

several things that taste the same. *Candy* may refer indiscriminately to gumdrops, cherries, and grape juice.

Toddlers also tend to use the same word to cover very different but somehow related situations. Your child may say *all gone* both when he finishes his juice and when he sees his father closing the door to leave for work. Or he may say *more* in the kitchen to mean he

wants another cookie and *more* upstairs by his crib to mean he wants a nap.

When your toddler overextends the meaning of a word, you may think he can't tell the difference between two things he calls by the same name. But often he can. Try this simple experiment to see what we mean. Show your toddler a ball and a light bulb (or any other two things he calls by the same name). Ask him to point to the ball. Say "Where is the ball?" or "Show me the ball." Then ask him to point to the light bulb. Chances are he'll point correctly. And words he understands in your conversation now, he'll soon be able to say himself.

Why does a toddler extend word meanings if he knows he's not using the right word? Part of the answer is that he wants to communicate, and he does the best he can with the words he knows. He uses the name of an object he knows for other objects that have features in common with it. That makes sense. If you were in a foreign country where you couldn't speak the language fluently, wouldn't you try to communicate through some combination of overextended words and sign language? Well, this is the situation your toddler is in, and he deals with it as you would: in the best way he knows how.

As new words enter a child's vocabulary and as new experiences clarify his concepts, or mental images, he restructures and reorganizes his early overextended meanings. New discriminations allow him gradually to refine his generalizations. The diagram on page 53 illustrates how this process works. A toddler first learns

what a dog (or bow-wow) is. He then overextends the meaning of this word to include all the four-legged animals he knows. A little later he learns that some of these bow-wows are actually cows (or moos). He still calls all other animals bow-wows. Eventually, he narrows his mental image of dogs even further, as he learns such words as *cat* and *lamb,* or, more likely *meow* and *baa-baa.* The whole process of refinement may take many months.

Sometimes a toddler learns words by a process that is the opposite of the one we've just described. Instead of first using a word in an *overextended* way, and then gradually refining its meaning and learning to use other words in its place, a toddler may begin by using a word in an *overrestricted* way, applying it more narrowly than it should be, and gradually extending its meaning until he is using it correctly. One scientist, Peter Reich, noticed this process in studying his young son's language development. He found that for this boy *shoe* meant only his mother's shoes and only when they were placed on the wire rack in her closet. Anytime the child was asked to find a shoe, he'd ignore all others and head straight for these. Peter Reich's son also used other words in an overrestricted way. For example, *car* to him, meant only a moving car passing by the living-room window. Parked cars or those moving by other windows in the house were simply not cars.

Putting Words Together

Some children have a rush of words as soon as they begin to speak. But it's more typical for new words to come slowly at first, perhaps at the rate of 1 to 3 words a month for the first few months. Around the middle of the second year the pace often picks up, and a child may learn between 10 and 80 new words each month. By their second birthday, most toddlers can say about 200 words. Children at this time will often go around asking for the names of objects, saying "What's that?" for example. Katherine Nelson, who has studied the language development of toddlers in great detail, found that the children she observed could say anywhere from 28 to 436 words at twenty-four months.

Before your toddler is two years old, you'll probably notice an even more exciting development in language learning: he'll begin to put words together to form simple phrases. This is a real milestone, because it reflects your toddler's ability to conceive of and express *relationships.* During the one-word stage your toddler could say *car* and he could say *Daddy.* Now he can talk about the relationship between these two concepts

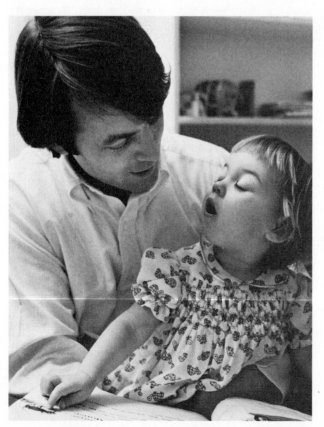

Bow-wows and Moo-cows
The chart on the opposite page gives an example of how a child might overextend and restructure the meaning of the word "bow-wow." (Adapted from E.V. Clark in T.E. Moore, ed., Cognitive Development and the Acquisition of Language. *New York: Academic Press, 1973.)*

step 1

BOW WOW

step 2

BOW WOW

step 3

BOW WOW   MOO

step 4

BOW WOW   GEE GEE   MOO

step 5

BOW WOW   OINK   GEE GEE   MOO
DOGGIE   HORSIE

step 6

BOW WOW   KITTY   OINK   GEE GEE   MOO
DOGGIE   HORSIE

and say "Daddy car" either to refer to his father's car or to note that his father is in the car.

The way your toddler puts words together shows his growing awareness of relationships between separate objects or events. And the way he *orders* the words in his early phrases shows he's beginning to learn some basic rules of grammar as well. For example, most simple English sentences have a standard form. They tell us who (the subject, or agent) is doing what (the verb, or action) to whom (the object). When your toddler wants you to pick him up, he's much more likely to say something like "Daddy pick me," ordering the words correctly, than he is to say, "Me pick Daddy," or "Pick Daddy me."

When your toddler's sentences do stray from this standard agent-action-object form, the variation itself is often another reflection of his awareness of the rules of English grammar. For example, when he says, "Daddy car," he is telling you one thing; if he says "Car, Daddy," he is expressing something else: perhaps he means "Look at the car, Daddy."

In the months before your toddler's second birthday he's not only saying more words, and putting them together to form simple phrases, he's also putting more expression into the words he uses. For example, when he sees a neighbor's dog lying in his yard, he may say, "Dog," simply identifying the animal. But if you're sitting on your front porch and a dog races by so fast that it's gone almost before your toddler notices it, he may say, "Dog?" The way he says the word puts a question mark after it. He thinks what he saw was a dog, but isn't sure, so he's asking you for confirmation. And if your toddler looks out the kitchen window and sees a dog digging up the flower bed in your back yard, he may say, "Dog!" In this instance he is passing a moral judgment on the dog, expressing his strong feelings about what the dog is doing, just as you would.

As your toddler's second birthday approaches and he begins to talk in two-word phrases, he continues to talk about what he knows and about the things that matter most to him, just as he did during the one-word stage of his language learning. You can gain insights into how his mind works by paying attention to what he talks about. One thing you'll learn by listening is that toddlers

are firmly rooted in the here and now. They are interested almost exclusively in what they can see, hear, feel, smell, and taste at this moment. They almost never talk about things that are in the past or in the future.

Toddlers are also innocently self-centered. They enjoy learning the names for the parts of their bodies and for their own clothes and possessions. They love to talk about what *they* are doing ("Eat cookie," for example), what *they* see ("Dog run"), and what *they* hear ("Baby cry"). They rarely tire of talking about what's going on around them, to get your attention, and to get you involved with them. Toddlers this age also use words to tell you what they want—"More cookie" or "Hug me," for example—and to tell you when they don't want your help: "Me do it!"

Since toddlers are fascinated by the world around them but know little about it, they often talk to request information rather than help. So the questions start coming, questions such as "Daddy gone?" or "Cup hot?" Other times your toddler may try to tell you about something he's done that requires your attention. He may say, "Uh oh," when he's knocked over a lamp, or "Juice all gone," when he's knocked over his cup and spilled its contents on his feeding tray.

The dramatic growth in your toddler's ability to communicate through words doesn't mean you'll suddenly begin having adult conversations with him. You still have a long way to go before that's possible. So you'll continue to pay attention to the nonverbal cues that help you understand what your child is trying to say. Tone of voice and facial expression are especially important for helping you figure out how your toddler is *feeling.* When a toddler starts to speak, he talks almost exclusively about objects and activities; he doesn't yet use words to describe his emotions. He still relies a lot on gestures, too. He will still hold out his arms to be picked up, or point to a toy he wants but can't reach. So words are only part of his communication system.

Actually this is true not only for a young child but for adults, as well. One scientist, Albert Mehrabian, estimates that when we are talking to another person, only 7 percent of the information we give to the listener comes from our words; the other 93 percent comes from

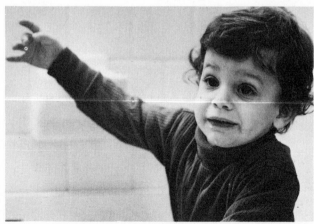

the tone of our voice, our facial expressions, and the way we hold our bodies.

Problems with Pronunciation

After the middle of his second year, your toddler will probably be making great strides in his language learning, but the way he pronounces his words will often be incorrect by adult standards. During toddlerhood, faulty pronunciation is the rule rather than the exception. This may be hard to believe, but studies show that perfectly normal children mispronounce at least half of their speech sounds at the age of eighteen or nineteen months.

When your toddler—or anyone else—talks, he uses his

lungs,
larynx (or voice box),
nose,
lips,
tongue,
teeth.

The different sounds we make involve different organs and muscles. Vowel sounds such as *ahh, eee,* and *oo* come from the larynx. Say "Ahh," and you can feel your larynx vibrate as it makes the sound. Even though the larynx is sometimes called the voice box, it isn't really a box. It's a place in your throat where air goes through a narrow opening like the neck of a balloon. The narrower the opening, the higher the sound; the wider the opening, the deeper the sound.

Other sounds, such as *ma, pa, ba,* and *wa,* are made using the lips. Try to say "Mayonnaise, peaches, beets, and walnuts," without moving your lips.

Sounds involving the larynx and lips are fairly easy to make. That's why so many of a young child's babbling sounds and first words are made up of these sounds. Certain sounds made with the tongue, such as *da,* and *ka,* are also among the easier sounds. On the other hand, other sounds that involve the tongue seem to be especially difficult to make. You have to use your tongue in a special way when you make sounds such as *ra, ya, sta, stra, scra,* and *spa.* Try this. Open your mouth and hold down your tongue with a spoon (or your finger). Now say:

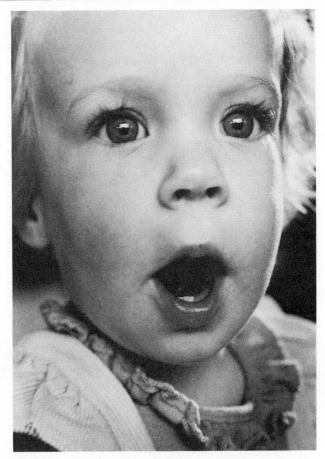

"Rainbows and railings, radios and rocks," or
"Lemons and lampposts, lockets and lace," or
"Stand straight while scratching spiders."

Can you do it? Until your toddler learns to use his tongue properly, he can't pronounce these words correctly either.

When a toddler has trouble pronouncing any sound, he may substitute an easier sound. For example, he may say *wabbit* instead of *rabbit;* or *poon* instead of *spoon.* Or he may omit the difficult sound altogether. For instance, he may say *oo* instead of *you.* He may even mangle the whole word. Perhaps he'll say *dya* instead of *flower,* or *maw-maw* instead of *lawn mower.*

Toddlers seem to mispronounce sounds at the middle and end of words more frequently than those at the beginning. For example, a toddler may say *basik* for *basket,* or *baw* for *ball,* or *docket for doctor.*

The Growth of Grammar

Sometimes your toddler pronounces his words correctly, but they sound strange even so. That's because he doesn't always follow the rules of grammar as we adults know it. But if you listen carefully, you'll see that the mistakes he makes have a logic of their own. Like his overextended word meanings, his grammatical errors tend to occur when he applies something he knows too broadly. Young children often make mistakes in forming the past tense this way. No matter what the verb is, when they want to make it past they add a *d* sound to the end. If your toddler is relatively advanced in his language development, he may begin using the past tense by the time he reaches his second birthday. And if he does, you're likely to hear him using words such as *goed* instead of *went,* or *comed* instead of *came.*

Similarly, since the plural of most English nouns is formed by adding an *s* or *z* sound to the end, many toddlers—and quite a few older children as well—extend this rule logically to all nouns and say *sheeps* and *mans* and *mouses.*

Fortunately, most parents quickly get used to their toddler's special speech, and few of them are bothered by mispronunciation or ungrammatical speech at this age. In fact, most "errors" either go unnoticed or provide a source of amusement. That's just as well, because it generally does more harm than good to worry about a toddler's speech. The child has a powerful drive to talk, and to learn new words. But when he's overloaded by pressure to "say it right," his language learning may actually slow down, because he's not capable of following instructions of this kind. Studies show that the more tolerant parents are of deviations from proper pronunciation and grammar in their child's early speech, the more rapidly the child will learn the proper forms when he's ready and the more new words he'll learn, too.

Eventually your toddler will decide that he wants to pronounce words correctly—if you speak correctly yourself. The desire comes naturally with increasing maturity. In the meantime, do your best to figure out what he is trying to tell you, and don't pretend you don't understand him when you do. Of course, there's no harm in responding to his "Doggy goed," with a pleasant "Yes, the doggy went in his house, didn't he?" But don't overdo it.

Sometimes it's a toddler's older brother or sister and not his parents who push him to talk. The older child may correct the toddler's pronunciation and make him repeat words and phrases. Fortunately, pressure from older siblings doesn't seem to be as difficult for toddlers to deal with as pressures from parents. Most likely, if you correct your toddler's mispronunciations and confused tenses matter-of-factly by simply repeating the sentence correctly and then continuing with the conversation, your older child will copy your method and ease up on the toddler. You can also remind your older child that it takes time to learn to talk. You can explain that your toddler still doesn't know all the ways to use his tongue to form speech sounds, that he still makes too many sounds with his lips, and that he's still learning rules for saying things correctly—*mice* rather than *mouses,* for instance. You might even show the illustrations in this chapter to your older child, and talk about the points we've made here.

Individual Differences in Learning to Talk

In general, children follow a very consistent pattern in learning to talk. The progress from crying to babbling to first words to simple sentences is nearly uni-

versal. But the differences among children in the pacing of this progression and in some of its details are too important to ignore.

As we've said, many children say their first words at about twelve months. But some begin as early as ten months and others as late as eighteen months, or even later. Katherine Nelson found big differences among the toddlers she studied in the number of words they could say at any given age. She paid special attention to the age at which the children could say ten words, since she considered this the point at which the toddlers were "really talking." On the average, the toddlers she studied were fifteen months old when they could say ten words, but some were as young as thirteen months, and others as old as nineteen months.

According to Dr. Nelson, the point at which a child can say fifty words is another important milestone in early language development. Once a child has reached this point, the number of words he learns each month usually increases rapidly, and he begins putting words together to form simple sentences as well. On the average, the toddlers Dr. Nelson studied were twenty months old when they could say fifty words, but some were fourteen months and others were twenty-four months old.

Parents are naturally tempted to compare the age at which their toddler begins to talk with the age at which other children they know start. They may think early talking is a sign of high intelligence. But there is no convincing evidence that a child who begins talking early is more intelligent than one who starts later. Most late talkers need no special attention or tutoring to catch up. In fact, Dr. Nelson found that many of the children in her study who reached the ten-word stage later than most others had already caught up to their peers in the number of words they could say by the time they were two years old.

Why Some Children Are Late Talkers

Why do some toddlers begin to talk later than others? Physically active children often concentrate all their energy on learning to use their bodies more skillfully. For them, learning to move about and manipulate things takes priority over learning to talk. They may start talking later than most other toddlers, but once they do start, they often do it all in a rush. At eighteen or twenty-four months their brains are more mature than they were a few months earlier, and at this age a child doesn't have to struggle so much through the trial and error and frustrations that younger toddlers sometimes experience in learning to speak.

There are some studies which suggest that *on the average* girls begin talking earlier than boys. This doesn't mean that all girls talk before all boys, or that the girls who do talk early will necessarily continue to be more verbal than boys. Some scientists who have noticed these differences among toddlers point out that girls tend to be slightly advanced in most aspects of development during the first few years of life. Others say that parents spend more time talking to girl babies, thus giving special encouragement to their language development. Whatever the cause, it's clear that these differences represent a temporary head start for girls, not a permanent advantage.

In families where parents put pressure on the child to learn to talk, the toddler may actually resist learning words, in order to escape the tension he feels. Sometimes, too, a toddler may learn to talk a bit later than his peers for just the opposite reason. Before a toddler can talk he has to rely on body language—primarily his gestures and facial expressions—and on preverbal sounds to get his parents' attention or to tell them he wants something. And some parents are so good at reading their toddler's nonverbal cues that the child

doesn't have much motivation to learn to express his needs in words.

There are many reasons why some children learn to talk later than others. And it's clear that in most cases there's nothing wrong with the child that is delaying his language learning. Still, delays in speech are among the most frequent indicators of developmental disturbances of all sorts. So if you are troubled by your toddler's language learning, it's a good idea to talk to your pediatrician. She may be able to reassure you that your child's language development is normal and that there is nothing wrong with him. And she can arrange specialized evaluation and treatment if these are needed. If your child is nearly two years old and has not begun to talk, you should definitely ask your pediatrician to examine him. She may be able to determine whether hearing difficulties or other medical problems are delaying his language development.

What You Can Do to Support Your Toddler's Language Learning

Being relaxed about your toddler's efforts to pronounce and use words correctly is important. But you can also take an *active* part in helping him learn to talk. You can do this by creating a rich verbal environment—which is to say, by talking to your child a lot. We're not suggesting that you need to drown your offspring in a sea of words. But as a general rule, the more words you say to your child, the more words he'll learn to understand and to say himself. A study by K. Allison Clarke-Stewart shows that the amount of talking di-

rected toward a child powerfully influences his ability to understand and use language.

The *way* you talk to your toddler can be just as important as how much you say. And parents seem naturally to speak to toddlers in ways that help them learn to talk. Parents seem to know that to communicate effectively with toddlers, they must speak to them differently than they speak to one another. So they generally use techniques that attract and hold the child's attention, and make it as easy as possible for the child to understand what is being said. For example, parents—

say "look" to attract the toddler's attention, and point to make clear what is being talked about.

exaggerate their facial expressions, pitch their voices high, and exaggerate their voice tones.

talk to toddlers about what's going on around them— things that the toddler can see, hear, and feel at that very moment.

speak more clearly and simply than they do when talking to adults, especially when the child is first learning to talk. They:

speak slowly.

use short words.

make an extra effort to pronounce words precisely.

stick to the present tense.

keep sentences as simple as possible.

repeat and emphasize important words.

talk to a toddler as if a real conversation were going on, even before the child can say a word. Much of what parents say to very young children is in the form of a question or a greeting. Both questions and greetings allow the parent to treat any response from the child—verbal or nonverbal—as a communicative response. A smile, squirm, glance, or gesture on the child's part is enough to keep the conversation going. The frequent pauses that characterize this sort of conversation are helpful, too, because they encourage a child to respond verbally and give him lots of chances to do so.

Almost anything you do with your toddler during the day can lead into the kinds of conversations that will help him learn to talk. Children this age love to look at picture books with a parent, and the relaxed conversations you can have about the things you see on each page can be marvelous language lessons. There are a wide variety of sturdy, well-illustrated books on the market designed specifically for toddlers.

You need only a few books to begin your child's collection. A book featuring pictures of animals or of familiar household objects is a favorite first book for many toddlers. Try to find a book with large, simple pictures. When you and your toddler look at the book together, you can point to each object and ask your child to name it. If that's a bit too hard for him, *you* can provide the name, and ask him to point to the picture. Then say, "That's right, it is a cup." You may want to go on to tell a little story about the cup; "That's like the cup you get your juice in, isn't it? Do you think it's filled with apple juice or orange juice?" Your toddler will get the most enjoyment and learn the most from these book times if you remember to

point to the object you're talking about;

emphasize its name;

keep your descriptions short and simple;

ask questions that involve him in the "reading."

Nursery-rhyme books are also popular with toddlers. Children enjoy the rhythm of these familiar rhymes. Many rhymes, such as "Pat-a-cake" and "This Little Piggy," can also be turned into games. And you can make up songs based on familiar rhymes, too. For instance, to the tune of "Here We Go 'Round the Mulberry Bush" you can create verses about "what we are going to eat for breakfast," "what we are going to do today," and so on. The gamelike atmosphere of these language lessons will make it fun and easy for your toddler to learn from them.

Your toddler will also enjoy books you make yourself with pictures of familiar objects cut from old magazines. You can also put together a book using family snapshots and simple drawings to tell a story about your toddler. The story can be real or made up. Many children treasure these homemade books about family members and familiar activities, and enjoy looking back at them as they grow older. For more suggestions about book play with toddlers, see the chapter titled "Pictures, Books, and Stories" in the "Play and Playthings" section of this guide.

Your child is eager to learn about the world. So remember to talk about what you are doing as you work around the house, whether you're mopping the kitchen floor, making the beds, washing the car, or setting the table. Talking as you work doesn't take any extra time, and your toddler will enjoy the attention.

When you are bathing your toddler, talk about the parts of his body, and about how different things such as the slippery soap and the rough washcloth feel when they are rubbed against his skin. You can also ask him to point to his own body parts.

When you are putting your toddler to bed, talk over the day's events. This sort of conversation will help him see an order in the day's activities, and contribute to his sense of security.

When you're getting dinner ready, talk about foods you're preparing and how you're preparing them. Talk about the shapes and colors and sizes of each food, and

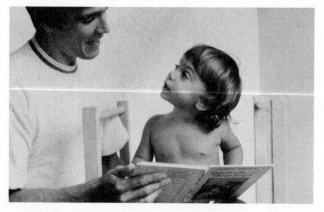

about how hungry you are, and how good the food will taste. You can also talk about flavors, sharing bites of foods that are sour, sweet, or salty. Be sure to talk slowly and in short sentences with lots of expression.

Studies show that the more exposure a child has to the world outside his home, the more advanced his language learning will be. So take your toddler on outings as often as you can—to the supermarket and other stores, and to parks, zoos, museums, and libraries. And when you're riding in the car, talk about sounds you hear, and point out and name interesting things you see.

We can also offer some other specific guidelines for gently encouraging your child's mastery of language. You probably do many of these things naturally; we're simply pointing them out to make it easier for you to keep them in mind.

Ask questions. And pause to give your toddler a chance to answer. In this way you invite him to get involved in conversations with you. Ask him to name something you're looking at, to tell how he's feeling, to describe what he is doing or would like to do, to say what he thinks of the weather, or anything else.

Repeat the words he uses. Your repetition will help him bring his pronunciation closer and closer to yours.

Elaborate on what he says. You can go a step beyond simply repeating to add more information and help increase your toddler's understanding. If he says, "Hot!" after tasting his oatmeal, you can say, "It is just a little hot. It will make your tummy feel warm inside. It tastes so good, too."

Let him see what you're talking about. It's easiest for your toddler to learn a new word if he can see the object, expression, or action that the word refers to at the same time that he's hearing the word. So match what you say with what you do. When you whisk off his shirt, say, "Off with your shirt." You can also match what you say with what you feel. If you feel tired, tell him so, and yawn and stretch, and rub your eyes or close them as if you're dozing off.

Make your talking times together fun for your toddler. Some of the best language learning takes place during playtime. Whether you and your toddler are playing with dolls or toy trucks, or playing pretend games with toy telephones or dress-up costumes, you have countless opportunities to talk with him and to encourage him to talk with you. Games such as "Eentsy Weentsy Spider," "Simon Says," and "Ring Around the Rosy" are also enjoyable ways to encourage language learning. There are some very attractive records you can buy to accompany such games.

Since fun is such an important ingredient in learning to talk, if you enjoy using baby talk you should go right ahead and do it. Baby talk won't hurt your toddler's language learning, as long as you don't use it exclusively —and no one does—and and as long as your toddler understands you. Many of the pet words toddlers make up are so endearing and amusing that it's hard not to repeat them.

Act as an interpreter for your toddler. Some of your toddler's words will be perfectly clear, while others will

be comprehensible only to people who know him very well. So help him communicate with other people by acting as his interpreter when he needs one. Don't go overboard. Give him a chance to try himself, but be prepared to step in when it's obvious that he needs your help.

Try to be patient with him. We've mentioned that by the end of their second year many children begin to ask questions. They ask questions about everyone and everything. From morning to evening, it's questions and more questions. Most of the questions a toddler asks are simply requests for information. Still, it's probably true, as many parents suspect, that sometimes a child asks questions just to get attention—especially if his parents are preoccupied with other matters at the time. When the questions are coming one right after the other, try to remember that the brighter a child is, the more questions he will ask, and do your best to answer. But don't feel you have to answer every question. It's okay to tell your child that you're tired and need a break.

Whenever you're talked out or answered out, it will be easier to get a break from your toddler if you have a good substitute to offer him. Records of songs or nursery rhymes designed for toddlers can provide some relief for you, and a good source of amusement and verbal stimulation for him. It's important to shop wisely for these, since most children's records are a bit too advanced to hold a toddler's interest for long. Don't forget that many public libraries lend children's records. A few television programs, such as "Sesame Street," also provide good language-learning experiences for toddlers. And, of course, your toddler loves to play with other children. When you give him a chance to do so, he'll be able to practice communicating with someone at his own level—and you'll get a break into the bargain.

The way a child learns to talk is a miracle, true, but it's one in which you have an important part. When you create a rich verbal environment for your child, you foster his language development the natural way. When you make his early conversations as easy and enjoyable as possible, you increase his motivation to learn new words and use them properly. By talking, listening, understanding, encouraging—by demonstrating a thousand times a day, in a thousand ways, the usefulness and expressiveness of language—you are putting at your child's disposal the most powerful, most versatile resource of civilization. There are few more wonderful gifts that you could give him.

7
How Toddlers Learn About Their Bodies

As we stress throughout this book, a toddler explores nearly everything she can get her fingers on. Handling objects helps her learn more about them: what they feel like, how heavy they are, how their parts move, what makes them work. One "object" that toddlers find especially fascinating is the human body. Young children love to explore their own bodies and their parents' bodies, to mouth and pull and poke and finger and discover what each part looks and feels like. And they enjoy learning names for body parts. You'll probably see a lot of body exploration throughout this period as your toddler grows to understand who she is and what she is made of and what she can do.

Exploring Her Own Body

Your toddler's interest in exploring her body isn't new; it began when she was a baby. When she was no more than four or five months of age, she started exploring her hands and fingers, feet and toes. Later she discovered her other body parts as well. These explorations continue throughout early childhood and are a part of normal, healthy development. After all, understanding more about herself and how *she* works helps her develop her identity. So all during toddlerhood you can expect to see your child explore her own body, sometimes with keen concentration, and at other times quite casually, when she's busily involved in some other activity. Such explorations will probably include fingering her navel; fondling and tugging on her hair; looking down the front of her clothing; mouthing and pulling on her fingers and toes; staring at herself in the mirror; touching parts of her face; and handling her nipples, buttocks, and genitals.

Before long, your child's fascination with her body and her growing interest in words will lead you into the nearly universal body-part-naming game of toddlerhood: "Where's your nose? Can you point to your nose? Yep, that's your nose! Now where is my nose? That's right! I have a nose like you. Now can you find Mommy's nose?" This game is an excellent way to help your toddler learn about herself, and we'll describe some other activities that serve a similar purpose later in this chapter. But first we'd like to discuss a concern that many parents have mentioned to us: genital play.

No matter how natural it is for young children to explore their bodies, you may feel a bit uncom-

fortable when your toddler handles her genitals. That's not surprising. Many adults consider sexual organs private, and in a different category from other parts of the body. So they may feel embarrassed when their toddler explores her genitals. Some parents also hear that playing with the genitals in toddlerhood is a sign of sexual development that's inappropriate for this age; they believe, therefore, that this should be discouraged. Other parents are just plain puzzled by the behavior. Whatever the reason, many parents discourage genital exploration by frowning, by removing the toddler's hands from her genitals, by telling her, "No, no, that's not nice," or by other means. If you are inclined to react this way to your toddler's genital explorations, we recommend that you consider the following points.

Most psychologists and child-behavior specialists believe that genital play is a healthy part of body exploration and that parents should accept it as such. No matter how you may feel about the specialness of the sexual organs, to your toddler they are just another part of her body. She can't possibly appreciate your sensitivity, because she lacks your sexual experience. If you actively discourage her genital exploration, you may give her the impression that there is something wrong with this part of her body. Because she doesn't understand why you find this exploration unacceptable, she may develop feelings of guilt and shame about herself and her body.

Since most of us feel that our sexual organs—indeed, our sexual selves—are personal and private, many parents have another concern about genital exploration in toddlerhood. They fear that if they let their toddler explore her genitals openly at this age, she'll *never* learn to share their feelings and beliefs about privacy. They fear she'll form distorted views of sexuality, or even become sexually interested in other children. This just isn't the case. When your child is older, she'll be able to learn about privacy and sexuality. That's the time to begin teaching her the difference between acceptable and unacceptable behavior regarding her sexual organs.

Helping Your Toddler Learn About Her Body

By the time they're twelve months old, most children have played body-naming games of the "This is your eye" variety. Most toddlers can readily point to parts of their faces when asked ("Can you show me your nose?"), and some can even point to the major parts of the body. Teaching your toddler the names of body parts is an important way of helping her learn about herself. And it's a delightful way for parents and toddler to share some time together. Now that she takes an active interest in all of her body, you can teach your child some new body-parts names.

We recommend that you start with the obvious ones: arms, hands, fingers; legs, feet, toes; and stomach or tummy. As you point to a body part, repeat its name a few times in different sentences. For example, "See here, Allison? This is your arm. You have two arms—here's another one, almost just like it. I have arms, too. We use our arms for drawing and throwing a ball and especially for hugging each other. I love to do that with my arms. I just love hugging you in my arms."

Of course, these sorts of activities needn't be dull or formal. You can help your toddler learn body-part names wherever you happen to be, using any sentences that come to mind. When she's exploring her toes during a diaper change, you might name them or play a simple nursery-rhyme game like "This Little Piggy Went to Market," using the toes of first one foot and then the other. When you're giving your toddler a bath, you can talk about body parts as you wash or dry them. Just keep these conversations lively, and your toddler will enjoy these important learning experiences.

After you've named a body part a few times, invite your toddler to point to it herself as you talk about it. You might say, for example, "I see your hand. Where, oh, where is Megan's hand? Can you show me your hand?" Again, this sort of verbal exercise shouldn't be conducted like a classroom test. Just incorporate body-part names into your conversations with your toddler any time you see fit. Now and then you might enjoy adding a song or rhyme game to these finding-the-body-part activities. Compose your own ditty, or use this popular one:

Put your finger on your nose, on your nose.
Put your finger on your nose, on your nose.
Put your finger on your nose, put your finger on
  your nose.
Put your finger on your nose, on your nose.
Put your finger on your head, on your head.
  (Etc.)

Once your child has learned the names of the major

body parts and can point to them, try adding the names of parts like elbows, knees, wrists, ankles, nipples, armpits, penis or vulva, and (a special favorite) the belly button. The belly button almost always evokes a particularly gleeful response, partly because it feels so tickly when you touch it, and party because its name is so funny. When you and your toddler are standing in front of a mirror, name body parts she can't normally see: her shoulders, back, and buttocks.

You might feel a bit hesitant about naming your toddler's nipples, buttocks, and genitals, just as you might be uncomfortable when she explores these parts of her body. However, we recommend that you try to overcome this reluctance and teach her the names of every body part. Ignoring some of them in your name games can have the same effect as discouraging her genital exploration. Sooner or later your child will wonder why your enthusiasm for teaching her about her body suddenly dies when her interest is directed toward certain parts of it. So if you want your toddler to feel comfortable with *all* of her body, try adding the words *vulva, vagina, clitoris, nipples,* and *anus* or *buttocks* to your games. If you have a son, use the names of his genitals: *penis,* and *scrotum.* You're bound to feel awkward at first. In fact, you may even catch yourself blushing or glancing self-consciously over your shoulder to see if anyone is listening. But you'll soon overcome your inhibitions. And if you feel more comfortable using family nicknames for the genitals or anus, go right ahead. In fact, it's best to avoid making a big deal about the subject one way or another. Setting a comfortable tone and providing in-formation in an open, relaxed manner is more important than the particular words you choose.

Over time, you may find that a relaxed attitude toward all of your toddler's body parts pays off in a number of ways. Several parents told us that when it came time to begin toilet training, they were quite comfortable discussing urination and elimination because their children already had a matter-of-fact attitude toward their private parts. This openness made toilet training a lot easier than it might have been otherwise.

She'll Explore Your Body, Too

In addition to exploring their own bodies, toddlers delight in exploring their parents' bodies. Your toddler will probably poke into your nose and mouth, rub her fingers against your scratchy cheek (if you're male) or smooth cheek (if you're female), pull on your neck, finger and chew on your hands, poke at your breasts (especially if you're female—even through your clothing), and otherwise show an interest in manipulating your body. This is to be expected. Your child is curious to find out about you, what you are made of, and how you and she are similar and different. These explorations are some of her ways of learning she's a member of the human kind. Use these sessions to teach her the names of your body parts, and mention that she has many of the same. If you're female, you might want to tell your small daughter that when she gets older, she'll grow breasts, too.

Sometimes your toddler's explorations may become a little too venturesome, if not downright dangerous.

She may reach for your eyes, or pull your hair, or try to bend your fingers the wrong way. When her poking and probing get to be too much for you, hold her wrist or hand and tell her gently but firmly how you feel. You might say something like "Don't pull so hard because it hurts me. Be gentle."

Some of your toddler's explorations can be embarrassing, too, especially when she conducts them in public places. If you feel uncomfortable when she touches your breasts or genitals, remove her hand as before. If her probing persists, try distracting her with another activity. For example, start playing a nursery-rhyme game, or hand her a toy, or just carry her around and talk about the things you both see. On those rare occasions when distraction isn't successful, deal with the situation directly by saying something like "I don't want you to touch me there." A remark like this does run the risk of implying that your breasts or genitals are somehow wicked, and it's true that you ought to avoid making your toddler feel guilty about her natural interest in other people's bodies. But in a situation like this, you needn't put your toddler's concerns above your own.

Using Playthings to Teach Your Toddler Names

You can also use playthings to teach your toddler names of body parts. Naming games involving toys will add an interesting new dimension to her learning of words, because they help her better understand the basic concept of a name. By using a number of different objects to illustrate the concept of eyes, for example, you help teach your toddler that an eye is an eye whether on a human body, a doll, a picture of a person, or a favorite teddy bear. Besides, toys can make vocabulary-building games more fun. The following suggestions will help get you started:

1. When your toddler is playing with a doll, take a minute to talk about parts of its body (including its face), and then some corresponding parts of your body and your toddler's body. You might also name the facial features on stuffed toys that have detailed faces.

2. Draw or paint a brightly colored face on a paper plate. Talk about the facial parts, and encourage your toddler to point to them.

3. Whenever you and your toddler are reading a book together, talk about the different body parts of the pictured characters. This activity is especially appropriate when your toddler snuggles up to you while you're reading a magazine. You can surely find at least a few people in the advertisements to talk about.

4. Make a body poster of your toddler. For this you'll need a large sheet of paper, such as a piece from a roll of wide shelf paper, the back of an old roll of wallpaper, or a white shopping bag opened up. Have your toddler lie naked (or diaper-clad) face up on the paper, and trace the outline of her body with a crayon or marker. Then have her get up so you can draw in some of the features: the face, the belly button, the knees, and maybe the nipples and genitals. You might also add your toddler's name and age for future reference. Tape the finished poster to the wall so the drawn feet just about hit the floor. This way your toddler can easily see the poster, and even stand

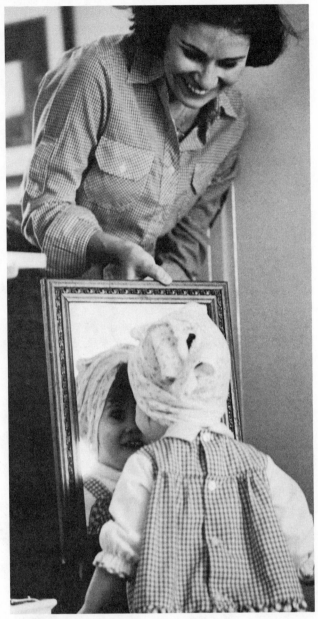

in front of it to match her body to the drawing. You can use this poster as a life-size chart for teaching the names of body parts—and as a wonderful room decoration, too.

5. To make a smaller poster, trace your toddler's hands and hang the drawing on the wall within easy reach so she can match her real hands to their pictured counterparts. You can also use tracings of her hands as illustrations in a homemade book. (See the chapter "Pictures, Books, and Stories" for more book-making suggestions.)

Understanding Changes in Appearance

Another aspect of learning about the body is understanding that a person remains essentially the same even when his or her appearance changes. Your toddler understands this concept about you. Even if you change your hairstyle, wear a new outfit, or put on a different pair of glasses, she still recognizes you. And it's lucky she does; otherwise we parents would have to look exactly the same every day!

Many toddlers have little experience with seeing changes in their own appearances, however, so you can add to your toddler's understanding of herself and her body by letting her see her face in different guises. Let your toddler look at herself in the mirror when she's wearing swimming goggles or sunglasses, or just glasses frames without any lenses. If you don't have any frames available, make a pair of fake glasses for her out of long pipe-cleaners. You can also stand your toddler in front of a mirror and put different hats on her head, or even a wig. If you have a flair for theatrics, you might even paint her face like a clown's for a special treat.

She'll probably be fascinated by the different ways she can look.

Learning about her body helps your toddler develop her self-image. When you take an active and enthusiastic part in your toddler's self-discovery by teaching her names of all her body parts, letting her explore your body, and playing other learning games with her, you let her know that you share her interest in finding out who she is. This is one way you tell her how important she is to you, and how much you love her.

8
Toilet Learning the Natural Way

Sometime during the second year of your child's life, you will probably start wondering about the best time to teach him how to use the toilet. Your next-door neighbor insists that her Jimmy never needed a diaper after he was one and a half, and your mother-in-law reports that your husband was completely trained by his first birthday. We advise you to take these stories with a grain of salt. Psychologists have observed that mothers tend to misremember the age at which their babies achieved important developmental milestones, and that the error is usually toward a younger age than was actually the case. In addition, learning to use the toilet is a gradual process, with the different stages occurring at different times. The completion of the process is not obvious in the way that the first word or the first step is.

Research in child development shows that the average child does not achieve reliable daytime control until two and a half or three years of age, and that nighttime control comes between the third and fourth birthdays for most children. On the whole, boys take longer to gain control than girls do. It is interesting to note that these findings hold equally true for toddlers whose parents began trying to train them at nine or ten months and for those whose parents held off until twenty-four months. In other words, starting early does not guarantee finishing early. All an early start guarantees is a long time spent rushing to bathrooms, cleaning up accidents, feeling lots of frustration, and fearing failure. On the other hand, if you wait till around your child's second birthday, when he has shown both physical and psychological readiness, toilet training can be quick and easy and not at all unpleasant for you or your toddler. We strongly suggest that you do both your toddler and yourself a favor and wait until he is ready, able, and willing.

Learning from the Mistakes of Others

A generation or two ago, mothers were advised to start training their babies very early, even before the first birthday. They were instructed to begin by holding their infants over a pot at the time of day when a bowel movement was expected. Sometimes this practice "worked" because the baby was fairly regular and the mother trained *herself* to catch the baby's bowel movement. Often the practice didn't work, though, especially if the baby's movements were irregular, which is quite common. Bladder training was similar; the mother was required to be constantly on the alert to try to get her toddler to the potty just before he urinated. Again, it was a matter of the mother's training herself, not her child, and because failure was practically inevitable, the whole business was very frustrating and upsetting. There was so much social pressure to try to train children early, though, that mothers tended to blame themselves, or worse, their toddlers, when failures occurred, instead of questioning the wisdom of trying to toilet train so early.

A number of second-time mothers have told us that they wish they hadn't tried to train their first child as early as they did. Sadly, they describe the pressures from grandparents and neighbors, the struggles and tears and anger, and the inevitable failures of their bewildered toddlers. And they say firmly: "With this second baby, I'm going to wait till *he's* ready! I'm never going through that again!"

Why You Should Wait

Learning to eliminate in the toilet involves a complicated series of steps, and it is impossible for a young toddler to master them. Think about what is required: first your toddler must understand what you want him to do. Second, he must realize that he is *about* to urinate (not that he is *already* urinating). Third, he must get himself to the nearest bathroom. Fourth, he has to be able to remove his clothing and sit on the potty or toilet. Finally, he must *relax* his sphincter muscles and let the urine out. All in all, you can see that a very complicated set of skills is required.

You may have heard that the period of toilet training is a very difficult and upsetting time, and you may be dreading it. But most of the difficulties and upsets people talk about were the results of parents trying too early and expecting the impossible. A toddler becomes upset because he's being asked to do something that he can't do. He loves his parents and wants to please them very much, and he begins to feel like a failure when he can't. The experience is frustrating for the mother, too, and she often gets angry and emotional, even though she meant to be patient. A few lucky successes may make her think that her toddler really *does* understand what to do and that he is just being uncooperative when he fails. She feels like a failure herself, too, so she increases her pressure on the child, and an unpleasant battle results, which no one can win.

If you wait until your child is ready, both in physical maturation and in his ability to understand what you want, you can avoid all this turmoil. If you wait until after his second birthday, he will want to stay dry and clean "the big-boy way" and he'll feel good about himself when he succeeds. Furthermore, if he's older, toilet training will take only a couple of weeks or months, instead of a year or more. In this day of disposable diapers and cheap, dependable diaper service, the wait is well worth it.

Getting Ready

Somewhere between eighteen and twenty-four months, you can begin to prepare your toddler for the toilet-training period, if you wish to. (Maybe you're already doing this and haven't even realized it.)

The first, most important step is to get your child to understand what you want him to do. He's worn diapers all his life. You will have to help him begin to understand what urine and feces are, where they come from, and where you want them to go—eventually. One way is to let your toddler join you when you use the bath-

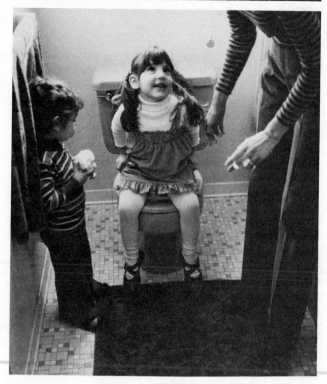

room. (A mother may have no choice: many toddlers go through a phase where they're so upset over losing sight of you that bathroom togetherness is the rule, like it or not. But it's important for fathers to take part in teaching their toddlers about how men use the bathroom, too.) When your child follows you into the bathroom, tell him what you're doing and why. Let him flush the toilet for you, if he wants to. Second and third children always seem easier to toilet train, and part of the reason is that they often observe big brothers or sisters using the bathroom and want to copy them.

Teach your toddler the words you use in your family for urinating and defecating, and then help him apply these words to himself and what he does. For instance, you can often tell when your toddler is having a bowel movement in his diaper: he stops all activity and gets a very concentrated look on his face. One father described this look as that of an army sergeant arriving to inspect the barracks. Use such opportunities to label what he's doing matter-of-factly. Just say, "B.M.? Billy making a B.M.?" to make him aware of the feeling of defecation and the word that goes with it. Encourage him to begin telling *you* about it. Later, when you change his diaper as usual, it's a good idea to show him his bowel movement and name it again, before you flush it away. Some toddlers get upset at actually seeing their bowel movements being flushed away: if your toddler is one of these, respect his wishes. Ask him if *he'd* like to do the flushing; that may make it okay. If not, do it later when he's become interested in something else.

Keep your toilet talks positive. As you chat with your toddler about what you do in the bathroom and what he's doing in his diapers, avoid acting as if his body

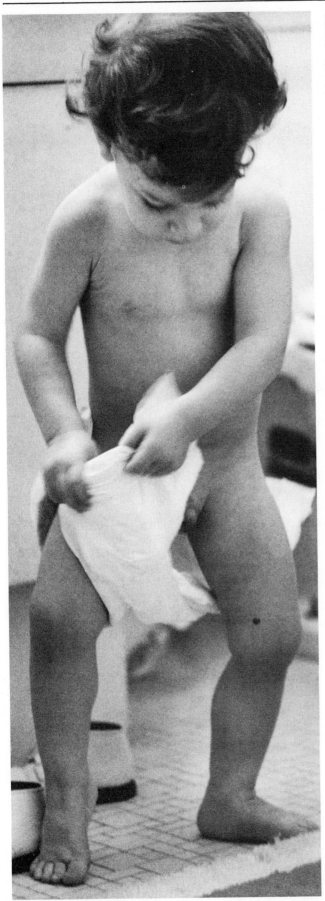

products are dirty or "yucky." You don't want to teach him to be ashamed of urinating or defecating, because then he'll start hiding from you when he needs to eliminate. Later, when you want him to give you a signal before he urinates or defecates so that you can help him use the toilet, he'll be afraid to let you know. Besides, if you make a child think the products of his body are bad or dirty, he'll begin to believe that he's bad or dirty, too.

Before you begin toilet training in earnest, it's important for your toddler to be capable of pulling his own pants down. Many two-year-olds resist toilet training because they have to run to Mom for help in removing clothes every single time, and they hate to be dependent. So make sure that your toddler has shorts or pants with elastic waists, and let him practice pulling them down all by himself when he gets undressed at night.

Last but not least, as your child's second birthday approaches, you may want to introduce him to the potty chair or toilet seat that he'll be using when you toilet train him. The point is just to get him accustomed to it, not to put him on it yet. Talk about how he'll be using this seat, after he's two, to go to the bathroom the way big people do. Let him practice sitting on it (if he wishes) with all his clothes on. He might try perching his doll or teddy bear on it or use the pot itself as a hat for a month or two. That's fine too.

Then—be patient. The next step is up to your toddler.

When Your Toddler Shows Readiness

Your toddler will let you know in two ways that he is ready to take the next step in learning to use the toilet. First, he'll signal his physical readiness by staying dry for longer and longer periods of time. And then he'll show his intellectual readiness by beginning to use the words you've taught him for both urination and bowel movements and by actually telling you that he's urinating or defecating as he does so. (Telling you *before* he does so is far more difficult; don't expect that for a while yet.)

Now it's time to suggest that he sit on his potty several times a day. Pick likely times: right after a meal or a snack, while you run his bath water, or any time you notice that his pants are still dry after a couple of hours. Talk about what you expect of him, using the words that he has become familiar with over the past months. Keep his time on the potty short and cheerful in order to keep him cooperating. Five minutes is probably long enough. If he resists, let him get off the potty right away. Never strap him to the seat.

Each time your toddler urinates or defecates in the potty praise him for his success. There's no need to reward him with candy or any other bribe; in fact, it can be detrimental to do so. The reward of your pleasure in his accomplishment, and the simple comfort of dry pants will soon be enough to keep him trying.

Make sure that your toddler is in charge of as much of the toilet-training process as possible. He is at the "*me* do it!" stage, and he feels proud of his growing

Trials and triumphs of toilet learning

independence and his new skills. He *wants* to be grown up and to have control over his body, and all you need to do is assist him in this effort.

To this end, you might switch him from diapers to training pants, which he can pull off and on, when he seems ready for actual toilet training. (Continue using diapers during naps and at nighttime, though, until he shows considerable daytime reliability.) The switch to training pants will symbolize for your toddler the big change in his life; it will help him feel more grown up and therefore dispose him to be cooperative. An additional benefit of training pants is that, with them on, a toddler is more aware of what is happening when he urinates or defecates. The results are more apparent than they were when he had diapers and plastic pants on. Buy or borrow at least a dozen pairs of training pants, by the way; wet pants will be very common during the next several weeks.

Never punish or scold or shame your toddler for his accidents. Treat them casually, but as helpful lessons for both of you: "Oh, you wet your pants. Next time

try to pee in your potty and keep your pants dry, okay?" Then let him toss his wet pants into the hamper and put on some nice dry ones from the handy pile in the bathroom or bedroom, all by himself. Note that you should have reminded him to try sitting on the potty a little sooner.

You may think your toddler is ready to be trained, and earnestly start a campaign, only to discover after a week or ten days that no progress is being made. Successes in the potty are few and far between, and your child doesn't seem to understand what is expected of him. If this happens, you might as well put him back in diapers and forget training for a month or two. Try again when you note more signs of readiness.

Learning to use the toilet is a very complicated process and usually takes several months, even when you wait until your toddler is ready. Don't expect your toddler's progress to be smooth. Sometimes he will improve more slowly than you might like, and at other times he may even seem to lose ground, apparently forgetting his new skills under the stress of illness, a move, a new baby, or some smaller problem in his life. At such times, be patient and extra loving, and assure him of your confidence in him. Remember, two and a half to three years old is only the *average* age at which toddlers learn to stay dry through a day; the range of ages is great. Some children are trained at two, but many cannot manage to stay dry till after their third birthdays. One mother who was discussing her son's toilet training with us had just the right attitude. "He'll do it when he's ready," she said. "I *know* he won't get married with his diapers on."

PART TWO
Personality and Behavior

1
Introduction

This section of the guide is about how a toddler gets along with others. We will talk about two major topics that come under this heading: discipline, and a toddler's relationships with people besides his mother.

Discipline is a central concern for the parents of a toddler. Once a child can move about on his own, the whole house is his for the taking. And take it he will, unless his parents find some way to control his explorations. Dealing with the toddler's propensity to get into everything is the first real disciplinary issue many parents face. And finding an approach to discipline that is firm without being restrictive can be a complicated business. Often, the first question parents must answer is what they mean by discipline in the first place. And unfortunately, many of them answer it by saying that discipline means punishment for bad behavior.

For us, discipline means something different. It means guiding a child toward desirable behavior. This definition of discipline is fundamental to our whole approach to child rearing. It rests on our most basic understanding of what a toddler is like, how he thinks and reacts. We believe a toddler is not mature enough to control himself to be either bad or good. Therefore he is not mature enough to make any sense out of punishment. As long as he lacks the ability to control himself, his parents must provide the control. And the more sparingly and lovingly they do so, the easier it will be for them to manage the child's behavior, both during toddlerhood and in the future.

In the first chapter of this section we will talk more about our general approach to discipline. We will explain how it differs from the approach by which many

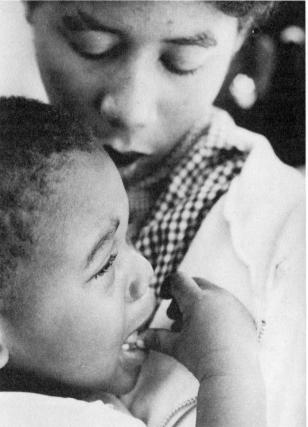

of us were raised, and why we believe our approach will help you get discipline off on the right foot. In the chapter "Adjusting to Life with Your Explorer" we will suggest a plan which steers clear of the traditional "no, no!" and hand-slap approach to keeping a toddler away from things he shouldn't touch. Our plan is designed to respect two basic needs: the toddler's need to touch, since for a young child touching is learning, and his parents' need to protect both the child and their household valuables.

Of course a toddler's tendency to get into everything isn't the only disciplinary issue with which parents must deal. The child soon begins asserting himself in other ways as well, becoming much less cooperative and agreeable than he was as a baby. Contrariness is a fact of life during toddlerhood. Essentially it's a healthy sign of growth, a kind of declaration of independence by which the child signals his need to leave behind him the total dependency of babyhood and to begin working toward the relative independence of childhood. But a toddler's contrariness can be really hard on his parents, especially if they react by fighting back. In the chapter "Coping with Contrariness" we will offer specific suggestions to help you get through this period in a toddler's development.

Parents often ask questions about their toddler's dawdling. A young child can take forever finishing his bath or walking to the store. And parents say that this can be really frustrating when they are in a hurry. We talk about why toddlers dawdle and what to do about this in the chapter "Dealing with Dawdling."

There's probably no single behavior that confuses and upsets the parents of a toddler more than temper tantrums. When a toddler has a temper tantrum, he seems completely out of control. It's often impossible to figure out exactly why he's having the tantrum or what to do about it. In fact, many parents find that *nothing* they try seems to help once a tantrum is underway. Distressing as temper tantrums are, they actually serve a useful purpose for the toddler. In the chapter "Surviving Temper Tantrums" we will talk about why toddlers have tantrums, and offer suggestions for preventing those tantrums that can be prevented and for managing those that can't.

Toddlers have many fears. A toddler may suddenly seem much more reluctant than he was only a few weeks ago to let his parents out of his sight. Or he may begin violently resisting the baths he used to love. Or he may seem terrorized by a neighbor's dog. Figuring out how to deal with these fears can be a real problem for many parents. Often the fears seem to make no sense. But a child is never fearful without reason. In the chapter "Helping Your Toddler Overcome Her Fears" we will discuss the common fears of toddlerhood, trying to account for them, and will offer specific guidelines for helping a toddler overcome each one.

One of the things toddlers need most in managing their struggle to grow up is love. Love and discipline (in the form of effective guidance) go hand in hand; neither is possible without the other. A toddler's needs

for affection, physical closeness, and comforting are very powerful. But while a toddler depends heavily on his parents for love, approval, and encouragement, he also has his own resources for gaining comfort and security. Thumb and pacifier-sucking as well as attachment to a "cuddly" are signs of a toddler's growing resourcefulness in managing the normal tensions of growing up. In the chapter titled "Loving and Comforting Your Toddler" we will talk about the countless opportunities parents have every day to show their toddler they love him, and will also address the worries parents often have about their toddler's reliance on his thumb or a pacifier or cuddly.

Toddlers live in families. No one questions the importance of a toddler's relationship with his mother. But until recently, much less importance was attached to the toddler's relationship with his father. Fortunately, times are changing. Fathers are becoming increasingly involved in the lives of their young children, and scientists are paying more attention than ever before to the benefits the whole family derives from this growing involvement. We feel strongly that when a toddler has two parents, they should share both the burdens

and the benefits of parenthood. At the same time, we recognize that a father who works all day can arrive at home with little time or energy for his toddler. In the chapter "Fathering: A New View" we will talk about the unique contribution many fathers make to their toddler's development. We will also suggest some ways a father might find time for his toddler without neglecting all the other things he needs to do after work.

Many people used to think that one-year-olds were too young to relate to each other. But we're beginning to realize that one-year-olds who have a chance to play together regularly do enjoy each other's company, and that they are even capable of forming real friendships. Also, any toddler who is not an only child has to learn to get along with his brothers and sisters as well as with his parents and peers. And his brothers and sisters have to learn to get along with him. The relationships among children in the same family are always marked by some conflict. But parents can do a lot to minimize these conflicts, often, ironically, by simply staying out of them. We will talk about all of these issues in the chapter titled "Helping Your Toddler Enjoy Other Children."

A child's first birthday is a landmark. When the first year ends many mothers find themselves looking outward again, wanting to have more part in the world outside their homes. Still, many mothers have mixed feelings about leaving their toddlers, especially since many one-year-olds seem particularly sensitive to separations. Mothers wonder whether it's all right to leave their toddlers in the care of another person; they have questions about how to find someone they can trust to care for their children. Such concerns are most pressing for the growing number of mothers who have jobs outside their homes. In the chapter "When Someone Else Cares for Your Toddler" we'll talk about the effects on a toddler of being cared for by another adult, and discuss several possible baby-sitting and day-care arrangements.

Finally, many parents of toddlers must cope with special situations. Single parenthood, moving to a new home, taking a toddler to the hospital, and living with a handicapped toddler are all discussed in the chapter titled "Special Situations."

2
Getting Discipline Off on the Right Foot

Once your toddler is able to walk, discipline becomes a major issue. Now that she can get around on her own, she's into everything. So you have to find a way to keep her out of trouble and danger. Within a few months, she will begin asserting herself in other ways, as well. *No!* will become her favorite word. And you'll be faced with the problem of balancing her need to test her budding independence against your need to maintain a degree of reasonable control over what she does and doesn't do.

The Meaning of Discipline During Toddlerhood
Nearly every parent sees discipline as an important issue. But there's a lot of basic disagreement among parents about what discipline really means. For us, disciplining a toddler means two things. It means guiding her behavior, and it means teaching her how to cooperate.

It's important to guide a young toddler's behavior rather than insisting that she behave the way you want her to, because she's simply not mature enough to control herself yet. She can't be good, or wait, or see things from another person's point of view. If you demand that she be more self-controlled than nature made her, your efforts at discipline are bound to fail. For instance, if you require her to pick up her toys when she doesn't feel like it—as she often won't—you may end up with a full-fledged battle on your hands. So you're better off

taking a less insistent approach. You could suggest a game—perhaps a race in which you put the pop beads into one container while she puts the blocks into another. When you take this sort of approach, you're much more likely to get a toddler to do what you want without fussing or fighting.

It's important to see that this approach to discipline doesn't simply involve avoiding conflict (though this can be advantage enough, given the level of tension in the homes of many toddlers). More important, this approach also helps *teach* a toddler how to cooperate. A cooperative impulse is the essence of any effective self-discipline; it's basic to getting along with parents and with other people all through life. And though a one-year-old isn't yet capable of cooperating consistently, she is ready to begin to learn if we teach her in small steps. When you truly cooperate with her, as you do when you turn clean-up into a game you both play, you are teaching her cooperation in the most effective way possible: by example. You are helping her learn that while she must clean up after playing, cooperation can be fun, and that you care about her enough to help her with her work.

"That's Not the Way I Was Brought Up!"
This notion of discipline may be quite different from others you've come across, or even from your own ideas. Many parents interpret a toddler's independent behavior as a sign of defiance. They feel they must "train" a toddler in order to curb her behavior before it becomes a pattern. Instead of trying to avoid conflicts, these parents feel they must try to win them. And they see punishment, in the form of yelling or hitting,

as a weapon in this struggle. Unfortunately, parents who approach discipline this way are making the process harder than it needs to be, both for their toddlers and for themselves.

A recent study by a group of psychologists, Drs. Donelda Stayton, Robert Hogan, and Mary Ainsworth, shows that a mother's efforts to train or discipline her child by slapping the child's hand or by physically forcing her to do as her mother wishes are not successful in the long run. In this study it turned out that the young children who responded earliest to commands such as "Come here" and prohibitions such as "No," were those whose mothers had always responded warmly and supportively when their children needed something—not the children whose mothers had tried to train them through punishment. This study suggests that guidance and cooperation, not punishment, are the keys to effective discipline during toddlerhood. The more sensitive and cooperative you are with your toddler, the more you'll provide the experience she needs to learn to cooperate with you. Her desire to please you will grow, and so will her understanding of *how* people go about cooperating with one another.

It's not hard to understand why the punitive approach to discipline is still used. It's tough to be supportive when you're feeling angry or frustrated or confused by your toddler's behavior. Besides, punishment was very much a part of the way most of us were brought up. The notion of discipline as something you did *to* a child rather than *with* her, went almost unchallenged in our parents' generation, and most of us grew up in families where spankings and threats of lost love were common practice.

Our mixed feelings about punishment are generally hardest to deal with when we see our children do something for which we remember being punished ourselves and which we have come to think of as "bad."

The effects of being raised this way are often paradoxical. Many of us who were punished as children have come to think of punishment as natural or even necessary. But at the same time, we have deep feelings of anger, resentment, and humiliation about the way we were disciplined when we were young.

Our mixed feelings about punishment are generally hardest to deal with when we see our children do something for which we remember being punished ourselves, and which we have come to think of as "bad." At these times, we may be so uncomfortable that we feel an almost overwhelming pressure to nip the behavior in the bud. And all too often we fall back on precisely the techniques to deal with this behavior which our parents used with us—even if these techniques didn't work and caused a lot of pain.

Dr. Therese Benedek takes a very optimistic view of this complicated and troublesome issue. She points out that grown-ups get a chance to resolve some of these early childhood struggles by being parents themselves. When we stop ourselves on the verge of reacting to our toddlers in some ingrained but unproductive way, we may be able to see with a special clarity how our reactions are rooted in the unrealistically high standards that *we* were forced to live up to as children. Comparing these standards with a realistic view of our toddlers' capacities and needs may help us to be more accepting of them and to be more accepting of ourselves, as well. And the self-acceptance we gain this way may ultimately make us happier people and better parents.

Expressing Anger Without Hurting the Toddler

By handling your toddler in a loving and understanding way you won't necessarily avoid all the troubles of toddlerhood. You'll probably escape the worst possible moments, but from time to time you're just bound to find yourself in a situation that makes you really angry. After all, it *is* frustrating to live with someone who wants to do more things than her skill and understanding really allow.

When you feel angry you need to admit it. But as a parent you need to find a way to admit and express and relieve your anger without hurting your toddler. In fact, if you can show her how to release and rechannel negative feelings, you'll actually be helping her. She certainly gets angry often enough, and you want her to learn to express her hostile feelings rather than bottling them up inside until she has to explode. But you also want her to learn to express her anger without deeply wounding other people.

Children always learn more about how they should behave from the way we treat them than from what we tell them to do. So it's especially important that you express your anger to your toddler without treating her disrespectfully. You want to let the child know, in no uncertain terms, that you are angry about what she's done. But you don't want to make her feel that she's a bad person just because she's done something bad. And you don't want to bully her or frighten her either. So you say, "I'm really mad that you did that," in a firm voice, and then you just as firmly stop her from doing it again, if she's about to. But you don't yell at

her, or hit her, or yank her away roughly, or call her names, if you can possibly help it. Put yourself in your toddler's shoes. Wouldn't it be awful if you made some mistake at work and your boss made you feel like a fool, and screamed at you and grabbed your arm, and shook you? (Especially if he were three times as big as you!)

All too often, that's just the way we treat a toddler when she doesn't behave the way we want her to. This *doesn't* help her learn to control herself. In fact, over time it teaches her just the opposite. At first, when we lash out at her she simply feels afraid and hurt. But gradually she begins to get the message; yelling and hitting are the way to behave when you're angry. And if we continue to stifle her every time she shows her temper while at the same time giving free rein to *our* temper, she will sooner or later learn another lesson: might makes right. She'll try to keep her angry and resentful feelings under control with us and with older children, but beware when a baby or small pet crosses her path. Defenseless creatures may become the target for all the feelings that have been building inside of her with no place to go.

Of course, no matter how well you understand and channel your frustration and anger with a toddler, occasionally you're going to fly off the handle. Sometimes things go so far that you just have to let off steam by yelling at your child. Or, on rare occasions, you may feel the urge to smack her bottom. A spanking won't do her any permanent harm, as long as this technique plays only a small part in your general approach to discipline.

When you've blown up at a toddler, you'll probably feel guilty soon afterward, and then it's a good idea to think about what you'd like if you were in your toddler's place. You'd probably appreciate a simple, honest apology. Apologizing isn't so hard to do, and usually everyone feels better once the air is cleared, after hugs have been exchanged and tears kissed away.

Helping Your Toddler Learn How to Behave: Clarity and Consistency

In many ways a toddler is still little more than a baby. She is barely talking, she can't think ahead, and she's incapable of making any but the most basic discriminations and choices. So when you decide how you want your toddler to behave, you must communicate your expectations to her in as clear and consistent a way as you possibly can. Otherwise, the limits you set will go right over her head.

Most of all, being clear means being brief. Since your toddler has just begun to talk, a long-winded discussion of what she can and can't do and why will only leave her confused. Tell her what you want her to know as simply and quickly as possible.

Being clear also means setting limits *firmly,* so that there is only one possible interpretation: "This is for real. We mean business." If your child is throwing blocks, for example, and you don't want her to, you must tell her so immediately, and be prepared to remove her—or the blocks—right away if she can't control herself. Whenever possible, you should be as clear with your toddler about what she *can* do as you are about what she *can't.* You do yourself and her a favor if you suggest an alternative to throwing blocks: perhaps a pillow toss, or a game of catch with a ball. The message should clearly and firmly direct the toddler toward acceptable behavior: blocks are not for throwing; pillows are.

Providing alternatives like this to behavior that's out of bounds will make the limits you set easier for your toddler to follow. But setting partial limits is only asking for trouble. Your toddler can understand the difference between splashing water and not splashing water while she's taking a bath. But when you say, "You can splash as long as you don't get too much on the floor," you are courting conflict, because you are asking your toddler to make a discrimination she is simply not capable of.

Clarity and consistency go hand in hand. The clearest rule will do no good if it is not applied consistently. Some inconsistency is inevitable, though. From time to time we are simply too tired to enforce a rule we are usually firm about, or we may make an exception for a special occasion. There may be minor differences between the disciplinary styles of the two parents, or between the rules of a child's parents and the rules of another adult with whom she spends time such as a grandparent or baby-sitter.

In general, a child can adjust to small differences, and she can even learn from them. But serious inconsistencies are another story. They can confuse a child of this age and make it much harder for her to learn how she's supposed to behave. Self-confidence is the basis for clear, consistent discipline. When parents are sure of themselves, it's easy for them to be firm. When they have basic disagreements about how to discipline their child, on the other hand, it's virtually impossible for either of them to feel self-confident.

Parents who find themselves in this bind need to try to talk about their differences in order to work out a plan they can both live with. Talking can be tough, but ignoring or denying differences is worse. When parents don't talk, they feel a tension that gets expressed in all sorts of other ways, leaving the whole family on edge and confused. If you and your spouse have serious disagreements about child rearing, it might help you to keep in mind that humor sometimes makes compromise easier. If the two of you can first laugh together at your toddler's antics, and at the comical side of your serious differences of opinion, after a while you may feel relieved enough to begin trying to resolve some of those serious differences through productive discussion.

To sum up, effective discipline during toddlerhood involves guiding and teaching, not pushing and punishing. It respects the child, accepting the needs, capacities, and limitations that are part and parcel of this stage in her development. Effective discipline is also clear and consistent; it is designed to make it as easy as possible for a toddler to learn how to get along with us and with other people. With these general principles in mind, let's turn to some of the practical problems that most concern the parents of toddlers and see how these principles apply.

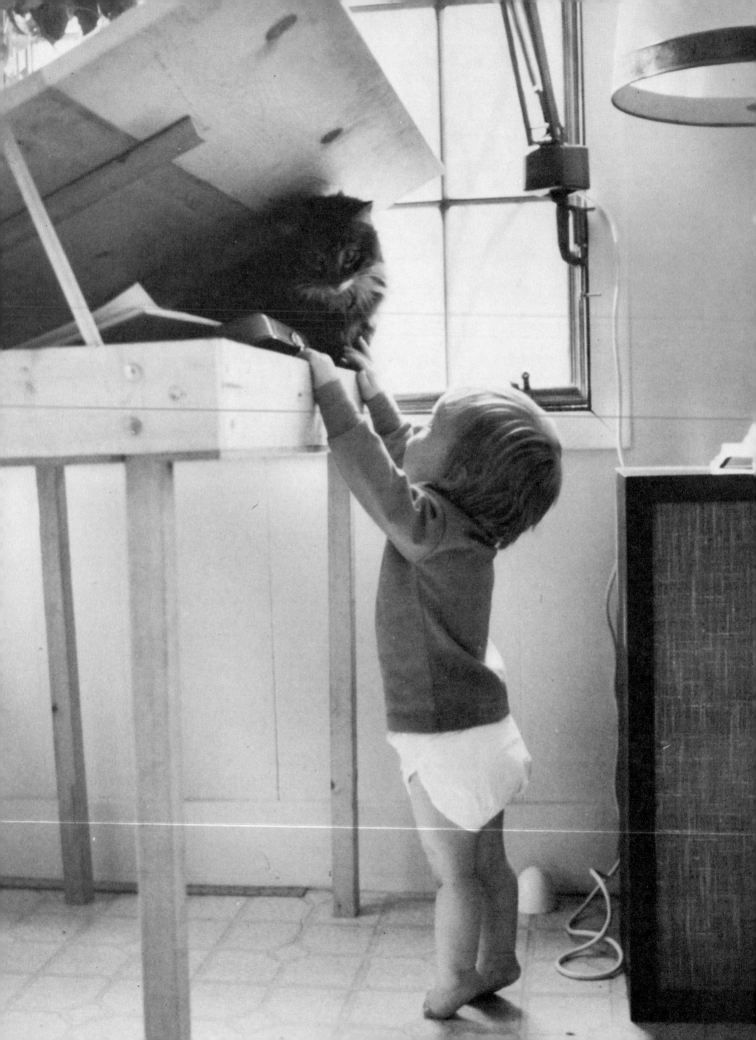

3
Adjusting to Life with Your Explorer

Every parent is thrilled when her baby takes his first steps. It's an exciting sign that the child is growing up. But growing up also means changing, and your child's first steps are a signal that your life together is about to change dramatically. You had a preview of what it's like to live with an explorer when your baby was crawling. But he can reach many more things standing up, and once he's a confident walker, he gets around much faster. Now he spends endless hours moving from room to room poking into everything.

One minute he's playing happily in his room. The next minute you hear the bathtub running full blast. You rush into the bathroom to find the bathmat drenched, the contents of the wastebasket spread about the floor, and your toddler trying to flush several of his bathtub toys down the toilet. Or you leave him in your bedroom for a moment and come back to find he's emptied your dresser drawers into the hamper and piled every pair of shoes you own on top. Later, he'll be involved with his toys on the kitchen floor while you cook dinner. But before you know it, he's into the cabinets under the sink where you keep the bleach and detergents.

In fact, the first weeks with your new toddler may make you feel that your house is a deathtrap. If he's not trying to stick his finger into a baseboard electrical socket, he's dipping his hand into an ashtray full of cigarette butts. And don't think he won't try munching on them, because he will. If you have pets, your toddler will be into their food and water bowls. And the kitty litter will draw him like a sandbox.

Of course, the television, stereo, and telephone are irresistible, too—they can be as fascinating to one-year-old explorers as they often are to adults. And houseplants are another favorite plaything. If you have any of these within reach, your toddler is sure to try pulling off the leaves and scooping out the soil. He may even nibble a leaf or taste a mouthful of dirt. Unfortunately, this can be dangerous; some houseplants have poisonous leaves, berries, or roots.

Finally, there will be the day your offspring teeters toward you, a proud smile on his face, and the teapot that's been in your family for generations clutched in his hands. And just before you can take it from him . . .

One thing is clear. As soon as your child can walk he will begin getting into everything. You can count on it!

Why He Needs to Explore
Of course, your toddler's urge to get into things makes life with him a real challenge for you. You may feel as if you spend all day saying, "No!" It's especially frustrating when a particular untouchable has caught his fancy and he keeps going back to it no matter how many times you tell him not to.

Controlling your toddler's expeditions can be a complicated matter, but the reason it's hard to stop him is pretty simple: *he has to touch.* What do we mean, "He has to touch?" Let's look for a moment at what we know about all young children, babies, toddlers and preschoolers alike. We know that young children are curious. They are born with a desire to learn—a drive as basic and as powerful as their need for food, sleep, and comforting. But young children don't learn in the same ways that adults do. Adults can read, they can solve problems by thinking them out, and they can understand what other people say. Young children learn in different ways. They learn by *looking,* by *touching,* and by *doing.*

At every stage of development young children use all their available skills to satisfy their need to learn. In his first few months of life, a baby spends most of his waking hours looking and staring. He can't control his body well enough to do much else. By the time he is three or four months old, he begins reaching for and grasping things. Now he can use his hands as well as his eyes to satisfy his curiosity, and with the help of his hands he pops anything he can get hold of straight into his mouth. He isn't really trying to find out what things taste like. He just wants to learn as much as he can about what objects feel like, and that means exploring them with every means he has available.

It's good that your toddler's curiosity is as powerful as it is, because he has so much to discover. But when he was a baby, his curiosity created fewer problems for you. Before he could get around on his own, *you* decided what he could touch and mouth and handle. Now that he's walking, he decides. He's spent many months looking at a world of fascinating things that were out of reach, and now he can't wait to get his hands on them.

Preparing for the Age of Exploration
And that's the problem for you, he can't keep his hands off of anything. For all his curiosity about the world of

It's nearly impossible for a naturally curious toddler to stay out of trouble in a house filled with attractive untouchables.

objects, he doesn't know much about it yet. He has no idea what's safe to touch and what isn't. He's as likely to touch a hot radiator as a chair leg, and a glass ashtray will draw his attention just as fast as one made of plastic.

You know it's important for your toddler to touch and handle in order to learn. But you can't let him touch things that could hurt him, and you don't want him to touch things that are precious to you and that he could destroy. Besides, you have lots to do during the day, so you can't spend all of your time cleaning up the mess a young explorer can create.

What is the right approach to living with an explorer? How do you strike a balance between his need to handle things, and your need to limit his activities—for his sake and your own? There are really only two ways to keep a toddler from touching things. You can stop him (or try to stop him) as he reaches for them; this is the "no,

no" approach. Or you can put things where he can't get at them. This is the toddlerproofing approach. The main advantage of the toddlerproofing approach is that it minimizes a whole lot of problems that are unavoidable if you rely on the "no, no" approach alone. The "no, no" approach creates problems for your toddler. And it creates problems for you, too.

What the "No, No" Approach Does to Your Toddler

During toddlerhood, the roots of your child's most basic feelings about himself are being formed. If your home is arranged so you don't have to thwart his urge to explore every other minute, he starts to feel confident about his ability to do things, and he feels good about himself. He senses that you support his efforts to learn through handling. But if you have to stop him from touching things countless times each day, he begins to doubt his ability to do things, and he feels bad about himself. He senses that his need to explore is in direct conflict with another need that is at least as strong: his need for your love and approval. If he could think it through clearly, he would express the conflict something like this: "I need to learn and I need your approval, but you seem to disapprove of me whenever I'm trying to learn." Of course a toddler can't think about the conflict this clearly, but he feels it strongly.

No toddler can completely curb his curiosity. But the toddler who feels his explorations are costing him his parents' love and approval will try hard to learn the "don't touch" rules. This is a very difficult job for a child so young, and he can only accomplish it by learning to rely on his parents completely to tell him what he can and can't do. So forcing a young child to learn more rules than he can comfortably handle actually hinders his ability to develop the capacity to control himself, and teaches him to be overly dependent on control imposed by other people.

Of course, there's another possible outcome of too many restrictions, especially for unusually sturdy, persistent toddlers. That's the "so what" reaction. The toddler may become a tiny rebel. If his parents place too many limits on him, he may act as if he's thinking: "I'm just not going to pay attention when my parents try to stop me. They get upset every time I do anything at all. I've got to explore, so I'm just going to stop listening and go about my business."

Different toddlers respond to an overdose of "no, no" in different ways. But they all have one thing in common. They are paying a heavy price simply because they are curious and trying to learn—a price they wouldn't have to pay if their homes were toddlerproofed.

What the "No, No" Approach Does to You

The "no, no" approach creates serious problems for you, as well. First off, it's exhausting. You've got to chase your toddler around all day, trying to stop him from touching things. So you're constantly on the run, and you have less time than you need for the many other things you have to do.

And it's frustrating. It takes an enormous amount of emotional energy to wage hundreds of minibattles with your child every day. Let's face it. It's nearly impossible to teach a toddler to stay away from tempting untouchables if there are hundreds of them around the house. And no matter how carefully you watch him, you can't keep your eyes on your child every minute. So you worry he's in some sort of trouble whenever he's out of sight. And your fears are well founded: there are just too many hazards for an unsupervised toddler in a house that hasn't been toddlerproofed.

Last but not least, if you spend hour after hour saying "no, no," to your child, you can get to feeling really bad about yourself. At some point, after your fiftieth battle of the day, you're sure to lose your temper and get angry (if you haven't before). Your toddler will dissolve in tears, and you'll be torn between guilt and righteous indignation. The former generally prevails. After all, he's still little more than a baby, and you are the parent. You're supposed to be able to deal with the situation. Trying to keep an explorer from touching things in a house that hasn't been toddlerproofed is enough to drive any parent nearly crazy.

TODDLERPROOFING

As we've said, toddlerproofing means putting things you don't want your toddler to touch in places where he can't get at them. When you do this, you cut down tremendously on the problems of living with a toddler. According to safety experts, between 50 and 90 percent of all serious accidents suffered by babies and toddlers in their homes could have been prevented if parents had thoroughly childproofed the house. In the chapter of this guide titled "Designing Your Home for Play" we offer detailed suggestions for toddlerproofing your home. Here we'd just like to mention a few highlights. Be sure you pay special attention to—

poisons. Just about any household cleaning agent and any medicine is potentially poisonous to your toddler. So are certain houseplants, and decorations such as mistletoe.

vases, china, glass objects.

electrical outlets. Place safety caps on all outlets that are not in use.

trash cans. Get cans with lids your toddler can't open, or place the cans high enough so that he can't reach them.

stairs. Put safety gates at the tops and bottoms of stairs. (Don't forget the top of the basement steps.)

matches.

Also think about where you put things down. Your toddler will go for anything you place within his reach—especially items on the floor or on coffee or end tables. By thoroughly toddlerproofing in this way, you will save

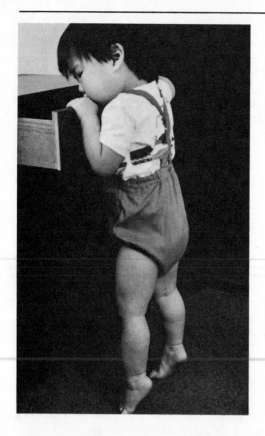

stereo, or the kitchen and bathroom wastebaskets. It's a nuisance to have the cleaners and polishes and other household products that contain poisons on a high shelf or in a locked cabinet rather than right at hand under the kitchen sink.

Still, with the stakes so high, you really should toddlerproof as thoroughly as you can. Two things we can mention may help you adjust more easily to the idea of a toddlerproofed home. First: it won't last forever. In less than a year, your toddler will be past the stage where he's into everything. Then you can begin to re-arrange your home to suit you again. Second: it's all right to limit your little Columbus's explorations to part of your home. So if there are particular rooms you don't want to or can't toddlerproof, create off-limits areas. Use safety gates to keep your toddler out of certain rooms, or close doors to rooms that are off limits. The bathroom, your bedroom, and the den are good candi-dates for this closed-door policy. If you have large houseplants that you keep on the floor within your toddler's reach, and he can't leave them alone, you may have to create an off-limits plant room as well.

Drawers and stairs are particularly tempting to a young explorer, so you must be sure they are toddlerproofed.

both your toddler and yourself all the aggravations that result when parents spend their days vainly trying to control a toddler's explorations with "no, no." And you will significantly reduce the chance of your child's being hurt in a serious accident.

Toddlerproofing doesn't only prevent aggravations and accidents, however; it also helps us curb our natural tendency to overprotect the young toddler. In the course of your toddlerproofing you will identify and remove obvious hazards. Carpeting the steps, putting a rug un-der the crib, and moving furniture with sharp corners from the paths your toddler follows: measures such as these will assure you that you have made your house safe for your tipsy traveler. And once you have done your best to protect him from serious harm, you will be able to stay calm in the face of such minor injuries as bumped noses and scraped elbows, which are a nor-mal and inevitable part of early childhood.

We Know It's Not Easy

Despite the advantages of toddlerproofing, many parents have trouble making themselves do it. For one thing, they like their home the way it is! That's understand-able. Most people take pride in their homes and their possessions. They spend a lot of time accumulating things they like and arranging these in ways that please them. Toddlerproofing puts a crimp in their life-style that's hard to accept.

Most people also like to have things in the house arranged for their convenience. They don't like the idea that they can't put ashtrays and drinks on the coffee table. They don't want to move the telephone, or the

Some parents limit their little Columbus' explorations to part of their home. If there are certain rooms they don't want to or can't toddlerproof, they create off-limits areas.

You Can't Put Everything Away: Dealing with Untouchables He Can Still Get To

You can't put everything away no matter how conscientiously you toddlerproof and create off-limits areas. There are still countless things, from radiators to records, that your toddler can get to, if he wants. Some of these are objects your toddler absolutely must not touch because they are dangerous, things such as

fireplaces (especially when they are in operation),
radiators,
stoves,
lamps (especially floor lamps, which can't be put out of reach),
electrical wires,
lawnmowers, tools (in garage or basement).

There are other things your toddler can still get to after a thorough toddlerproofing which aren't really dangerous, but which you want him to leave alone anyway. These include

telephones,
stereo, television receivers,
magazines in the magazine rack,
books on bookshelves,
records.

These are a few of the most common trouble spots remaining after a thorough toddlerproofing. We suggest that you take a tour of your house and make up lists of your own troublespots. Make one list of dangerous things that your toddler absolutely must not touch, and another list of things that aren't dangerous but that it's a real nuisance to have him get into. The second list is likely to be a lot longer than the first, but you should make both lists as complete as possible.

The distinction between things your toddler abso-

lutely must not touch and things you just wish he wouldn't touch is an important one. Your toddler has to learn as quickly as possible to stay away from things that could hurt him. So when he goes for something dangerous that can't be moved, you really have no choice but to stop him and say, "No." On the other hand, using the emphatic 'no, no" approach for things you merely wish he wouldn't touch will make the whole matter of setting limits for him a lot harder for you both. You are operating under an enormous handicap if you try to teach *lots* of "no, no's" before your toddler can talk and understand your explanations. It's really not worth the battles. Eventually your toddler will learn to keep away from all untouchables. Very few preschoolers leave phones off the hook, pull books and records off the shelves, or pluck the leaves off plants. Once they are old enough to understand what these restrictions are all about, they learn quickly and easily to stay away from things their parents wish they wouldn't touch.

So do yourself a favor. Just concentrate on teaching your child to stay away from the things he *must* not touch. And when it comes to the many things you *wish* he wouldn't touch, settle for simply keeping him away from them. It's a whole lot easier.

Teaching Your Toddler to Stay Away from Things He Must Not Touch

Parents have an almost automatic way of warning their toddlers that they are about to get into trouble. A mother will frown, raise her voice, point her finger at the toddler, and vigorously shake her head from side to side. If you've managed to keep the number of things your toddler must not touch to a minimum, he'll know you mean business when you warn him this way. But he really doesn't know why he's being told "no." You can help him learn why he's not allowed to touch if you give him more information.

For instance, when he goes for a hot stove or radiator or reaches for a bowl of steaming food on the table, don't simply say "No." Tell him that the thing he's reaching for is *hot,* and that if he touched it it would *burn* or *hurt.* He's had some experience with hot food, and he may catch on to what you mean pretty quickly. If he's willing, you can gently hold his hand near the hot object so he can feel the warmth. This will help him get the idea. You can use this approach to help your toddler learn to stay away from other things, too. To a simple *no,* add a few words (such as *sharp, break,* or *hurt*) that communicate gently and firmly the nature of the danger and your concern for your toddler's safety.

No one can promise that your toddler will understand what you are saying the first time. In fact, if you think about it, it must be pretty hard for him to know what you're warning him about unless he's experienced it himself at least once. But he will certainly understand that you are warning him against some real danger—if you're sparing in your use of this kind of warning.

Of course you can't let your child toddle toward danger while you deliver a little lecture on the harm that

on his own and go about your business. It's a rare toddler who will head back for a forbidden object in another room after a few minutes of enjoyable play, as long as he has something else to do and you stay close by. Removal from the scene combined with a few minutes of play is your ace in the hole because it can be counted on to work and because it avoids the drawn-out battles over irresistible untouchables which can ruin a parent's—as well as a toddler's—day.

Keeping Your Toddler Away from Things You Wish He Wouldn't Touch

It's aggravating to have to hang up the phone every time your toddler knocks it off the hook, or to replace the magazines in their rack a dozen times a day, or to have to readjust the controls on your television or stereo every time you turn it on because your toddler's been fiddling with them, or to reshelve your books endlessly after your toddler's "borrowed" them. Who has the time to be a librarian?

But these aren't situations where there's real danger to your child or to the objects involved. Your primary goal in situations like these isn't to teach your toddler not to touch; it's just to avoid the extra work that results when he does. Of course, some parents really don't care if their toddler gets into things like these. Their list of things they wish he wouldn't touch is short. They just let him have his fling—sometimes literally—and either clean up after he's moved on or wait until naptime or some other convenient occasion to straighten things out. If they've toddlerproofed fairly thoroughly, they say this isn't too much of a job.

But many parents feel they've done their share by toddlerproofing, and they want the toddler to leave all remaining nontoys alone, whether they are dangerous or not. How do you keep your child away from things you wish he wouldn't touch? Your toddler's distractibility is the key. Any time he goes for something you don't want him to touch, offer him a substitute. "Look, I have a wonderful surprise for you!" The quicker you act and the more attractive the substitute, the better this tactic works. If you don't move until your toddler already has the untouchable in his grasp, it's much harder to distract him. And if your substitute isn't very interesting, you'll have problems, too. Keys usually work very well, as do any other little doodads that make noise and move in interesting ways. To make this kind of switch successfully, you have to be positive. Your enthusiasm will go a long way toward making the substitute attractive. If you are irritated and show it, your toddler will feel that you are trying to trick him.

Of course, there is one really foolproof substitute for an attractive untouchable: you. If you are willing to get down on the floor to play with your toddler and *mean* it, you can distract him from just about anything —especially if you take him into another room. Sometimes being enthusiastic can seem like a pretty tall order. You may be frustrated and not have much time. But if you offer even a few minutes of genuine play with your toddler, he'll not only forget about whatever it was

might befall him. If the danger is imminent you've got to move quickly and scoop him up. The lesson is best delivered while you're holding him. And remember, as with any kind of lesson, it'll be easier for your toddler to understand what you're trying to teach him if you're not in a panic. It is frightening to see your toddler nearly hurt himself seriously, but try not to overreact. Your lesson will have the most impact if you are calm, clear, and firm.

If the warning doesn't seem to sink in and your child heads right back to the danger as soon as you've put him down, you'll have to help him take his mind off it. This is most easily done by offering him something else to play with. Fortunately, toddlers are highly distractible. They're curious about everything, and their memories and attention spans are blessedly short. So while you can't block your toddler's urge to explore, you can redirect that urge. You can substitute an acceptable plaything for something dangerous and get away with it most of the time.

If your toddler doesn't fall for the switch—and he may not if he's a really persistent kid or if the forbidden object is really attractive—you may have to play your ace in the hole. Just pick him up as calmly and positively as you can, and remove him from the scene. Please be sure to do this *before* your patience has run out and you're feeling angry. Take him into another room—preferably one where you have some work to do—and sit down on the floor and play with him for a few minutes. Then give him something he can play with you didn't want him to touch, he may also shift from restless "search and destroy missions" to playing happily, at least for a while.

If you find yourself fresh out of ideas for distracting your toddler, remember that his restless roaming is probably a sign that he's bored. He's always interested in finding out how things work, so you can keep him out of trouble and help him learn by setting up little experiments. If you give him a large unbreakable bowl of water and a couple of plastic containers, a washcloth, a sponge, and some things that float, he'll probably stay happily occupied for a long time discovering that—

floating toys will pop up again after he pushes them under water and lets them go, while other things stay sunk.

pouring gets water out of a container, and squeezing gets water out of a washcloth or sponge.

the water in a container is visible but the water in a washcloth isn't.

water always falls when it's poured or squeezed, but it can go up when it's splashed.

If you're working in the bathroom, you can even pop your child in the tub and let him try the same experiments.

If you're busy in the kitchen, give your toddler some cans and packages of food, and encourage him to build a tower. Does he seem to know how to go about it? Or put a can between two of his building blocks and ask him to get it out. Does he do this by unstacking the pile, or by knocking over the pile, or by trying to poke out the can? Then put the can on the bottom of the pile and get him to try again. In giving your toddler a chance to work out this problem, you're not just keeping him occupied. You're also helping him learn important concepts such as "on top," "underneath," and "in the middle."

When you're at someone else's home, or anyplace else that's not toddlerproofed, distracting your toddler and keeping him out of trouble can be a special problem. For advice on how to handle this situation, see the "Special Play Reference" chapter in the "Play and Playthings" section of this guide.

Helping Your Toddler Learn to Handle Things Carefully

There's a third category of objects you may not have moved in toddlerproofing. These are things that are not likely to harm your child but that may be harmed by him. This category includes things such as plants, pets, and certain precious decorations.

These are an important part of your life, and they need to be protected. It's not so much that your toddler can't touch them at all, it's just that he doesn't yet know how to handle them with the care they require. He'll learn this most quickly if you give him a chance to touch them occasionally, while you supervise and help him learn what's needed.

Sit your toddler on a carpet or on your sofa and let him handle an attractive figurine. Show him how to hold it. Say, "Carefully."

Let him pat the cat while you hold it. Show him how to do this. Say, "Gently." After a while, when they're both calm, you may be able to put the cat in his lap for a petting session.

Hold him in your lap or in your arms and let him touch the leaves of your houseplants. Show him how soft they are.

These are exciting experiences for your toddler. He senses that you are sharing the things you care about with him, and that you trust him. You don't have to do this sort of thing all the time, of course. But he's got to learn to live in a house that contains plants, pets, and other precious things, so help him learn to deal with these when you feel *you* would like to and when you want to give him a treat.

Here are guidelines for making these sharing experiences as enjoyable as possible for both of you.

Set up the situation so it's safe.
Supervise your toddler so he doesn't harm or throw.
Teach him patiently what's needed.
Don't expect too much. At the first sign that he's had enough, gently remove the object, letting him know that you're proud of what he's been able to do, and that you'll give him another chance soon. Don't yank him away with the message that he can't deal with the situation on his own. You already knew that.

Move on to some other interesting activity, preferably in another room, so he won't try to get you to let him handle beyond his capacity.

CREATIVE TODDLERPROOFING

One of the best ways to minimize conflicts over untouchables is to have lots of good things around that your toddler *can* touch. When you toddlerproof, you put as many untouchables as possible out of reach. Creative toddlerproofing puts touchables within reach of your explorer.

Creative toddlerproofing gives your child the opportunities for discovery and learning that he craves and needs. And it makes life easier for you, too. We've just talked about using distraction and substitution to keep your toddler away from untouchables. Creative toddlerproofing goes distraction and substitution one better. For example, a variety of unbreakable ornaments spread out on a low table in the living room makes a very appealing alternative to the fragile objects you've placed just out of your toddler's reach. With a distraction like this at hand, he's less likely to struggle to get at the things you don't want him to touch, and you're less likely to have to spend time trying to stop him.

Your toddler takes a special interest in touching the things he sees you use. He wants to act grown-up and be like you. So add to his tabletop collection an old watch that has stopped running, or some costume jewelry you no longer wear. While you're busy shaving in the bathroom, you can keep him occupied by giving him an old razor without a blade and spreading a little lather on his face, so he can shave himself.

There are two steps to creative toddlerproofing. First, think about the troublespots in your house—those things you wish your toddler wouldn't touch that seem to be just irresistible to him. Then think of alternatives that come as close as possible to looking, smelling, tasting, and feeling like the real thing. Here are some creative toddlerproofing suggestions for common troublespots.

If your explorer can't leave the books on your bookshelves alone, put a selection of old magazines, dog-eared paperbacks, old phone books, comic sections from the Sunday papers, and the like in a box near the bookshelves. Or put his "reading materials" on a separate shelf. Then he can handle, turn pages, throw, and even tear to his heart's content. Another hint: stuff your own book (and record) shelves *tight!* It's not too hard to pack these so you can get out what you want while your toddler can't. Within a year your toddler will have lost interest in yanking books off your shelves, and you'll be able to loosen them up again.

You spend a lot of time in the kitchen, so your toddler does, too. It can be especially frustrating to have to keep an eye on your little explorer while you're busy preparing meals. But that's just what you'll have to do unless you do some creative toddlerproofing here. Instead of worrying about what he's getting into in your cabinets and drawers, give him his very own shelf or drawer with his own kitchen supplies. Make sure his area is away from the main traffic pattern of the kitchen, so you won't be running over him. Stock his shelves with pots, pans, lids, dishrags, and unbreakable containers and utensils such as used coffee cans, stirring spoons, and strainers. You might even add a few small unopened cans of soup or tuna. Your explorer's kitchen play will probably get a little noisy. But it's almost sure to keep him happily occupied unless he's hungry, and putting up with a little noise is a lot better than having to pay full-time attention to him when you've got a lot of other work to do.

Think about stocking a low bureau drawer in your bedroom or your toddler's room with a few articles of old clothing, small toys, and other safe, interesting objects he can play with. If the drawer opens *very* easily, he can get to these things on his own. Otherwise, you can open it for him whenever you're working or relaxing in that part of the house. It'll be like his own little treasure chest. He may want to add things to the drawer. Let him put in a few of his own toys and books. This gives him lots of opportunity for two of the activities children this age love most: filling and emptying.

There's something your toddler is just beginning to learn that helps make creative toddlerproofing as effective as it is. He's just starting to learn about "me" and "mine." His awareness of himself, his powers, and his possessions will blossom in the months to come. It will soon be a major issue for you to deal with.

But for now this dawning awareness helps you. You'll see he responds to the idea that he has *his* space, *his* kitchen supplies, *his* drawer to play in, and *his* telephone. When you have to draw him away from your things, identifying the alternatives as *his* will make it easier. One mother we talked with summed up creative toddlerproofing in these terms: "Pulling things out of boxes was the main problem, so we gave him a box to put his little toys in. That was his box—his very own. And that seemed to satisfy him really well." The mother didn't have to add that she was satisfied, too.

That's the point of all the suggestions we offer in this chapter and the next ones: making your life with your toddler better and easier for both of you. That's what you do when you keep "no, no's" to a minimum and control your toddler's behavior by—

toddlerproofing: removing as many untouchables as you can.

helping your toddler learn about dangerous things he absolutely *must* not touch.

distracting your toddler from things you would rather he didn't touch and offering him acceptable substitutes.

teaching him how to handle fragile things carefully.

creative toddlerproofing: minimizing conflicts by having lots of good things around that your toddler *can* touch.

4
Coping with Contrariness

At about eighteen months, your toddler enters a new phase in her journey from babyhood to childhood. She is almost halfway between the total dependency of the newborn and the relative independence of the preschooler, and suddenly everything she does begins to reflect the intensity of her struggle to grow up. She seems almost driven to assert herself, as if to convince everyone, herself included, that she is no longer a baby.

Often a toddler's self-assertion takes the form of contrariness. She tries to prove she's growing up by refusing to be controlled by you as she was when she was younger. Of course, she's not resisting you at every turn, but it may often *feel* to you that she is. She's talking more now, and *no* is far and away her favorite word. She seems to use it constantly. You ask her if she's ready to have some lunch, and she says, "No!" You ask her if she wants to go to the laundromat with you, and she pouts, stamps her foot, and yells, "No!" Her need to think for herself is so strong that she even says *no* to things she wants to do. For example, if you offer her a cracker, which you know she loves, there's a good chance that as she reaches for it she'll be shaking her head and muttering, "*No.*" This may seem strange; you might even conclude that the child doesn't know what *no* means. She does. It's just that she wants to defy you, on principle, and she wants to have the cracker, too. Her solution is so simple it's beautiful. She does both.

THE DECLARATION OF INDEPENDENCE

Your toddler's contrariness is like a declaration of independence. It's easy to see her contrariness as negative, since it involves a denial of your right to control her. But from her point of view, the situation is quite different. For her, contrary behavior is essentially positive. It's her way of saying that she doesn't feel like a helpless baby anymore, and that she won't be treated like one. She needs room to grow in. She wants to begin making decisions for herself. So she tries to create the space she needs by forcing you to back off a bit. She isn't being contrary in a conscious effort to get your goat, though it may feel that way to you at times. It's just that you're so big and powerful and she's so small and powerless. So she often fears that she'll lose her new-found sense of herself as a separate, independent person altogether unless she digs in her heels and forces you to recognize that she's growing up.

No! becomes your toddler's favorite weapon in her struggle for autonomy, because she recognizes that there's power in the word. She's heard you say no again and again to control her, and now she wants to feel a little of that power herself. In fact, though she gets a certain amount of pleasure out of saying no to anybody about anything, she gets a special charge out of turning no against you. For the next few months she'll probably be saying it to you every chance she gets. Often it seems that she chooses the worst possible moments to exercise her budding independent spirit. Let's say you've had a really busy day, and now, with just an hour left before dinner time, you're trying to put the evening meal together. Suddenly you realize that you're out of oil to fry the chicken in, and you have to go to the grocery store right away to pick some up. Usually your toddler loves a trip to the grocery. Today, however, she's of a different mind. When you ask her to come so you can put her coat on, she takes one look at you and runs as fast as she can in the opposite direction. You finally get hold of her, but she is kicking and screaming, "No, Mommy! No, Mommy!" at the top of her lungs. When you try to get her into her coat, she pulls her arms away. You keep trying to get the coat on, because it's too cold for her to go out without it, but she goes stiff all over. By the time you finally get out the door, half your hour is gone, and you're both really upset and angry with each other.

More and more now your toddler tries to deny your right to make decisions for her. She won't go to her nap willingly no matter how exhausted she is; she won't agree to stop playing to come in for lunch even when you know she's hungry; she refuses to take the baths she used to enjoy; and you may feel that you now need four hands to change her diapers. She expresses her resistance in a variety of ways; saying no is only her favorite. She also runs away from you, and pulls away from you, and kicks you, and screams at you, and goes stiff or limp all over when you try to insist that she do something she doesn't want to do.

Defiance Is a Healthy Sign of Growth
During this stage of your toddler's development, her defiance of you is perfectly normal. As we've said, it's

a healthy sign of growth. Her awareness that she can choose *not* to do something is an essential first step to her learning that she can choose *to* do something. Just about every one-year-old passes through a phase of contrariness, which tends to subside—temporarily, at least—sometime around her second birthday. At that point the drive to imitate grows stronger than the drive to oppose, and toddlers usually become quite cooperative for a while. So, when your toddler's defiance begins to feel intolerable to you, remember, this too shall pass. And while it lasts it'll be useful preparation for your life together during the teenage years. As a matter of fact, the willfulness of the second half of the second year has a lot in common with the rebellion of adolescence. During puberty your child will once again declare her independence by seeming to oppose on principle every request you make of her and every view you hold.

Friction Is Inevitable

At times your toddler's defiance is so direct that it's bound to be threatening. Even if you understand that her contrariness reflects a striving for independence that is essential to her psychological growth, friction is inevitable. Sometimes her willfulness can leave you ab-

solutely infuriated, and you may be shocked by the intensity of your reaction. When she stomps her foot and shouts, "No!" at you, you may feel your face flush, your heart beat faster, and your hands begin to shake. It can feel as if you're losing control altogether—control of yourself as well as of your toddler. When you feel this way, it's no wonder that you overreact, yell at your child furiously, or even strike her. You feel like you have an insurrection on your hands. You react harshly because you feel desperate.

We have all been driven to the very edge of our patience, and even beyond, by our toddler's willfulness. But in fact, it only makes matters worse if we treat this stage as a revolution that has to be quashed rather than as a normal, if difficult, phase of growth. When we react too harshly or repressively, we risk prolonging the struggle, and making it more furious. And we end up adding to the emotional strain that is an inevitable by-product of this stage anyway.

Different toddlers have different ways of reacting to parental rigidity and overcontrol during this phase. A feisty child may bitterly resist her parents every step of the way, throwing temper tantrums over practically every demand they make of her. Another child, faced by what seem to be overwhelming odds, may bury her willfulness instead, trying to get her parents off her back by becoming outwardly compliant. But her instinctive contrariness is almost sure to surface again in a more passive form, and before long she may be getting back at her parents by refusing to eat or sleep. Or she may seem to give up the struggle altogether, and instead become more babyish, clinging to her mother all the time and taking a timid approach to life's challenges. Other children who conform on the outside are actually raging on the inside at the parental pressure they feel. Though they usually do what's expected of them, they're likely to express their anger in sneaky ways, breaking things, pinching their baby brothers, or kicking the dog when they think no one is looking.

GETTING YOUR NAYSAYER TO OBEY: GUIDELINES AND SUGGESTIONS

Balancing your toddler's need for independence with your need to maintain your authority is like the greatest high-wire act of all time. You feel yourself constantly slipping off to one side or the other. In one direction are your fantasies of raising a tiny tyrant who is undermining your parental powers altogether. In the other direction are your fears of breaking your toddler's spirit and becoming too bossy yourself. How can you maintain your balance?

Let Her Have Her Say

When your goal is ultimate cooperation rather than instant obedience, you're much more likely to succeed. And letting your toddler express her defiance is the first step in an effective plan for getting her to do what you want. It can cut down on her resistance by giving her a chance to get her feelings out. Your easy acceptance of her initial defiance will keep her feeling good about you, so she'll want to cooperate—within the limits nature places on her.

About five minutes before you want your toddler to do something, make a simple, friendly, matter-of-fact statement to that effect. For example: "In a couple of minutes it will be time to go in and have dinner." That's it. It's important to make this an announcement only, not the lead-in to an argument. So don't say anything else, no matter how your toddler reacts to your warning. She may seem to be agreeable, or she may start crying and arguing, or she may ignore you. Forget it! The point of your announcement is simply to give her a chance to wrap up what she's doing and to save face by defying you a little. Let her deal with the news that her fun is about to end in her own way. She has a right to be upset, but you should stay cool. You know you have a plan for getting her to do what you want, and giving her a chance to express her disappointment is a sensible part of that plan. If you find it hard to keep from arguing with your toddler once you've delivered your message, leave her on her own for a few minutes and go back to whatever you were doing.

Help Your Toddler Deal with Her Feelings by Reflecting Them

A few minutes after your first warning, make a second announcement: "It's just about time to go in now." The chance to play a few more minutes and express her resentment at having to stop may have been enough, and your toddler may be ready to go in already. But likely as not she won't be, especially if she's been having a lot of fun. She'll probably continue to resist, or continue to ignore you, if that's her style. Now's the time to add a new element to your strategy (if she's still resisting) by helping her put her feelings into words: "You're having so much fun playing that you don't want to go in. I know, it's hard to stop when you're enjoying yourself, but it's time to go in to eat."

She may not understand every word you're saying—though using simple words and short statements helps—but she won't miss your tone of compassion and support. Your expression of understanding will make it easier for her to put up with her disappointment and come inside. At the same time, your description of her mood will help her begin to learn a very important lesson: expressing her feelings in words instead of acting them out. This is a crucial skill. Obviously, it's a thousand times easier to help a child who says she's angry and upset than to help one who kicks and bites or acts out her anger in other ways. And a child who's able to talk about her feelings is less likely to be swept by rampant emotions in the first place, because language gives us a handle on a situation and lets us control it. Your toddler won't really get the hang of putting her feelings into words for quite a while, probably—it's a lesson most grown-ups haven't entirely mastered yet —but hearing you describe her disappointment now will at least give her the idea and get her started.

Act; Don't Argue

If your toddler isn't willing to cooperate even after you've given her an initial chance to defy you and then reflected her feelings for her, you can feel comfortable that you've tried hard enough to coax her. Now it's time to take matters into your own hands. It's important to do this without arguing. Maybe this time your respect for your toddler's need to defy you didn't bear fruit, but eventually it will; it's just bound to. So don't destroy the important groundwork you've laid by getting angry with her at this point. Remember, your goal is to get her to do what you want, not to win a battle. So pick her up firmly but in as cool and friendly a manner as you can manage, and carry her into the house. You might want to repeat that you understand that she feels disappointed and upset and angry because she can't play anymore right now. But try not to argue or scold. She's not being bad, and you won't persuade her to feel differently about the situation by debating. All you'll do is make yourself more frustrated.

Of course, some days your patience is going to run out. You're bound to get angry and argue with your toddler and yell at her sometimes. Every parent does this, and as long as it's not the way you deal with your toddler most of the time, there's no serious harm done. The important thing is to keep the scales tipped toward a more supportive, positive approach to discipline. After you've blown up at your toddler, try a very simple, matter-of-fact apology, if it makes you feel better. Everyone, including your toddler, can understand that people have bad days and bad moments.

One of the most common mistakes parents make in disciplining young children, especially during this stage, is to talk too much. It's important to reflect your toddler's feelings in terms she will understand, and it's useful to offer a simple apology when you've flown off the handle at her and want her to know you're sorry afterward. But long-winded explanations of why she should do something will only confuse her. If you find yourself talking a lot but getting no results, here's an exercise to try which may be helpful: pretend your child is deaf. There are times when a single gesture says more than a hundred words anyway, so communicate what you want her to do by gestures and action alone. If you want her to go upstairs for her bath, just walk over to her, give her a big friendly smile, pick her up in a warm, loving way, and carry her off. Or go over and hold out your finger. It's surprising how often a child will simply grasp an outstretched finger and go along, no questions asked.

This exercise seems to contradict our advice that before you try to make your child do something, you should give her a chance to express her rebellious feelings. And it does, in a way. But wordless intervention can be a refreshing change of pace, especially if you have a tendency to overuse words and the situation is one in which your toddler isn't likely to resist too much anyway. Try it to see how it works for you. You may find a few situations in which this turns out to be the very best strategy of all.

Make Cooperation Fun

Sometimes you can gain your toddler's cooperation by turning obedience into a game. This is basically the old carrot-and-stick ploy, and it can sometimes enable you to avoid confrontation altogether. Try to tempt your toddler into doing what you want her to. A toddler who bitterly resents having her play interrupted to take a bath may feel differently if the process is turned into a contest. Instead of "Now you have to pick up your toys and go upstairs," try "Let's see who can pick up all the blocks first" and then "Let's race up the stairs. You start and I'll try to catch you." This strategy works even better if you can enlist an older brother or sister in the act; when there are several enthusiastic competitors your main intention is all the better disguised.

If your toddler, once upstairs, still refuses to take her bath, try putting some of her favorite washable toys in the tub, especially those she's not used to playing with in the water. After a while it may be as hard to get her out of the tub as it was to get her in, but if you find yourself with this problem, you can invent other games. Try enticing her out by doing some magic with a towel. Hide a little surprise under it, or turn it into a tent, or make it into a turban for your head. Then see if your toddler wants to get out of the water and back on dry land to join the fun of finding the hidden prize or crawling under the tent or having you make a turban for her to wear. As part of the game you can dry her with another towel.

Nourish Your Toddler's Autonomy

Sometimes you can avoid battles and nourish your toddler's drive to make her own decisions at the same time. Give her a choice whenever possible. If you let her choose between her red shirt and her yellow one, she may forget about refusing to put on any shirt at all. Similarily, letting her choose between washing her hands in the bathroom or washing them in the kitchen may get the job done far more quickly and with less fighting than simply insisting that she wash them in one place or the other. When it's time to clean up her toys, the choice of picking up her blocks or her cars may get her working willingly—while you pick up whatever she didn't choose.

Unfortunately, the choice technique isn't foolproof. If your child's feeling tired or irritable when the choice is proposed, or if you offer more options than she can easily choose among, you can end up with an emotional catastrophe on your hands. So if you're going to use this technique, make sure that you offer only two choices, that both are equally acceptable to you (since

Making cooperation fun for your toddler is often the key to coping with contrariness. Use your imagination to find ways of enticing your toddler when you think she may resist otherwise.

you won't be able to follow through comfortably otherwise), and that your child is more or less on top of things when the choice is presented. Then, once she's made her choice, work along with her to help her complete the job.

It's also a good idea to let your toddler "win" every once in a while when you see a battle developing. This tactic lets her flex her muscles a bit. Choose situations in which the stakes aren't too high for you, times when it doesn't matter that much whether your toddler cooperates with you right away. Maybe you want her to come in for lunch, but once you give a warning and she protests, you realize she is more involved than you thought. If it's just as easy for you to do a load of laundry first and then feed her lunch in half an hour, you may be willing to let her continue playing for a while after all. When this happens, tell her what you're thinking, so she'll understand what's going on. Say, "You're right, you should have a little more time to play, since you're in the middle of your game. I'll do a load of laundry, and then we'll have lunch." The important thing here is that you've let your toddler know that you respect her legitimate rights while at the same time you've maintained control of the situation.

Giving Your Toddler a Chance to Do Things for Herself

During the age of self-assertion, a toddler naturally wants to do more things for herself. This drive is especially evident at mealtime. As soon as you start to feed your child breakfast, she'll probably try to take over, grabbing the spoon and plunging it into her cereal with great purpose and concentration. Chances are, if she

maneuvers any food at all actually onto the spoon, she'll spill at least half before she even lifts it from the bowl, and spill even more before she manages to steer the spoon to her mouth. But she'll probably be thoroughly satisfied with herself for having accomplished this much. Before you can interrupt, she'll have jabbed the spoon back into the bowl for another go.

By the end of a meal like this, there's generally a great deal of food on the outside of your toddler and very little on the inside of her, and you may be hard pressed to feel any sympathy for her aspirations to self-sufficiency. Your toddler's mealtimes are just part of a busy day for you, after all, and before she began trying to take over you could get through a meal and on to other things pretty quickly. What's more, you knew the food had actually made it into her. Now, when she feeds herself, the kitchen's a mess by the end and the project takes three times as long as you'd like. So you're probably tempted to go on feeding her yourself.

The trouble is, when you try this you're likely to meet a closed mouth. Often a toddler at this stage will simply refuse to open up; no matter how hungry she is, she'll turn her face away whenever the spoon approaches. And if you do manage to pry her mouth open and ram a bit of food in between her teeth, she'll get back at you by holding it in her mouth and then slowly letting it dribble out between her lips and down her chin. You simply can't win.

She Needs Encouragement

It's important to encourage your toddler's efforts to feed herself. She feels proud when she gets a spoonful of food into her mouth without spilling it or when she

her spoon. Most parents feel a natural temptation to do a task for their toddler when they think they can do it faster and save her the frustration. But it's important to let her try it herself, unless what she's doing is dangerous or she asks for help. She needs to learn what works and what doesn't. To do that she needs practice; watching you put her puzzle together isn't enough. Of course, when she asks you to get involved, you should be ready. But when you step in, remember how long it takes to learn things. Do your best to be patient. And try not to expect too much. Let her know that she's doing very well already and that she'll be doing even better before long. Make it clear that she doesn't have to push herself too hard, because you're not rushing her.

She'll Try to Dress Herself

Toddlers want to be able to dress themselves, but most things are just too hard for them to put on properly. As often as not a toddler who tries to put on her shirt ends up with her head sticking through an armhole. Or if she manages to get all her body parts to come out the right holes, the shirt itself will be inside out and backwards. Sometimes she'll let you give her a hand, but other times she's bound to insist, "Me do it!" When that happens, just back off matter-of-factly until you think she's getting frustrated. (She may let you know just when that is by looking at you pleadingly or by demanding help.)

When you do step in, it's best to offer the least possible help to start with. Just steer her legs into the right holes, for instance, and let her pull the pants up herself. Or point out which foot goes into which sneaker and then let her work with you to actually get the shoes onto the feet before you tie them. It's important to talk as you work together in this way. Say: "*Here's* the pant leg. Now push your leg through. Push! That's right! Where's your foot? Here comes your foot. Very good. Yes! You did it." A running commentary like this helps your toddler learn the names for the parts of her body and her clothes. But more important, it reinforces the point that your toddler's doing the most important part of this job, and that you're only there to help her finish (or get started, as the case may be).

The easiest article of clothing for a toddler to put on herself is a hat. That may be why toddlers like hats so much, even in a non-hat-wearing society like ours. But before her second birthday a toddler can also learn to put on her jacket all by herself, if you teach her this simple trick: Put her jacket down on the floor front-side up, with the collar at her feet. Make sure the zipper's open. Help her stoop down and stick her arms through the right holes. Then have her stand up and swing her arms over her head, bringing the coat into position. Presto! Your toddler may want you to demonstrate the procedure with your own coat before she is willing to try it herself. But once she's had a few practices, she'll feel completely in command of the technique. In fact, after a while you may find that she

can finally use a cup by herself. And she feels even better when you admire her accomplishments too. Your encouragement provides extra fuel for your toddler's drive to grow and can also take the edge off the inevitable hassles between you during this stage of development. So do the best you can to be patient and supportive even though your toddler's meals are often slow and messy. You'll find specific suggestions to help you minimize strain during this trying period in the "Feeding and Weaning" chapter of this guide.

Giving your toddler a chance to do things for herself also means letting her make her own mistakes. Can you think of a single important skill you learned without making mistakes? It doesn't matter if what she's trying to do won't work: fitting a shoe on the wrong foot, for instance, or squeezing a puzzle piece in the wrong space, or trying to lift a piece of food that won't fit on asks to put her jacket on even when you're not going out.

The more you teach your toddler to do for herself, the less contrariness you're likely to see; after all, one of the main reasons she acts contrary is that she feels frustrated by what she can't do. Unfortunately, though, helping her learn to feed and dress herself won't do the whole trick. There are bound to be days where she feels riotous no matter how patient or sensitively helpful you've tried to be. There *is* a cure for these negative moods of hers, but it's not one you can administer: it's time. Maybe just knowing that as your child balks and fumes at you, she's growing toward a day where she'll be able to react to life much more calmly, will help you keep your composure during this trying period. The more composure you can master, the better off your whole family will be.

5
Dealing with Dawdling

It takes a toddler a long time to feed himself and an even longer time, often, to try to dress himself. In fact, when you think about it, it takes a toddler a long time to do just about anything. When you walk to the store together he stops to examine every discarded cigarette butt and bottle cap in his path. He has to climb the front steps of every house you pass as well. If you try to hurry him along he may refuse to walk at all, and insist on being carried.

Why Do Toddlers Dawdle?

There are lots of reasons for dawdling. The most basic is just that it's hard for toddlers to move quickly. The toddlers who dawdle most may simply be ones who are a bit slower than their peers in developing muscle coordination. Or they may be very persistent sorts, children who have a harder time than most switching activities.

Most toddlers don't have a clear concept of time, anyway, so they are basically unable to think in terms of getting someplace sooner or later. In fact, a small child lives so thoroughly in the present that as far as he's concerned, the attraction of the moment is all there is. Everything he stumbles on is new and interesting. With so much to explore, no wonder he dawdles.

Besides, when you think about it, grown-ups are the really incurable dawdlers. Much of a young child's life is lived to a refrain of "not now" or "soon" or "later" or "in a little while." Making your toddler wait in these ways is sometimes unavoidable, because you're often busy and can't respond right away. But think about how these postponements sound to him.

What to Do About Dawdling

Of course dawdling can also be a form of self-assertion: a way for a toddler to express himself by setting a pace that suits him, and even a clever way for him to manipulate a situation without being downright uncooperative. So dawdling that happens at home—taking forever to finish a bath, for example—is best dealt with the same as any other form of self-assertive behavior. You should avoid confrontations, arguments, and anger. Let your toddler know in a calm, friendly way that it's time to move along; try to get him moving on his own by turning cooperation into a game; and take matters into your own hands *before you get angry,* if all else fails.

Dawdling is a special problem if it happens when you're out with your toddler away from home. Some-

times you need to get back to your phone or your desk or your kitchen quickly and it's very inconvenient that your toddler's dawdling is slowing you down. But with other people around you may feel embarrassed by your inability to control your toddler, and especially disinclined to get into a fight that could lead to a temper tantrum. So when you have to get someplace quickly, it's a good idea to drive or take a bus or cab. If you really want to walk, take along your toddler's stroller or backpack. That way you can pop him in it if you feel he's moving too slowly.

When you're out with your toddler without a stroller or backpack and want to keep moving along, the best policy is just to keep walking at a slow, steady pace. You don't have to stop and wait for him—except if there's traffic, and at corners, of course. As long as you keep walking slowly, he'll more or less match your pace, catching up with you after every side trip, because for all his interest in exploring and his budding independence, he would be very upset if he lost sight of you in an unfamiliar place. In fact, if you resort to that old standby of exasperated parents, "Bye, bye, I'm leaving you," you'll probably absolutely terrify him. (Of course, if you use this line a lot, eventually he'll realize it's just a ploy to trick him into hurrying, and he'll no longer be so upset by it. In fact he may start to figure that all your threats are hollow and that he can afford to ignore just about any command you give.)

So don't ever threaten your toddler with abandonment. Just encourage him to move along by strolling steadily forward yourself at a pace he can manage, occasionally offering a supportive remark or two, such as "I know there are lots of interesting things to see, but we have to get home, so let's keep moving. When we get there we can play in the yard together." If you've got a free hand and your toddler wants to hold it, you may be able to guide him along at a quicker pace, but you should be prepared to let go now and then and allow him to make a few side trips along the way. You can also play a game as you walk along. If you have a belt, you can hand one end to your toddler and pretend that you are a puppy he is walking on a leash (or you can switch the roles). Carry on a running conversation as you move along: "Woof, woof. I'm looking in the window. Woof, woof. I'm hurrying home to get my dinner." You may even find that this kind of dawdling along with your toddler is fun.

6 Surviving Temper Tantrums

At times the struggle to become independent can be terribly frustrating for your toddler. She has a drive to do things that are simply beyond her abilities, such as dressing herself completely, or doing a puzzle intended for an older child, or even turning a doorknob. So she's bound to fail a great deal. And your sensible regulations and limits frustrate her as well. You're not going to let her roll her ball into the street or take off her shoes in a park where there's broken glass, but sure enough, she's going to feel driven to do just these things, and she's going to feel unfairly hindered when you interfere. Frustration is simply a fact of life during toddlerhood, and that's why temper tantrums are so common during this period.

A temper tantrum is like a blown fuse; it's a sign that the load of frustration has become too much for your toddler to bear. The problem is, her tolerance for frustration often seems so low. Sometimes the slightest issue can be enough to set her off. If a cracker you've given her breaks in half, she may stare in horror for a minute and then fling the pieces across the room and throw herself down on the floor, screaming so loudly that you're sure she's going to make herself sick.

Temper Tantrums Are Hard on Everyone

Temper tantrums are obviously hard on your toddler. They leave her emotionally and physically exhausted. And they're hard on you, too. Most of the time you're not really sure what the problem is or how to fix it. In fact, nothing you do seems to help once a tantrum has taken hold. All too often you find yourself caught up in a vicious cycle: Your child's frustration triggers a tantrum, which makes you frustrated and angry, which makes her feel even more frustrated and helpless, which makes the tantrum worse.

Avoiding the vicious cycle demands a great deal of patience and ingenuity, because there is no way to eliminate frustration from your toddler's life altogether. In fact, you wouldn't even want to. She can't learn to feed herself or dress herself or draw or do puzzles or express herself in words without feeling frustration. And the natural impulse to overcome this frustration is one of her best incentives to go on trying and learning. But it's hard to keep from exceeding her tolerance for frustration; she's bound to feel an overload from time to time. And when she feels this way, only the explosion of a tantrum gives release. That's why it's the very rare toddler who hasn't had a temper tantrum or two by the time she's two years old. In fact, more than half of all two-year-olds have a tantrum at least once a week.

Some toddlers are definitely more tantrum-prone than others, but even the happiest, most easygoing children have tantrums occasionally. "Difficult" children, those unusually sensitive kids who have had a low threshold for uncomfortable feelings since they were babies, will have more tantrums than "easier" tots. Similarly, toddlers who are frustrated too much will have lots of tantrums. And toddlers who are unusually lively and who may be highly intelligent are also likely to have an unusually large number of tantrums. They want to do a great many things. And they mind a great deal when someone or something stops them.

Your toddler will have fewer tantrums when she becomes more skillful, because then she'll feel helpless and frustrated less often. Learning to talk will help, too, by enabling her to release her anger and frustration through words rather than through tantrums. This is another reason why it's a good idea now to begin reflecting your toddler's feelings for her and showing her how to express them through words herself.

HOW TO PREVENT TEMPER TANTRUMS

You can't always prevent tantrums, and you can't always relieve them once they're underway either, but it's a good idea to learn some techniques of tantrum prevention and tantrum relief even so, because sometimes what you do or don't do can make a difference.

Of course, your first goal should be to keep a tantrum from ever getting started. Once in the grip of a tantrum, a toddler is so overwhelmed and confused by her own violent emotions that there's a good chance your earnest efforts to help at that point will make her feel worse, not better. So the best favor you can do her —and yourself—is to prevent the tantrums from happening in the first place.

The Key Is Controlling Your Toddler's Frustration

Try to keep her out of situations where she is likely to feel overwhelmed. Some toys and equipment designed for older children can be very frustrating to toddlers, for instance. A riding, swinging, or rocking toy intended for preschoolers may be so fascinating to your toddler that she'll struggle with it till she's furious, if you don't intervene. She won't be able to use such a toy successfully unless you help her, and of course you won't always have the time or energy to do this, so the sensible thing is simply to keep this sort of toy out of the way until she's older. In general, make sure all the toys and equipment you make available to your toddler have been designed so she can play with them herself.

Of course, if there aren't enough interesting toddler-size toys around for your child to play with, she'll be frustrated by boredom. She'll head for things you don't want her to touch, and your efforts to stop her will lead to battles and tears. So don't try to avoid the problem of difficult toys by sticking your child with toys that are too simple, or by no toys at all. It's important to take the time to come up with playthings that are really appropriate. We have suggested a number of suitable toys for children this age throughout the "Play and Playthings" section of this guide.

Offer Help, But Don't Interfere
Another thing you can do to minimize your toddler's frustration is to give her assistance when she needs it.

This isn't nearly as simple as it sounds. You've got to help without interfering. Sometimes you can see or hear your toddler become frustrated with something she's trying to do. If you can help her in a way that lets her complete what she's doing and feel successful about it, you will probably have headed off a temper tantrum. But if you try to take over from her, you're likely to increase her frustration, and in fact make a tantrum more likely. It's hard to do the right thing in a situation like this, but it's not impossible. You have to be really calm and patient, tune in to the frustration your toddler is feeling, and figure out the least you can do to help.

Sometimes when you come to help your toddler after she's expressed frustration with something she's doing, she'll give up altogether and insist that you finish the job for her. In this case, you should try gently to encourage her to work with you to solve her problem. If she still refuses to participate, you can demonstrate what needs to be done in a calm, supportive way, mentioning that you know this *is* hard to do, that you saw she *almost* succeeded on her own, and that you're confident she'll be able to do whatever it is completely by herself before too long. Stay with her for a few moments, since she might want to try again after recharging her emotional batteries in your lap.

Don't Thwart Her Unnecessarily Yourself
You can also reduce the frustration your toddler feels by not thwarting her any more than you have to. It's amazing how often we say no to our children without even thinking about it. For example, your toddler may suddenly have become attached to a particular doll. Maybe she dragged it around all day long, propped it up next to her in her chair when she ate dinner, and even took it into the tub when she had her bath. But now it's bedtime, and when she insists that you get the doll out of the bathroom so she can sleep with it, you refuse. For some reason, you just decide to put your foot down, and your toddler feels confused and upset by your sudden and unexpected refusal.

It's especially important to think before you say no to a toddler in a situation like this, because your decision can influence not only whether or not your child will have a temper tantrum right now, but also whether or not she'll have a lot of tantrums in the future. How can this be? Well, think about it. If you're a sensitive parent, you'll realize, after impulsively saying no to some reasonable request, that you're not being fair. Unfortunately, by this time a tantrum may be well underway. And if you reverse field and go along with your toddler's request after a tantrum has begun, you're encouraging her to think tantrums have some advantages. She'll reason something like this: "It's no fun to get so upset, but sometimes that's the only way I can get what I want." It's much better to listen carefully and respond thoughtfully the first time your toddler asks for help than to give in after your unconsidered reaction has provoked a tantrum. This doesn't mean that you will always do what your toddler asks of you, of course. It simply means that you will say no only after you've thought about it, and when you intend to stick by your decision.

Watch for Signs That Your Toddler Has Reached Her Limit
You can sometimes prevent a blowup by paying attention to your toddler's signals that she is exhausted, hungry, or overstimulated. See to it that she has a nap when she's tired, and a light snack, if not a meal, when she needs food. When she's getting too wound up, help her switch to a calmer activity. You might sit and read to her, or help her drop some clothespins into a milk carton, or give her a refreshing bath.

What Can You Do Once a Temper Tantrum Is Underway?

You can't prevent tantrums completely; you can only cut down on the number you have to deal with. So you still need a plan for coping with a tantrum once it's underway.

You Don't Need to Stop a Tantrum— It's a Form of Release

The first thing to realize is that you don't need to stop a tantrum. Your toddler's temper tantrums aren't a sign that you've failed as a parent, unless she's having them every day, day in and day out. Nor do they indicate that there's anything wrong with your child. Try to remember that a tantrum serves a purpose. It works as a release—albeit an explosive one—for the unbearable pressure of frustration. After all, adults have tantrums too, and they feel like having them even more often than they actually give in to the impulse. Can you remember the last time you felt like having a tantrum? Or perhaps did have one? Be honest: ask your husband or wife to remind you of the last time you looked as though you were going to explode. Take a minute to picture yourself—

missing a bus or train.
being unavoidably late for an appointment.
being locked out of the house.
running out of paint on a Sunday morning when the room you're working on is three-quarters done.

finding a button off your only clean shirt when you're already late for work.

How did you feel the last time you found yourself in a situation like one of these: tired? angry? desperate? depressed? frustrated? Did you want to swear or scream or hit someone or cry? If you can remember how you felt, you will have some idea of how a toddler feels: swamped by a strong emotion and needing to let it out. Of course, adults usually express their strong negative emotions without resorting to temper tantrums; they sigh, stomp their feet, slam doors, or swear. They are also much better able than toddlers are to put their feelings into words, and putting your feelings into words is a release in its own right, besides being a good way to get help from someone else. But toddlers don't have all these resources. When their feelings get out of control, they may not have any release available except a temper tantrum.

Toddlers have tantrums, then, because they need them. Still, some parents feel that if they don't stop their toddler's tantrum quickly, she may hurt herself. Given the fury of a toddler's emotions at the height of some tantrums, this is an understandable fear. But cases in which children injure themselves during tantrums are extremely rare. Realistically, your goal should not be to stop your toddler's tantrum, but simply to control it.

Basically, there are two good approaches to controlling a temper tantrum. You can ignore the tantrum. Or you can hold and comfort your child during the tan-

Toddlers aren't the only ones who have tantrums. Often, adults too feel unbearably frustrated.

trum. The strategy that works best for you will depend on your style and your toddler's. Many parents combine the two approaches effectively, ignoring the tantrum until it begins to subside, and then holding and comforting the child.

Controlling Tantrums by Ignoring Them

Parents often find that they have no choice but to ignore the tantrum, at least for a while. At the height of a temper tantrum, many toddlers vehemently refuse to be comforted. They need to release their frustration, and they're simply not ready to be soothed. One mother who talked to us about her toddler's tantrums said, "I leave her alone to cry it out; she just gets angrier if I go near her." And another mother added, "I let mine scream and kick. It's really not worth picking her up, because she'll just throw herself out of my arms." You'll be able to tell if your toddler needs to be left alone for a while to cool down by the way she reacts when you try to comfort her.

There are a couple of different ways to ignore a temper tantrum. You may want to stand silently by your toddler, or to go about your business quietly where she can see you. Or you may feel better leaving the room until her screaming subsides. You may even need to carry her to her room, or some other special place, so she can cool off away from the rest of the family.

Acknowledge Your Toddler's Feelings, But Don't Get Your Own Involved

If you know what touched off your toddler's tantrum, tell her. Even if you don't know, you can say something such as "I can see that you're very angry and upset. I'm going to leave you until you cool off. When you're ready, just let me know." A calm, simple statement of this sort tells your toddler that you are still in control even if she isn't, that you understand how upset she is and why, and that once she has calmed down (which you are telling her she ultimately has the power to do), you'll be ready to pick up where you left off with no hard feelings. Despite her rage, your toddler will probably hear at least some of what you say, and she's sure to catch your calm, matter-of-fact tone. Don't overdo your explanations. And forget about trying to argue her out of her tantrums. She's not beyond hearing what you are telling her, and she's certainly not beyond feeling your love and presence, but she *is* beyond dealing rationally with the situation.

If your toddler gives no sign at all of responding to your simple, supportive message, forget it. Don't let her get to you. She may even increase her screaming and carrying on when you try to talk to her. Just walk away. Ignoring her tantrums not only gives your toddler a chance to calm down, it also helps you keep your natural reaction of anger and frustration in check. Unfortunately, it's almost invariably disastrous when a parent gives vent to these natural feelings. If you let loose your anger at your child's tantrum, before you know it you'll both be completely out of control. Your toddler will learn that she can't count on you to stay calm when the going gets rough, and you'll develop some pretty bad feelings about yourself, too, especially if you end up shaking her or screaming at her, or even spanking her.

Ignoring your toddler at the height of her tantrum

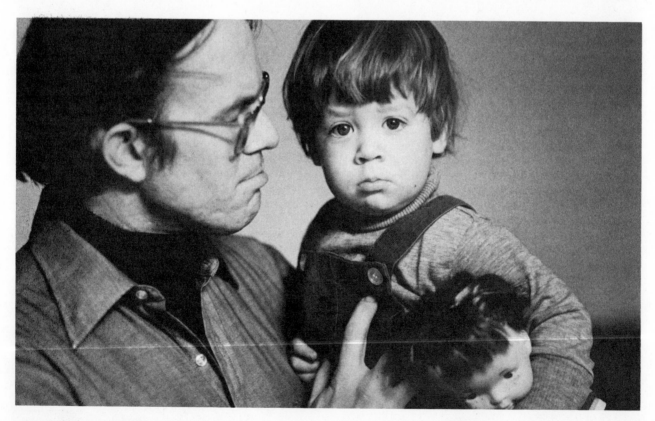

will also make it easier for you to avoid the worst pitfall of all: capitulating to your toddler's unreasonable demands in a desperate attempt to get the tantrum to end. Of course, if you give in to a tantruming child you teach her that tantrums are an effective way to get what she wants, and pretty soon you'll have her throwing tantrums right and left. What you want her to learn is that her overwhelming feelings are understandable, that you aren't undone by them, however, and that her tantrums aren't an effective way to get you to do what she wants.

Comfort Time

Sooner or later it's comfort time. Most parents find that it helps to return to the toddler as soon as her tantrum begins to subside. Now you can help her contain her tantrum and pull herself together. (Some toddlers seem to appreciate being cuddled and comforted all the way through a tantrum. They like the sense of security that comes from being held very close when their feelings inside are exploding.) As your toddler calms down, you can kiss her, and tell her you're sorry that she was so upset, and you're glad she's feeling better. There's really not much point in saying more than this—rehashing the causes of her tantrum, for instance. If you've stayed out of her way during the worst of her tantrum, you're probably calm enough to give her the kind of compassionate support she needs now. As long as you haven't been too involved with her furious behavior, you'll be clear in your own mind that the comfort you're offering as the behavior subsides is a way of controlling the tantrum and not an indication that you condone it.

Some toddlers need a longer cooling-off period than this before they're ready to be comforted. Your toddler may tell you to "Go away!" even after she seems to have calmed down quite a lot. If that's the way she reacts, accept it. Don't get indignant. Go matter-of-factly about your business and come back later. The point is to get to know your child well enough to choose the approach that will suit her best. Depending on her individual temperament, she may want to be held, talked to, distracted, or simply left until she's ready to reestablish contact with you on her own. In any case, your goal is simply to offer her a graceful way out. If you stay calm and give her room, you're sure to come through in one piece.

SPECIAL PROBLEMS WITH TANTRUMS

Public Tantrums Are the Worst

You may be at the end of a morning of shopping. You know that your toddler is hungry and tired, and that you've been out too long, but you need to get your groceries. Your toddler has been whining ever since you put her in the cart, and giving her a cracker from the box you just bought hasn't helped much. Trying to hurry through, you park the cart for a moment beside a pyramid of soup cans while you look for the noodles that should be around here somewhere . . . Egad. You deflect your toddler's arm just in time to avert a soup-

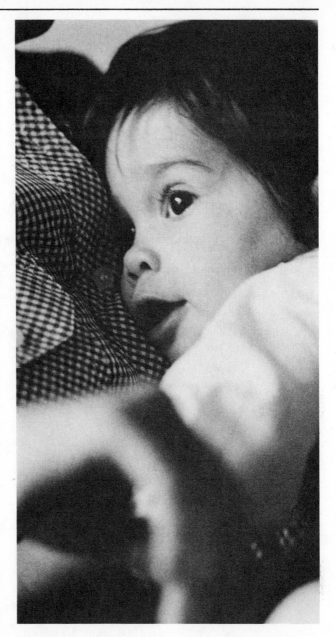

can catastrophe, but she yanks her arm away from you and starts screaming bloody murder. You take her out of her seat and put her down on the floor in a hopeless attempt to short-circuit the tantrum you know is on its way. At the same time, you pretend she's not yours. With no sympathy at all for your embarrassment, your toddler shifts her tantrum into high gear, hurling herself down and kicking her feet on the hard floor as loudly as she can. *Why did I let her wear her cowboy boots today?* you wonder helplessly, as the screams issuing from your aisle attract the attention of everyone in the store who wasn't already lined up to watch.

When you're out shopping or visiting friends or relatives, your toddler's tantrums will probably upset you more than when they take place at home. It's so embarrassing when your child explodes in front of other people that it's often hard to deal with her as calmly in

public as you usually do in private. It's still important to try, of course, because after all, your toddler's needs are the same no matter where her tantrum takes place. Besides, if you can stay cool, other people will be impressed by your self-control, and by the effectiveness of your sensitive but matter-of-fact approach, as well. So do your best to focus on your toddler's discomfort rather than on your own.

There is one special suggestion we can make for public tantrums: look for a quiet, relatively secluded place where your child can cool off. Perhaps you can take her to your car, if it's nearby, and let her cry out her frustration in some privacy there. If you're at a friend's house, ask her if she has a fairly childproof room where you can take your toddler. You may want to sit in the room with your child until she calms down, or you may prefer to wait just outside the door. If you're at a shopping center or in a store, find a quiet corner or go outside for a couple of minutes until your toddler begins to calm down. Obviously, in these situations you'll have to stay closer to your child while she winds down than you would at home. But at least create as much privacy and room for your child as the circumstances allow, and take some comfort from the knowledge that, in however small a way, you're helping her cope with the distress she feels.

When Both Parents Work
In families where both the father and the mother have jobs and in families where there is only one parent and he or she has a job, a toddler's tantrums seem to be concentrated during the evening hours that the whole family spends together. There are probably several reasons for this. The toddler may feel it's safer to be out of control with her parents, and in the security of her own home, if she is cared for somewhere else during the day. She may also find it frustrating that her parents, who are tired and busy with other important activities such as getting dinner, can't give her the attention she wants so much after being separated from them all day long. Besides, by the time her parents get home after a long day's work, they may be too worn out either to take the necessary steps to head off temper tantrums before they get started, or to deal with tantrums effectively once they are underway. And of course these difficulties are intensified when there is more than one child in the family and they all need attention.

If you and your spouse both work all day, it's especially hard for you to feel confident that your toddler's tantrums aren't a sign that you are failures as parents. You should try not to feel guilty, though. Instead, turn your energy to creating some special time with your toddler when you get home from work. Of course you're tired, but she really needs you. Maybe you can bring your spouse and your toddler into the kitchen with you, so while you cook dinner he can hold her and play with her and generally include her in the conversations he wants to have with you. Then, after dinner you may decide it's worth putting off doing the dishes so you and your toddler can do something together before she goes to bed. She doesn't need lots of time. But she does need at least some of your undivided attention, lovingly given. Playing with her, reading stories to her, and taking her for walks are good ways to share your time with her and to unwind a little yourself.

Sometimes there's work that just has to be done and you can't play with your toddler no matter how much you'd like to. This is an especially common problem for single parents. If you find youself in this bind, give your toddler something to do right next to you as you work, and while you go about your project talk to her about how her day went. If there's any way to let her feel she's helping you with what you're doing, that's even better. For a fuller discussion of the special concerns of working parents, see the chapter in the guide titled "When Someone Else Cares for Your Toddler."

Tantrums are probably the biggest problem parents have to deal with during the toddler years. And probably no parent ever feels confident that she's constantly met the challenge well; tantrums seem to get the best of everybody at one time or another. But by making an earnest effort to recognize your toddler's needs, to respect her intense and complicated feelings, and to provide a secure, loving framework within which she can work to achieve eventual self-control, you will be doing the most that anyone can to help a toddler weather this stormy stage. And in the process you may be growing up a little more yourself.

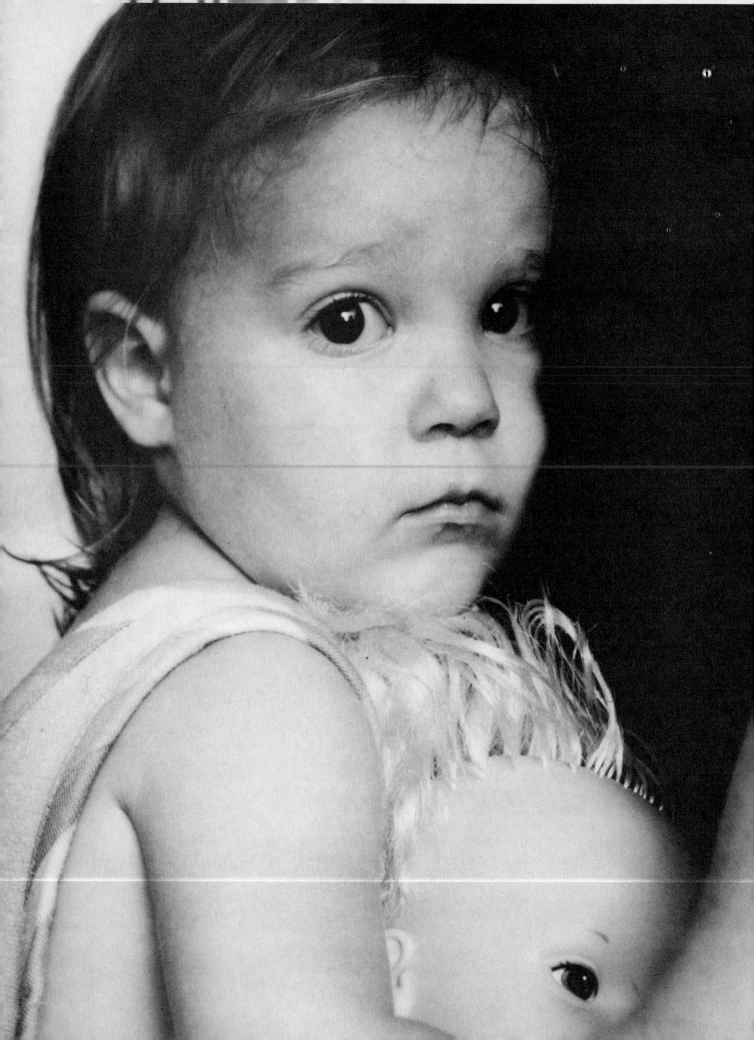

7
Helping Your Toddler Overcome Her Fears

The struggle to grow up can be frustrating for your toddler, and at times it can be frightening as well. Her independence is still very fragile, and, in many ways, her dependence is deeper and more real. So the months around your toddler's second birthday may be marked by a sudden upsurge of insecurity and fearfulness. She may have a lot of difficulty dealing with even brief separations from you, though she took these completely in stride only a few weeks ago. And she may become frightened by things that never scared her before, the sight of a tiny ant, for example, the rambunctious affection of a neighbor's dog, or even the baths she used to love.

When your toddler feels insecure or frightened, she may become much more whiny and demanding than usual. This sort of behavior can be hard for parents to deal with, and your reaction may be tinged with feelings of annoyance. You may think, *Usually you don't seem to want my help, so why should I come running to help you now?* This is an understandable reaction on your part. But if you push your toddler away—perhaps because you think it's time for her to stand on her own two feet—your efforts are likely to rebound. John Bowlby, a British psychiatrist who has spent many years studying the effects of separation in young children, says the result of such a parental rebuff is not likely to be a more capable and confident child but rather a more anxious, clingy one. So you don't reduce your toddler's whining by refusing to help. If she knows you are always there when she needs you, she'll feel free to be her independent little self most of the time.

Separations Can Be Especially Difficult Now
During this period, your toddler may be much more upset than she used to be by normal short separations. She may cry or seem depressed or angry when you leave her. She may also spend a lot of time clinging to you when the two of you are together, as if she's afraid you're going to abandon her suddenly. Surprisingly, she may continue to feel comfortable about initiating a separation from you; she may wander away quite heedlessly when you're out shopping or in a park. But as soon as you leave her, she'll feel desperate.

Actually, a toddler's anxiety about separations is a sign of growth. It's an indication that she's now mature enough to puzzle over and begin trying to understand your disappearances. When she was younger, you ceased to exist for her almost as soon as you left her; her short memory brought quick relief from her unhappiness over your departure. Now she is old enough to begin asking herself simple questions about your disappearance. "Where are you? How will I manage while you're gone?" Since she can't answer these questions, she becomes frightened and upset. Later, when she is old enough to begin answering such questions for herself—sometime between two and a half and three years of age—her fears will subside.

For the time being, if your toddler hates to see you go, nothing you can do will eliminate her fear of separations. But you can help her manage her fear. Try not to leave her alone unless you have to. Give her as much opportunity as possible to be with you, even if this only means letting her follow you from room to room as you work. And prepare her for the separations that are bound to take place. Tell her simply and honestly what's going to happen, and reassure her that you will return. It's not a good idea to prepare her way in advance, because her sense of time is so undeveloped. "In a little while" or "this evening" will mean nothing to her. But ten or fifteen minutes before you plan to go out, you can tell her very simply that you're leaving, where you're going, when you'll be back, and who's staying with her. Give her a chance to be upset, as you stay calm and reflect her feelings.

This policy is definitely the best one to follow whenever you have to leave your toddler for a while, but it is not the easiest. Your child will put up much more of a fuss when you prepare her this way than she would if you just slipped away after the sitter arrived. After all, now she understands what you mean when you say you're about to leave her, and the news makes her fearful and angry. But stealing away would create more serious problems in the long run, by betraying your toddler's basic trust in you. If you've sneaked away from her once, she has good reason to worry that you'll do it again, and she's likely to become more clingy even when you're home with her, because she won't ever be sure she can count on you to stay around.

Another step you can take to help your toddler handle separations from you is to get her started on some familiar, enjoyable activity before you leave. To your toddler one of the most upsetting things about your departure is that, without you, she's on her own; she feels as if she has more freedom and responsibility for herself than she knows what to do with. It reassures her, therefore, to have you tell her what to do while you're gone. A recent study of two-year-olds found that the children who were least upset by their mothers' departures were those whose mothers helped them this way. By setting their toddlers up with specific projects before they left, these mothers gave their toddlers the comforting sense that everything was still under control. (And they also gave their toddlers something else to think about besides the separation itself.)

Some kinds of separations, such as those involved when you or your toddler must be hospitalized or when a parent leaves the family as a result of divorce or death, create special problems. We discuss these problems in the chapter of this guide titled "Special Situations."

often deny this sort of fear; they see that the child won't be hurt badly even if she does fall, and they put her off with what's meant to be a reassuring line: "You aren't scared," or "Go on, you're having fun," or "That's not too high for you." Parents who respond this way have looked at the situation from their point of view, not their toddler's, and this is unfair.

Sometimes parents recognize that their toddler is really frightened, but feel that her fear means she's turning into a crybaby who needs to be "cured." It's pointless, though, to expose a child to something she's really afraid of in the hope of easing her fear. This is not only cruel but also self-defeating. A toddler who's afraid of the water is certainly not going to feel any more secure about it after being thrown into a swimming pool.

Often a toddler's fears seem to make no sense at all—

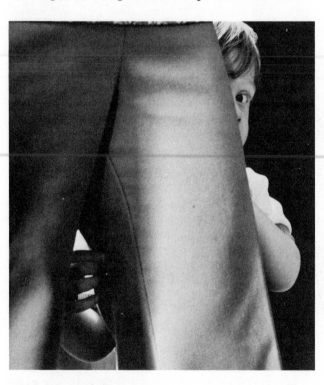

Other Fears Are Common, Too

Besides separations, the common fears of toddlerhood range from dogs to doctors, and include baths, insects, and loud noises. A particular toddler's fears depend on her general level of anxiety, her unique experience, and the working of her own individual imagination. How adults behave with her can either heighten or alleviate these fears.

The first step in helping a toddler deal with her fears is to see the situation from her point of view. Of course she can't take you by the hand and say, "Daddy, I'm scared." Until she can talk, you have to notice without being told. Unfortunately, some parents fail to do this. For example, their toddler may struggle gamely to climb a jungle gym, get stuck at a certain point, and begin to cry in fear; because she's little and inexperienced, the danger of falling seems very great to her. But parents

from an adult point of view. A toddler's terror at the sight of a dead crab on the beach may seem silly. But a young child can't always distinguish fantasy from reality. From her point of view, it's possible for that crab to come to life and chase her across the sand. It might even catch her and eat her up with those big claws. You may think she should know better, but how could she? It's important to respect *any* fear that your toddler expresses. Inside she feels she has a very good reason to be afraid.

When you think about it, of course, everyone has fears. Can you remember some of the things that frightened you as a child? Were you scared of shadows? Of something under the bed? Of branches tapping at the window? Of faces in the patterned wallpaper of your room? What frightens you still? Perhaps you shiver instinctively when you see a spider, or recoil from those

Everyone has fears. And while many of them don't "make sense," none are silly. Your fears deserve respect, and so do your toddler's.

little bugs that live under rocks. Maybe the sight of a harmless garden snake parting the grass beside your feet would make you jump. None of these fears "make sense," but they're not silly. You don't deserve to be ridiculed or punished or scolded for your unbidden feelings, and your toddler doesn't either.

Of course, some children are more hesitant and fearful than others. There are children who are simply slow to warm up to *any* new experience. This is a tendency born in them, and if your toddler is one of these, she'll need extra time and the most gentle reassurance to get over her initial fear of trying something new during this stage of her development. Pushing her will only make her more fearful and clingy. If you don't push, she'll eventually make all the adjustments she needs to. So be patient, accept her style, and let her get used to things at her own pace.

Fear of Dogs
Many toddlers are afraid of dogs, especially big dogs. That's not hard to understand. Dogs bark and leap up and move around fast and unpredictably. Don't ever force your toddler to approach a dog if dogs frighten her. If you do, she may develop a terrible fear, technically called a phobia. A child who has a dog phobia is not only intensely fearful every time she sees a dog, no matter how small or how far away the dog is, but

she also gets frightened by pictures of dogs, toy dogs, and even by any shape that looks like a dog.

If you want to help your toddler overcome a fear of dogs, do it gradually. She may feel more comfortable meeting a dog if you hold her during the introductions. But even this kind of supervised contact may be too much for her. If it is, respect her feelings and offer her reassurance. You can say something such as "I won't let the dog hurt you, but I see you're frightened. So I'll take you away from it now." Later you can talk to her about dogs when there isn't one around, or read her a book about dogs.

Giving her a toy dog to play with may also help. Then the two of you can play a game together with her toy dog, and you can help her work through her fears by acting them out. A few days later, you might try to introduce her to a dog again, maybe just by talking to one who is safely contained behind a fence in its yard. Pick a small, quiet, friendly dog if you can, perhaps a puppy, if it is even-tempered and not too rambunctious. Your toddler will eventually grow to feel comfortable with her canine neighbors if you introduce her to them gradually, and pay attention to any sign along the way that you may be moving too fast. If she does get upset at any point, back off as quickly and calmly as possible and try again another day. If her fear persists, do her the favor of helping her avoid dogs (or anything similar that she fears) altogether until she's older and stronger.

Bath Fears

Fear of the bath is very common among toddlers, and it's a particularly tricky fear to deal with since parents are seldom willing to let their offspring forego bathing altogether. The fear seems to come on unpredictably, often striking children who for weeks or even months before have seemed to love their baths. Suddenly, every time anybody tries to put them in a tub they start kicking and screaming. The change is so complete it can leave parents really baffled.

Part of this sudden fear is probably caused by a toddler's growing awareness of her unsteadiness in the tub; she's afraid of slipping under the water. But there's also another, rather fascinating reason for the new fear of the bath which hits children this age. Before this stage, playing with the plug—pulling it out of the drain and putting it back in again—was a favorite game for many toddlers. But suddenly, the sight of the bath water whooshing down the drain when the plug's pulled out makes the child worry that she, too, just like the noisy, swirling water, may be sucked down the plug hole. (Some toddlers develop a fear of flushing toilets for similar reasons.) Of course there's no danger of this at all, but at times of stress it's hard for a toddler to distinguish what really can happen from what can't. So if your toddler suddenly becomes terrified of the tub, you've got to treat her with respect. It may be enough just to make sure no one pulls the plug until she's out of the water, but you may have to take more steps than this. Often children this age are so afraid that the water might start to run out—taking any bathing toddler with

it—that you can't even get them to sit down in the tub for a bath. (In fact, you may have trouble getting your child into the bathroom at all.) If your toddler's reaction is this strong, try keeping her clean for a while without putting her in the tub. Use the kitchen sink, or a dishpan, or the wading pool in your back yard if it's summertime. Try a sponge bath, bathe your toddler on the bath table you used when she was a baby, or see if she'll take a bath together with you, sitting on your lap.

Above all, try your best to be especially gentle and reassuring. Do everything possible to help her become comfortable using the tub again. Start off letting her stand up in the tub, with just an inch or two of water at the bottom; you don't need more than that to get her clean. You might let her stand by the side first and throw a few of her toys in before she "takes the plunge" herself. Another good way to help her get over her fear is to set up some water play she can control herself. For example, she might enjoy playing with her bath toys in the bathroom sink, where she could pull out the plug, let the water drain, and see the results without feeling endangered herself. If she plays this game, she'll soon see that her toys don't get sucked down the drain, and you'll have an opportunity to point out gently that if her toys don't go down the drain she won't either, since she's even bigger than they are.

Basically, when you start tub baths again, just do everything you can to make the experience fun for your toddler. Let her play with the bath water, perhaps using a funnel and a length of rubber hose with her water toys. And always be sure to keep her bath water lukewarm, not hot: children seem to prefer cooler water than adults do.

Sometimes hairwashing—not the tub itself—is the

Many toddlers fear baths. One reason seems to be the concern that they may be swept down the drain with the swirling water.

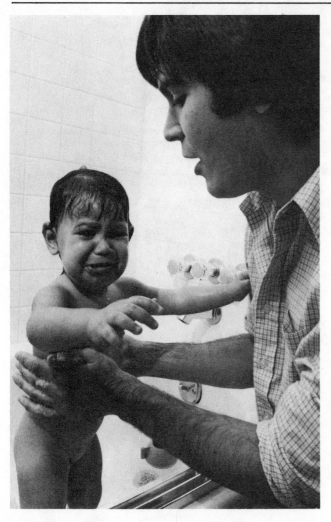

out a major battle, and that parent should be relied on to do the job most often.

Fear of Doctors

Many toddlers develop a fear of doctors. Being undressed, handled, poked, and probed in the doctor's office is bad enough. But even more upsetting is the fact that the doctor does things that hurt. And most upsetting of all, you don't stop him. It's not surprising that some toddlers start protesting as soon as they arrive at the pediatrician's office.

There are some things you can do to allay your toddler's fear of doctors. First off, it's important to prepare her ahead of time for what the doctor will be doing, including injections. Don't tell her injections won't hurt,. because they do, but assure her the pain lasts for only a few minutes. It might be a good idea to rehearse the whole scene beforehand. "Playing doctor" with a toy doctor's kit for use on dolls (and parents) is a good way to help a child work through some of her fears.

Once you're in the examining room, it will help if you keep your own natural feelings of embarrassment at your toddler's carrying on under control. After all, this isn't the first time your pediatrician has seen a crying child. In fact, most pediatricians have developed ways to ease the discomforts of both toddlers and parents in this situation. Perhaps you can help, too, by undressing your toddler, by holding and comforting her during the examination, and by dressing her when she's finished. And be sure to praise her when she only cries a little. No one enjoys going to a doctor, but your toddler is much more likely to take the experience in stride if she knows you're there to support her.

Dentists and barbers often bring out the same reaction in young children (and in some adults) as doctors do. One mother told us that her toddler was particularly upset by trips to the barber. A friend suggested she buy a toy barber's kit and play haircut with her toddler at home for a while. The next time this toddler had to go to the barber, she was allowed to take her kit with her. And this time the barber played with her for a few minutes before taking up his scissors. Thanks to all this preparation, the child was relaxed enough to submit to the haircut without any fuss—and her mother reports that she was delighted with herself for the whole rest of the afternoon.

The keys to success in this situation were the ones that help any toddler overcome any fear: having her parents understand and accept her fear in the first place; getting a chance to work through the fear in gamelike practice sessions; and feeling her parents' active support each time the fearful situation arises. If you can give your toddler this much help, you can feel confident that eventually she'll overcome whatever fear is upsetting her now, and that she'll gain in self-esteem, as well, from having faced something hard and dealt with it. You will have helped her grow.

toddler's greatest bugaboo. Unfortunately, this fear generally lasts for years, but there's no question that careful management on your part can reduce the distress your child feels because of it. You should certainly use a reputable baby shampoo, since it won't sting your child's eyes as some regular shampoos can. In addition, you'll need to figure out what part of the process bothers her most. Many children are most distressed by the feeling of water running over their faces and into their ears. If your toddler is one of these, try to find a shower ring that shields the face and ears and keeps the water on the hair only. Or use a cup for rinsing, to control the flow of water, and help her keep her head tilted back so the water will run away from her face.

Any way you do it, you have to be prepared for some fussing during hair washing. Some toddlers are also upset by having their faces covered while their hair is being dried. If your toddler feels this way, try a blow drier on a low setting and held not too close to her head, or let her hair dry naturally if the weather's not too cold and she doesn't have to go right to sleep. In many families one parent seems to have more success than the other in washing and drying the toddler's hair with-

8
Loving and Comforting Your Toddler

Clear, consistent discipline is an essential ingredient of good parenting during toddlerhood. But your child needs more than effective guidance. He also needs love. Of course, the way you discipline your toddler is itself a reflection of your love for him: it can take a *lot* of love to deal patiently with a cranky child at the end of a day. But your toddler needs more direct, obvious love, too. You express your love for him most directly through the comfort and pleasure you provide when you cuddle him and kiss him and talk to him lovingly.

We all relate to babies in a close, physical way. But our behavior changes a little when a baby becomes a toddler. For one thing, a one- or one-and-a-half-year-old child doesn't seem to want to be cuddled as much anymore. He's able to move around by himself, and he's becoming more and more interested in the world beyond his parents' arms. Often when you try to hold him, in fact, he'll squirm out of your lap before you've even got settled. His urge to be off on his own is very strong.

Telling Your Toddler You Love Him
But though your toddler's needs for physical closeness and comfort are changing, they're not gone altogether. Almost certainly, when he's frightened or hurt he comes running, and you pick him up, hold him close, and do your best to soothe him with a few soft words as you did when he was a baby. The comfort you provide at a moment like this lets your toddler know for sure that he can count on you for help whenever he is upset. Sometimes too, you can console your toddler by simply assuring him that you are nearby. During a thunderstorm, just being in the same room with you may calm your toddler's fears, not because you're actually doing anything to protect him, but because in his eyes your very presence has an almost magical power. Being in touch with you makes him feel safe.

Your toddler expresses his need to be "in touch" with you at other times too. He loves to share with you the discoveries he's made in the new world that walking has opened up for him. And when his adventures leave him weary, it feels wonderful to him to find a cozy perch in the lap of one parent or the other, and to exchange smiles and kisses and hugs with the people he loves best of all.

It's important that you meet your child's early needs for affection, because the affection he receives when he's little is what nurtures *his* ability to love in return. By hugging him and kissing him and telling him that he is the best kid in the world (at least most of the time), you help your child feel that he's lovable—and so help him feel secure enough to reach out and respond to you in turn, and to other people, as well. If he gets a good start this way, he will be comfortable making friends, being affectionate, and giving and receiving love all his life.

It's Not Always Easy to Be Loving with a One-Year-Old
Of course, it's not always easy to be loving with a toddler. His behavior can be exasperating at times. He *has* to explore, so he's often getting into things he shouldn't. And he must test his wings by asserting himself, too. So he often refuses your help even when he's struggling with something he can't possibly manage on his own. Dealing with your child when he's behaving this way can make you angry, and acting affectionate when you're feeling angry can be a pretty tall order. At times such as these, it's important to maintain a clear perspective on your toddler's behavior, so that nothing stands in the way of your basic love for him.

Much of the behavior that parents find so irritating during toddlerhood is perfectly normal and healthy for a child this age; it is simply characteristic of the trying stage through which all toddlers pass. Giving a child less affection than he needs at this point won't help matters in the least. It will only make him feel hurt and fearful and angry. In fact, a child who's denied the affection he wants during this stage may resort to clinging and whining and making lots of demands in an effort to get the emotional nourishment he needs. So instead of withholding love during this period, you should do your best to provide all the affection you possibly can. The more loving and supportive you are, the more easily and completely your child will transcend this stage—and the more likely it is that he will continue to develop as a person who is happy, and emotionally sound.

Being Affectionate with Your Toddler Helps You, Too
When you are loving to your toddler, he isn't the only one who benefits. Your affection helps you as well.

When you give love, you get love back. And you experience much more powerfully the positive side of this stage of development: the warmth, the tremendous openness to the world, and the almost boundless joy of living which are as real a part of a toddler's makeup as his contrariness and his "search and destroy missions."

Maybe the greatest benefit of a loving relationship with your toddler is that it makes you feel good about yourself. Many parents feel just the opposite when at the end of a day they look back and realize that they've been involved in a nonstop battle with their toddler since breakfast or even before. It's really hard to break out of this struggle mentality. But you can change the whole course of your day if you can just force yourself to stop. What a difference it makes when, instead of responding angrily to your toddler's testing and contrariness, you just reach out to him and draw him into your lap for a cuddle and a kind word. Often a simple gesture like this can change the whole tone of an afternoon. Your toddler may respond by melting against you lovingly, and the tension between the two of you may subside almost magically. It can make your day, a moment like this when you practice the true art of parenting, turning conflict into closeness through the gift of love.

When Do You Cuddle?

Life with a toddler can feel like one long round of feeding and diaper-changing, with lots of housework in between. Sometimes it seems as if you just don't have any time for a decent cuddle. But cuddles are at least as important to your child as the food he eats. Is your toddler getting enough from you and, if you work, from the people who care for him in your absence?

When you're home with your toddler, you can cuddle or offer a smile or a word of praise anytime. Sometimes you may want to race through your chores so that you can give your child your undivided attention for an hour or so when you are done, but cuddling needn't be separated from routine care and household chores. So other times it may suit you to go through your work at a more leisurely pace and make time for cuddling whenever you feel like it along the way.

In the course of a normal day you have dozens of opportunities for a quick cuddle with your child. Here are some of the times when you may want to take a few seconds to show your toddler how much you love him.

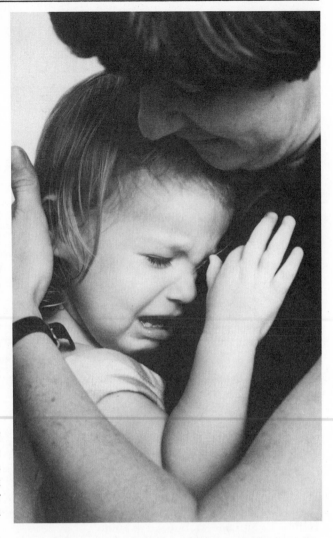

First thing in the morning, take a moment to hug your child and tell him what the day has in store.

When you settle him in his chair for breakfast, give him a kiss and talk about what he'll be eating.

While you prepare a meal and he plays nearby, smile at him occasionally and show interest in what he's doing.

While you read him a book or actively play with him, pause from time to time for a smile or a squeeze or a hug.

While you take a coffee break, settle in with your toddler in your favorite chair and talk for a few minutes about how the morning has gone and what he'd like to do next.

While you change his diaper, softly stroke his body and tell him how beautiful he is to you.

While you give him a bath, help him enjoy the feeling of water spilling over shoulders and down his back and arms. And help him learn the names for the parts of his body.

When you get him dressed to go out, snuggle him in your lap as you pull up his pants, and talk about where you'll be going together and what you will see and do.

When you say good-bye to him, take a moment to hug and kiss him; tell him that you'll miss him and you'll be back soon.

When you arrive home from work, scoop him up and swing him around, and talk to him for a couple of minutes about how his day went, before you go about your business.

While you take a walk with him, stop occasionally to kneel down beside him and share his discoveries.

When you get him ready for bed, take a few minutes to talk about the day that's ending, and about the

new adventures tomorrow will bring. And once you have him tucked in and have read him a story, sit by his bed or lie with him quietly for a few minutes before you leave him to fall asleep.

The best guide to how much you should cuddle your toddler—and to when he enjoys it most—is the child himself. Children differ, and even the same toddler is more cuddly some days than others. But all toddlers thrive on warm, loving attention. So make sure that your child gets all the hugs and kisses he needs every day.

COMFORT THROUGH SUCKING

Your toddler depends on you for love and affection. But he also has his own resources for providing comfort and security. If your child sucked his thumb or a pacifier as a baby, he'll probably continue to do so as a toddler. In fact, he may suck even more. Studies show that the second year of life is the peak period for non-nutritional sucking. That's not surprising. The second year brings a stage of development marked by tremendous achievements and the tension that often accompanies rapid change. Sucking is comforting. Because it's rhythmic and absorbing and repetitive, it's a very effective way of relieving stress. In fact, at his age, it's just about the *only* way your toddler can soothe himself. He can't turn on the TV, or call up a friend, or leave the house to take a walk.

Sucking is a sign of your child's perfectly healthy continuing need for security and comfort. And it's a sign of his growing resourcefulness, too. More and more he uses sucking to help him manage on his own the normal tensions of growing up. Of course, not every child sucks to comfort himself. Some use special objects such as cuddlies or comforters to relieve stress and gain pleasure. Still other toddlers, especially those who are unusually easygoing, seem to need no obvious security devices at all.

Thumbsucking During Babyhood
Even as infants, many children gain security and a sense of self-control through their sucking. You may have noticed that it was easier to leave your baby in his crib when he was sucking his thumb. Instead of crying (as he might have done if he wasn't sucking something), he could just suck harder when he sensed you were leaving him. In this way he could use the comfort of his thumb to replace the comfort you provided.

Your toddler is a much more complicated person than he was as a baby. He's developing and practicing more complex skills, and in the process he's feeling all sorts of new frustrations and anxieties. He needs to have a way to soothe himself now even more than he did as an infant. You may notice he sucks his thumb when—

he's playing with a group of children and things get too active or demanding for him. Maybe there are

too many children, or an unfamiliar child has joined the group, or perhaps his playmates are a bit older and more skilled than he. He can relieve the tension at moments like this by retiring to the sidelines and sucking his thumb while he watches the activity. He is taking a time-out, giving himself a chance to absorb what's going on in a way that's not overwhelming to him. Chances are he'll rejoin the group once he's recharged his emotional batteries.

he's tired or bored or frustrated. Sometimes the pressures he feels come from within. When he's exhausted, or fed up with the lack of excitement on a particular day, or frustrated by a toy he can't quite get to work, he may retreat to that big comfy chair in the corner and curl up in it with his thumb in his mouth.

Pacifiers, Too

Many babies and toddlers suck pacifiers instead of thumbs. Others use their bottles the same way. In a recent study involving toddlers and their mothers, one-fifth of the parents reported that their toddlers were attached to a pacifier at twelve months.

Sucking on a pacifier can relax a child and help him get to sleep, and it can protect his sleep as well. Noises and other disturbances that would otherwise wake a child just make the toddler with a pacifier suck more vigorously.

Another recent study shows that a pacifier can help a toddler in more surprising ways, too. In this experiment, twelve-month-old children were placed by their mothers (one at a time) in a room where a variety of toys were spread about on the floor. Each mother left her child immediately; half the mothers gave their toddlers a pacifier as they left, and half did not. The children were free to follow their mothers, play with the toys, or do anything else they wanted. What the researchers hoped to find out was whether or not having a pacifier made the toddlers more comfortable when they were on their own: whether the toddlers with pacifiers stayed in the room longer than the children without, and whether they explored more actively or played with more toys. This is exactly what did happen. And most interesting of all, the benefits of the pacifier were so powerful and immediate that when they were given pacifiers for this experiment, even toddlers who had never used a pacifier before stayed longer and played more than the children who didn't have this aid.

Concerns Over Sucking Needs

Even though sucking fingers, thumbs, and pacifiers is normal for toddlers, parents sometimes worry that this sucking may become a habit that can't be broken. But recent research shows that sucking subsides on its own, without any special efforts on the parents' part to stop it. In one study of children whose mothers didn't try to prohibit their sucking, there was an upsurge in the amount of sucking during the second year of life, followed by a natural decrease by the time the children were about two and a half. So you don't have to put bad-tasting stuff on your toddler's thumb, or pull his fingers out of his mouth, or hide his pacifier to help him get over this dependency. In fact, more often than not tactics like these are self-defeating. They tend to increase the tension a child feels, and since at this stage his primary means of relieving tension is sucking, any aggressive attempts you make to get him to stop sucking could easily end up causing him to suck *more*. For your child's sake as well as your own, it's a better bet to simply wait for his sucking urge to fall off naturally with the passage of time.

But even if you let your child suck to his heart's content now, the process of weaning when he's older will still be a gradual one. Even after they reach the age of two and a half, many children continue to suck their thumbs or pacifiers at bedtime and at times of stress, when they are sick or uncomfortable in a new situation. They may continue to suck on these special occasions until they are four or five or even six years old.

Sometimes parents worry that all this sucking may make a child's teeth grow crooked. There is no universal agreement on how long a child can suck without affecting his teeth, but the best evidence suggests that sucking is a problem only if it continues after a child's second teeth come in. The baby teeth of thumbsuckers are often pushed out of line, it's true, but it's a rare child who's still sucking his thumb or a pacifier with any regularity by the time his second teeth begin coming in, at six or so. So chances are your child won't do any harm to his permanent teeth no matter how often his thumb is in his mouth when he's one.

Special Issues for Pacifiers

Parents tend to be more concerned about pacifier sucking than about thumb sucking. Maybe that's because they feel they have more control over pacifiers. You can't take a toddler's thumb away from him; you can't make him use it in a certain way (such as sucking) any more than you can keep him from doing so. But a pacifier comes from a parent in the first place—children aren't born with them—and many parents feel they should have some say about the way it's used. Some parents try to control pacifier use by deciding when to withhold it. They restrict the times and places where the pacifier's allowed to be sucked. Other parents do the opposite, influencing not their child's abstinence but his dependence. In effect, they use the pacifier to plug him up.

To tell the truth, every parent probably uses her

Some parents fear that their toddler will never give up her sucking habit.

toddler's pacifier as a plug now and then. There are times when you're just too busy or too tired to cope with a fussy toddler any other way. But it's important to keep these occasions to a minimum. As a general rule, a pacifier should be the toddler's crutch, not his parents'. If he is given his pacifier every time he starts fussing, he soon learns that his parents view the pacifier as their form of comfort, and he may begin to use it not only when he feels he needs to suck but whenever he needs stimulation or comforting from his parents, too. So try to pay attention to whether your toddler is asking for his pacifier or really asking for you. And make an effort to find the time and energy to give him a little of yourself when that's what he really needs.

You may not mind at all seeing your child suck his pacifier in the house, but you may feel quite anxious when he does the same thing outside in the yard, in the car, or while you're together shopping. A neighbor may have looked disapprovingly the last time you strolled your toddler by with a plastic dohickey sticking out of his mouth, or your mother-in-law may recently have wondered aloud when you were going to put a stop to this nonsense. At times like these, it's hard to balance your toddler's need to suck against your natural feelings of embarrassment.

Ideally, you should recognize the importance of your toddler's need, and simply live with your own temporary discomfort. But your feelings deserve respect, too, so if your toddler's pacifier causes real problems for you, try to work out a compromise. You'll need to use tact and caution in setting limits; don't try weaning him from his pacifier suddenly. Take it by steps, if you do it at all. First try restricting the pacifier's use to the house (or house and car rides). Later, try keeping it for use only when you and your toddler are in a particular area of the house (upstairs, for example). Still later, try restricting it to your toddler's bedroom. Finally, he may be ready to use it only at bed- and naptimes. This weaning process may take months, and by the end of it your toddler's sucking urge will be diminished anyway, unless you've prevented him from satisfying it. So, if you meet powerful resistance in taking any of these steps, you'd best back off and wait for nature to have its way. Your toddler is telling you he still really needs the comfort his pacifier provides him. Give him a break now, and you won't have problems later.

Sucking Needs by Any Other Name

As we've said, your child's sucking needs will get less intense by the time he is two and a half or so, unless you've prevented him from satisfying his need earlier. But chances are he'll still suck on special occasions. Even adults depend on forms of gratification similar to the thumb- and pacifier-sucking of early childhood. Smoking pipes or cigarettes, chewing gum, sucking toothpicks, blades of grass, or pencils, thoughtfully fingering one's mouth; these are common adult expressions of the basic oral needs of human beings. Toddlers really aren't so different from the rest of us.

> One little boy we know retreats to a quiet spot whenever he's tired, and alternately sucks and plucks an old blanket.
> Another wants to hold a piece of cloth right against his cheek, while he strokes his nose or lip with a free finger.
> A third child cuddles his teddy bear to his chest when he's put to bed, then slides it down under his stomach and rocks himself on it; this is a crucial part of his falling asleep ritual.
> Other children fondle their own soft, warm hair at quiet times. They may stroke it or twist a strand of it over and over again, often sucking their thumbs at the same time for added pleasure.

Many toddlers adopt special objects like these, usually soft cuddly things ranging from cloth diapers to old blankets to soft toys, to use with or instead of sucking. A cuddly may be slept with, chewed, hugged, loved, and talked to. It may even have its own special name. A toddler who has grown attached to such an object is likely to become very upset whenever he can't find it.

Children often become attached to cuddlies at about eighteen months, and continue to use them for several years. In fact, one recent study found that 60 percent of a group of toddlers were already attached to such special objects by the age of eighteen months, and an almost identical proportion (58 percent) of the older children in the study were still attached to their cuddlies at the age of three years.

Dr. D. W. Winnicott, a pediatrician and child-development expert, has labeled these special comforters "transitional objects" because, like pacifiers and thumbs, they are useful to the child in making the transition from dependence to independence. Like old friends in a new place, cuddlies are reassuring to a child because they're familiar and accepting. They can't make demands or judgments, and they offer no surprises. And the toddler himself is in control of his cuddly.

Even adults take comfort from special objects. When you find yourself in a situation that makes you feel insecure, you may absently finger a favorite piece of jewelry or rub your thumb against the back of your ring—partly just to keep your hands occupied, to be sure, but also because it's reassuring to touch something familiar. And toddlers behave the same way, only more so.

In fact, your toddler's cuddly can be almost as important to him as you are, at least in certain situations. Recent studies, similar to those showing the benefits of pacifiers for toddlers, have demonstrated that for a

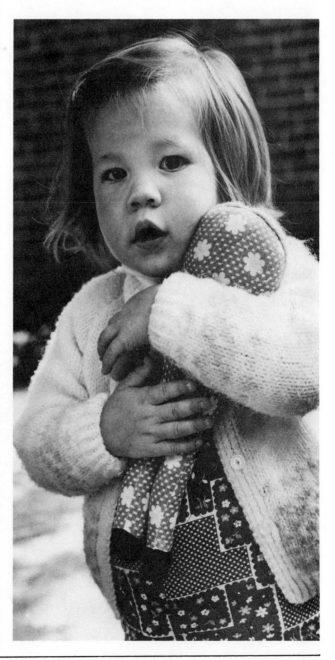

toddler who is attached to a security blanket, the blanket is as effective as his mother in keeping him from becoming upset in unfamiliar settings while at the same time freeing him to play and explore. So don't forget to take your toddler's cuddly along when you go away on vacation. Strange places won't distress him as much and he'll have a much easier time settling down to sleep in an unfamiliar room if he has his cuddly right there with him, like a piece of home. If you ever need to take your child to the hospital, be sure to take his cuddly along too. And before you go out for an evening, tell your baby-sitter where the cuddly is and what its special name is.

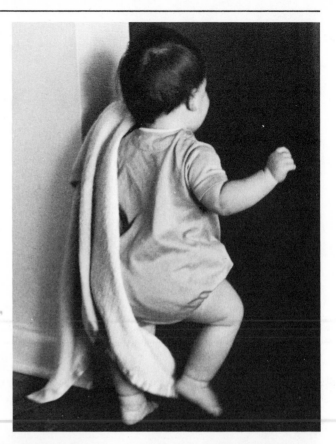

You'll probably find your toddler becomes so attached to his cuddly that you won't be able to wash it as often as you'd like. When you do wash it, he may become really upset, because you'll have ruined its precious familiar smell. To minimize problems, wash the cuddly as infrequently as your own standards of personal hygiene allow, and when you must wash it, use a soap or detergent that doesn't have a powerful smell of its own.

Once you see how attached your toddler is to his cuddly, get duplicates of it if you possibly can. There are years of use ahead. If the cuddly is a soft toy, buy a second and put it someplace safe. If it's a piece of blanket or rag, you may be able to cut it in half as insurance against the day when the first one becomes so

threadbare that you have to throw it away. The "second" won't be perfectly satisfactory, of course, because it won't smell or look or feel quite like the original. But it's a lot better than nothing. You might try tying or sewing the old cuddly to the new one until the second is broken in. Then, and only then, the old one can be thrown away (or cast in bronze).

A few toddlers are willing to accept two cuddlies from the start, switching off between them. Naturally, this alternation tends to prolong the life of each one. Most toddlers remain attached to their cuddlies for two years or even longer. Weaning them before they are ready can be at least as difficult as forcing them to give up a pacifier, and it's best not to try. But if you are really uncomfortable about your child's use of his cuddly, try setting some limits, along the lines of our suggestions for controlling use of a pacifier.

The more you respect your child's dependency on special objects and special sucking rituals at this stage, the more likely it is that he will outgrow these dependencies soon and without great suffering. By accepting his tattered blanket and his calloused thumb, you will be acknowledging his need for security and at the same time supporting his increasing resourcefulness. And what better way could there be to help him grow through this important, but so often unsettled, period of his life?

9
Fathering: A New View

It used to be assumed that the mother was the only significant person in a child's life during her first few years, and that the father, though nice to have around, wasn't really essential. But times are changing. Fathers today are much more involved with their young children than they used to be. And researchers in family life are beginning to emphasize their importance.

Today many fathers are becoming full partners in parenthood from their babies' first days of life—and even before. In many parts of the country, a father is able to participate in his wife's preparation for childbirth. He may even be able to see his own baby being born. The fathers who take such an active role in their children's lives from the start seem to sense in a very immediate way that they are responsible for the development of another human being. And their experience calls into question one of the major myths of fatherhood, the notion that a father doesn't have the same capacities as a mother when it comes to caring for a young child.

Can Fathers Be Competent Care Givers?
There is no certain evidence that women have a biological, psychological, or other natural advantage that automatically makes them better caretakers. They simply have more experience. In our society, boys get less practice caring for children than girls do. And the experience gap widens later in families where the father goes off to work every day while the mother cares for their children. Men often shy away from child care simply because their wives seem so much more competent at it; fathers feel uncomfortable about their own lack of skill.

You may not be as skilled at child care as your wife is, but the more you can assume these responsibilities, the sooner you will learn. Remember she had to learn at some point, too. With practice, you can become an expert at fixing bottles and meals, changing diapers and clothes, wiping noses and tears, and giving baths and reading stories. These tasks are really not difficult, and they often turn out to be fun and satisfying besides.

With practice, fathers quickly become competent enough as caretakers for mothers to feel perfectly confident when they leave their husbands alone at home with a toddler. Toddlers rarely get upset about their mother's departures when Dad is the "sitter." In fact, they often seem to get a special kick out of being left with their fathers. And mothers often tell us that they return refreshed after such a break, and with a renewed appreciation of their husbands and their children.

Some parents we know say that in certain aspects of child rearing—discipline in particular—fathers actually seem to have an advantage. They say that at times their toddler will "mind" Dad much better than Mom. If this is true, it may have something to do with the fact that, seeing her father less often than her mother, a toddler may feel less sure of herself with him and so be more likely to do what he asks. Or perhaps it's related to the image of greater authority many fathers project through their larger size and deeper voices. This image of fathers can also be helpful in calming a child's fears. Dad may be able to convince a toddler there are no crocodiles hiding under her bed by simply appearing so confident and unafraid that the child loses all sense of danger in his presence.

Finding Time for the Father-Toddler Relationship to Flourish
Of course, uncertainty about their competence as caretakers isn't all that prevents many fathers from becoming full partners in parenthood. Too often, fathers have very little time and not much energy. After a rough day at work a father may drag himself through the front door longing only for a shower, a change of clothes, and a chance to relax for a bit. Roughhousing with his toddler may be the last thing he feels like. But the child is clamoring for attention, and of course mother is tired and needs relief as well.

If you are a father, this is probably a familiar predicament. It can be hard to balance your needs against your wife's and your toddler's at times like this. But it's really important to try. Ignoring your wife and toddler and collapsing into the nearest chair to read the paper or watch television, or retiring to your bedroom or the basement—none of these is a good solution. Sometimes a weary father will justify this sort of copout by falling back on the traditional distinction between a man's job and a woman's job. But this rigid distinction rarely applies anymore. It is especially outmoded in the growing number of households where both parents work outside the home.

Hard as this may be to believe, there *are* ways to

respect the reasonable needs of both parents, and at the same time make weekday evenings especially warm occasions for everyone. What you need to do is to plan and to share. When you arrive home from work, try to spend a few minutes with the whole family, talking about how each person's day went, unwinding a little, and planning for the hours ahead. If your wife is in the middle of fixing dinner, you might take your toddler into the kitchen—if she's not already there—for your little *tête à tête*. Then you could take your youngster upstairs to "help" you change your clothes and clean up before dinner. Let her try on a pair of your shoes, help you hang up your shirt or throw it in the hamper, and wash her hands and face when you do. She'll probably be delighted to be part of your routine, and involving her in it will enable you to spend time with her and begin to unwind at the same time. Your wife will really appreciate the break also. Once you've changed, you'll probably feel a little more like playing with your toddler. If you've had an especially hard day and you're really wrung out, you can read her a story or take a quiet walk or stroller ride around the block with her. If you're feeling more energetic, you can get involved in some active floor play or general roughhousing, or even take a trip to a park, if there's one close by and you have time before dinner.

Of course there are often things you need to do when you get home. You may have errands to run before the stores close, for instance. Your toddler loves being with you and where the action is, so she'll probably be delighted to join you on your trips to the grocery, the hardware store, the drug store, the laundromat, even on your trips to the service station to get your oil changed. She'll probably enjoy going just about anywhere you have to go.

You do need to plan ahead, though, and think of your toddler's comfort before you go off on these jaunts. You may run into problems if she's exhausted or starved or if the experience involves lots of waiting. (She probably won't be comfortable entertaining herself for thirty minutes in a hardware store while you give your undivided attention to all the available sizes of galvanized screws.) But if she's not too tired, put a few bite-size snacks in a bag, and head off on your appointed rounds. You should also be sure to take along a diaper or two just in case. Running errands with your toddler gives your wife a chance to finish dinner, put the house in order, or just relax a bit, if that's what she

really needs. (You can also keep your toddler close by while you do chores around the house or in the yard. Just make absolutely sure that dangerous materials and equipment are safely out of your toddler's reach.)

By sharing and caring in this way when you first get home from work, you can set a warm tone for your whole evening. After dinner you and your wife and toddler can do something as a threesome, or a more-some if you have other children. You might also want to find other special times to be alone with your toddler. You could give her a bath and get her ready for bed. Many fathers take this responsibility and enjoy it, play-ing with their toddler while she's in the tub, reading her a story, tucking her in, and lying with her for a few minutes, savoring the closeness that is such a special part of bedtime rituals.

Many fathers also share certain weekend rituals with their toddlers. They may take the toddler off for break-fast at a local diner, or put the toddler in a backpack for a scenic walk, or take the toddler on a weekend visit to relatives or friends. Fathers who have to get up early in the morning to go to work tell us this can be another good time to spend with their toddlers. Father and child can talk together while Dad is dressing, and then have

breakfast together, too, letting Mom have a little more sleep. (You can add extra fun to morning routine if you let your toddler "help" you pick out the clothes you'll wear.) Turning early mornings into enjoyable times to-gether in this way takes only a little thought, and it's really worth it. It can send you out the door with a smile on your face that will carry you through at least your first traffic jam.

A Father's Special Contribution to His Toddler's Development

Fathers can share both the burdens and the benefits of parenthood with their wives. But fathers are different from mothers, of course. And these differences have a special importance for their young children. Fathers look different, sound different, smell different, feel different, and react differently from mothers. The dif-ferences between her father's bigger body and her mother's smaller one, her father's deeper voice and her mother's higher one, her father's scratchy face and her mother's smoother one, all help a young child learn about contrasts between people. Contrasts provide variety. And for everyone, toddlers included, variety makes life more interesting, Experiencing differences between her mother and father helps a toddler learn to live in a world that is full of contrasts, and helps her learn to feel comfortable with people of widely different appearances and personal styles.

There's one difference between fathers and mothers which has special importance for young children. Fathers generally play more actively with their toddlers than mothers do. They roughhouse more; they're more likely to throw a toddler in the air and catch her; they're more likely to give vigorous, bouncy piggyback rides and shoulder rides; they're more likely to wrestle and roll about on the floor with a toddler; and they're more likely to enjoy chasing a small person around the room or around the house.

Of course, mothers also play with their toddlers in an active, involved way, but this kind of play appears to be more characteristic of the way fathers relate to young children. There are probably a number of reasons for this. First of all, an active, physical style is characteristic of male relationships in our culture. And of course, most fathers are around their children far less than their wives are. So they want to relate in an active, intimate way during the short time they do spend together. If mothers played as actively as fathers do during the much longer stretches they usually spend with their toddlers, both mothers and toddlers would probably collapse from exhaustion. Many fathers also seem to be less concerned than their wives are with the mess that active play sometimes creates. They don't spend all day cleaning, so the disorder doesn't seem like such a problem to them, even if they're the ones who clean it up. Whatever the reason, fathers tend to play more boisterously than mothers, and it's clear that most children love it. Researchers who've watched mothers and fathers play with their young children have found that in most cases the children are more involved, more excited, and more cooperative when they play with their fathers.

It's obvious that toddlers love their playtimes with their fathers. What's less obvious—but no less important—is that a father's greatest contribution to his young child's intellectual development comes from these active sessions. Playtimes are highly stimulating experiences for toddlers; for a young child, play *is* learning. And the give-and-take, the direction, the encouragement and praise that are a natural part of play with fathers have a powerful influence on the children's cognitive growth. In fact, the contribution that these play periods make to a toddler's physical and mental development, emotional security, and trust is out of all proportion to the amount of time fathers and toddlers spend together. So it ought to be clear that fathers aren't just bystanders in their toddler's lives at all. They're critical.

10
Helping Your Toddler Enjoy Other Children

As a toddler becomes more independent and begins exploring the world around him, he also becomes more and more interested in other children. You may have noticed that even before his first birthday, your child showed a special enthusiasm for other small people, responding to the approach of a child with wide smiles and excited waving of arms and legs. Most babies react positively to a strange child's approach even during those periods when the appearance of a strange adult can send them crying to mother or father. They learn to recognize other children and show a desire to interact with other small human beings from a very young age.

When you think about how important the abilities to make friends and to get along with others are to us as adults, it is not surprising that the foundations for these abilities develop very early. In the second and third years of life, a toddler's relationships with his main caretakers (usually mother and father) are definitely *the* most important to him, but he will be ready to start actively developing relationships with members of his own generation, too. His social life will include both his peers and older and younger children, be they relatives, neighbors, or the children of your friends. Helping him to form friendships with these other children, and to enjoy them, will be one of your most important jobs during these early years.

TODDLERS AND THEIR PEERS

Why Do They Want and Need Friendships?
Your toddler's "peers" are those children who are approximately the same age and stage of development as he is. He's likely to have the most fun with his peers because it's with them that he has the most in common. Two psychologists who do research on toddler friendships summed up the affinity this way: "Peers share an interest in such activities as jumping off a step twenty times and wearing pots for hats."

Your toddler may admire the four-year-old next door and often follow her around, but his interests and capabilities are so different from hers that it isn't likely they'll form a real friendship. Likewise, he may show great interest in his six-month-old cousin, hang over the carriage to talk to her, and show real concern when she cries, but their relationship can't be called a friendship either. (For the time being, anyway. Of course,

when your toddler is seven and his cousin is six, they may be inseparable.)

You may have heard that toddlers are too young to really play with one another, or that if they're put together for an hour or two they'll spend the whole time fighting over toys. These were the views of many child development experts until very recently. The notion was based on a handful of studies on toddler interaction, all of which observed groups of toddlers who did not know each other, gathered in a strange laboratory playroom. Naturally, these toddlers spent a lot of time just staring at each other (that's their way of learning about something new), or turning to their mothers for comfort (it was a strange playroom, after all). It's hardly surprising that under these circumstances some of the toddlers were observed snatching toys, hitting, and pushing one another. Recently, scientists have thought to observe toddler friends who are *used* to playing with each other, and to conduct their studies in the toddlers' own homes. And not surprisingly, they have come up with some very different findings about toddler social life. (A researcher observing you in a large gathering where you didn't know anyone would undoubtedly draw different conclusions about your social style than a researcher watching you greet your best friend as she arrived at your house for a cup of coffee and a chat.) The new research has found that toddler friends show far more interest in each other than in their mothers, and that positive actions (offering toys, smiling, laughing, babbling, touch-

ing, and imitating) account for most of their interactions. One study reports that conflict between toddlers who know each other occurs in only about 3 percent of their interactions.

Even if your toddler has a brother or sister or two, he will still benefit greatly from friendships with peers. In important ways, play with siblings is different from play with friends. It's influenced by the differences in skill and power that inevitably follow from age differences, and it's also affected by the rivalry that two children in the same family naturally feel as a result of their day-in and day-out competition for their parents' attention. If your toddler's sister or brother is older, and if your toddler plays only with his older sibling, he is likely to learn that he is always second best, never as skilled and competent at things as he wants to be. (*You* know that he's doing fine—for his age—but he doesn't understand that.) Of course, a toddler should play with his siblings often, and there are lots of positive aspects to that relationship, but for your younger child it's particularly important to balance this play with experiences with one or two friends of his own age and abilities, so that he can get a realistic sense of himself and his skills. Later on in this chapter, under "Toddlers and Their Siblings," we'll say a little more about helping your toddler get along with his older brother or sister.

Arranging for your toddler to spend time with others his age is important not only because he'll enjoy this play, but also because he'll learn a lot from it. Play with a fellow toddler will be very different for him from play with Dad or Mom. When you play with your toddler, you take far more than half the responsibility for how the interaction goes. You try to do what your toddler wants to do, you take it easy on him, you let him go first, and if he wants the toy you're holding, you probably let him have it. That's marvelous: play with the adults who love you is an important part of a toddler's development.

But your toddler will also benefit greatly from beginning to learn how to cooperate with others like himself, age mates who indeed will jump off the step with him twenty times in a row but who will then insist on playing with the wagon *he* was trying to climb into. From play like this, your toddler will begin to learn the give-and-take of daily life. It's nice to know you're the center of Mommy's and Daddy's universe when you're only one year old. It's also useful to start learning that you have to earn friendships in the outside world, practicing social rules such as sharing or lending toys, waiting your turn, respecting other people's feelings and possessions, and saying "please" and "I'm sorry." Your toddler won't master all of these sophisticated behaviors for many years, of course, but if you provide him with lots of opportunities for supervised play with other toddlers, he will be showing remarkable progress by his second and third birthdays!

Not only is having a friend over fun for your toddler, but you'll find that it has benefits for you, too. Once the toddlers get to know each other, your child will need very little attention from you when his peer is

around. Although you'll have to stay close by to keep an eye on things, you'll be able to go about your own work with far fewer interruptions than usual. Or maybe you'll enjoy a two-hour chat with the other toddler's mother and discover that the two of you have as much in common as your toddlers do!

Arranging for Your Child to Meet Other Toddlers
If your toddler hasn't been around other children much yet, and particularly if he's young (only thirteen or fourteen months old), it's best to lead him into the social world gradually. The best way to start is to introduce your toddler to only one other child, either in your home or at hers. Plan to keep the first visits short, and be sure they come at your toddler's best time of the day. (If he's usually grumpy after his nap, then that's not the time for guests.)

Mothers should definitely plan to stay with their toddlers during these visits, at least until the toddlers get used to each other and to one another's houses. Although some one-year-olds toddle right off to play with each other, those who are new at this may need to use Mommy or Daddy as a secure base for several visits before they are really comfortable with the situation. While your toddler is getting used to the idea, he'll

probably touch you often or even want to be up on your lap for a while, studying the situation from the safety of your arms. He will probably interact a lot with *you* at first—talking to *you,* showing *you* toys, and barely seeming to notice the other toddler. Let your child use you for his security base for as long as he needs to, and he'll be off and exploring when he's ready.

After a while, when the toddlers are comfortable with each other and their respective houses, you might try trading off with the other mother. You can take care of both toddlers at your house while she has a morning off, and then she'll repay you by having your child visit at her house. This sort of arrangement is cheaper than a baby-sitter, and toddlers often enjoy it a lot more! Both mothers should remember, however, that two toddlers take an even more alert eye than one. When you're the mother on duty, keep both children in sight, or check on them frequently. Don't let a long silence lull you into feeling that you shouldn't disturb them when they're so contented. They may be absorbedly taking turns sticking bobby pins into an electrical outlet!

Many mothers and fathers have formed informal play groups where three or four toddlers are brought together on a regular schedule. One or two parents stay and care for the whole group while the others are free to relax or do errands. A regular play group for your toddler can be especially helpful to him if he has an older sibling who goes off to school each day, leaving him behind and lonely. Besides simply enjoying the companionship his play group offers, he'll probably be proud of having a regular place to go to, too. (There is a more detailed discussion of play groups in the chapter entitled "When Someone Else Cares for Your Toddler.")

What to Expect with Peer Interaction

Toddlers are more capable of enjoying play together than we once thought. But interacting happily with others is a skill that has to be learned through lots of practice. Toddlers differ in their reactions to others in many ways, depending on their basic personalities, their age and peer experience, and on what the other toddlers are like. Naturally, as they mature and become better coordinated and better able to communicate verbally, they become more skilled at forming and maintaining friendships. The important thing is to be sensitive to your individual toddler's reaction to new situations and new people and to move at a pace that keeps him feeling comfortable.

Although each child is an individual, your toddler will probably exhibit some of the following types of behavior as he learns to play with others: (1) timidity; (2) watching; (3) parallel play, imitating; (4) treating other toddlers as objects; (5) acting selfish, sharing; (6) acting aggressive; (7) playing cooperatively; (8) showing sympathy and empathy.

1. *Timidity.* Some toddlers can dive right into their first group experience, ignoring their parents completely. But the more common reaction is hanging back, acting shy, and needing to stay close to Mommy or Daddy for a while. As we mentioned earlier, you're your toddler's secure base. If you let him stay close to you, even on your lap, as he studies the situation, he'll fulfill his security needs more quickly and be able to move away from you fairly soon. If you push him away, telling him to be a "big boy" and go play, your rejection may make him feel even more timid and nervous, and he may end up clinging to you longer.

If after quite a while your toddler is still shying away from the other child, try moving into the interaction with him. Sit down on the floor, with your toddler still in your lap, near the other child and her toys. Try playing with her a little and talking to her, ignoring your own toddler. He'll probably join in pretty soon, if only

to earn your attention. Just play it by ear and see what happens. Maybe nothing will, this visit. But don't give up; try another visit soon. With patience on your part, this, too, will pass.

2. *Watching.* All toddlers spend a large part of their day staring. They'll sit and stare at the surroundings both at home and outside in the community, and they'll study both people and objects intently. Staring is one way to learn about things, so you should expect a lot of this when your toddler first encounters another child or finds himself in a new place.

Sometimes your toddler will stare openly, at other times out of the corner of his eye while he appears to be concentrating on something else. He may be learning a lot in this quiet way. Realize that this watchfulness is a type of interaction with the world, and don't try to push your child into more active interaction if he's not quite ready.

3. *Parallel play, imitating.* When two toddlers play close by each other without seeming to notice each other, their behavior is called parallel play. This sort of play is quite common during the early stages of toddlerhood, when children are still relatively inexperienced at playing together. If you'll observe closely, however, you'll see that even parallel play entails a certain amount of interaction. Often two children who appear to be ignoring each other are in fact playing with similar objects in similar ways—which means that they are not only noticing each other, but also silently copying one another. They're probably enjoying this "togetherness" the way a husband and wife might enjoy sitting and reading in the same room, each aware of the other even though no obvious interaction between them occurs.

4. *Treating other toddlers as objects.* If your toddler is not accustomed to being around others, he may treat a new child as he would a new toy: he'll try to explore her with his hands and mouth. This sort of investigation, particularly if it involves exploration around the other child's face, may look like an aggressive act (and may be reacted to as such by the other child), but it isn't. As long as your child appears to be curious, not angry or upset, chances are his poking and probing of the other child are not hostile.

But if your toddler repeatedly explores other children as he would a toy, he needs a little help in learning that other people don't like to be poked, shoved, or pulled on. If it's fairly gentle exploring, you can try just waiting to see if the other toddler will take care of the situation. If it's rough, you'll need to intervene, for both toddlers' sakes. Stop your child as you explain to him that he *cannot* hurt people like this. Also comfort the toddler who got poked. She doesn't care if your child was exploring or being aggressive, all she knows is that it hurt! Your comforting the other toddler and apologizing will help your child understand that he has hurt someone.

When we meet someone new, we have lots of ways of beginning the interaction, and most of them (except shaking hands) are verbal. We can say, "Hello, how are you?" We can ask the stranger's name and where he's from, or what he does. These spoken exchanges help break the ice. Nonverbal toddlers have to devise other ways of meeting and greeting, and most of them will greet each other with a physical act of some sort. Offering a toy is a common toddler greeting. Or your child's poking and pushing may be his way of saying hello. It this technique seems to bother his small friends, you may be able to get him to stop it by simply suggesting an alternative greeting. After you've explained (again!) that people don't like their eyes poked, suggest, while demonstrating, that instead he rub Carrie's arm when he meets her. Watch him carefully for a while, *especially* when he first enters a room and is most likely to go into his greeting routine. Be right next to him, ready to protect Carrie's eyes and reinforce the new form of greeting until he learns it.

If your toddler continues to explore all his friends

will learn what types of exploration are acceptable, and which ones people don't like.

This lesson may take a while, because toddlers are basically egocentric: they have trouble understanding that other people feel pain because of their acts of hitting and pinching. But you *can* teach your toddler not to do these things, by consistently stopping him. Even before your toddler is old enough to understand the cause and effect—pinching causes pain, which makes someone unhappy—he'll understand that this behavior is unacceptable. You'll be doing your toddler a favor in teaching him this lesson now, too, because if you don't teach him, who will? His peers, that's who, and they won't be patient and gentle about it the way you can be. They'll clobber him, or refuse to play with him, and that will make him miserable.

5. *Acting selfish, sharing.* When toddlers really do begin to interact with each other and their toys, the problems of selfishness and refusing to share may come up. A toddler is very likely to hold a toy out as a gesture of friendship. Chances are, though, when he does this he's just showing the toy; he doesn't want it to be taken. As an adult, you undoubtedly know to smile appreciatively at the toy without making any move to possess it, but his toddler visitor, confronted by an offered toy, will almost certainly try to get hold of it. When this happens, your toddler may let the toy go, looking surprised, or he may howl in protest, or he may hold on and struggle over possession. By the same token, your toddler is likely to walk up to a visiting friend and just take (or try to take) whatever toy she's playing with. And he'll probably look astonished if she struggles to grab it back.

In both of the above cases, the toy-taking results from a lack of understanding of the rules of possession. If Laurie is playing with an airplane, the rules of social life say it's hers (for the moment) and that Tom should not grab it. He should wait or ask if he can have a turn. These rules have to be learned, however, and learning them takes time. A docile toddler may learn the rules of sharing fairly quickly and without much suffering, but a more aggressive toddler will probably have to go through many struggles for possession before he com-

too roughly, even after you've stopped him over and over again, you should ask yourself how you let him explore *you.* Most parents let their babies pull their hair and poke and pinch them. Of course, exploring parents' bodies is one way babies and toddlers learn about people. Because such explorations by a baby rarely hurt, parents usually don't need to restrict this behavior. But toddlers are bigger and stronger, and some of their body explorations *do* hurt. And even if you can stand the occasional pain, another child can't. So if your toddler continues to hurt other children through his physical explorations, it might be because you've never taught him to restrict himself. Now is the time to start.

As we said, gentle explorations of your body are good learning experiences, and should be allowed. However, when your toddler gets too rough—say, he really pulls your hair—you should stop the painful activity *at once.* Remove his hands, restrain them with your own, and tell your toddler *firmly,* "No. Don't pull hair. It *hurts* people." Your physical action and sharp tone may work. If he continues pulling your hair when his hands are freed, put him down so he can't reach you. Finding himself abruptly out of your arms may make him think twice about what he was doing. Every time his explorations—be they pulls or pokes or pinches—get too rough, stop them in a similar fashion. Over time your toddler

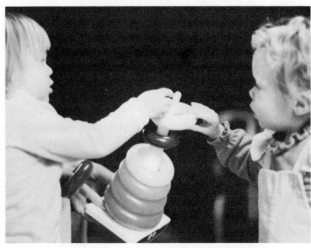

prehends. As long as neither toddler gets angry enough during one of these struggles to hurt the other, it's usually best to let children work the conflict out for themselves. They may screech at each other and push and shove, but their flare-ups are usually short-lived. Before you know it, they're playing together amiably again. And along the way they've learned something about how to settle disputes—which is certainly a more valuable lesson than how to run to an adult for help.

If your toddler occasionally takes toys from others or sometimes doesn't want to hand his possessions over to visiting friends, be assured that this is perfectly normal behavior for his age. A baby is so cheerfully generous with his toys that parents are sometimes caught off guard by the changes that occur somewhere between twelve and eighteen months, when a toddler develops feelings of ownership. As he practices his new awareness of *"Mine!"* his parents may worry that their generous child has suddenly turned into a selfish pig. He hasn't. If you give him lots of experiences with other toddlers, he will gradually learn about sharing and selfishness from them—and they'll learn the same from him.

We've talked a lot about "selfishness" because that's what parents worry about. But among toddlers who play together regularly, acts of sharing and taking turns are far more common than acts of selfishness. Without much adult intervention, toddlers can be counted on to teach each other the basic rules of getting along and enjoying it.

There are two situations where it makes sense for an adult to intervene, however. The first is the situation where one toddler continually has his toys taken away and seems to be upset about this, but doesn't know what to do. The other situation is where one specific toddler seems *always* to be snatching things away from others.

A child who consistently loses all his toys may need a few lessons in assertiveness. Talk to both participants at once: assure Billy that he is playing with the rings and that if Tom tries to take them he can hold them *tight* and say to Tom, *"No!* They're mine!" Also explain to Tom that when Billy has the rings, Tom should play with something else for a while, and wait till Billy has finished. Keep your voice calm. You're just teaching a short lesson on respecting other people's rights, not accusing anyone of being good or bad or right or wrong. You will probably have to repeat the lesson over and over before it takes.

When one child seems to spend all his time taking toys from other children, the problem may be a little harder to solve. If you've already waited and watched, and the other toddlers' protests haven't changed the offending child's behavior, try this method next: each time the snatcher takes another child's toy, calmly direct him to an unused toy, and return the grabbed toy to

whoever was playing with it. If aggressiveness (hitting, banging, biting, shoving) goes along with the snatching behavior, read the next section, on "Acting aggressive," for suggestions.

6. *Acting aggressive.* As we have already pointed out, some behavior that looks like aggressiveness really isn't; it's simply a matter of one toddler's treating another like an object. In this section, we'll discuss true aggression, that is, an attack on another, caused by anger or frustration. Aggression against both peers and adults is normal at this age, just as selfishness is, because a toddler is trying to develop his independence and sense of self. His *"Mine!"* and "Gimme that!" to a fellow toddler are similar to the "No!" shouted at his mother. His reactions are often extreme because he isn't sure of himself.

Mild aggression includes not only physical pushes and pokes but aggressive speech, too. Verbal bossiness is very common at this age. A toddler who is hearing "No, no" and "Bad boy!" all day from his caretaker is likely to try to use words to shove his small friends around when he has the chance. Don't worry, though. Toddlers usually work this sort of problem out for themselves—often by pushing or bossing the aggressive toddler back, so he learns what it feels like.

You should always be close by and alert to what's happening, however, because toddlers' social controls are not well enough developed for them to be left entirely alone together. If one toddler begins pushing hard, hitting, clobbering others with toys, biting, or kicking, it's time for an adult to intervene—and swiftly. To say that aggression is normal in this age group does not mean that it's admirable. You will want to begin helping your toddler learn to handle his aggression in more acceptable ways than by hurting other people.

Stop the aggressive toddler instantly and firmly. He *needs* to be stopped; he isn't happy when he's totally

out of control. And, of course, his friends need protection from him.

This doesn't mean that you should lose control, too, and rush in shouting and physically punish anyone. After all, it's completely illogical to strike an offending child while shouting, "You must *never* hit people!" It won't help to tell the child that he's bad or selfish or a mean little boy either. Your intervention should be prompt, firm, and above all, calm: you simply restrain the toddler from kicking, and in a very definite tone, say, "You may *not* kick people like that!" This may be enough. If it isn't, at the next bit of aggressive behavior, remove the child from the group. If he's calm enough, explain things to him again in a loving way. Suggest better ways of handling whatever the problem was (it's usually a property dispute). After all, that's what all toddlers are struggling to learn. "Next time you want the truck, *ask* Lisa if you can play with it. She likes to play with trucks, too, honey. You can't just grab it from her. Let's see if we can find some more trucks in the toy box so everybody can have a truck."

If you're the only adult present, you may have to do a momentary balancing act, because the aggressor will need restraining and, perhaps, removal, but at the same time the child who was hurt will need comfort and protection. A good first step, if you're alone, is to pick the hurt child up quickly; that way you can comfort her and prevent any further blows. At the same time, start talking to both children. You may even have a free hand left to pat the aggressor with as you try to cool him down.

Don't let yourself get put into the role of judge about who started the fight or who's right. This is an impossible task and only prolongs the battle. All that matters is that a fight erupted and it has spoiled the play for everyone, so the fight must be stopped. After you point out better methods of handling disputes, cheerfully suggest

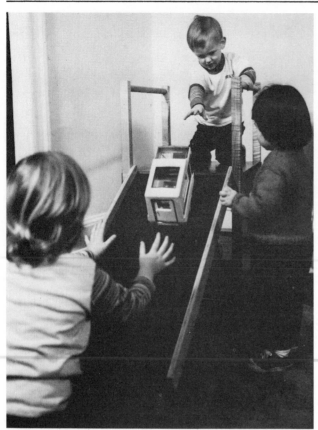

Occasionally a toddler will act like a real bully. He'll hurt other children constantly, and none of the suggested ways of controlling or channeling aggression will work with him. If this is happening with your child, you should examine his daily life carefully. Is he experiencing some stress at home: a new baby? A move to a new house? Daddy and Mommy separating or divorcing? Or is someone acting aggressive toward him: a parent or sitter who gets angry often or uses lots of physical punishment? An older sibling who is beating him up? Either (or both) of these circumstances could make a toddler quite upset and physically aggressive. To help him out, you will need to remove as much of the stress as you can. What you can't remove, you can at least talk to him about. If there's some big change in his life (like a new baby or a divorce), you're going through it, too, and that may make it pretty difficult for you to be extra patient and loving with your toddler, but do your best. Read the sections called "Toddlers and Younger Siblings" and "The Single Parent" for further suggestions.

7. *Playing cooperatively.* The ability to play cooperatively does develop eventually. (With some tod-

a new game and supervise the toddlers as they begin it. If tempers still seem high, a total change of scenery may be best. You can march everybody off to the kitchen for glasses of juice, or arrange a trip to the backyard swing set to help everyone forget.

What about the idea of teaching your child to "stand up for his own rights" by leaving the toddlers to settle their own disputes? We're talking here about physical assault, not just some tug-of-war or a verbal "Mine!" battle. Allowing toddlers to handle the milder forms of aggression themselves probably will help them learn to stand up for their own rights. Permitting painful assaults, however, will only teach small children that "might makes right," that the stronger or crueler person can take whatever he wants. That's probably *not* the lesson you want your toddler to learn.

dlers it's there from the very beginning.) Two children who have approximately the same level of physical and verbal skills can have a really wonderful time together. As we've said before, the better they know each other, the better they will get along. Stranger toddlers are the most likely to fight over toys or attack each other; toddler friends will spend most of their time together happily, at first playing in parallel ways and, as they get older, playing more and more cooperatively. They will offer each other toys, take turns, and even divide the blocks or toy people without a single reminder. Once they become verbal, they will use language in cooperative play also—sometimes in a most amusing way, as you'll discover if you listen for a while.

8. *Showing sympathy and empathy.* These surprisingly grown-up signs of true friendship have frequently been observed in toddlers who spend a lot of time together. For a toddler to learn to care for a friend takes time and exposure, of course, just as it would for you to learn to really care about someone. But toddlers in small day-care groups or play groups that meet regularly often show such feelings toward each other, rushing eagerly to greet each other in the morning with hugs or kisses and lots of touching. During the day they show their feelings with smiles, touching, and offerings of toys or food. If one child gets hurt, a friend will act sympathetic and upset, often patting his buddy or crying along with him. On leaving each other, these toddlers show real regret, and when they're apart, they clearly miss each other. One mother describes her toddler's friendship as follows: "When Bruce arrives, Joey gets all excited. He says, 'Want play?' and runs to his playroom. When that little guy left last week, they were hugging and saying good-bye."

Toddlers do want and need some time with other toddlers. They enjoy it, and they learn a lot during it. When toddlers play with one another, their parents get a bit of a break from them, as well. So don't let the hassles that accompany toddler friendships discourage you from giving your child this broadening experience. No matter how complicated toddler play sessions may be, their advantages far outweigh their annoyances—for all of you.

TODDLERS AND THEIR SIBLINGS

Why is it that your toddler can play with the four-year-old next door for hours with almost no bickering, yet can't spend half an hour with his four-year-old sister without three major fights? Because of "sibling rivalry," that's why. Your toddler and his sister are competing for the love and attention of the same parents; your toddler and the neighbor child don't care at all about each other's parents. Jealous rivalry between brothers and sisters is universal. The only sure way to prevent it would be to have only one child. Although you cannot hope to eliminate sibling rivalry if you have two or more children, you *can* work to minimize it and to help your children learn how to handle it. The next three sections will examine some of the ways in which you can help

improve your toddler's relationships with his older or younger siblings.

Toddlers and Older Siblings
The toddler's point of view. Your toddler will probably absolutely adore his older sister. He'll want to be right where she is, doing just what she's doing, as often as possible. He will light up when she comes home from nursery school, run to her for a hug after he's been punished, "brrmm" his cars just the way she does hers, and try to help her color in her coloring book. Admiring her so much, he'll be amazed and confused when she suddenly yells at him to get away or hits him for no reason that he can comprehend. In his unhappiness, he'll cry for help or wildly scatter her blocks in uncontrollable frustration.

The older child's point of view. Most older brothers and sisters do *not* absolutely adore their toddler siblings. As a matter of fact, unless they're four or more years older than the toddler, they can often be annoyed with the small household explorer. Older siblings

are less than enthusiastic about having a toddler around the house for the same reasons that parents often find this stage a difficult one: the toddler's growing mobility and independence, and his great curiosity.

As a baby, he was okay. He just stayed in his playpen or infant seat; the older child could go over and show him a picture or make him giggle when she felt like it and she could ignore him when she was busy. Now, though, the toddler can come to her when he wants, and that seems to be all the time. Furthermore, when he arrives, he wants to touch everything. But he's clumsy, he doesn't understand verbal commands yet —and another carefully built block tower bites the dust. No wonder many parents report that the jealous behavior and fights between their children that they were expecting just didn't happen—*until* the younger child became mobile. Naturally, your older child is upset when that toddler messes up her doll tea party or destroys her coloring book. And when she takes the law into her own hands and tries to teach him a lesson, she has trouble understanding why Mom and Dad come rushing in and get angry with *her!*

On the other hand, the older child really enjoys the admiration of the younger. It's hard to be annoyed for very long with someone who obviously thinks you're wonderful. She's probably found out what fun it is to teach him things, that he's the only family member who will sit still while she "reads" to him, and how useful he is when she wants to play "Mommy and Baby" or "Doctor and Hurt Person." He may not play his role to perfection, but at least he's there. And it certainly is twice as much fun in the bathtub or under the sprinkler with that silly little brother sharing the giggles.

The parents' point of view. Actually, most sisters and brothers get along quite well most of the time. But the arguments are more noisy and obvious than the peaceful times, and sometimes you may be convinced that those two do nothing but fight. As a parent you love both of your children very much, and you want them to love each other. It's upsetting when they appear to hate each other instead, even momentarily. But take a deep breath, and repeat to yourself that sibling rivalry happens to all siblings. Think about the battles you and your brothers or sisters had, *and* think about the warm, good times. You probably feel really friendly and close to your brothers or sisters now that you're all adults. It all worked out for you, and it will for your children, too.

Sibling Rivalry

How can you best help your children to get along well with each other? First, you can identify and reduce many areas of stress and competition between them, thus greatly reducing the number of fights. Second, you can teach your children some simple psychology lessons on how to get along with each other. And third, you can learn how to stop the occasional big fight without getting mad yourself and making things worse.

The chief cause of the stress your children feel is simply that they have to share your love and attention.

The younger they are, the harder this is for them to do. Be sure you give out lots of hugs and kisses and compliments every day. In addition to the time all of you spend together, try hard to find some special time to be alone with each child each day. The special time might be when you and your toddler read a book together while your older child plays with her friend. Or when you and your older child have a long discussion about what clouds are, while your toddler is napping. Be sure that both parents give special attention: Daddy can take Ann over to the hardware store with him on Saturday morning, while Mom and Jerry weed the garden together. Or Dad can stay home with Jerry while Ann and Mommy take the dog to the vet. (Be sure to switch around and not get in a rut where, for instance, Daddy always takes the older child on excursions while Mommy always stays home with the younger.) It's nice for every young boy and girl to feel like an only child every once in a while, even if it's only for fifteen concentrated minutes at night, when Dad sits on your bed and talks about what happened today.

Researchers have observed that the closer in age two siblings are, the more frequent and intense the fights between them will be during the preschool years. The farther apart they are in age, the better they'll get along. This finding may come as a surprise to parents who deliberately spaced their children close, thinking that nearness in age would make their offspring close friends. But think about what causes sibling rivalry. What it really amounts to is competition for the parents' time, love, and attention. And since the younger a child is, the more love and attention she needs, if a new baby comes along when the older child is only one or two years old, still needing to be babied herself, her needs are likely to go unmet, no matter how hard the parents try. In this situation the "old baby" is bound to feel a lot of resentment toward the new one. If the older child is already three or even four when the baby arrives, on the other hand, she is fairly independent and has interests outside the family, so she needs a lot less time and attention from her parents. She won't find the new sibling so much of a threat. Children who are older when their siblings are born are more capable of helping to take care of the newcomer also, and this can make life easier all around.

Another stress your children feel is the sibling's invasion of their private space. This may be a more serious problem for your older child than for your younger one; as we said before, a toddler is much more eager to play with or near his older sibling than vice versa. An older child definitely needs a safe place where she can set up games and plan to play in peace, without invasion from the toddler. If she's four or older, this could be her bedroom with a door that closes, but if she's only two or three herself, she may still prefer to be near you instead of shut off in the bedroom. Tell her she can use the kitchen table or some other special area and that you'll keep her little brother away.

Occasionally a toddler will set his toys up in some

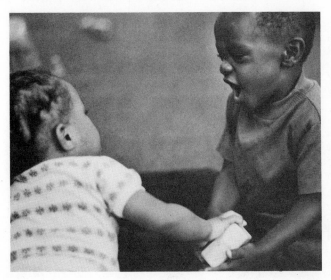

mysterious order also, and loudly protest when his big sister interferes. Respect his rights, too (even if the order isn't clear to anyone but the toddler), and remind your daughter of how she sometimes wants to play alone, too.

Teach your children a little child psychology as they interact. It's amazing what they can learn if you give them a chance. Teach your older child, for example, how distractible toddlers are: "If you want the horse he's playing with, show him the doggy with the bell in it. Ring it so he'll be interested, then make a trade." Now isn't that a lot easier (and quieter) than just grabbing the horse? And everybody is still happy, too!

You might also explain to your older child that her little brother keeps coming around because he admires her so much. He wants to build block towers *just like hers*. So if she's busy building and he comes toddling over eagerly, she can be taught to deflect him from her precarious seven-block tower with a quick lesson on how to pile up three blocks, and "That's Eric's tower!" Eric will love this sort of play and may work away at his pile of blocks for quite a while before threatening his sister's again.

Sometimes it's important to help your children divide toys up evenly, but don't do this every time. Cooperative play can be lots of fun, too, with each child adding one more block to a tower until it collapses—and the playmates collapse, too, in wild laughter.

The younger child can learn some simple psychology lessons, too, if you stop to explain things to him: "Better stop banging the pots together," you might say, "because Ellen's head aches today." Then, as you help put the tempting pots away, say, "All those big bangs make her head hurt *more.*" Next thing you may notice is your toddler rubbing Ellen's head and offering her his special blanket! If you'd suddenly forbidden pot banging with no explanation, your toddler would have been left feeling angry and resentful—and would have learned nothing.

As you teach your two young children how to be sensitive to each other's needs and moods, remember that the most effective teaching method is not what you say but what you do. Don't stop explaining things—that's helpful too—but remind yourself that *your* sensitive behavior toward each child's needs, and the ways in which they observe you handling disagreements with your spouse and other adults, will have a more powerful effect on their learning the golden rule than all the words you ever say.

Last, but not least, comes dealing successfully with the big fights that are bound to erupt between your children even after you have reduced as many stresses as possible and taught them a few simple getting-along-with-others lessons. First, reread the section under "Toddlers and Their Peers" about sharing and selfishness and aggression. You're dealing with the same problems with a pair of siblings, and you need to find the same balance between knowing when to let the children work things out for themselves and when to take matters into your own hands. Most small and even medium-size hassles are probably best ignored; figuring out solutions by themselves will help your children learn the give-and-take necessary in daily life. But when tempers flare and behavior gets really out of control (or if you're alert, just *before* this happens), you should quickly step in and help your children work things out.

This does not mean that you should become a referee. It's usually impossible to judge who is right or wrong or who started what. Often there *is* no right or wrong anyway; if you try to reconstruct the argument to assign blame to one child or another, you'll only prolong the battle and probably make both children resent you as well as each other. It's important for you to stay as calm and detached as possible. When two people are already heated up about something, having a third person lose her cool only makes the situation worse. The kind of help your children need from you is threefold: They need you to end the hostilities before someone gets hurt. They need you to help them deal with the strong feelings that have been aroused. And once everyone has cooled down, they need you to suggest better ways for them to handle things next time.

Remember, both the attacker and the attacked (if you can even tell which is which!) need comfort—the attacked because he just got hurt, and the attacker because inevitably she feels guilty and upset about what she's done. While you firmly state, "Karen! You may *not* hit people," you pick up the crying child to remove him from further harm (or to keep him from retaliating). As you hug him, you may be able to pat Karen to help calm her down. If she starts telling you that Adam took her doll out of the high chair and she hadn't finished feeding it, agree that this must have annoyed her, and then talk about better ways of handling annoyance. The important lesson here is that it's okay to feel angry at someone, but not okay to vent anger in a physical attack. Next time, could Karen offer Adam another doll and cup and spoon and help him co-

operate instead? Remove her doll to some other room to feed it? Grab her doll back and resume her game without slugging Adam?

An older child is at an advantage in learning to handle interactions without hurting people: she's stronger than her toddler sibling and can either win a tug-of-war over an object or run away from the attack, and because she's more verbal she can *say* what she feels rather than acting it out physically. The toddler has a lot of handicaps: he's smaller, less well coordinated, weaker, and unable to express his feelings in words. He's also less aware of his ability to hurt people than his older sibling is. Although you can begin explaining alternative behaviors to him, usually the most effective tactic is just to remove him from the scene. Luckily, it's fairly easy to get him interested in other activities, and he forgets fast.

Keep in mind that family fights are probably at their worst when one sibling is a toddler; a year from now the sibling relationship will be more peaceful. Your toddler is going through a particularly difficult phase of his own development, he's mobile but he doesn't yet have much self-control, and he's just not very verbal yet. What this means in practical terms is that the toddler gets frustrated and angry *more* than older children, but has *fewer* ways of handling his strong emotions. Naturally he lashes out physically. When he really becomes verbal—not just able to name objects, but capable of expressing feelings—you will probably be amazed at how much more peaceful *all* interactions with him will suddenly seem.

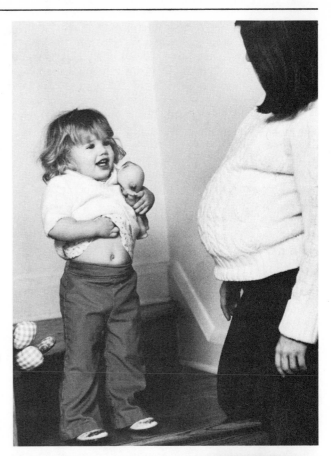

Toddlers and Younger Siblings

Are you thinking about becoming pregnant again now that your last baby is a toddler? Pediatricians have noticed that the most common time for mothers to ask for advice about child spacing is when the first child stops being a helpless, agreeable baby and becomes a mobile, often stubborn toddler. Perhaps that's why so many families do have their first children only two years apart: the urge for another cuddly, dependent infant hits women when their first child is thirteen or fourteen months old.

Spacing children two years apart is so common in our culture that people have come to assume, without thinking about it, that a two-year interval is best. Pressure is put on parents to live up to this norm. (If your child is nearing twenty-four months and you're not pregnant yet, observe how many people start asking you, "Well, when are you going to give Andy a little sister?") But psychologists, and some young parents, are beginning to question the two-year interval.

Throughout this book we have emphasized what a difficult period toddlerhood is for a child, *and* for his parents. Clearly it takes a lot of stamina and patience to be a good parent to a toddler, even without additional stress. If you're going through the last clumsy months of a pregnancy or getting up three times a night with a newborn baby, you may have no reserve of patience left when your toddler needs it most. The situation can be

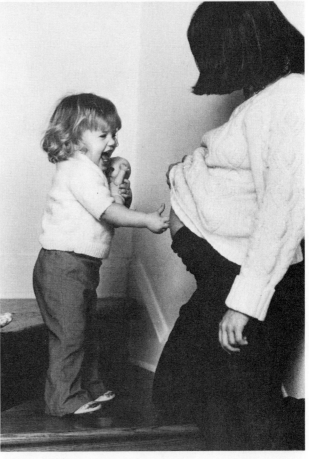

lived through, of course: many mothers and fathers have survived closely spaced children. But close spacing makes those early years a lot more difficult. If you're not yet pregnant but are thinking about when to have another child, consider the needs of your toddler—and the new baby—and, of course, yourself and your spouse and the marital relationship. You may decide that spacing your children three or even four years apart would be in everybody's best interest.

If you're already pregnant and the new one will arrive while your first is still a toddler, read on. The next few years are a potentially stressful period, but the difficulties will seem easier to handle if you have some warning about what to expect and some practical tips on how to cope. In the following pages we will discuss:

preparing your toddler for the new arrival.
leaving your toddler for the hospital stay.
coming home with the new baby.
adjusting to the new baby.

1. *Preparing your toddler for the new arrival.* No matter how young your toddler is, it's important to be honest with him about what's going on. So if you haven't done so earlier, by the time your pregnancy starts showing, tell him about it. Tell him that there's a baby growing inside you, that it will grow and grow, and then when it's big enough it'll come out. Show him how your abdomen is getting bigger because of the baby growing, and let him try to feel the unborn baby's kicks. (He may not succeed for months, of course, but trying is fun and will make him feel part of the process.) Throughout the next few months, you should repeat the facts whenever a chance arises, because naturally a toddler (or even a three- or four-year-old) can't grasp so amazing an event all at once. He may ask further questions if he's verbal enough, or he may not. If he asks, answer simply. If he doesn't ask, you may wish to add a few more facts anyway, just because pregnancy is such a convenient time for introducing the rudiments of sex education. Some people will object: "But he can't understand yet!" Of course he can't yet comprehend all the complexities of reproduction; he can't fully understand justice or fair play yet either, but that doesn't stop you from telling him about sharing toys and not clobbering playmates. He has to start somewhere, and the simple fact that a new baby is growing inside his mommy is a fact that he will accept perfectly happily, especially if it's repeated several times and he gets to feel the baby moving around in there.

Toward the end of the pregnancy, you will want to explain to your toddler several times that Mommy will have to go to the hospital for a few days, to have the baby, and that Grandma (or whoever) will be taking care of him for those days. If you're planning a home birth, you won't have to warn your toddler about a separation, but you should still let him know that you'll be resting in bed for a few days and that Daddy will be staying home from work to run the house, or a friend will be living in for a while, or whatever.

If your toddler is not used to having other people

take care of him, take advantage of these months before the baby's birth to get him used to other adults, especially the one who will be his caretaker while you're gone. If your husband hasn't had full charge of your toddler very often, now is the time to let the two of them practice. Even if your husband won't be the *main* caretaker at the time of the birth, you'll find it necessary to ask him to take over the toddler's care many times in the months following the birth, and it'll be hard on everyone if he's not really sure how to do it.

Toward the end of your pregnancy, make an effort to visit friends or neighbors who have just had new babies as often as possible. Or "borrow" one and baby-sit. Hearing about the new baby is all very interesting, but actually *seeing* several will obviously give your toddler a much clearer picture of what to expect. Prepare him for what's in store by talking realistically about the new baby, too. Don't promise a nice little sister or brother "to play with" or your toddler will be disappointed when the month-old infant just lies there and sucks its fist instead of sitting up and playing peekaboo. Do warn your toddler that Mommy will have to spend a lot of time caring for the newcomer, too.

Buy your toddler a doll that is fairly babylike, and supply it with a few old receiving blankets, diapers, and a nightgown. Give it a box for a bed and make sure it can be submerged in water, because your toddler will want to bathe his "baby" while you bathe yours. If you're planning to bottle-feed, add a dolly bottle to the supplies. If your toddler is nearing his second birthday, buying one of the simpler books about having a new baby, and reading it often, may help him to understand the whole situation even better.

Try to make sure that your toddler doesn't have to make any *other* big adjustments in his life during this stressful time. If you're planning a move, do it six months before or six months after the new baby is born. Even if you're just moving your toddler to a new bedroom or a new bed, make a point of doing so long before or after. And be sure you explain such a move tactfully; you're giving your toddler a new bed "because you're a *big* boy now," not "because the new baby needs your bed," a reason almost guaranteed to cause resentment.

2. *Leaving your toddler for the hospital stay.* If you are planning to deliver in a hospital, find out which hospitals in your area allow siblings to visit. If none does, raise the issue with your doctor and see what can be arranged. The separation will be much easier for your toddler if he can see you each day. (You'll relax better too; you may be amazed at how much you miss your firstborn during those days in the hospital.) If you can't find any institution that will let your toddler visit you, you may wish to arrange an early discharge. Many doctors nowadays are quite willing to sign a healthy mother and newborn out of the hospital only six or twelve or twenty-four hours after the birth. If you can't arrange toddler visits or early discharge, keep in touch with your toddler in every other way possible. Talk to him on the phone several times. Send little presents home to him. Consider borrowing an instant camera so Daddy can go home every evening with new pictures of Mommy and the new baby.

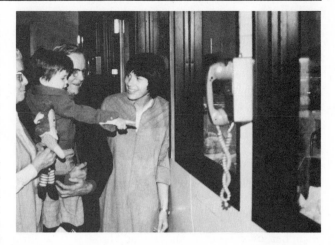

3. *Coming home with the new baby.* Make sure that when you arrive home you can concentrate completely on your toddler. Let someone else carry the baby in and put it to bed. But be prepared for surprises. Even though you're all ready to hug and kiss your toddler and tell him how you missed him, he may act stand-offish or appear not to notice you. This is his way of telling you that *he* really missed *you,* and that he's upset that you left him like that. Of course he can't understand that you had to, so don't react angrily to his rejection or try to force him to come to you. If he's not verbal yet, this is his only way of telling you how confused and upset he feels. Be patient; go at his pace. After he works through his feelings, he'll be in your arms and as affectionate as ever.

Your toddler may or may not be interested in the new baby when she first gets home. Again, follow his lead. He may glance at her once and then walk away, or he may hang over her cradle, watching every move. Either reaction is perfectly normal, and neither predicts their future relationship. If he is interested in holding or touching the new baby, encourage him to, but supervise the interaction very closely. You will need to explain to him over and over just how gently he must treat his baby sister. Don't shout a lot of "no, no's" at

him all of a sudden. Instead, try to be alert enough to prevent pokes and bangs *before* they occur.

4. *Adjusting to the new baby.* In the weeks and months after the birth of the new baby, try to keep the "old" baby's needs in mind. It's not easy when you're feeling exhausted and pulled in two directions at once, so plan to get lots of help (husband, relatives, friends) and to let other things (like housework or outside work, clubs or classes) go for a while. Give your toddler lots of special times alone with you, while the baby's asleep or someone else is watching her.

At first you will be spending a large portion of your time caring for the baby's physical needs: feeding, diapering, bathing. If you turn away from your toddler at these times, he will not only feel your lack of attention, he'll be smart enough to figure out that the baby is to blame. But actually, it's not too hard to turn these caretaking times to your (and your toddler's) advantage instead. Take feeding, for example. You can make it clear to your toddler that whenever you sit down to feed the baby, you're also available for a cuddle or quiet play with him. Feed on a sofa or bed, so that there's room for both children. Tell your toddler to bring a book or his puzzle or some other activity the two of you can share quietly. If you're breast-feeding, you'll have a free hand and arm for him. If you're bottle-feeding, you may need to use a little more ingenuity but

you'll still manage. Fortunately, newborns don't require your constant eye contact while feeding, and three or four weeks from now, when the baby needs more interaction with you while feeding, your toddler will feel secure enough to let that happen. Once your toddler learns that feeding times are his special-attention times, he'll look forward to them rather than resenting them. And of course, once he finds out that you *are* available to him, he'll decide he doesn't need you so much anyway, and you'll find that he'll be climbing up there next to you less and less of the time.

Burping the baby turns out to be a marvelous opportunity for a toddler to "help" while perhaps getting rid of a few mildly aggressive feelings at the same time. Teach your toddler how to pat his sister's back as you hold her over your shoulder, and if he pats a little harder than you might, it won't hurt her. (Be sure to compliment him on the big burps she brings up when he assists you.)

During diaper changes and baths, encourage your toddler to help as much as he wishes to. He can bring clean diapers, powder the baby's bottom, and even help wash her tummy. Or he may do all these things to his doll. It helps many a toddler to be told that you took care of him just like this when he was a baby, too.

Show him the trick of putting his finger next to baby's hand so that she will reflexively grasp it. He'll be enchanted and feel that she really likes him. Teach him to *gently* rock her cradle or jiggle her carriage to help her stop crying when she's fussy. When friends stop by, be sure to boast about what a helper he is and how much the baby likes what he does.

Expect some regression in your toddler's behavior. He may want to be spoon-fed again, or he may suddenly have problems going to sleep. He may want to be carried around or cuddled and held more than before the birth. If he's given up his bottle, he may want it again for a while, especially if he sees the baby being bottle-fed. It's best to let him try these things without comment, while praising him for acting like a big boy whenever he does act more mature. He'll soon find it's

not that rewarding to act like a baby, and stop. If you forbid the babyish behavior or try to shame him out of it, he'll feel more insecure and upset, and act even more babyish.

If you're breast-feeding, your toddler may want to try sucking again, especially if he's been weaned fairly recently. If he asks, it's easiest just to let him, unless the idea really bothers you. He won't remember how to suck anymore anyhow, and if he does get any milk from you, he won't like the taste. Mothers report that one or two tries usually end the experiment. If you don't want him even to try, just tell him firmly that nursing is only for babies and direct his interest to something else.

Although there will be many loving interactions between your toddler and the newcomer, there will also be times when it's clear that your toddler wishes the baby had never arrived. These feelings are inevitable no matter how carefully you prepare your older child and no matter how much time and attention you've managed to give him. Talk about the feelings. He'll be so relieved that you understand and aren't angry! When the baby

begins crying hard, and you have to stop playing on the floor with your toddler to go amuse her, shake your head and say, "Boy! Babies sure get annoying sometimes! She was so hungry she couldn't even wait till we finished our game!" Your toddler will feel better hearing that you find the baby annoying at times, too.

The toddler will need to learn, however, that although it's o.k. to feel anger toward the baby, it's not all right to hurt her. But no matter how well you've explained this distinction, you should never leave your toddler alone with the baby; he is simply too young to be trusted to resist the impulses. If you keep a close eye on the two children, you'll be able to stop most roughness before the toddler actually hurts the infant. If he seems to be feeling particularly hostile and talking about it isn't helping, you can suggest other ways for him to vent his feelings. Some parents have found that

having a punching bag or large punching toy around is a good idea. When necessary, they just tell their toddler to go bang on his toy, not on the baby.

Be prepared for the possibility that jealousy and rivalry toward the new baby may appear months later, rather than right when she's born. Some toddlers don't seem to mind the new baby until she starts crawling and can get into their possessions.

Everyone has difficult adjustments to make when a new baby joins the family. A toddler has a particularly difficult time coping with these changes because he is barely past babyhood himself. He'll need lots of patience and reassurance from you during this period. But the rewards are worth the effort. The more love and understanding you are able to give your toddler during these months, the more he'll be able to give to his younger sibling in the months and years ahead.

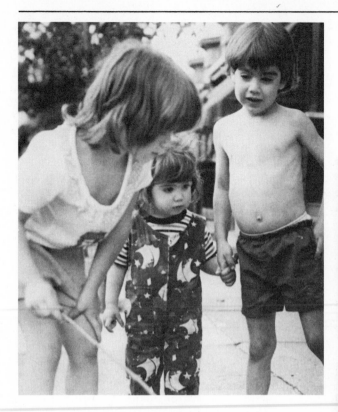

11
When Someone Else Cares for Your Toddler

Before your child was even a year old, you had probably discovered that there are many situations when baby-sitters are useful. The need to share the parenting responsibilities will continue through the toddler years as well. All parents need help from baby-sitters for short periods of time every now and then, if only to keep an appointment or get out for dinner and a movie on Saturday night. And if both parents work outside the house, help on a long-term basis will also be necessary. So in this chapter, we will talk about your needs for time off, your toddler's feelings about being separated from you, and the best way to look for reliable caretakers to fill both your short-term and your long-term child-care needs.

BALANCING YOUR NEEDS AND YOUR TODDLER'S

Keeping up with your adventurous toddler seven days a week can be an exhausting occupation. Being the parent of a toddler has its delightful moments and rewards, but it can also wear you out, especially if you are the toddler's main caretaker. You may find that occasional relief from the unending demands of parenthood is even more important this year than it was during your child's first year, when she was relatively placid and immobile. And yet your toddler may choose just this time to become upset and anxious when you leave her, even though, only a few months ago, she didn't seem to mind your going at all. How do you balance your need for a break against your toddler's need to be near you every minute?

Most children go through a period of anxious clinging to their parents when they start to feel something psychologists call "separation anxiety." This anxiety about being separated from their parents tends to show up when babies are somewhere between six and twelve months old, and usually disappears around the middle of the second year. In general, the peak of anxiety often coincides with the child's first birthday. These ages are just averages, however; each individual child is different. Some children show almost no separation anxiety, or seem fearful for only a couple of weeks. Others act really panic-stricken and miserable for months. Most toddlers fall somewhere between these two extremes.

What Is Separation Anxiety?

Separation anxiety develops as your child's ability to comprehend the world and the people about her grows. Sometime between the ages of six and twelve months, she becomes aware of just how much you—her parents—mean to her. At the same time, she begins to comprehend that you can leave; that you're not *always* available. This can be a frightening discovery when she's so small and helpless! You may remember a period when your baby tried to crawl after you every time you left the room, even for a minute, and then cried if she couldn't find you promptly. She may still be doing this!

The real problem is that the baby or toddler becomes aware of her dependence on you at a time when she still has the primitive idea that if you are out of sight, she may never see you again. We have already discussed how this anxiety can cause bedtime problems for a toddler, because going to bed involves a type of separation.

A mother may feel her toddler is being pretty ridiculous if she cries sadly and tries to follow when her mother is merely going down to the basement to put a load of laundry into the washing machine. "She *knows*

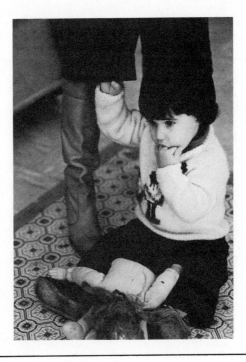

I'm coming right back!" the mother says in exasperation. Actually, though, at this age, a toddler doesn't know that. The concept that objects are permanent is much too complicated for her to comprehend yet, and all she knows is that her mother has left, and she feels abandoned. Over the next few months, she will learn that things which disappear usually reappear—especially mommies and daddies and other beloved people. But the development of this understanding will take a lot of time and experimentation.

Why Are Some Toddlers More Anxious About Separation Than Others?

One-year-olds who have been cared for only by their mothers during the first year of life are likely to experience more separation anxiety than toddlers who have learned to trust two or three other special adults, such as a father who has been very involved in child care, a grandparent living close by, or a regular, loving sitter. That's because the toddlers in the first group have all their feelings and dependencies invested in one person, while the second group has already become accustomed to trusting several adults.

Other children may experience more than the usual level of separation anxiety because of basic personality traits, because they're just a little shyer and more anxious than an average toddler about *everything* that happens to them. And still other toddlers may feel unusually strong anxiety about being left because they experienced a traumatic separation sometime during the first year. Perhaps the baby herself had to be hospitalized, or her mother had to leave town for an emergency and couldn't take her child along, or some other situation caused an unavoidable separation.

How to Survive the Separation-Anxiety Period

If your toddler is one of those who experience moderate to strong separation anxiety, getting through this phase may be difficult at times. It helps to remember that this *is* just a phase and that your child will grow

out of it soon. It also helps to keep in mind that she's going through it because she loves and needs you so much; you're so special to her that she panics when you leave. When you can't wait to go out to that great movie everyone's been talking about, though, and your toddler is crying piteously and clutching your legs, you may be forgiven for wishing that she occasionally loved you a little *less*.

There are several things that you can do to help your toddler through this anxious period, and some of these suggestions may also hasten the day when she will be able to let you leave without becoming miserable. You can help by taking her fears seriously, by making her feel as secure as possible when you do have to leave, and by helping her develop the concept of object permanence.

1. Take her fears seriously. They may seem silly to you: *you* know you're coming back. But your toddler's anxiety is very real to her, and in terms of her stage of understanding, it is entirely reasonable. If you ignore or make fun of her feelings, pry off her clinging fingers and leave abruptly and angrily, she will be even more anxious and upset. And the more anxious she feels, the more she will cling to you and protest your departure next time. If your toddler is going through a period of separation anxiety, try to keep your separations to a bare minimum for a while. Try taking her with you when possible. Have friends over on Saturday night instead of going out.

2. Make your child feel as secure as possible when you do have to leave. Perhaps her daddy can arrange to be home when you have to go out. Or you can make a special effort to use only her favorite baby-sitter for a while, even if this takes extra planning. Now is no time to try a new sitter.

Always warn your child that you are leaving; never just sneak out. Slipping out may seem easier at the moment—for you. But when your child suddenly discovers your absence, she'll be much more frightened than she would have been if you'd prepared her and given her a chance to express her anxiety in your presence. After a betrayal like this, your toddler may well have trouble trusting you at all for quite a while. Her understandable fear that at any moment she may look around and find you gone is likely to make her even more clinging and anxious than she was.

3. Help your child develop a concept of object permanence. There's a good reason why "Peekaboo" and "Find the Hidden Toy" are favorite games of toddlers going through this developmental stage. Toddlers use these games to experiment, in a nonthreatening way, with objects and people disappearing—and returning. Your toddler will need to make you or that block disappear and reappear hundreds of times before she can really understand the concept of object permanence. But when she finally does, she will at last be able to let you go out of sight without panicking.

Labeling your goings and comings is another way to help your toddler understand that after each departure you'll return. When you tell her that you're leaving she's upset, but at least she doesn't feel abruptly abandoned. And if you use the same words each time—"Mommy's going out now, but she'll come *back soon*"—and if you tell your toddler's sitter to remind her of your return in the same words, even before your toddler can really understand the phrase, the words will be comfortingly familiar to her. Another helpful departure ritual one mother reported was having a "bye-bye window," where her sitter held her son up to wave to her each time she left. This boy used the same window to spot his mother's return, and soon began to understand that the return could be counted on to happen each time his mom was gone. Another method that is often helpful is to let your toddler walk away from you, to play with her sitter. This makes her feel more in control of the situation and, therefore, less threatened by it.

If your toddler acts very upset when you leave, ask your sitter how long the behavior lasts after you have disappeared. If she reports that the wails stop completely two minutes after the door closes behind you and that your child plays happily for the rest of the time, then you know you're not dealing with acute separation anxiety anymore. Your toddler dislikes departures but has learned to handle her separation anxiety.

Remember, the period of separation anxiety won't last forever. Sympathy and understanding on your part will probably shorten the stage considerably. In any case, most toddlers seem not to mind separations as much anymore by the time they are two or two-and-a-half.

SHORT-TERM SEPARATIONS

During the weeks or months when separation anxiety is at its peak, you'll probably leave your toddler as seldom as possible. But during the less anxious periods of your child's second and third years, there are bound to be many occasions when you want or need to leave home for several hours at a time, and when your toddler will not mind being left with a sitter. It's a good idea to have one or two regular baby-sitters available who are familiar with your toddler and her habits. Naturally, your toddler will feel more positive about your leaving if she's in the care of an old and trusted friend.

Even when your toddler is over the most intense period of separation anxiety, it is still important to remind her of your return. Psychologists studying two-year-olds' reactions to their mothers' methods of leaving found that some types of leavetaking were more upsetting to toddlers than others. The mothers fell into three groups: those who just left abruptly; those who explained that they were leaving and would be back; and those who not only explained leaving and returning but explicitly told their children what to do while they were gone. The children of the first group of mothers showed the greatest upset and anxiety while their parents were gone, and the children of the third group showed the least.

How Do You Find Baby-Sitters?

Parents who are lucky enough to have relatives living nearby generally feel that the very best source of reliable, loving baby-sitters is this extended family. A toddler's grandparents, uncles, and aunts are likely to love her in a special way, of course, and probably share many of your child-rearing philosophies, too, so they can make marvelous parent substitutes.

Another good source of sitters is your close friends, especially if they have small children of their own. Your best friend is likely to have special loving feelings toward your child that a stranger simply wouldn't have. You know just how she will treat your toddler because you've observed her caring for her own child. And what's more, you can trade baby-sitting with her—pay her back by sitting for her children next week—and never have to spend any money.

Don't completely rule out friends who don't have children or those whose children are older. Your childless friends may welcome the chance to "borrow" a child; in fact, practicing on yours may help them decide whether they want children of their own someday or not. And your friends with older children may really enjoy reliving the fun of having a cute toddler around again—for a few hours!

Many couples have found it helpful to get together with other parents of small children to form baby-sitting co-ops. A baby-sitting co-op is a group of parents who take turns baby-sitting for each other, so that nobody has to pay cash for a sitter. (You are expected to pay by giving time: you baby-sit for the other mothers and fathers for as many hours as they sat for you.) A co-op is not only a cheap and easy baby-sitting source, it's also a great way to make new friends. If you can't find an existing baby-sitting co-op, you might consider forming one. All it takes to begin is a notebook, a pen, and a few interested parents.

Another way to find baby-sitters is to ask other mothers whom they use. Most women will generously trade names and phone numbers of good sitters. Ask neighborhood teenagers or older people if they like to baby-sit. Call local colleges, nursing schools, churches,

visit to the prospective sitter. After putting her at ease, ask her how she'd handle some everyday problems that come up in caring for a toddler. For instance, what would she do if she saw your daughter getting into the wires behind the TV? What if she put your toddler to bed and she cried and wouldn't stop? Obviously, you'll get a clearer picture of the sitter's child-care philosophy if you don't discuss your own views on these matters until after she's had a chance to air hers.

If you feel good about the sitter's answers, about the way she relates to your toddler, and the way your toddler seems to feel about her, trust your gut reaction. You're the parent, and after a year or more of living with your toddler you probably have a special sensitivity to what (and who) is right for your child.

The first time a sitter works for you, be sure to have her come half an hour or so early. This will give your

synagogues, senior citizens' centers; these organizations often have lists of students or members who wish to baby-sit. Don't discriminate by sex; the football player next door who says he enjoys baby-sitting may turn out to handle your active, negative toddler far more appropriately than the grandmotherly lady from down the street. And chances are your toddler will have a blast!

How Do You Know They're Reliable?

You feel safe entrusting your toddler to relatives or close friends, because you already know a lot about them and how they treat small children. But how do you evaluate a stranger before leaving your child alone with him or her? Ask the prospective baby-sitter to come over for a visit ahead of time. It's important to find out how you feel about this person, learn her views on child care, and see how she interacts with your toddler. If all goes well and you *do* hire her, this preliminary visit you've had will mean she's at least somewhat familiar to your toddler when she comes to baby-sit.

Be sure to explain the purpose of the preliminary

toddler time to get used to her while you're there for security. How soon you can leave will depend on your toddler. Your new sitter will do a better job of making your toddler feel secure in your absence if you take the time now to tell the sitter about your child's little idiosyncrasies and rituals. If she always has her cup of milk before her finger food, mention this. If the sitter's going to put your toddler down to sleep, be sure you describe the bedtime rituals. Be particularly careful to tell a new sitter the best ways to soothe your toddler if she gets upset. Mention where her lovey is, if she has one, and how she uses it. This careful preparation will be less important once your toddler gets past the age of separation anxiety. Then she'll probably thrive on the differences between her various caretakers.

Whenever you leave your child with someone else, be sure the sitter has a phone number where she can reach you, as well as the number of a close friend or neighbor, just in case an emergency arises while you're in transit. A permanent list of important numbers, such as those of the police, fire department, pediatrician, and poison-control center, should be prominently displayed by the telephone. Point this list out to a new sitter. Also take her on a tour of the house so that she knows where to find a flashlight that works; where the fuse (or circuit breaker) box is, and how to use it; where the water and gas valves are, and how to operate them.

Play Groups

Toddlers enjoy being with other toddlers. Unlike babies, they are capable of forming friendships, and they clearly enjoy visiting at each other's houses, playing with one another whenever their mothers happen to get them together. Going a step further, some mothers have found it convenient and interesting to form regular play groups for their toddlers.

Ideally, a play group for children this young should consist of only three or four toddlers, and its meetings should be kept short (two or three hours) so that no one gets really tired or out of sorts. Often mothers choose a regular time for their play group to meet, and take turns volunteering their houses as meeting places. (When the weather's good, they may elect to spend the time instead in a local park or at the zoo, both of which are more fun if you're with a group.)

When a play group is first formed, all the mothers generally stay, giving their toddlers a chance to get to know each other without the worry of separation from Mommy. Participating mothers often seem to enjoy this chance to chat with other women whose children are going through the same stages. At the very least, the other mothers can listen sympathetically to your toddler tales, and at best they may offer some useful anecdotes about how *they* coped with temper tantrums or sibling battles.

Once the toddlers get to know one another and feel comfortable in the group, their mothers can start taking turns leaving the group if they wish; while one or two mothers supervise, the others can spend a couple of hours doing whatever they want. Before a play group gets to this point, however, the mothers need to decide how they want the sessions structured: a midmorning snack? stories? games? crafts? free play for several hours? And they need to decide what kind of discipline they want to aim for.

Play groups can be a very enjoyable way for a toddler to learn how to get along with others and for a mother both to share ideas with other young mothers and to gain a little time for herself, secure in the knowledge that her toddler is happily occupied while she's gone.

LONGER SEPARATIONS

Mothers Who Work Outside the Home

Many mothers return to outside employment soon after giving birth. Some do so because of financial need. Others do so because they feel a personal need: they fear they will lose ground professionally if they take very many months off. In many families, however, the mother finds it possible to postpone returning to a job until her baby is a little older. She and her husband start thinking about her returning to work now that their baby has matured into a toddler. They wonder what the best time for returning is and how best to go about it. Unfortunately, there is no sure place to find the answers. Mothers of babies and toddlers have started working outside the home in substantial numbers so very recently that psychologists and sociologists have only just begun to study the effects on both the child and on the parents. So far there isn't much good scientific information available to help parents make these decisions. You will have to balance your own particular needs—both financial and psychological—and your toddler's individual needs, and do what *you* feel is best. No one can tell you how things will work out in *your* particular situation.

You might be interested to know, however, that some research *has* been done on the effect of having an employed or a full-time mother on grade-school age children. This research shows that, for this age-group, the best-adjusted children are those whose mothers are happy with what they're doing, staying at home *or* working outside the home. The more poorly adjusted children belong to discontented mothers: stay-at-home mothers who wish they had a job and employed mothers who wish they could stay home with their children. What should you conclude? Only that the decision must be your own and carefully thought out.

Pressure on Mothers to Stay Home

There have long been strong pressures in this society for mothers to stay at home with their children for at least the first three to five years. Most of the current psychologic and psychiatric literature takes it for granted that mothers should be constantly available to their preschool children. This is such a commonly held idea that you'd think there were scores of solid studies documenting the terrible effects of a mother's leaving her young child for several hours a day. But there aren't. There really isn't much information available at all. There is research showing that babies who lose both mother and father and are put into institutions are likely to develop severe problems. But a baby whose parents are gone for only six or eight hours out of the twenty-four, and who spends those hours in the competent care of a warm and loving day mother, is certainly not similarly deprived. So mothers who really want or need jobs should not stay home just because they think psychologists have proved they'll damage their toddler by working; the research has not yet been done.

Pressure on Mothers to Seek Outside Employment

The pressure on educated young women not to "waste" their training but to have babies and return almost immediately to outside employment is relatively new. Undoubtedly, though, lately some people have begun to look down on mothering as a boring, unliberated, and even unnecessary job. So some young women feel they must prove themselves by returning to work as quickly as possible, whether they really want to or not. This new pressure is just as foolish as the old stay-at-home-no-matter-what ideology. Any social myths that force people to make decisions they're uncomfortable with are bound to cause a lot of unhappiness. Mothers who really want or need to stay home, and can afford to do so, should not let their friends' or colleagues' opinions push them back into their jobs before they or their toddlers are ready.

The Juggling Act

Having a full-time job, mothering, and keeping up a close husband-wife relationship is a difficult juggling act. Our society is simply not set up to help women take on this much responsibility, and the stresses can be incredible. Yet some women do manage to play all three roles and even to enjoy the diversity. How do they manage? With lots of planning, our own research shows, with supportive husbands, somewhat flexible jobs—and by finding good child-care arrangements.

1. *Lots of planning.* In a family where so much is going on, successful employed mothers say everything has to get planned and scheduled down to the minute. You probably found that just having a first child made your life a lot less flexible and spontaneous than it had been previously. Having a child *and* a job remove almost all flexibility. Working mothers of very young children say that they really miss spare time and seeing friends. They say they almost have to schedule an appointment to be alone with their husbands for an hour or two! But they find that the time they spend being with their spouses and playing with their babies is far more valuable and special, just because it is so scarce.

2. *Supportive husbands.* Mothers who are working outside the home and who are married say that a husband who fully supports them in their decision to work is invaluable. By support, they mean not only a willingness to pitch in and do half the shopping, cooking, laundry, and child-care, but also an emotional or philosophical commitment to the goals of an employed wife and mother. A supportive husband doesn't just accept the idea; he's proud of his employed wife.

3. *Flexible jobs.* The more flexible a woman's job is, the easier it is for her to combine it with mothering her toddler. Most of the successful working mothers we talked to reported that they were able to start back to work gradually, only a few hours a day or a few days a week at first. Those who were their own bosses reported taking their infants to work with them at first, for up to six months. (After that the babies needed entertainment, and having her child in the same room kept Mom from doing her work.) Several of the mothers purposely lived near their offices and made a point of returning home to have lunch with their toddlers, thus making separations shorter and easier. Many were able to work partially at home, especially when their babies were young. Two new mothers successfully split a full-time job between them, each going in every other day. They found that the mother who was home on a given day was able to take care of both toddlers and get some housework done, too. Some other couples reported scheduling their jobs so that one parent was always home with their toddler while the other worked. In one case, the mother, who was a nurse, worked the evening shift. In another, the husband, who was a systems analyst, arranged to put in his eight hours between 6:00 A.M. and 2:00 P.M. His wife left for her job when he got home.

4. *Finding a good child-care arrangement.* The employed mothers we've talked to all emphasize that it takes a lot of determination, time, and trouble to find a good source of child care. Many reported going through several sitters before finding the right one for their toddler and for their own needs. Here are some of the arrangements that the employed parents we know have found useful: an individual sitter, who takes care of only your toddler; a small-group sitter, who cares for several toddlers, either in a play group or in a day-care home; and a day-care center.

You might decide to hire an individual sitter for your child because you want her caretaking to resemble being-home-with-Mother as much as possible. If the sitter comes to your house, your toddler will be able to stay in a familiar place. And you'll only have yourself to get up and out each morning. Some sitters are willing to do light housework and to prepare some meals, too—services that can be very helpful to busy employed parents. Look back to the section called "How Do You Find Baby-Sitters?" for suggestions on how to look for an individual caretaker. A relative who is willing to baby-sit might be the perfect choice, but first be sure that you get along well with this relative and can communicate freely with her. If you wouldn't dare give her suggestions about how to raise your child, then you're better off finding someone else. It's very hard to fire a relative if things don't work out.

If you try all the other sources for baby-sitters listed and still have not found anyone who is interested, you can try placing an ad in your local newspaper. Be sure to take the time and trouble to ask the applicants for references, and then to check them out. Then, anyone who still sounds like a possibility should come to your house for a lengthy interview. Follow all the steps sug-

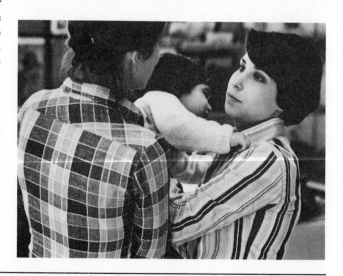

gested for interviewing short-term sitters, but plan to ask more questions and observe longer interactions between the prospective caretaker and your toddler. This sitter is going to be spending a lot of time with your toddler and will be a big influence on her life and on yours; it's important that you feel very good about her.

After you find someone you feel comfortable with, ask her to come to your house for several long visits. Explain to her that you'll pay for her time but that this will be a trial period; she doesn't have the job yet. Any good sitter will understand your concern and be willing to cooperate. These visits will give your toddler a chance to get to know the sitter gradually, with Mother still around for comfort and assurance. If things go well during the trial period, you and your toddler will both feel much more relaxed on that first morning when you finally leave for work than you would have without this preparation.

Some parents prefer having their toddler cared for in a small group, with a few other babies or toddlers. There are definite financial advantages to this plan; you share the sitter's salary with other parents, so none of you is paying as much as you would for individual care. Some day-care mothers take two or three children into their homes to care for them; sometimes one of the children is their own. These women may be licensed by the state, or they may not be. (Call the Department of Social Services or the Health Department to find out about licensing requirements and to get a list of available day-care homes.)

Remember that as important as licensing is, it means only that the woman and her home meet a bare minimum of physical requirements; it says nothing about the day mother's personality or child-rearing philosophy. Plan to go visit the home with your toddler, and to stay and chat a while. While you're there, you'll be able to see her in action caring for her other charges. Observe whether she talks to the children and seems to enjoy them or whether she tends more toward just keeping them quiet and out of her hair. Does she seem in command of the situation, or does chaos reign? Is she warm

and affectionate, or distant and stern? Does she seem energetic enough to keep up with several toddlers? How about her house: is it bright and cheery and toddler-proofed? Is there lots of room to play and a good selection of sturdy toys? Is there a safe yard for outside activities when the weather is good? You may have to visit several day-care homes before you find the right situation for your toddler.

Instead of placing your toddler in an established day-care home, you may wish to get together with another working couple or two and hire a caretaker to come to one of your homes and care for your children as a group. For the day-care location you might choose the home most convenient to your workplaces, or the one with the nicest fenced-in backyard. If you plan to organize cooperative day-care with several couples in this way, you will need to meet with the other parents first, to discuss what each person is looking for. Once you've all agreed on your objectives, you can begin interviewing prospective caretakers. All the parents should be in on this, so that all are satisfied in the end with the person who's hired. And the prospective sitter should go through a trial period during which all of you observe how well she actually manages to keep up with two or three toddlers. Needless to say, a prime requisite for this demanding job may well be a high energy level!

Day-care centers are another option in some areas, but they aren't often available for this age-group. Most centers won't take a child until she's at least two, or sometimes three. If you do find a day-care center that accepts toddlers, visit the premises when the center is in session and stay a while. Watch the caretakers and their interactions with the toddlers. You should look for the same qualities here as you would look for in a day-care home. Regulations for the group care of children this young require that there be one adult to every three or, at most, four toddlers. Centers should also arrange for each toddler to have one special caretaker, who will take particular pains to get to know that child.

A toddler is bound to be cared for by others at various points, but she needs one focal person to turn to among the sea of people at a day-care center, and good centers recognize this need and provide for it.

Day-care centers can be costly, but many have government funds that enable them to help low-income families. So if you need financial help, don't hesitate to ask. Often fees are set according to your income.

Other Considerations

Now that you have decided to return to outside employment and have found the best possible caretaking arrangement for your toddler, what else should you think about or plan for? Following are several tips to help you avoid potential problems.

Plan for sickness before it happens. If your toddler gets sick, you or your husband will want to stay home with her, and you will probably have to use up your own sick leave or vacation days. Sitters get sick, too, so have available an alternate caretaker, whom your toddler already knows.

Plan for relaxed mornings before you leave for work. If your toddler is cared for in your own home, this won't be too hard. If you must get her up, feed and dress both her and yourself, and drive to the sitter's or the day-care center, allow plenty of time. When you are away from your toddler all day, it is especially important that you make your morning together a pleasant time. There will be mornings when your child wants to dress herself or spills her milk all over her clean overalls and needs changing. You should allow enough time to take care of her needs and still remain calm yourself. Of course there will be a few mornings when a rush is unavoidable, but you can keep these to a minimum by simply setting your alarm fifteen minutes earlier than you used to. A little less sleep is a small price to pay for a cheerful beginning to the day.

scenes, let your husband take the child to the sitter for a while. (Or, if your toddler is cared for in the home, make a point of leaving earlier than Dad for a week or two.) Men sometimes seem to be more matter-of-fact about these necessities, and your husband's calmness may do the trick.

If your toddler leaves her home to go to another house or to a day-care center, let her take some familiar objects with her to help bridge the gap between the two places. Her lovey or several special toys, even some pictures of Mommy and Daddy and siblings, can help a lot.

Some toddlers seem to adjust easily and happily to their new care situation and then suddenly, months later, start going through a rebellious, unhappy time. Treat separation problems with the same understanding

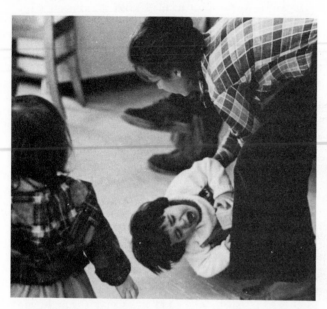
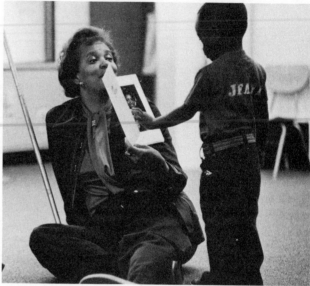

Prepare yourself for your toddler's daily reaction to the new caretaking situation, which can be anything from happy eagerness to clinging and crying. Especially at first, you should allow extra time so that you can stay with her and help her ease into the new situation. If after several weeks your toddler is still protesting your departure every single morning, check your own feelings. If you're feeling guilty and uncertain about leaving her, she may be sensing this and reacting to your anxiety. ("If Mommy thinks she shouldn't leave, maybe she's *right!*") Try making your departure matter-of-fact and firm, while remaining loving and sympathetic, of course. At a moment like this it's important to remember all the thought and care you put into finding the very best day-care situation for your toddler. You really *do* have confidence in the sitter, so be assured that she will help your child get over her upset. (In the evening when you pick your child up, you might take a few minutes to discuss the problem with her caretaker. She might be able to reassure you that your toddler always stops crying the minute you're gone and then seems fine all day.)

If you can't get out of the rut of anguished departure

and sympathy no matter when they occur. Plan to spend some time staying with your child at her day-care home, or remaining in your own home after the sitter comes, to help her through the fearful period. If she's old enough to talk, you may be able to get her to verbalize her worries. Her caretaker may be able to offer some insights and help.

Plan to keep up close communication with your toddler's day mother. In the morning, you should share with her some of the important events of your child's evening and night, especially if she had any problems. In the evening, when you pick your child up, the day mother should take a moment to fill you in on your child's day. It takes time to arrange this communication, but it's very important to your toddler to keep a continuity between her two worlds.

Take time to consider your own reaction to the separation. You may feel relief from constant child-care demands and pleasure at being back on the job, and *at the same time* guilt and doubts about what you have decided to do. Almost every employed mother we have talked to has reported that she has a guilt problem, no matter how important her work and how excellent her child-care arrangements. It may help you to find support in friendships with other mothers who work outside the house.

Another problem employed mothers commonly report is jealousy. You want the caretaker you chose for your toddler to love her, of course. And you want your child to have a nice warm affection for her day-care mother, too. That's the healthiest situation for your child. At the same time, though, you may find that you feel a bit left out. You may fear that your toddler will learn to love her day-care mother more than she loves you. Rest assured that this will not happen. The special bond between parents and their children is not threatened by the child's receiving love and care from other adults. As the mother, you have a very special, strong concern for your toddler and what happens to her each day, and your toddler senses this. No day-care mother can *ever* feel as strongly about your toddler as you do. Several recent studies have compared the mother-attachments shown by home-raised toddlers with the

mother-attachments of toddlers in day-care. And the researchers have found that day-care toddlers are just as attached to Mom as their home-raised counterparts. When both Mommy and the day caretaker are available in a strange situation, a toddler is far more likely to turn to her mother for comfort and reassurance.

Remember this, too: most fathers leave their toddlers for nine or ten hours every day, and yet we can observe that our toddlers are tremendously attached to their daddies. Your child will continue to prefer her parents to the most loving day caretaker.

Some parents report that when they go to pick their toddler up at her day-care home in the evening, she'll act as though she wants to stay there. Don't let it upset you if your toddler does this occasionally. She may just need to finish the game she's in the midst of, or she may need a little help in making the transition from one segment of her day to the next. If she runs to the climbing dome and climbs, then goes to touch a puzzle and look back at you, perhaps she's trying to tell you about the high points of her day in the only way she can, since she isn't very verbal yet. Parents who join in and take a little tour around the day-care home before suggesting putting on the jacket and leaving, generally have more peaceful departures than those who ignore their toddlers' needs and just rush them out.

Plan for some relaxed time together when you first get home each evening. Don't rush off distractedly to

prepare dinner. Everybody needs to unwind after their respective busy days, and having dinner a half hour later than usual won't hurt. If you're hungry, have a healthful snack as you relax on the floor with your toddler and talk about your day. Later, when everybody is more settled, go into the kitchen and get dinner going. Some mothers appreciate having Dad take over toddler care at this point so they can whip up dinner without distraction, or having Dad cook so Mom can play with the toddler. Other employed couples enjoy making dinner preparation a joint project, with the toddler happily underfoot or in her feeding chair with finger food. Then Dad can run the chicken liver through the food processor while Mom tosses the salad, and they both catch up on the day's news as they work together.

Other Caretakers
Your toddler will make tremendous strides in her understanding of other people and social relationships. Experiencing separation anxiety, overcoming it, and learning that adults other than her mother and father can be trusted and enjoyed are some of the benefits she will gain through her exposure to other caretakers. There are bound to be difficulties along the way, of course, but don't let these deprive your child—or yourselves—of the many advantages of baby-sitters.

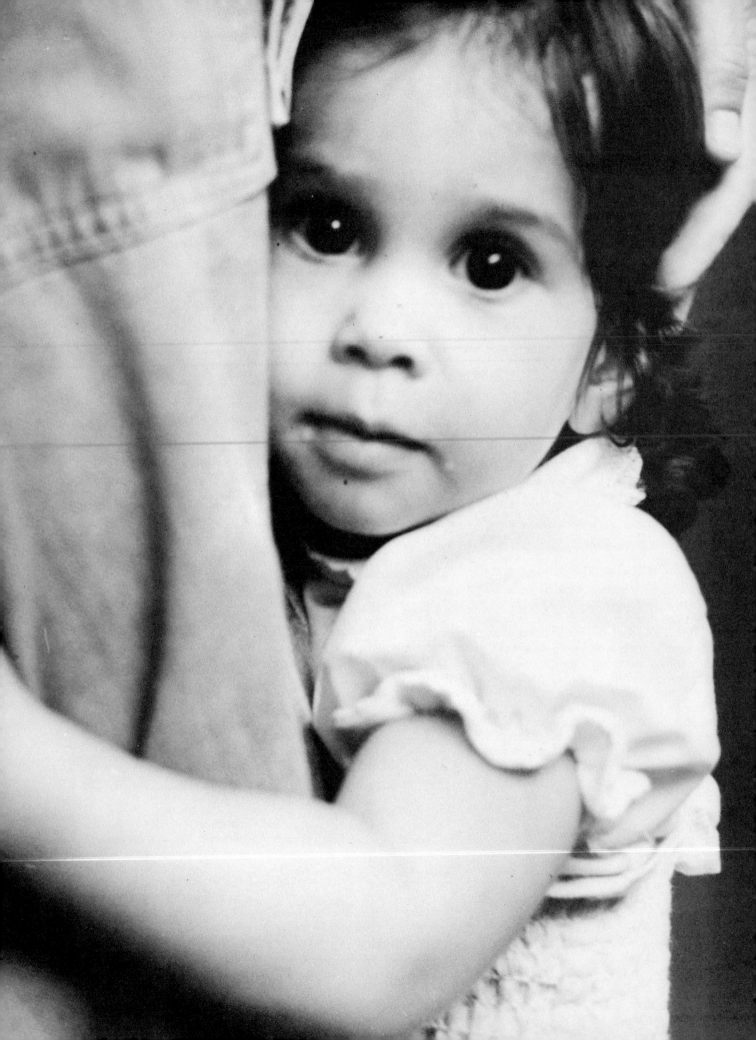

12
Special Situations

This chapter talks about some of the special situations which sometimes confront the parents of toddlers. The topics we have chosen to include aren't the experiences of every family, to be sure, but we think they are the experiences of a large enough minority to warrant our consideration. In the following pages we will discuss

Being a Single Parent
Moving to a New Home
Taking Your Toddler to the Hospital
Adjusting to Your Toddler's Handicap

BEING A SINGLE PARENT

The number of single parents in America is growing rapidly. According to figures from the Census Bureau, in 1970 there were about three and a half million single-parent families with children under the age of eighteen. That represents a 25 percent increase since 1960. In 1975, more than eleven million children (approximately one out of every five) were being raised in single-parent families. Five years earlier, the proportion had been one out of seven.

Single-parent families are created through any of a number of circumstances: marital separation, divorce, long-term illness or death of a spouse, an unwed mother's decision to keep her baby, a father's separation from his family by military duty, and so forth. The official statistics don't even take into account all the "unofficial" single-parent families in our society: those in which the father is so busy working and traveling that he rarely shares in the child rearing, or in the life of his family. For all practical purpose, the mother in such a family is really a single parent, too.

Single parents face lots of problems that are caused by the very fact of singleness. The practical pressures and responsibilities of parenthood sometimes loom very large when there is no other steady adult to share them with. Many single parents suffer financial problems. And inevitably they have fears about the child's psychological development. Can he be raised successfully with only one parent? Will he ever be happy? These concerns are all real problems when you're a single parent. But like almost all problems, these can be managed and, with conscientious effort, solved. Remember: *all* families have problems, regardless of how many parents

they contain. It's just that some of a single parent's problems will be a little different. And remember, too, that two-parent families have some problems that the single-parent family escapes, such as disagreements over methods of discipline, which church (if any) the child should attend, or how time together as a family should be spent. As a single parent, you have freedom to choose and monitor the influences that will guide your child's development.

All of this is simply to say that every situation has pluses and minuses. Sure, you will probably have a much harder time raising a child alone than you would with a compatible partner, but it can be done. And the job will bring special rewards in the bargain. In this chapter we'll try to help you deal objectively—and we hope, optimistically—with the stresses and fruits of single-parenthood.

Since 96 percent of all single-parent families with children under six years old are headed by the female parent, this chapter is addressed primarily to single mothers. Many problems faced by single parents aren't gender related, however, so single fathers should also find this information useful.

Popular Assumptions About Single-Parent Children
According to popular American mythology, the "normal nuclear family" contains two parents, one of each gender, who are married to one another. And a child or children. Any family with different composition, such as only one parent, is considered an exception, and usually in the negative sense of the word. We often hear about the evil effects of single-parenthood: children from "broken" homes, we are told, tend to do worse in school, have more emotional and behavioral problems, and are generally less well adjusted than children from two-parent families. Well, serious research into this area is revealing some interesting facts. It turns out that the *quality* of the parenting—the *quality* of the family life—is far more important to a child's happiness and social adjustment than is the number of parents.

Let's look more closely at some of the other assumptions surrounding single parenthood.

Assumption: *Single-parent homes are broken homes.*

A home that has lost one parent, especially through divorce or separation, is usually called a "broken" home. The word "broken" has many negative connotations here, suggesting at best a state of disrepair. But Gladys Jenkins, a specialist in family life, disagrees with the implication that a family which has been through a divorce has been somehow shattered. She argues: "The single-parent home is not a broken home. The home that was broken no longer exists. The present single-parent home is a different home, stronger, perhaps, and less breakable. The discords and tensions of the first home may be over."

Sometimes, of course, there wasn't any discord preceding the single-parent situation. The family has lost a parent not through divorce or desertion, but because one parent has died or because the mother never had a spouse. In many of the cases, the single parent and her child or children enjoy a particularly close relationship, not a fragile one. They form a strong, not a "broken" family.

Assumption: *Children who have only one parent tend to have more emotional and behavioral problems.*

This may be the hardest assumption to shake, because there is some empirical evidence linking single-parent families to delinquency and other behavioral problems. However, many studies point out that having a single parent does not in itself cause behavioral problems. Rather, the causes often lie in other stresses placed on a family—stresses that may or may not be caused by single parenthood. Consider these studies and opinions.

An impressively thorough, ongoing British research project, called the National Child Development Study, has spent the last twenty years following the development of 17,000 children, all born in Great Britain during the same week of March 1958. So far the study has evaluated each of these children four times: at birth, and again at the ages of seven, eleven, and sixteen. All aspects of each family's situation are taken into account in each evaluation. The latest report, published in 1976, describes the effects of one-parent families on those children in the group who have ended up in such families for one reason or another. Patricia Ashdown-Sharp sums up the findings thus:

The most striking conclusion of the study is that it appears to be the economic difficulties associated with single-parent families that most affect a child's development. When economic circumstances were taken into account (by comparing one- and two-parent families with similar incomes) the differences between the children's social adjustment and school performance were small and often disappeared altogether.

Statistically, the study found that "compared with children living in unbroken homes, *all* groups which lacked a parent tended to suffer from a disadvantage in terms of their material environment and standard of living." In other words, it was *poverty* (associated, as it is, with poor housing, health care, nutrition, and substitute child-care when the single parent must work) rather than the absence of a parent that was the major cause of child deprivation.

In the United States, just as in Great Britain, single-parent families tend to be less affluent than two-parent families. As we said, nearly all single-parent families are headed by women. In 1974, the median income of women who were single-parent heads of families was about $4500—less than half the median of families headed by males. In 1975, over three *million* women with dependent children were on welfare. When you consider the findings of the National Child Development Study, it's no wonder that a large percentage of single-parent children have behavioral problems: a large percentage of them are poor! Economic deprivation, rather than the psychological effect of having only one parent, is usually their biggest problem.

Most people have heard that children of divorced parents—and divorce is the leading cause of single-parent families—have more problems than children with two parents. Again, there are statistics that point to this correlation. Having only one parent is *not* the main source of a divorced child's problems, however. Most experts now lay the blame on the tension in the home which typically precedes most divorces. The quarreling, fighting, dissension, and general unhappiness between parents before (and even after) a divorce have a far more serious effect on their children than the actual divorce. In fact, the divorce often results in happier parents and children.

Still, many parents are tempted to hide their dissension and stick out a bad marriage "for the sake of the children." We've found that this rarely works well. Children, even toddlers, are capable of perceiving their parents' emotional state, and living with constant tension is likely to cause emotional problems for them. A recent study by Dr. Michael Rutter found that there is more delinquency in tense, unhappy—but intact—families than in harmonious single-parent families.

Assumption: *A child needs a parent of the same sex in order to develop an appropriate and healthy sexual identity.*

This is a real concern of single mothers who have sons (and fathers who have daughters, though this situation is far less common). It's a tough concern to address. Though there are lots of theories, we don't know *for sure* how a child develops his sexual identity. And the various theories differ in the amount of influence they assume parents have over the development of sex-role identity in their children. One theory says that fathers are absolutely necessary for both girls and boys. Another says that fathers are helpful, but not essential. Still another maintains that parents are practically immaterial to the child's formation of sex-role identity—that a child will develop this over time by watching television, observing the behavior of familiar adults, and just generally interacting with people of both sexes throughout his life. Of course, each theory has the support of experts.

We hope this disagreement among the professionals will help a single parent take an optimistic view (always the best path when controversy rages). Remember: there *is* support for the idea that a child doesn't need a parent of his own sex to form his sexual identity. It's important to recognize, though, that *all* theories agree that a child needs contact with adult members of each sex. So if you're a single mother with a son, make sure he forms some friendships with men, be they neighbors, your own parents or brothers, special male friends of yours, or whoever. Your son probably doesn't need to form a lasting, powerful relationship with these people; a casual but frequent acquaintance will do. But a strong friendship isn't a bad idea.

We could continue to bring up popular assumptions for debunking, but you get the idea by now. Having only one parent does not necessarily place a toddler at a disadvantage. A single parent can offer her child the most important ingredients of healthy, happy, emotionally stable development: love, a warm, supportive relationship; and help in forming social relationships with other adults and toddlers. But let's be really honest. It won't always be smooth sailing. Single parents and their children do often have problems that are either directly or indirectly caused by the single-parent situation. Of course, if you've been a single-parent for a long time you already know some of these problems—and potential solutions. But if the situation is relatively new for you, you may feel overburdened by all your responsibilties. It might help you to know that many other families have found themselves in similiar situations, and have devised their own ways of coping. Here we'll pass along some of the ways other single-parent families have dealt with the stresses they have encountered.

Helping a Toddler Adjust to Divorce
Divorce is usually hard on everyone—parents, children, grandparents, and other members of the extended family as well. And whole books have been written that help families cope with divorce. Here we'd like to concentrate on the problems toddlers often have as a result of divorce, and on ways parents can help their toddler adjust to the new single-parent family.

Most young children go through a period of marked behavioral change when adjusting to a divorce. Depending on how close the toddler was to the missing parent and how successfully the remaining parent is coping with her own emotional stress, this period of adjustment may last for weeks or even months. A toddler's physical development may slow or even seem to take a step backward; he may return to crawling when he had been walking for months, or demand a bottle when he had successfully switched to a cup. A toddler may show changes in his emotional state as well; he may become demanding and clingy when he had previously seemed quite independent, or he may cry far more than he used to. He might even become very angry, hitting you or other people for no apparent reason. You may notice these changes particularly at certain times of the day: early in the morning, for example, or around suppertime, or right before bedtime. Such changes in behavior are a toddler's natural expression of grief and anxiety. He's responding both to the loss

of a person he loves and to the loss of familiar routine. That's why you often see these marked changes at predictable times of the day; these were the times when your toddler's Daddy was usually home to interact with him.

If you see these changes and regressions in your child's behavior, we recommend that you deal with them in a loving way. He needs these opportunities to exhibit and "play out" his emotions. If you scold him for expressing his natural anger and grief and anxiety in the only way he knows how, you will just confuse him and make him feel worse. Instead, you should hold him, talk about why he's sad, let him know that you understand his problems. These might also be the times when you feel sad. If so, don't be afraid to share some of your own unhappiness with your toddler. When you openly express your pain, you help your child deal with his own. Of course, we recommend that you keep your expressions within reasonable bounds. Hysterical outbursts will be more frightening than helpful. At times like these you're bound to feel hostile and angry; however, it's probably best not to condemn the missing parent. Your spouse will have visiting rights, and it's unfair both to him and to your child for you to set up strife between them. Also, it might hurt your toddler to hear his beloved Daddy being maligned.

When a toddler loses one parent, he becomes especially dependent on the remaining one. You'll need to reassure your toddler constantly that you won't be leaving also. In fact, any separation from you that isn't part of your ordinary routine will probably cause your toddler extreme anxiety. When you must leave him for a while, be sure to explain that you love him, that you'll be gone only a short time, and that you will soon be home with him again. Also be sure that he is very familiar and comfortable with his baby-sitter.

Because your toddler is already experiencing a loss of a parent and a disruption of normal routine, you should try to keep other changes in his life to a minimum. However, divorce often causes financial burdens that necessitate your going to work or changing residences. Try to avoid making these drastic changes, if you can, at least for a few months yet. But, of course, you must consider what's right for your whole family, not just for your toddler; and you may decide that moving or going to work is your best—or your only—course, all things considered.

One final thought on this subject. Many parents have told us that talking to a toddler about divorce beforehand often helps him deal with it. You might want to try this with your own child. Of course, he won't understand the term itself so you shouldn't dwell on explaining it. Instead, simply tell him that Mommy and Daddy will no longer be living together, but that you will still be his Mommy and Daddy (or whatever terms you use). Be sure to emphasize that the absent parent will visit him often, and that he and Daddy (or he and Mommy) will still have a warm, loving relationship, even if they don't see each other every day. Experts recommend that each parent discuss the divorce separately with the child so that he feels the love and support of both of them. When explaining the divorce before it happens, you should be careful of the words you choose. Don't say something like "Daddy's going away," for example, or else every time Mother leaves, the toddler may fear that she, too, will no longer be living with him. And reassure him repeatedly that each parent still loves him. You may have to offer these explanations and reassurances many times following the divorce, but in doing so you will be helping your toddler understand the enormous changes he's experiencing in his life. And the fact that you're willing to share your own life with him will go far toward making him feel secure in your love for him.

Helping a Toddler Adjust to a Parent's Death

Some toddlers lose a parent through death. Although death usually changes a family much more abruptly than divorce, it causes many of the same disruptions in a toddler's feelings and behavior as divorce, and it calls for the same sort of supportive care from the surviving parent. Accept the changes in your toddler's behavior, and use them as opportunities to talk about the pain both of you are feeling. Respect his feelings of grief and loss, and grieve openly with him if you feel like it. Reassure him that you love him even though you are sad, and that you will stay with him. And expect that for a long while he will react violently to even short separations from you; you will need to help him through each one.

The death of a parent also creates some new concerns the remaining parent should try to deal with. One is the concept of death itself. How should you explain to your child that he will never see his deceased parent again? Most experts agree that children under the age of three are incapable of grasping this idea, so it's futile trying to explain the concept of *death* or *dead* to them. However, even a toddler is old enough to feel the reality of the situation that results from death: Mommy or Daddy is no longer there. Just as you talk about the loss of a parent through divorce, you should discuss with your toddler the loss he has experienced through death. Again, though, you should be careful of the words you choose.

Avoid saying something like "Daddy has gone away forever." The word *forever* has no meaning for a toddler, who has no understanding of time, but the "gone away" will be understood—and each time the remaining parent goes away (to work or on a trip) the toddler may fear she will never return either. It's far better to use a simple explanation like "Daddy is dead, and dead means that he can't be here with us, that he'll never be home again." Your toddler won't fully understand this statement either; he may even look forward to Daddy's return every evening for weeks or months. But at least this plain explanation won't complicate his grief by further confusing or misleading him. The times of the day when your toddler especially misses his deceased parent will be hard on both you and him. As we said

before, these are times when you should hold him gently and explain, over and over, that Daddy is dead and can never come back, and share your grief with one another.

Since a toddler simply cannot grasp the finality of death, if his deceased parent's clothing and other belongings are left in their usual places—for instance, pants and shoes in the bedroom closet, sport gear in the back hall—the toddler is likely to conclude that his parent will be returning any time. So to help your child understand that Daddy isn't expected home as usual, you might want to store the deceased parent's clothes and other things in trunks or cartons somewhere out of the way. Making this change is bound to sadden you, reminding you, as well as your toddler, of the finality of this separation, and of course you shouldn't feel obliged to take on such a wracking job before you feel up to it.

But by making such a change you're not trying to wipe out the memory of your deceased spouse. Nor should you. Children—even toddlers—usually remember a parent they've lost, and most surviving parents want to keep these memories alive and pleasant throughout the child's life. If you like, you can talk about your spouse to your child frequently, show your child scrapbooks, and reminisce about the wonderful times you all shared as a family. Such quiet memories may bring some pain to both you and your toddler, and even some shared tears. But this sort of sharing of your grief will help both of you understand and accept the sad reality of your shared loss, and will probably bring the two of you closer to one another as well.

After a spouse has died, the surviving parent is naturally full of grief and trouble, and having to deal with a toddler on top of everything else can seem like too much of a burden. In this situation you might feel that you'd like to send your toddler to Grandma's for a few days while you try to recover your composure and perspective on life. But we recommend otherwise. For one thing, the sudden trip away from home would itself unsettle your toddler; and returning to a one-parent family instead of the two parents he had before the trip would leave him extremely confused and upset. Besides, sharing in his surviving parent's grief is the best way for a toddler to understand and express his own. If you need help dealing with your toddler right after your spouse's death, you may want to have a family member live with you for a few days, to help you run your house and care for your child until things become fairly normal again.

Of course, your feelings about the death of your spouse can sometimes overwhelm you. If you need more support, see the "Where to Go for Help" section at the end of this chapter.

Helping Your Toddler Adjust to a New Adult

If you're like most single parents, you'll probably begin dating before too long, and if you find another love you might consider remarriage. When you become seriously involved with another adult, it can create problems for your toddler, however. Many a younger child balks when his single mother brings a new male adult into their life together.

Such objection is perfectly understandable when you look at things from a toddler's point of view. Since he lost his other parent, you've easily become his most powerful source of love and attention and support. When another person enters your life, your toddler may well feel very jealous and threatened. And if you are divorced rather than widowed, your toddler may be specifically confused about the role of this new man as compared to his father's.

If you decide to remarry, you should introduce your child to your fiancé gradually. To start with, maybe have him over for an early dinner a few times, so he and your child can meet in a familiar place. You might even warm your toddler up by letting him help fix the meal and talking to him during the preparation about your visitor. After a few dinners and get-togethers at your home, you might try some day excursions that involve the three of you, such as a trip to the zoo or park. When the three of you are out together this way, be sure to pay as much attention to your toddler as he seems to need. And most important, be patient if your toddler has some reservations. Eventually, with enough support and help from you, he will begin looking upon your fiancé as his friend, too.

Of course, some toddlers accept new adults better than others. And no matter how well you handle introductions, and how gradually you bring these two people together, you should expect at least some resistance at first. So don't give up. If you stay calm and supportive, things will probably work out. You should also be mindful of your behavior toward your intended spouse. The more comfortable and confident you feel about the relationship, the happier you seem, the easier it will be for your toddler to adjust to this new person. If this is a good relationship for *you,* chances are it will be a good one for your toddler as well.

Helping You Help Yourself

Helping your toddler adjust to a new situation is one thing; once you've made the initial adjustment, though, coping with life day in and day out is quite another. Even happily married parents agree that raising a child can be very taxing, and when the child is a toddler—who is naturally full of changes and surprises and difficult periods—well, raising him alone can seem almost overwhelming. Suffice it to say that nearly all single parents need some special help: help with the daily caretaking routines, help with the emotional and psychological tensions of parenthood, and help with the financial burden of running a household alone. Often the practical problems and emotional struggles of single-parenthood seem out of hand. Hard, yes; but not impossible.

One way successful single parents cut their difficulties down to manageable proportions is by getting help when they need it. It would be wonderful if there were someplace you could call or walk into that would supply all the help you need. Unfortunately, there's no central agency that's equipped to handle all the problems a single parent is likely to encounter. So it's up to you to create this agency for yourself.

In your search for helping hands, it's always good to start in your own backyard. For most single parents, help comes from many areas: friends, neighbors, relatives, baby-sitters, clergy, and co-workers. You should also seek out other single parents in your neighborhood or surrounding area. You can meet them through single-parent groups (often sponsored by churches or women's organizations) or just ask friends if they know anyone they could introduce you to. Since other single parents face situations and problems very similar to your own, they may be able to give you particularly valuable insights and tips.

This brings up another point: don't let yourself become isolated from the world because you're a single parent. It's very easy to devote your whole life to home and toddler, especially when you feel you have so little time and emotional energy to spare after domestic needs have been taken care of. But such isolation is bound to cause problems. If you center your life around your child, you'll eventually become bored and restless and begin resenting your toddler for having tied you down. And then you're bound to start reacting to him more sharply and negatively than you really should—and to feel even worse about yourself and your situation for doing so. So do yourself and your toddler both a favor and avoid falling into the isolation trap. You need adult company, breaks in routine—and fun. Getting away from your household occasionally will help you be more relaxed and optimistic about life, and your toddler is bound to benefit from your well-being.

Forging a new social life for yourself won't necessarily be easy, because as a single person you'll probably feel uncomfortable around your old married friends. You may have to make some new friends, or join groups where you can meet other people who might be single. Just keep searching; as we said in the beginning, there are more than three and a half million single-parent families in this country.

Friends, neighbors, and relatives can do far more than help you feel less isolated. They can also help you deal with both the practical problems and the emotional tensions of parenthood. Trading children for a day or part of a day, forming an informal play group or day-care arrangement, helping out in emergencies—by offering practical aids such as these, your friends will help you ease your financial problems. And here's another thought to keep in mind. If your house is large, you might consider sharing it with another single parent. Then the two of you could split housekeeping costs, benefit from adult companionship, and generally gain the support another adult brings to a family. Or maybe you could rent a bedroom to a college student. In return for room and board, he or she might help you by baby-sitting, working around the house, and supporting you in times of stress. Or work out your own survival plan, using methods and resources you think are especially suited to your situation.

Friends usually prove to be the most useful and certainly the most used sources of help. In addition, you should consider the other types of help available in your local community, or even on a statewide and national basis. When you start to explore all the possibilities, you'll see you're not as alone and helpless as you might have thought. And to keep all these potential sources straight, why not create your own Single-Parent Survival Guide?

To start, set aside a few hours and draw up a list of every kind of help you might ever need. Include services that will help you cope with running a home as well as agencies that can help you deal with emotional or family-type problems. Some categories to consider are

baby-sitters;

plumbers who are on call twenty-four hours a day;

taxis (for emergency aid and mornings when your car won't start);

electricians;

emergency services: poison control center, doctor, ambulance, fire station, police, hospital, and so forth;

legal aid.

Don't skip some unpleasant category like an emergency counseling hotline even though at the moment you're convinced you'll never need this sort of help. One day you just might, and this is precisely the number you'll want in a hurry.

Once you've listed the services you might need to call in an emergency, expand your resources book to include the names and addresses of organizations designed to help single parents and families in trouble. These are the people to contact when you want more than quick help with a particular problem. Consult the resources section at the end of this chapter for some organizations that you might include on your personal resources list.

Of course, once you've begun keeping a list of resources, you'll probably become more attuned to the different types of services that are available in every community. How many public-service announcements about counseling services have you ignored on the television? Probably lots, because at the time you didn't need them. Well, now that you might, pay closer attention, and write down in your resource book names and numbers of appropriate agencies. Also check services offered by your local library, unversity, hospital, and city welfare department. The last might be especially helpful if you suffer financial problems. And since money can be such a worry, you might also make an appointment with a good financial consultant. He or she can help you better budget the resources you do have, and can suggest ways for reducing debts if you have them.

If single-parenthood begins to get you down in spite of all your efforts to rise to the occasion, it might help you to remember that, in spite of all the problems, there

are some advantages to going it alone. Consider these:

1. A single parent is free to choose her own friends, and the types of people she wants to have influencing her child.

2. A single parent is free to choose her own style of child rearing, from how to handle discipline all the way down to how to dress her child. And don't forget: she's also free to raise her child according to her own principles regarding masculinity and femininity, aggression and pacifism, and other political and personal issues.

3. A single parent and her child often share a very special closeness. When there are only two of you, and especially if you have come through some rough times together, the love you share can be beautifully strong.

Where to Go for Help

General Organizations

The following organizations offer a variety of services for families in need, including families headed by single parents.

United Way of America
801 North Fairfax Street
Alexandria, Virginia 22314

If you're not sure where to go for help with a specific problem, it's a good idea to start with the United Way. Their Information and Referral Service works with you to assess your personal needs, then recommends agencies in your area which are equipped to deal with your problems. Most large cities have branches of the United Way, so you might want to contact the nearest office instead of the national one.

Family Service Association of America
44 East Twenty-third Street
New York, New York 10010

National Council on Family Relations
1219 University Avenue, S.E.
Minneapolis, Minnesota 55414

Parents Without Partners
7910 Woodmont Avenue
Washington, D.C. 20014

Parents Without Partners has chapters in over six hundred communities. Check your local phone book or write the national office for information about meetings in your area. This international organization is almost wholly concerned with helping the single-parent family.

Parents Anonymous, National Office
2810 Artesia Boulevard
Redondo Beach, California 90278

Most parents have times when they feel like lashing out at their young children and even harming them. Single parents, who don't have anyone to share the emotional burdens of child rearing with, may experience these impulses more often than they like to admit. Of course, when you think about it, you know you don't want to hurt your child, but there are times when control wears very thin. Before you reach your breaking point, contact Parents Anonymous. It is designed to help parents who abuse, or fear they will abuse, their children. PA has over eight hundred chapters, all of which are prepared to take emergency calls at any time of night or day. Check the listing in your local phone book or call the toll-free number, 1-800-352-0386. Better still, put this number, and the number of the local chapter, in your resource book.

Books

For Divorced and/or Single Parents:
Edith Atkin and Estelle Rubin, *Part-time Father* (New York: Vanguard Press, 1976).

Although primarily written for the divorced father, this warm and sympathetic volume will help both parents understand a little more about the effects of divorce. Besides, it offers lots of sound advice.

Susan Gettleman and Janet Markowitz, *The Courage to Divorce* (New York: Ballatine Books, 1974).

These authors, both clinical social workers, believe that for many families divorce is a far more destructive and painful experience than it need be. They say: "We do not advocate divorce as a universal panacea, nor do we disqualify marriage as a happy, healthy life-style for many people. Our concern is to minimize the suffering of those for whom divorce is a logical and healthy decision."

Earl Grollman, *Talking About Divorce: A Dialogue Between Parent and Child* (Boston: Beacon Press, 1975).

When your child is slightly older and begins to ask questions about divorce, or if you have an older child as well as your toddler, this is a book to get. The first section is a storybook with text, the second a helpful guide for parents describing children's typical reactions to divorce. As the title implies, the book is designed to help you talk about your divorce with your child in an open, honest, sharing way.

Carole Klein, *The Single Parent Experience* (New York: Avon, 1973).

The publisher's blurb on the back cover of this paperback says: "*The Single Parent Experience* gives a warm but realistic picture of (this) brave new kind of parenthood, a frank appraisal of all its problems, and a great deal of honest and moving testimony from the single parents themselves." We agree. This is a very handy book.

Bernard Steinzor, *When Parents Divorce* (New York: Pocket Books, 1970).

This book concentrates on how divorce affects children, and how divorced parents can best handle visitation rights, divided loyalties, and other emotional and practical concerns which follow from divorce.

For Stepparents and Parents Considering Remarriage:

Brenda Maddox, *The Half-Parent* (New York: Signet Books, 1975).

This book is directed toward helping a stepparent become part of an established family. Although most of the text and examples really refer to living with children older than toddlers, there is also extensive discussion of the psychological adjustments potential stepparents have to make to the new family situation, and these aren't so age-related. If you are considering remarriage, have your partner read this book.

June and William Noble, *How to Live with Other People's Children* (New York: Hawthorn Books, 1977).

The authors, who have both experienced the step-relationship since their marriage a number of years ago, worked with professionals and step-families alike to compile this book, which identifies problems and offers advice and insight to everyone connected with the step-family situation: parents, children, in-laws, and family friends. Very helpful if you're planning to remarry.

Helping Yourself and Your Child Deal with Death:

Earl Grollman, *Talking About Death: A Dialogue Between Parent and Child,* rev. ed. (Boston: Beacon Press, 1976).

Like his book about divorce, Grollman's book about death will help parent and child talk about this painful subject in an open way. Again, this book is really intended for young children past the toddler age. However, it has an excellent resource guide in the back (listing helpful organizations to contact, additional books to consider), so don't necessarily pass it by as inappropriate.

Elisabeth Kübler-Ross, *On Death and Dying* (New York: Macmillan, 1969).

This is one of the finest books ever written about the subject of death and dying. Kübler-Ross writes movingly both about how to care for the dying person and about how to care for the survivors.

MOVING TO A NEW HOME

Americans are constantly moving. Father gets transferred, Mother wants to live closer to her new job, the old place is too small for the growing family, you find a wonderful (and affordable!) home in a more attractive neighborhood, the city's putting an expressway through your front yard, your old place is so dirty you'd rather move than clean, it's springtime—there are hundreds of reasons why people decide to change addresses.

Moving to a new place can open up a whole new world of excitement and opportunity. But it can also be very hard, especially for young children. Unless you've moved a few times in the past year, your toddler has come to feel her present home is a base of comfort and security. She depends on its familiarity, its predictability. Removing her from this safe, familiar environment is bound to cause some problems.

But, of course, these problems aren't insurmountable. Moving is a fact of life, and just as you help your toddler adjust to other major changes in her life, you can help her make a successful move. This section will lend you a hand. And we'd like to thank Susan and Barry Rosen for lending us a hand in preparing it. During Susan's second pregnancy, they moved to a new house with their fourteen-month-old, Catherine, and lived to tell us about it. With a great deal of humor, too.

Preparing for Moving Day
Sound preparation is the cornerstone of any successful move, and you should start by preparing yourself emotionally. Of course moving is a hassle, of course you have some reasons for wanting to stay where you are. But even if you aren't particularly looking forward to the move, try to psych yourself up. Tell yourself over and over how much of an adventure moving will be, how the changes will really benefit everyone, how you won't let the annoyances get you down. Once you've convinced yourself, start convincing your toddler. Talk to her about what will be happening in the coming weeks: the packing, the cartons everywhere, the new house and her new room, the adventure, the excitement. Remind her that she'll be taking all her toys, that Grandma will continue to visit, that Mommy and Daddy will still be there. Repeat these reassuring litanies often.

When you begin the actual procedures of moving—gathering boxes, sorting possessions, packing—explain the importance of each step as you take it. Your toddler is too young to understand all your explanations, but your efforts to include her and your enthusiasm about the project will go a long way to relieve the anxiety she's likely to feel about these many disruptions. If your move is caused by some misfortune—death of a spouse, divorce, or financial difficulties—your mood will be understandably subdued. A combination of moving and personal problems is particularly hard on everyone. But it's important to remember that your toddler is especially vulnerable. For her sake, try to sound somewhat encouraging.

You should also do your best to plan the logistics of the move itself. Your toddler will need lots of attention and support during this time; the better organized you are, the better you can tend to her needs and the responsibilities of the move. Most large moving companies (and even some rent-a-truck businesses) offer free brochures that help you plan a move. Call the company of your choice and request all the information they can send. And do this well in advance of moving day. You'll need all the time you can get to plan things. We also suggest that you talk to other families with young children who have recently moved. They'll be able to offer lots of practical tips.

Here are some of the tips we received from our sources.

1. Let your toddler help you pack whenever you have the time and the patience for a little dawdling. Being involved this way will make her feel more like a willing participant in the project. Ask her to bring you piles of towels and linens, encourage her to put her books in a carton, let her scribble her mark on cartons containing her toys and personal items, have her gather up shoes—basically let her pack anything she can't ruin. And be sure to thank her enthusiastically for her help.

2. Pack your toddler's things—toys, clothes, bedding, personal articles, room decorations, and so forth—apart from the rest of the family's. Mark these cartons clearly and try to keep them together as much as possible. You'll want to unpack your toddler's things first, for reasons we'll mention later.

3. Be sure you pack at least one special suitcase for your toddler. You'll need to keep this on hand, both for the ride to the new house and for unpacking as soon as you get there. This suitcase should hold things like:

> a change of clothing;
> clean diapers (disposable are most convenient);
> caretaking items for diaper changes;
> sleepwear (in case your toddler wants to nap when she reaches the new house);
> a few favorite books and toys.

The morning of the move, add some additional items:

> a bag of nonspoilable finger foods (raw vegetables, raisins, fruit, and the like);
> a bottle or thermos of juice or other liquid refreshment;
> your toddler's special security blanket or lovey (unless she prefers to carry this with her).

4. No matter how tempted you may be, don't throw away any of your toddler's toys when you're packing (unless of course, you'll have absolutely no room for them in your new home). Things you think she has outgrown may be the very items she cries for in the new environment.

5. When you really consider all the complexities of moving, you'll probably be tempted to ship your toddler off to Grandma's or Auntie's for a few weeks. Having her safely out of the way for a time sure would make your job easier. If you think about it, though, you'll realize a step like this would make the adjustment much harder for your toddler. Imagine how *you* would feel if you took a vacation only to discover on return that you had been moved to a new house. More than likely, such an experience would make you apprehensive about ever leaving home again! Your toddler would probably react the same way. She will eventually adjust to the move no matter what, of course, but her adjustment will be a whole lot easier if she's allowed to be part of the process from the beginning.

Moving Day
Moving day finally arrives—with so much commotion that you'll need extra planning. We suggest that you divide responsibilities: one parent be in charge of the

toddler, the other in charge of the movers. If you have more than one child, it's also a good idea to ask a friend, neighbor, or relative to come over and help out. However you arrange things, be sure to keep a special eye on your toddler. She's probably going to be very anxious and will need your repeated reassurance that everything is going to be fine. Also, with so much going on in the house, she could get caught up in the bustle and end up tripping one of those sofa-toting moving men.

Have the moving men load your toddler's furniture and other items last, so they can be unloaded first at your new residence. Then while one parent oversees the remainder of the unloading, the other can set up the toddler's bed and start unpacking toys and other personal things. Remember: moving day can really exhaust your child. If you set up her bed right away, she'll have a familiar place to nap while you unpack additional things. Or if she'd rather play than sleep, she'll have playthings available and a safe play area.

In fact, we suggest you organize your toddler's entire room before starting to unpack other household items. As we said, moving to a strange environment can really unsettle your toddler. If you furnish her room first, with her familiar bed and bureau and curtains and wall decorations and toys, she'll adjust to the new home far more quickly. It's particularly important that the bulk of her room be set up before nightfall, so she'll have a familiar, comfortable place to sleep her first night in the new house.

If your new house is fairly close to your old, you might even drive over to it the night before the move and get a head start setting up your toddler's room—lay her carpet or hang her curtains or put up her favorite wall decorations. The new room doesn't have to be a duplicate of the old, of course; you've probably planned some changes, like a new wall color or different window treatments. But everything shouldn't be changed at once.

Helping Your Toddler Adjust to Her New Home

Once the confusion of moving day is over, it's time to help your toddler (and yourself) adjust to your new home. Arranging her room first was an important first step. Here are some others you might also take.

Let your toddler help you unpack the types of things she was allowed to pack: sheets, shoes, towels, books, and so forth. Her participation will undoubtedly delay the whole process a bit, but it will help her feel more comfortable and involved in her new house, and it will also help her learn where the familiar things are now kept.

Ask your toddler's opinion as you arrange dishes in your glass-front china closet or set knicknacks on the mantel or hang pictures on the living-room wall. Phrase your questions so her agreeable response is almost assured: "I think this painting of the sinking ship would look lovely over the fireplace, don't you, Rebekah?"

If the weather is good, take a walk around the neighborhood every day. You'll meet new people, discover exciting treasures, and otherwise learn more about your new environment.

Take your toddler on daily house tours. As you carry her or walk with her around your new home, point out things you see on walls, bookcases, tables, and so forth. Open closets and talk about the things inside them. Show your toddler where you now keep household playthings like pots and pans, cooking utensils, and the like. Help her become familiar with the whereabouts of her clothes, toys not stored in her room, secret play-spaces, and other useful nooks.

Above all, try your best to maintain your toddler's regular daily schedule. If you used to read a bedtime story, continue this routine. If she regularly played with Daddy in the evening, make sure you take time out of your busy schedule to provide this necessary playtime. If the family always had breakfast together on the weekends, continue this practice. In the midst of all the new experiences moving can bring, these bridges to the past are welcome indeed.

TAKING YOUR TODDLER TO THE HOSPITAL

At some time during this age period, your toddler may require hospitalization, for tests, surgery, illness, accidental injury, or some other temporarily disabling condition. A hospital visit, whatever the cause for it, usually has a powerful impact on a young child. Going to the hospital means being separated from familiar surroundings, very often being separated from loved ones, and experiencing a complete disruption of the daily routine. Suddenly, home, with all its comfort and security, is replaced by a strange environment filled with unfamiliar people, some of whom must perform painful procedures. And since these changes occur when the child is feeling uncomfortable and vulnerable anyway—if something weren't wrong she wouldn't be in the hospital—it's no wonder that the hospital experience puts a toddler under enormous stress.

Parents can't eliminate all the pain and problems created by hospitalization, but they can help make these rare occasions less traumatic. In this chapter we'll discuss ways you can care for and support your toddler—and yourselves—should she ever require hospital treatment. Some of our suggestions are pertinent only if you know about the hospitalization in advance, such as when your child is scheduled to be admitted in a few days, for instance, for tests or a nonemergency operation. Other suggestions deal with both scheduled and unexpected hospital visits. All are intended to give you a little better understanding of the special needs of the hospitalized toddler, and ways you can help meet them.

This section was prepared with the help of Jerriann Wilson and Carlesa Finney of the Child Life Program at The Johns Hopkins Hospital. These warm and wonderful women have worked very hard to improve hospital care for children of all ages, and we thank them for their thoughtful contributions.

Choosing a Hospital for Your Toddler

The pediatrician, surgeon, or other physician attending your child will usually decide which hospital she should be admitted to. Luckily, pediatric medicine has lately come a long way in acknowledging the special physical, social, and emotional needs of hospitalized children. Thanks to the efforts of the Association for the Care of Children in Hospitals and other concerned groups, almost all modern hospitals are now well-equipped to meet the needs of pediatric patients. Still, obviously, some hospitals are better than others. If you are in the position of selecting a hospital for your toddler, we recommend you look for the following features.

1. *Living-in, or Rooming-in, Arrangements.* Living-in arrangements mean you are allowed to spend the night with your toddler. Your presence will be important to your toddler when she falls asleep at night and wakes up in the morning in the strange hospital crib, and can be especially reassuring if she awakens unexpectedly with fears or nightmares. If living-in is forbidden, make sure the hospital has long visiting hours so you can at least be present at bedtime and morning wake-up time.

2. *Child Life Program.* A Child Life Program (it may have a different name in some hospitals) complements the medical program in caring for the hospitalized child. Child Life personnel are trained professionals dedicated to caring for the child's emotional needs and requirements for play and stimulation. In addition, Child Life Programs offer counseling services to parents and other members of the family to help them better understand and deal with the hospital experience. A program like this can be an invaluable support for both your toddler and you.

3. *Playroom.* If your toddler will be hospitalized for more than a day or two, and if she won't need total confinement to a bed, she should have a warm, attractive playroom to visit. As one astute hospital staff member told us, "A real problem for the hospitalized toddler is that a hospital takes away her opportunities to make choices for herself. Making choices—doing things for herself—is an important part of the older toddler's growing independence. But in a hospital bed the toddler is confined and everything is brought to her. Our hospital playroom is a place where toddlers have the freedom to make some decisions on their own: which toys to play with, which *people* to play with, what types of activities to play; those sorts of things."

In addition, a playroom will go far toward making your toddler feel comfortable in the strange hospital environment. Once she makes a few friends—with other children and with staff members—she'll be less anxious about being separated from the comforts of home.

4. *Flexible Policy About Bringing Things from Home.* One of the biggest problems of a hospitalized toddler is being separated from familiar people and environments. So you want to find a hospital that allows you to bring some of your toddler's favorite toys, books, room decorations, articles of clothing, and other reminders of home.

Preparing Your Toddler for the Hospital

As we mentioned earlier, hospitalization often frightens a toddler because the experience is so unfamiliar. So if you know about a hospital visit in advance, you should prepare your toddler *before* she's admitted. The following suggestions will help you.

One thing you might try is a preadmission tour of the children's ward where she'll be staying. This can usually be arranged through the pediatric nursing office, the Child Life Program, or if all else fails, through your child's physician. Schedule a tour for a few days before actual admission. If you do it too far in advance the significance will be lost on your toddler.

As you and your toddler tour the ward, talk to her about the people and places you come across. Be sure to visit the playground and, if you have time, let your child play with staff members and other pediatric patients. When you see medical personnel, talk about them, and tell your toddler some of their responsibilities. For example, "See that lady" (or man) "all dressed in white? She's called a nurse. A nurse takes your temperature and brings you things to eat and drink and helps care for you the way Mommy and Daddy do." Of course, your toddler won't understand all you say, but she'll begin to draw some connection between a nurse and herself, and will probably be more receptive to nursing care when the time comes.

As part of this tour, be sure to introduce your toddler to the hospital bed. Because of safety considerations, most hospitals use crib-type beds with very high sides. These beds resemble cages and can look quite ominous, especially if your toddler has graduated to a full-size bed at home. So talk about the hospital bed and try your best to link it with pleasant memories your toddler may have of her crib and playpen from the earlier months. You might say, for example, "When you visit the hospital, Catherine, you'll be staying in a bed like this one. See the bed? It's like your old playpen at home. Remember when you used to play in your playpen while I practiced the piano, and you'd stand up and sway and dance?" Of course she won't really remember, but if you approach the topic with a sunny voice, the pleasant association will probably sink in. If the hospital beds you see have toys in them, be sure to emphasize this play aspect.

Another tactic experts suggest is preparing your toddler at home, through toys and games. For instance, you might act out little hospital "dramas" with a set of doctor and nurse puppets. If you like, use your toddler as the patient, and have these medical puppets talk to her about what's going to happen when she goes to the hospital. Or maybe engage in some hospital fantasy play yourselves. Parents can be the medical staff, the toddler can be the patient. Some experts suggest acting out typical hospital procedures on your child's favorite doll or teddy bear. Try things like examining the eyes and ears, pretending to look down the throat, applying a bandage, hugging the doll because she's scared, and putting her in bed for postoperative recovery. For an older toddler who enjoys fantasy play with miniature figures and settings, you might consider purchasing a commercial play hospital set or a doctor's kit.

If your toddler enjoys "reading" with you, you might also try introducing the hospital experience through books. There are numerous going-to-the-hospital books on the market, but unfortunately, nearly all are geared to the preschooler or older child. Since most toddlers aren't interested in listening to the long explanations these books usually contain, you should find a book with lots of pictures. Then you can make up your own narrative, using the illustrations and printed text as a guide. You can also make your own book. Take pictures of the hospital your child will be visiting (maybe when you take that preadmission tour) and put them in a photo album. Or cut appropriate pictures from magazines. If you have trouble finding these in your regular magazines, beg a few medical journals from your pediatrician's office.

What to Take to the Hospital

Our experts tell us that separation from loved people and familiar surroundings is usually the most traumatic part of a toddler's hospital stay. That's why we urge parents to remain in the hospital as much as possible, including living-in if this can be arranged. In addition, you can take to the hospital things that will remind your child of home and make her feel less cut off from her everyday experiences. The following list will give you ideas, but follow it with caution. Each hospital has its own policies, so check with yours to see how much—and what—the regulations allow you to bring. Also, keep in mind that you'll be personally responsible for almost everything you take to the hospital. Few hospitals keep tabs on patients' belongings.

1. Your toddler's favorite lovey or comforter, be it a blanket, a teddy bear, a bottle, a doll, or whatever. This is very important!
2. Three or four favorite toys.
3. Some crib toys, even if your toddler has outgrown them at home. Since your toddler will sleep in a criblike bed at the hospital, you should choose toys that will make this a more interesting environment.
4. Your toddler's own pajamas. These will make the bedtime experience that much more comfortable and familiar. Some parents we spoke to even took in their toddlers' own crib sheets.
5. Your toddler's own daytime clothes to wear to the playroom. The opportunity to change from pajamas and diapers to her regular clothes will make the daily routine seem more normal.
6. Simple room decorations. Bring a few favorite pictures for the walls, especially if they are decorations your toddler has made herself. You might include a few photographs of your family members.
7. If you won't be living in, try to provide a tape recorder with "living letters" from home: tapes from parents and siblings. The hospital workers can play these for your child. And since both parents will rarely be present at the same time, have the absent parent call frequently, if only to let the toddler hear his or her voice.

Of course, if your toddler was taken to the hospital in an emergency, you won't have made these preparations. But there are still things you can do to help orient her to the hospital experience. Take her on a tour as soon as danger has passed (and the nursing staff says it's O.K.). Talk about the playroom, point out the personnel and talk about their jobs, and in general try to duplicate the tour mentioned previously. Each time a parent comes from home, bring some toy or room decoration or other reminder. You should also ask a member of Child Life or the nursing staff for more suggestions that will suit both your particular hospital and your toddler's physical condition.

When Your Toddler Is in the Hospital

No matter how thorough and loving your preparation has been, you should expect dramatic changes in your toddler's behavior once she's in the hospital. She may become very scared and spend much of her time clinging to you. She may become very angry and cry or even pretend to avoid you. This anger is probably a reaction to her feeling that she's been deserted, especially if you're not able to live in. Some toddlers, unable to express any particular emotion, just throw tantrums. Other toddlers react in the opposite way, by becoming very withdrawn and listless. Or your toddler may exhibit a succession of different emotions during any visiting period.

It's bound to make you mad when your toddler reacts in such a seemingly negative way, especially if you're trying your best to alleviate the stress of the hospital experience. But it's important that you work to accept these dramatic behaviors. Your toddler isn't being bad or disobedient or a tease. She's just reacting to a new and rather scary experience in ways she often employs when she's distressed. She needs you to stay as calm and supportive as you can.

In fact, it's important that you retain a positive attitude about the hospital, and especially the medical staff, and pass these feelings on to your toddler. The hospital staff will care for her in your absence, will treat her and give her medication and take her temperature and otherwise deal with her medical problems. Your toddler needs your help in learning to trust them. So remember not to drop idle threats like "If you're not good I'm going to call the nurse." Instead, work *with* the staff; you can serve as a sort of interpreter between them and your child. When a doctor performs a checkup, tell your toddler what she's doing and why she's doing it. The trust you have in the professional staff will be transmitted to your child.

Being in the hospital usually limits the amount of stimulation your toddler gets, both because she's in a bed much of the time and because she's tense. You should make sure she continues to get the same types of stimulation she receives at home. You can read stories with her, play quiet lap games, bring her a variety of toys for independent and social play, sing to her, give her soothing massages if you're allowed. Conscientiously playing with your toddler is especially important if the hospital doesn't have a Child Life Program or its equivalent.

You should ask the nursing staff to let you care for your toddler's nonmedical needs. Many hospitals allow parents to feed, bathe, and dress their toddlers as long as these activities don't interfere with the medical routine. In addition, some hospitals allow parents to perform minor medical procedures, like taking a temperature or administering medication. If you care for your toddler here as you do at home, you will help her feel safe and secure in this new environment.

If your toddler is going to be operated on, ask the doctor to let you be present when the anesthesia is given. Some hospitals allow the child to be sedated in her own bed, with you at her side or even holding her in your arms. Or else they allow you to stay with your toddler when she's given anesthesia in the preoperating or operating room. Your presence will help soothe your toddler's fears. And it might help you feel a lot calmer, too. As Joan Beck says in her excellent book *Effective Parenting,* "One of the most miserable experiences of parenthood is to hear your youngster being carted screaming down a hospital corridor for surgery while you sit helplessly behind in his room listening."

Sometimes *parents* need some help and comfort and support when their child goes to the hospital. You might have problems at home that make it difficult for you to visit your hospitalized child. Or maybe her illness causes financial burdens. Or maybe you just want someone to talk to about personal worries and feelings. Many hospitals will help you arrange an appointment with a professional social worker. Talk to your child's doctor, the nursing staff, or a Child Life member if you want some help.

One final suggestion: please don't be afraid to give your toddler extra love and attention when she's in the hospital. It won't spoil her. Remember that she's going through a very stressful time and really needs your reassurance and emotional support. When she gets home and things return to normal, chances are she won't continue to demand so much attention.

If You Have Other Children
When a toddler goes to the hospital, the whole family is affected. Parents, of course, are placed under a good deal of stress, what with worrying about the toddler's physical condition, helping to care for her special needs while she's in the hospital, perhaps sleeping over in the hospital with her, and at the same time trying to maintain order and continuity in their own lives. If your toddler must be hospitalized, you'll need to summon up your special reserves of patience and energy and love. If both parents are working, you may want to make some special arrangements; you might decide that one of you should take some vacation days or a temporary leave of absence from your job so you can be with your child more. This is also a time when parents should be very supportive of one another. If the two of you join forces to deal with this temporary crisis, you will both find it easier to face.

In addition to parents, the toddler's siblings may be affected by her hospitalization. Think about it. When a toddler is hospitalized, the parents (and usually the mother in particular) are away from home far more than usual. Indeed, sometimes a parent is gone all night. A toddler's siblings can become very jealous of all the attention their little sister is receiving. A pre-school-aged sibling in this situation may even feel abandoned by his parents. What's more, older children generally know enough about hospitals to realize that people sometimes die in them. When an older sibling hears his sister is going to the hospital, he may think that she, too, will die. If you have an older child (or children) as well as a toddler, keep the following in mind.

1. To help alleviate the older child's fear of death in the hospital, and to help him feel involved in the event, prepare your older child ahead of time for the toddler's hospitalization. Explain to him, at a level he can comprehend, that his sister must go to the hospital for a few days, because she's sick or needs an operation or whatever the cause. Don't try to dodge the issue by saying his sister has to go away for a few days. Chances are he'll hear, from a neighbor or anxious Grandpa, that his sister is being hospitalized. Then he'll really worry: he'll conclude that since you didn't tell him, something must be very wrong. Even if he doesn't find out where his sister is, he'll wonder why she gets to go away when he's stuck at home. And that sort of speculation might lead to unbridled jealousy. It's best to be truthful.

When you talk about why your toddler is going to be hospitalized, be careful of your choice of words. For example, suppose the toddler is going to have minor surgery, like removal of a cyst in her arm. It's better to say something like "Alexis is going to spend a few days in the hospital so the doctor can remove a bump in her arm," than to say she's going so the doctor can "cut a cyst out."

If the sibling is a preschooler, you might try "acting out" some hospital procedures for him as you did for your toddler herself. Operate on a doll, give a nurse-and-doctor puppet show, or read a going-to-the-hospital book.

2. It's also important to help your older child deal with separation from you. Explain that one (or both) parents will be spending lots of time at the hospital, even that one parent may have to spend the night away from home. Reassure your older child that you still love him and will do everything you can to maintain the routines of your family life. The younger your older child is, the more assurance he'll need. When you're visiting your toddler in the hospital, be sure to call home frequently so you can talk to your older child, and so he can say a few words to his sister. For more suggestions, you might want to refer to Chapter 10, under "Toddlers and Their Siblings," where we talk

about preparing the toddler when mother goes to the hospital to have a second child.

3. You should also encourage your children to keep in contact with one another. For example, have your older child draw pictures and get-well cards for your toddler. Be sure to tell him how much his hospitalized sister enjoyed his handiwork. If you have an automatic camera, take pictures of the older sibling to share with your toddler, and pictures of the toddler to show your older child. Of course, pictures taken in the hospital should be discreetly posed, so your toddler looks as well as possible. A picture of his younger sister hooked up to a tube of some sort would probably be more frightening than comforting to your older child. You should also try to arrange some visits by the older child. Some hospitals don't allow children to visit the ward. But even in this sort of hospital, if your toddler isn't confined to her bed, you can probably carry her down to a lounge where she can visit with her older brother or sister.

When You're All Home Again
Short or long, a hospital visit puts pressure on everyone in the family. For a toddler, the impact may last even after she returns home. So expect your toddler to take a few days or so to settle back into her daily routines and activities. She may be extra clingy for a while. She may have some nightmares. Just accept these changes in her regular behavior. She'll work them out over time. In fact, you can help turn the bad memories into more pleasant ones by making a scrapbook of her hospital visit for you to share together. Fill the scrapbook with images of the more agreeable aspects of the experience, such as photographs you took in the hospital of your toddler hugging her teddy bear, cards and decorations she received from siblings and friends, and any art works your toddler produced in her Child Life play sessions, as well as her hospital bracelet and any other hospital items you may have saved. By using such visual reminders of the more pleasant memories of your toddler's hospital stay, and by making up stories that recall the fun she may have had with the hospital staff or in the hospital playroom, you'll help her accept what was probably in most respects a very trying experience.

Where to Go for Help
Books
As we said, there are lots of books for children who are about to go to the hospital. One that we especially like is Sara Bonnett Stein's *A Hospital Story* (New York: Walker and Company, 1974). Although really geared for three- to eight-year-olds, this unique book contains both a story for children and insightful information for parents. It's written in a beautiful, straightforward manner that makes it a pleasure to use.

We also recommend that you write

Mr. Roger's Neighborhood
Family Communications
4802 Fifth Avenue
Pittsburgh, Pennsylvania 15213

and ask for up-to-date information regarding the Mr. Roger's *Let's Talk About It* Series. This series, which is being added to all the time, contains helpful books about going to the hospital, having an operation, and wearing a cast (among many topics). Each book in the series is designed to be shared—and talked about—by parents and child together.

For a comprehensive list of additional books, send for a copy of *Books That Help Children Deal with a Hospital Experience*. It's available from

The Office of Child Development
400 Sixth Street, S.W.
Washington, D.C. 20201

For additional suggestions about ways to help your toddler deal with the hospital experience, we recommend *When Your Child Goes to the Hospital,* which is also available from the above mailing address.

Organizations
If you'd like to learn more about the care of children in hospitals, or if you need some specific information about some aspect of care for your child, you can write

Association for the Care of Children in Hospitals
3615 Wisconsin Avenue, N.W.
Washington, D.C. 20016

ADJUSTING TO YOUR TODDLER'S HANDICAP

Nearly all parents have dreams and expectations for their child, even before he or she is born. They want their child to be healthy, to be happy, maybe to be very intelligent or very attractive or very talented, and certainly to develop to the best of his or her potential. And they want to help—by being loving, nurturing, stimulating, and otherwise well-fit parents. In addition, parents often have special expectations. Mark will be a carpenter like his father. Carol will follow her mother into medicine. One day Billy will run the family business, or Angela will transcend the family's past and go to law school. Courtney will be an actor, Maria will be the first woman president. Parents are anxious to help their children fulfill these and similar goals.

But what if the child is born with a disability? Or is born healthy, but later develops a handicapping condition through illness or injury? When this happens, parents are naturally keenly disappointed, both because their child may never come close to fulfilling some preconceived expectations, and because they fear the child might never enjoy a happy, successful life. In addition, parents are usually unsure of how best to raise a child who has a disability. In the presence of a handicap the burdens of parenthood sometimes seem to outweigh all its potential joys.

This situation is more common than many parents realize. It's estimated that about one child in five has some type of handicapping condition. Some of these, such as minor birthmarks or partial hearing loss, are relatively insignificant and have little effect on overall development. Others, such as blindness or missing limbs, are far more severe. A child's handicap may require constant medical monitoring or the daily use of special equipment. Some disabilities, such as cerebral palsy, are plainly visible; others, such as certain learning disorders or mental slowness, may not be apparent to the casual observer. But minor or major, any handicapping condition is bound to create problems for the toddler—and especially for his parents.

How Parents Can Help a Handicapped Toddler

Because there are so many different kinds of handicaps, we can't offer specific guidelines for dealing with each one. Every handicapped child has his or her own special needs—and, of course, special gifts. For suggestions about how you might handle your toddler's particular handicap, we suggest you consult your pediatrician or family physician, or contact the appropriate resource associations listed at the end of this section. Here we simply offer three general recommendations for parents of a disabled toddler, no matter what the nature of the disability. You should try your best to—

1. Accept the limitations the handicap places on your toddler's total development.
2. Concentrate on your toddler's strengths.
3. Keeping these first two thoughts in mind, treat your handicapped toddler as normally as possible.

Since these ideas are so closely connected, we'll elaborate on them together.

The real key to helping your disabled toddler is to see him as an *individual*. Throughout this book we stress that each toddler is unique, with his own personality, his own rate of development, his own likes and dislikes, and his own potential and limitations. Well, a toddler with a handicap is just like any other toddler, except that one or more of his limitations is obviously severe. His disability is only part of his total composition, his personality.

Of course, you have to take your toddler's special limitations into account when you consider his special growth pattern and anticipate his future. For example, a blind toddler will probably lag in many aspects of physical development, even though his muscles aren't directly affected by his loss of sight. Walking, climbing, running, and even using your arms are much more difficult skills to perfect when you can't visually orient yourself in space. But though blindness means that your toddler will inevitably encounter special difficulties, it doesn't mean he will be unable to develop his skills and talents. Blindness will prevent him from becoming a race-car driver or a brain surgeon, but it won't prevent him from becoming a lawyer or businessman.

As a parent, you must accept the fact that your toddler's handicap will slow down or even halt some areas of development. You must accept the fact that your disabled toddler will need special understanding. And you must accept the fact that he may require more of your care and attention than a nonhandicapped child. But remember: he is still a toddler with his own per-

sonality and set of strengths and abilities. When you accept his limitations, you're on your way to helping him develop to his greatest potential.

The main reason you must accept your toddler's limitations is so that your expectations won't exceed his abilities. But accepting his limitations doesn't mean giving up on him. Far from it. It's important that you concentrate on your child's abilities: think about his potential, and then make sure he has a well-rounded schedule of appropriate play and learning activities. Like any growing toddler, he needs a balance of active play, book play, art activities, games for the senses—in short, all the kinds of play which we discuss in detail in the "Play and Playthings" section of this guide.

Try to gear activities to your disabled toddler's special situation. For example, if he's lost the sense of hearing, emphasize his other senses. Draw his interest to the visual world with picture books, trips to the museum, games of looking out windows, and similar activities. And draw his attention to the textures of objects through touching games. If your toddler's handicap limits his large-muscle activity, concentrate on games with toys that stack, twist, fit together, and otherwise challenge both his small muscles and his growing intelligence. Or play lap games, emphasize reading, introduce lots of art activities. While you're at it, though, don't neglect his physical needs in the bargain. Be sure even the physically disabled toddler gets plenty of exercise. This is especially important if your child's disability confines him to a bed or wheelchair or other piece of equipment most of the time. Of course, make sure your toddler's doctor approves of the exercise games you play.

A disabled toddler, quite naturally, needs special treatment: maybe some extra understanding, maybe extra stimulation in certain areas, maybe medical treatment for the handicapping condition. Otherwise, though, he needs his parents to treat him as normally as possible. Remember: a toddler with a handicap is first of all a toddler. Like any other toddler he needs people who care for his physical and emotional development, people who love him and approve of him, people who play with him, help him learn about the world, discipline him, dispel his fears, teach him social skills, and otherwise help him grow into a happy, self-sufficient, and independent child.

Some parents are inclined to overprotect a disabled child: to relax rules of discipline, to cater to all the child's needs, and in other ways to "spoil" him as they would never dream of spoiling another child. Some parents also feel they should shield the disabled toddler from other children, so that he'll be spared embarrassing looks and questions. Most experts agree that such treatment is far more harmful than beneficial. As your child grows up, he'll become aware that his treatment is special, and wonder why he is being raised so differently from other children (especially his siblings, if he has any). He'll also fail to develop important social skills. The handicapped child needs and deserves the same chance as normal children to suffer all the ordinary setbacks and disappointments—and joys—that are part of growing up.

How Parents Can Help Themselves

Parents can help a disabled toddler by accepting him, by helping him develop all his abilities and by raising him as normally as they can. But it's usually not enough to help their toddler in these ways. They need to look out for themselves.

Like their toddler, the parents of a handicapped child often need some special help. Getting to the point when you can accept your handicapped toddler is usually a hard journey. Researchers have discovered that most parents go through a predictable sequence of emotional stages after they learn their child is handicapped. The first stage is shock, largely mixed with resentment. The prominent, although usually unspoken, question is "Why did this have to happen to us?" At some point this reaction dissolves into feelings of guilt. Parents often blame themselves, or even each other, for the child's handicap. Usually the guilt is entirely unfounded, but it can take lots of reassurance from physicians, experts, and family before parents will be able to accept this.

In the next stage, parents often become so preoccupied with the handicap they neglect to see the child's other abilities and qualities. Only after some more time and adjustment do they mature to the point where they can accept the child as a pretty fine person who just happens to have a disability. Working through these stages can be a long and painful process. If you've known about the disability since your child's birth, you've most likely reached the stage of acceptance by now. But if the handicap has shown up only recently, you're bound to be very confused and upset about it still.

Parents of a handicapped toddler often have other problems as well. Some of them suffer financial worries created by the need for special medical treatment or special equipment. Those who have other children as well are often so busy and worn out doing all the extra chores that are required for their handicapped child that they feel unable to care adequately for the rest of their children. Worst of all, the parents of a handicapped child often feel alone. Family and friends offer as much sympathy and help as they can, but these people, with their normal children, can never *really* know what it's like to raise a child who isn't normal. Often the parents of a handicapped toddler just don't know where to turn for real understanding and support.

Where to Go for Help

Fortunately, nearly every community has services to offer you. Some of these help relieve the financial burden of raising a handicapped child; some help you cope with the psychological problems; and some just steer you to other appropriate resources. In a city, you might contact the United Way, City Health Department, or Department of Social Services. You can also ask your doctor or a local health clinic to guide you to necessary aid. If you live in a town or rural area, chances are you'll have to go the state level to find out about services. We suggest you write the State Department of Health and the State Department of Social Welfare, in care of your state capitol building.

There are also many national organizations that will help parents. In fact, some were originally organized by parents. These associations offer printed materials, information-and-referral services, sometimes counseling, and lots of support. We include a list of some of the better-known organizations. You should seriously consider writing to the ones that seem relevant to your handicapped toddler's special case. These groups can support you over the years, can make your parenting job more pleasant, and can make you feel a lot better about both your child and yourself.

General Resource Organizations

The following groups are designed to function largely as information and referral services for parents whose children are afflicted with almost any type of disability. When you write one of these general agencies, we suggest you specify your child's age and the nature of his handicapping condition.

Closer Look
Box 1492
Washington, D.C. 20013

Closer Look, a part of the Department of Health Education, and Welfare, is also known as the National Center of the Handicapped. This extremely helpful organization will send you pamphlets and other useful information, and also describe steps you can take to find additional services for your handicapped child.

Council for Exceptional Children
1920 Association Drive
Reston, Virginia 22091

This organization is affiliated with the National Education Association.

National Foundation–March of Dimes
P.O. Box 2000
White Plains, New York 10602

One of the best-known organizations, The March of Dimes, was originally set up to fight polio. Its drive was so successful it has now undertaken to fight all birth defects and crippling conditions.

United States Public Health Service
National Institutes of Health
Public Information Officer
Bethesda, Maryland 20014

This government agency is equipped to give you information about specific birth defects. Remember: your tax dollars go for this, so you're entitled to its services.

In addition to general-resource organizations, there are many groups set up to help parents (and others) deal with specific disabling conditions. You might wish to contact some of the following:

Visual Handicaps

American Foundation for the Blind
15 West Sixteenth Street
New York, New York 10011

American Printing House for the Blind
1839 Frankfort Avenue
Louisville, Kentucky 40206

National Association for Visually Handicapped
3201 Balboa Street
San Francisco, California 94121

Cerebral Palsy and Other Neuromuscular Diseases

United Cerebral Palsy Associations, Inc.
66 East Thirty-fourth Street
New York, New York 10016

The National Easter Seal Society for Crippled
    Children & Adults
2023 West Ogden Avenue
Chicago, Illinois 60612

Foundation for Child Development
345 East Forty-sixth Street
New York, New York 10017

Muscular Dystrophy Associations, Inc.
810 Seventh Avenue
New York, New York 10019

Mental Disorders

Joseph P. Kennedy, Jr., Foundation
Suite 205
1701 "K" Street, N.W.
Washington, D.C. 20006

National Association for Retarded Citizens
2709 Avenue "E," East
Arlington, Texas 76011

American Association on Mental Deficiency
Suite 405
5101 Wisconsin Avenue, N.W.
Washington, D.C. 20016

Hearing Handicaps

Alexander Graham Bell Association for the Deaf, Inc.
3417 Volta Place, N.W.
Washington, D.C. 20007

American Speech and Hearing Association
10801 Rockville Pike
Rockville, Maryland 20852

National Association for Hearing and Speech Action
814 Thayer Avenue
Silver Spring, Maryland 20910

Various Handicapping Conditions

Center for Sickle Cell Disease
College of Medicine
Howard University
2121 Georgia Avenue, N.W.
Washington, D.C. 20059

Epilepsy Foundation of America
1828 "L" Street, N.W.
Suite 406
Washington, D.C. 20036

Cystic Fibrosis Foundation
3379 Peachtree Road, N.E.
Atlanta, Georgia 30326

The National Hemophilia Foundation, Inc.
25 West Thirty-ninth Street
New York, New York 10018

National Kidney Foundation
2 Park Avenue
New York, New York 10016

PART THREE
Play and Playthings

1
Introduction

For a small child there is no division between playing
and learning; between the things she does "just for
fun" and things that are "educational." She learns
as she lives and any part of living she finds enjoyable
is also play.

—Penelope Leach, *Baby and Child*

This "Play and Playthings" section is about all the
different things a toddler likes to do, both alone and
with parents or other playmates. Like Dr. Leach, we
define play very broadly. Play includes exploring the
world with all the senses; practicing physical skills;
manipulating objects and mastering the challenges they
can present; experimenting with new materials, "reading" books and listening to stories; making music;
dancing; roughhousing; helping parents with household
chores—in short, just about everything your toddler
does. All of these activities are important to your
toddler's development because, as Dr. Leach points
out—and we readily agree—playing *is* learning. And
a whole lot more.

Here are some ways your toddler benefits from play:

1. *Play stimulates a child's developing intelligence.*
Your toddler is born with the desire and ability to learn,
and play gives him the opportunity to "exercise" his
mind. Every new experience your toddler encounters,
be it a person, a toy, or an intriguing obstacle, presents
new information for him to understand and store.

2. *Play expands the senses.* Babies are born with the
senses of sight, hearing, touch, taste, and smell. Play
exercises each of these.

3. *Play develops the muscles.* Not only does play
make muscles stronger, but it helps your toddler develop skillful control and coordination of specific muscles. He will practice coordinating his hand, arm, and
leg muscles, for example, when he tries to climb up a
climbing frame.

4. *Play aids in organizing the world.* The world is a
very complicated place, filled with trillions of objects.
To make sense of it all, we have to learn to classify
these objects into categories. We adults do this all the
time without even thinking about it. Although there are
hundreds of different makes and models of automobiles,
for instance, we have no trouble calling them all cars. If
someone drives by in a completely outlandish foreign
model, we still recognize it as a car because it shares
basic characteristics with the cars we already know:
wheels, seats with people riding on them, lights, and so

on. A toddler learns to group things into categories this
way through play. In the course of his handling all of
the objects he finds around him, he begins to notice
properties that make various ones of them alike or
different, and he starts to organize the things he knows
in his mind.

5. *Play is a form of communication.* Since your toddler can't really talk, he communicates with you through
his actions. Through the way he plays with a toy, for
instance, he tells you something about himself: "I can
make music!" or "I'm strong enough to carry this
chair," or "I feel like knocking these down right now."
When your toddler feeds his doll, wipes its face clean,
and hugs it, he's telling you he understands and enjoys
the sequence of a typical caretaking routine. If he constantly shouts "No!" and "Bad boy!" at his doll, he
may be telling you something else about your relationship.

6. *Play helps form social relationships.* When you
and your toddler play, he's learning things about *you*
and ways he can relate to you. More broadly, he's
learning how to interact with other people. He learns to
share, to take turns, and to sense other people's emotions. He also learns how he influences people, what he
does to make them happy or sad or angry.

7. *Play offers opportunities for expressing many behaviors.* As your child's teacher and disciplinarian, you
often have to stop him from doing certain things, like
hitting another child or making too much noise in a
crowded place. Play allows a larger scope for many
expressions that would be considered negative in another context, but are perfectly appropriate in terms of
play. For example, punching a punching bag, yelling,
screaming, and roughhousing with people are all acceptable as part of a play session—but not necessarily
as part of a family dinner.

8. *Play is relaxing.* Your toddler is usually a bundle
of energy, and play enables him to use some of this
energy constructively.

9. *Play is fun.* This is the most important play
benefit of all.

Your Contributions to Play

All healthy toddlers play and learn to some degree
without parental involvement. But such experiences are
rather limited. You can enrich your toddler's play
enormously by providing two important elements. The

first is a safe physical environment offering a wide range of objects to explore. The second is a social environment that offers encouragement, attention, and plenty of exciting opportunities. The following chapters are filled with ideas to help you design play spaces, choose appropriate toys, and devise interesting games and activities for your toddler. But before you try out any of these ideas, here are some hints about how to provide the best social environment for play. As is so often the case, *how* you do something is as important as *what* you do.

Being Your Toddler's Play Helper

Your role in your child's play is not so much that of teacher as that of play helper. Your toddler usually likes to play near you and often welcomes your participation, but he doesn't need to be taught how to play. His play involves exploring and experimenting and discovering. If you constantly show him the "right" way to play with something, much of its play-and-learning value will be lost. Besides, with so much pressure on him to do things "correctly," he'll feel a lot less eager to try new things. So keep these suggestions in mind.

1. *Talk about what interests your toddler.* Pay attention to the things he explores and make a point of talking about these objects when you have time: "That's a gorgeous green frog you're playing with, isn't it?" When you get down on the floor to play with your toddler, talk about what you see and do. Talk about the different steps in games, and name the toys involved. Try to guess what your toddler is trying to learn. And when you think he wants you to be quiet, because he's really concentrating on a task, be quiet. A constantly chattering parent can become as boring as any nonstop speaker.

2. *Help him when he needs it*. Often your toddler's desires are bigger than his abilities. He has a goal in mind but lacks the wherewithal to carry a task through. When he has a real problem, help him with it. Offer suggestions and encouragement: "I think that piece fits there. Why don't you try it? You almost have it. There! You did it!" Sometimes your help should be more than verbal. If your toddler has spent several minutes struggling up the steps and finally begins to fuss in frustration, lend a hand. But don't help too much; stop when the immediate problem has been solved.

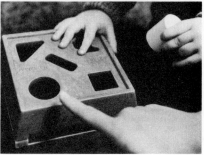

3. *Become a partner when he wants.* Many games require more than one. After all, how can you play "Chase" without a chaser and chasee? Try to allot time for these social games. Of course, you're too busy to play with your toddler all day long (and chances are he doesn't want you to), but try to be on hand when he indicates an interest in spending time together. And if your schedule permits, be a willing partner until your toddler loses interest.

4. *Introduce new experiences at appropriate times.* If your toddler is already absorbed in something, such as staring out the window, don't distract him with a new toy or game. Wait until he becomes bored with what he's doing and seems to want some interaction with you.

Another way to make sure you offer new experiences only at appropriate times is to look at what your toddler is already doing and build on it. Suppose he's playing with some small blocks. You might hand him a container and start some fill-and-dump play. Or you might construct a tower for him to knock down. When he's rolling a small car on the floor, you might pick up another one and demonstrate how to roll it through a mailing tube. If he's playing with pots and pans, show him how to fit the lids on in a matching game.

Be sure to offer these new experiences casually. Suppose you want to introduce a new game with a ball. Don't say, "Sit down and I'll teach you how to catch." Instead, show your toddler the ball, talk about it, bounce it, let him explore it, and then start rolling it back and forth. Later, try a game of catch.

5. *Help him to concentrate.* Most toddlers find it hard to concentrate on a challenging task, especially if it requires sitting still. So by himself, your toddler won't get too much satisfaction out of some complicated tasks like working puzzles or fitting things together. But if you sit with him, talk about what's going on and encourage and support him, he'll be able to concentrate longer, maybe long enough to get the great satisfaction of completing a new task. Remember, though: don't force him. Just help.

6. *Enjoy your toddler.* Don't push him to do something because you think he ought to learn a certain skill. Let him choose the task—by accepting or rejecting what you've made available—and let him decide when he wants to move on to something else.

There is one final element in truly successful, satisfying play, and it's something parents offer best: love. When you play with your toddler, let him know how much you love him, and how much you enjoy being with him. You can express your love in many, many ways: with words, hugs and kisses, encouraging hints, happy exclamations at your toddler's successes, comfort and understanding at his temporary failures. Warm and caring love from parents is absolutely essential to a toddler's happy play and learning; it fuels his curiosity and his drive and his desire and his whole pleasure in play. It's what makes his world go around.

Now, on to Play!

The remainder of this "Play and Playthings" section contains play suggestions for toddlers and their parents (or other playmates). Some will help you design your home to support safe, independent explorations. Some will show you how to make your own toys and equipment. Some will describe games you can enjoy with your toddler, and some will suggest activities for toddlers to play alone. A few are just to help you get through the trying times of the day. But all are offered to help you and your toddler share happy and rewarding times through play and learning. This section is intended as a play resource, not a curriculum. Use it as a recipe book for fun.

For convenience and clarity, we have organized the suggestions into eleven major chapters. We don't mean to imply by this that the various kinds of play the different chapters take up are distinct and independent of one another, however. In fact, the different kinds of play overlap considerably, and any kind of play will involve a child's whole personality.

As you read through these hundreds of suggestions, remember that all toddlers are individuals. Every toddler will like certain games and not others. Please don't push your child into any activity we've recommended if he doesn't seem interested. We have included a wide variety of suggestions so you can choose the games and toys that seem best suited to your particular child. Of course, as your toddler grows, his preferences and abilities will change, too, so you might want to give any game he rejects initially a few more chances before you abandon it altogether.

Throughout this section, you'll notice that we refer to our parent group. This is the large group of parents who cooperated with us in a number of helpful ways: taking part in interviews; allowing us to observe them and their toddlers both at home and in play groups; participating in discussions of toddler play; and reviewing drafts of this play section while we were writing it. Many of the ideas contained here have come from these parents, and we are truly grateful for their generous help.

Now, on to play!

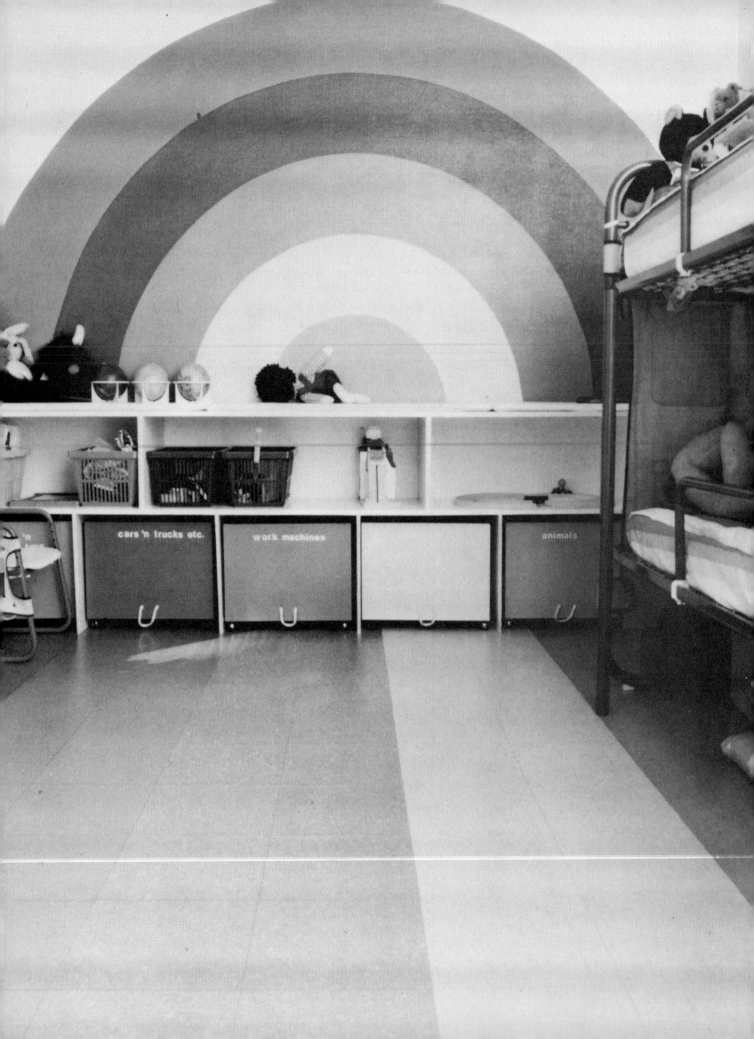

2
Designing Your Home for Play

Designing for play means arranging and equipping your home to suit your toddler's play needs. If this is your first child, chances are your home has been adult-oriented up to now. You've arranged things in ways that please you aesthetically or that suit your convenience. But now that your toddler can walk, adults aren't the only ones whose needs and tastes should be taken into account. It's important that your house also supports play.

For one thing, your house is your toddler's primary play space. It's where she plays most of the time, and since play is learning, it's where she does most of her learning during the toddler years. Every home is filled with fascinating objects to explore and opportunities to learn new things. The more your toddler can handle and experience—the more objects and settings you make available to her in your home—the more she's going to learn about the world.

Parents sometimes think it's enough just to create an attractive and well-stocked playroom for a toddler, but actually it's important to design your whole house for play. The reason? Your toddler usually loves to play where you happen to be. Studies have shown that in the early years, children want to be near an adult almost all of the time they're awake, even if the adult isn't directly involved in play. Your toddler will want to be close to you for security's sake, and so you can share her new accomplishments, talk with her, and just keep her company while she goes about her business.

The Goals of Designing for Play
Designing for play isn't as complicated as it may sound. When you design for play, you simply try to achieve three major goals:

You try to make your house safe for toddler explorations. Even though your toddler usually plays near you, where you can keep an eye on her, she'll frequently take short excursions to explore on her own. And there will be many times when you're too busy to give her your watchful attention. So it's important that your home be safe.

You try to create play spaces that are suited to a toddler's interests, needs, and size. Many things in our adult world are too big or too confusing for a toddler to comprehend or cope with. She needs some toddler-size

spaces, equipment, and toys that she can explore and handle.

You try to balance your toddler's needs and interests against your own.

Parents have rights, too. Few of us could be happy living knee-deep in toys all the time, or living in rooms so designed for children that adults feel like intruders. This chapter will help you create a house that suits both your toddler's play needs and your adult life-style.

Designing for play doesn't require special expertise. Armed with the following suggestions, you can create a stimulating environment for your toddler to explore and play in—and for you to enjoy with her.

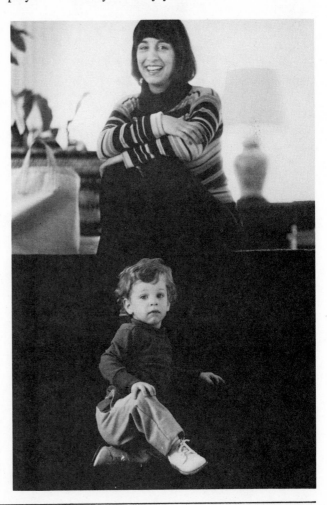

HOME SAFETY

The first step in designing for play is making sure your home is safe. At the risk of seeming overcautious, we include a very extensive list of possible hazards to make sure you've been alerted to almost all trouble spots, whether you live in a large house or a small apartment, in a city or a suburban area, whether you have one child or several. We don't mean for this section to sound overwhelming, or to imply that your house is a thoroughly dangerous place. But there might be some hazards listed here that you hadn't thought of.

If some of these cautions and precautions seem unnecessary for your child, remember: she is growing rapidly, and new abilities spring up almost overnight. Even if your toddler is just beginning to walk today, the day when she'll learn to climb to hazardous heights is just around the corner.

Here are some potential dangers to keep in mind.

Small Things

Because your child is still at the everything-goes-into-the-mouth stage, small objects can pose a choking hazard. So:

Keep your floors clear of buttons, coins, paper clips, screws, matches, even bits of fluff that accumulate on the carpet and under furniture.

Check the small knobs on your television, stereo, and radio. If they can be pulled off easily, replace them with larger controls. These can often be found at appliance, electronic, or electrical-supply stores.

Avoid giving your toddler small, hard foods like nuts and popcorn. Not only might she choke on them, but she might put them in her ears or nose.

Things on Tables

Remove all the breakables you might have on low tables: glass figurines, decanters, vases, china bowls, pottery, and so forth. (It's also a good idea to remove heavy objects from high tables if they're within the reach of a standing toddler.)

Be especially careful with ashtrays. Unappetizing as this may seem, some toddlers will chew on cigarette butts. Keep all ashtrays well out of reach.

On dining tables, use placemats rather than hanging tablecloths. Hanging cloths are so tempting to pull on.

Lamps on high tables present another problem. If your toddler tugs on a cord, she could bring a lamp

crashing down on her. Secure loose wires to the undersides of tabletops with strong tape or staple-type nails.

Electrical Things

Cover any unused outlets with safety caps. These are available at hardware or variety stores.

Keep small appliances—hairdriers, hot curlers, fans, and kitchen items—out of reach.

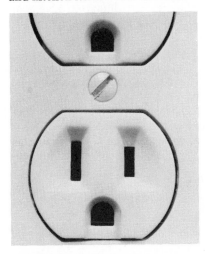

Hot Things

If your radiators don't have covers, block them with large pieces of furniture.

Space heaters are extremely dangerous. If you use them during the winter, place them well out of your toddler's reach.

Never, ever leave a hot iron unattended, even for a minute, if your toddler is awake and around.

A cup of coffee or other hot beverage can seriously burn your toddler if she upsets it. Be careful.

If your toddler joins you at the dining table, be sure that bowls of hot foods are out of reach.

Fire

Use safety screens in front of all working fireplaces. And even then, never leave your toddler alone in a room where there's a fire going. The same is true of charcoal grills in the backyard.

By the way, don't burn the Sunday funnies in the fireplace. Recent studies show that the brightly colored inks used in funnies and newspaper magazines contain lead; and when burned, the lead can be inhaled. Lead has been known to cause brain damage.

Keep matches and lighters out of reach.

Be careful with burning cigarettes, pipes, etc.

Sharp Things

Make sure knives, scissors, razors, and other sharp tools are kept well out of your toddler's reach.

Store sewing baskets, knitting baskets, and other handicraft materials on high shelves.

Dispose of broken glass in covered containers out of doors. If for some reason you can't, wrap the broken glass in lots of newspaper before throwing it away.

Even toddler art materials can be unsafe. So never let your child play with pencils, ballpoint pens, or similar items without close supervision.

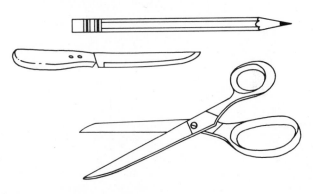

Wastebaskets

Because toddlers love to fill a container with smaller objects and then dump everything out again, they often find wastebaskets irresistible playthings. But trash cans can contain many hazards: spoiled food, small items that might be choked on, broken glass, cigarette butts, and so on.

Buy a wastebasket with a locking lid for the kitchen, or place the garbage pail behind a securely fastened cupboard door.

Empty wastebaskets frequently; better still, place them out of your toddler's reach if possible. Always throw dangerous trash into outdoor garbage cans. And

be sure you put these containers where your toddler can't get into them when she plays in the yard.

Plastic Bags

Thin plastic bags, such as those used to protect your dry-cleaned clothes, are particularly dangerous: they can smother a toddler very quickly. Dispose of them immediately in outdoor garbage cans. For extra safety, tie these bags into knots before you throw them out. It's also a good idea to keep plastic food storage bags, trash bags, and food wrap out of your toddler's reach.

Glass Doors

Make sure sliding glass doors, and large glass sections of storm doors, are made of safety glass. When broken, this kind of glass forms small rounded lumps rather than jagged pieces.

Put screens over the outsides of sliding doors to prevent your toddler from smashing into the glass when she's riding a wheeled toy on the patio. It's not a bad idea to put screens on the inside as well.

Windows

Upper-story windows pose a fall hazard. Be sure to lock all unscreened windows, and make sure that screens on open windows are securely shut. It's worth taking this precaution even if the windows are set well above the floor, because sometime your toddler might drag a chair over in order to look outside, often a favorite pastime of this age-group. Avoid putting large pieces of furniture near unscreened windows for the same reason.

Curtain pulls and venetian-blind cords pose a strangling hazard should your toddler become entangled in them. Secure these high on the wall if possible.

Things That Can Be Climbed

Many toddlers love to climb on things, and are oblivious to the dangers of falling off. To minimize this danger:

Place outdoor climbing equipment on sand or grass rather than hard pavement.

Put ladders away when you're not using them.

Use safety gates on all stairways until your toddler can easily go up and down the stairs.

Keep sliding doors to a balcony closed when you're not right there. Your toddler might try climbing the balcony rail.

Poisons

Accidental poisoning is a very serious health hazard for toddlers. Strange as it may seem, studies show that toddlers will eat or drink almost anything, no matter how foul tasting or smelling. So it's imperative that you take special care to prevent accidental poisonings.

Poisons commonly found around the house include:

Items stored in the kitchen: ammonia, bleach, detergents, drain cleaners, sink cleaners, floor wax, metal polishes, and other cleansers. These should never be stored under the sink; move them all to an upper cab-

inet. If you can, lock this cabinet also. Your toddler might climb up sometime. And be very careful when using these cleansers. Never leave them around your toddler while you go to answer the door or take a phone call.

Insecticides: Store roach sprays and the like in upper cabinets. And never use solid roach or rat poisons in low cabinets or other spaces accessible to toddlers. If you have pest problems, find another way to deal with them.

Alcohol: You should store liquor out of your toddler's reach, and be careful where you put your cocktails down if she's around. Also, if you have a party, empty all half-finished drinks before you go to bed. Otherwise, your toddler might find them when she awakens and goes exploring early in the morning.

Items stored in the bathroom or bedroom: aspirin, contraceptive pills, deodorants, hairspray, hair removers, iodine, laxatives, reducing pills, rubbing alcohol, sleeping pills, vitamins, and most other cosmetics and medicines. Store these in an overhead medicine cabinet.

Accidental poisoning from over-the-counter medications, especially headache remedies, is regrettably common. When you take an adult headache remedy, al-

ways replace the childproof cap before putting the bottle away. And when you're trying to get your toddler to take flavored children's tablets (or any medicine; even vitamins) never call it "candy." If you do, she may try to eat some more "candy" whenever she finds some pills in small bottles.

Items stored in the garage or workshop: cements and glues, gasoline, kerosene, lighter fluid, paint, paint thinner, turpentine, and varnishes. These materials should always be stored well out of your toddler's reach.

Plants: Many common plants have poisonous leaves, berries, or roots, and the rising interest in home greenery has unfortunately increased the risk of botanical poisoning. We don't suggest that you give up houseplants or gardening, but we do ask that you take a few safety precautions.

Rid your home and garden of plants that are known to be toxic. If you're uncertain which ones fall under this category, call your nearest Poison Control Center.

Whenever possible, place houseplants out of your child's reach.

Fence your garden with chicken wire or other suitable material.

If your toddler should eat part of a plant, call your physician or nearest Poison Control Center immedi-

ately. A Center will typically ask for the following information:

> Name of the plant. If you don't know it, the center will usually ask for a clear description. So clip a part of the plant and have it with you when you call.
> Amount eaten, if known.
> Age and weight of your child.
> How long ago the plant was eaten.
> Apparent symptoms of poisoning, if any.

In most parts of the country, the number of the local Poison Control Center is listed with other emergency numbers inside the cover of the telephone book, or else in the White Pages. If you're unable to find it, ask the telephone operator for assistance. In fact, it would be a good idea to post this number near your phone right now, just in case of a future accident. Poison Control Centers handle all types of accidental poisonings, not just from plants. Many Centers also supply literature and answer questions about poison prevention, so you might contact your nearest Center for more safety hints.

Now that we've reviewed all the major household

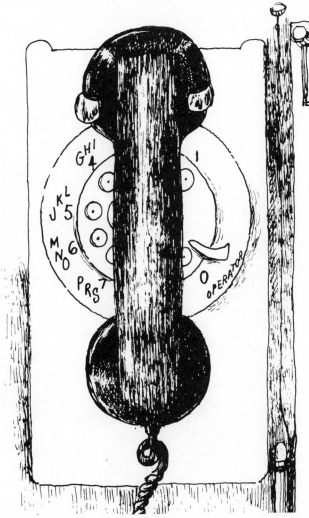

hazards, here's a quick checklist of safety steps you should take in specific areas of your house.

Kitchen

Although the kitchen is a terrific place for your toddler to play when you can keep an eye on her, you should never let her play there alone.

Keep appliances out of reach, and watch out for dangling cords your child might tug on to bring an object crashing down on her head.

Keep the high chair away from hot surfaces.

When you're cooking, turn pot handles toward the back of the stove so your toddler can't reach them.

Put knives and other dangerous cooking utensils in a high drawer, and make sure this drawer can't be pulled all the way out. If need be, install a safety latch to keep your toddler from opening it.

Keep your toddler away from pet dishes and cat litter boxes.

Nursery

To prevent falls from the crib, set your toddler's mattress at the lowest level and remove from the crib large toys she might use as "ladders" for climbing out.

Be sure all appliances, like fans and vaporizers, are out of reach. In fact, only use a cool-air vaporizer. It's just as effective as a warm-air one, and much safer.

Place the crib out of reach of windows, curtains, and venetian-blind cords.

At night, use a dresser lamp with a low-wattage bulb instead of a night-light that plugs directly into an outlet.

Bathroom

Never let your toddler play in the bathroom alone. The fixtures are hard, the floor is often slick, the toilet is *not* a suitable toy, and there's a chance she might turn on the hot water and burn herself.

Never leave your toddler alone in the tub, even for a minute. Tubs of water pose a drowning hazard. Or your toddler might turn on the hot water and scald herself. If you must answer the telephone or doorbell, wrap your child in a towel and take her with you.

To prevent your toddler from accidentally locking the bathroom door from the inside, remove the lock and replace it with a hook and eye, high on the door.

Make sure scissors, razors, medicines, and cosmetics are out of your toddler's reach.

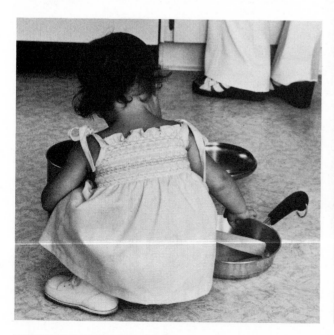

Garage or Utility Room

Make sure paint, gasoline, and pesticides are out of your toddler's reach.

Put tools on high shelves or hang them on the wall.

Keep the floor clear of nails, screws, other small pieces of hardware, and all tools, large or small.

Yard

Remove poisonous plants.

Keep the yard free of broken glass, rocks, animal feces, and the like.

To prevent neighborhood cats from using your backyard sandbox as a toilet, cover it when it's not in use.

Since standing water poses a drowning hazard, drain wading pools after use.

If you have a large swimming pool, even one that sits above the ground, be sure to fence it in. No exceptions to this!

Always keep an eye on your toddler to make sure she doesn't wander away.

There are two additional areas of toddler safety that concern materials found in every toddler environment, and these warrant special attention.

Car Safety

A safe car seat is an absolute must! Each year, thousands of children are killed or permanently disabled in automobile accidents, and many of these deaths and injuries could have been prevented had the children been using approved child-restraint car seats. Your toddler is not safe when held in your arms, even if both of you are strapped in an adult seat belt. In the event of an accident, your weight could crush her body. Nor is a toddler safe when wearing an adult seat belt by herself. Because her hip structure isn't fully developed, the belt can't fit correctly.

Since safety standards are periodically updated, and new seats are continually manufactured to meet the new requirements, choosing an approved child-restraint car seat may take some effort. But it's certainly worth it. We suggest you do some homework *before* shopping. The magazine *Consumer Reports* often evaluates car seats, and its recommendations are very trustworthy. Try to find a copy of their most recent article in your public library. Or you can write to either of these organizations for their latest recommendations.

Physicians for Automotive Safety
5 Union Avenue
Irvington, New Jersey 07111

Consumers Union
Mount Vernon, New York 10550

Once you buy a seat, be sure to install it correctly, and be sure your toddler uses it. Otherwise your money and efforts will be wasted.

Never leave your toddler alone in the car. She might wriggle out of her seat and play with the cigarette

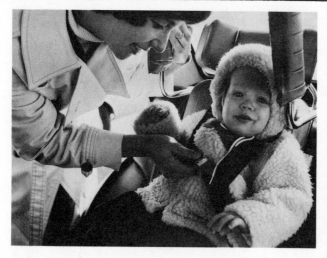

lighter, remove the parking brake, or open the door and get into traffic. Or someone might enter your car uninvited.

Don't allow your toddler to play with pens, pencils, or other sharp objects when riding in the car.

Keep the rear-window ledge free of objects that might fly around should you make a sudden stop.

Avoid disciplining your toddler in a moving car. If you must give her your attention, pull off to the side of the road.

Always check carefully before backing up the car in your driveway. Your toddler or your neighbor's child might be crouched behind it, happily playing

Toy Safety

Toys should be too large to be swallowed, should be free of sharp edges and points, and should have a finish that is safe for mouthing. Any painted toy should bear a label, on the object itself or on the box it comes in, certifying that the paint is nontoxic.

Stuffed toys should have strong seams and covers too thick to be bitten through. Eyes, nose, and mouth must be so firmly attached that *you* can't pull them off. Should your toddler remove one of these accidentally, she might choke on it. Painted, embroidered, or printed facial features are the safest. Stuffed toys should also be labeled as containing all new material, to prevent possible contamination from old material.

Even if toys are safe when new, wear and tear over time might render them dangerous. Plastics crack, seams split, wood splinters, and metal bends. So examine toys regularly to make sure they're in good condition.

Another point to keep in mind is the age-group for which a toy is intended. For example, although a construction set of girders and bolts might be perfect for a seven-year-old, small pieces and sharp edges make this a "hands-off" item for any child under three. Be sure you choose toys designed specifically for toddlers, and do your best to keep unsafe older children's toys well out of your toddler's reach.

If you're not sure about an item, check the label on the box to see what age the manufacturer recommends this toy for. Often age labels are awarded on the basis of safety considerations, not of skill level. So if a toy is marked "not for children under three," you probably shouldn't buy it, even if you think your toddler is bright enough to master the toy's intellectual challenges.

First Aid

Toddlerproofing your home is the best way to prevent accidents. And the suggestions given here—along with some special safety reminders sprinkled throughout the rest of this section—will greatly reduce the probability of toddler injury in your household. But there's no way all chance of accident can be eliminated.

So we can't disregard the other side of safety: treatment, or first aid. We don't have the space here to provide a comprehensive guide to first-aid techniques. But fortunately another book has already done so. We strongly urge you to buy *A Sigh of Relief* (produced by Martin Green for Bantam Books). This top-notch paperback will tell you almost everything you'll ever need to know about handling childhood emergencies, and its information is presented in an exceptionally clear, concise, and well-illustrated form.

These many precautions probably sound complicated and inconvenient, but your toddler's safety is of utmost importance. If you've seriously considered the points listed here, you'll be able to relax when your child plays and share her delight in exploring and learning about the world.

But enough of the grim part of life. Now that you've done your best to make your home safe, let's make it more fun.

YOUR TODDLER'S TOYS

Toys are about the most important things in a toddler's environment. They provide countless opportunities for practicing new skills, learning new concepts, sharing pleasant experiences with other people, and generally enlarging your toddler's understanding of the world. In a nutshell, toys are the tools of your toddler's play and learning, just as textbooks, lab equipment, films, and Frisbees are the tools of a college student's play and learning.

What Is a "Toy"?

Since you've been a parent for a year now, you're well aware of the commercial toy market. And, fortunately, there are many excellent toddler toys being manufactured now. However, these are only part of the plaything story. *Anything* that your toddler is interested in, and that's safe for her to play with, can be called a toy. Such objects are everywhere! Even a can of tuna can be an exciting plaything. To you it may be just a sealed container holding some edible seafood. But to a toddler it can be a wheel for rolling across the floor, a block for stacking on other cans of tuna, a small drum for striking with a spoon, or an object for placing in a container in filling-and-dumping games. Or take a large cardboard box. It can be a challenging gym for a toddler to climb into and out of, a car to drive in fantasy play, a giant block for building with, or a secret hideaway. If you take a creative approach to defining toys, you'll greatly enlarge the number of potential toys— and valuable play experiences—you can provide for your child.

Where to Buy Commercial Toys

A section called "Where to Buy Commercial Toys" sounds a bit silly, because everyone is familiar with toy stores. But here are some additional sources you may not have thought of:

Preschool Supply Centers. There are businesses that sell school and preschool supplies in many large cities. They carry materials you often can't find in conventional toy stores, especially books, art supplies, children's records, puzzles, prereading skill games, and the like. Look in the yellow pages under "School Supplies," or ask a preschool teacher next time you bump into one.

Catalogues. In addition, there are many mail-order companies that handle preschool products. These are usually excellent sources for hard-to-find items and large play equipment from top-quality commercial and independent toy manufacturers. Here are two of the more popular mail-order companies; you can request their catalogues by writing to them.

Johnson & Johnson Baby Products Co.
Customer Service Center
6 Commercial Street
Hicksville, New York 11801

Childcraft Education Corporation
20 Kilmer Road
Edison, New Jersey 08817

Novo Educational Toy and Equipment Corp.
124 West Twenty-fourth Street
New York, New York 10011

You might also check with people who run toddler day-care centers. They usually have a library of good toy catalogues and may be able to help you select which ones you could send away for.

Garage Sales and Flea Markets. These can be terrific sources of fairly cheap toys, especially large items like wooden indoor slides and outdoor climbing equipment you might not be able to afford new. Remember: always check secondhand toys to make sure they are safe and in good basic condition: no splinters, cracks, or

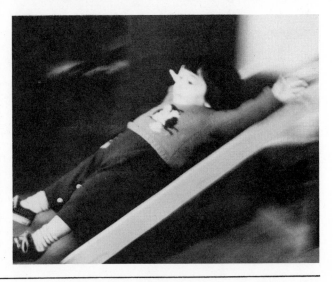

other potential causes of injury. If the painted surface of a wooden toy is chipped, you can add a new coat of nontoxic paint to restore its showroom appearance. Garage sales and flea markets often offer a variety of smaller toddler toys also, still in good condition but outgrown by their previous owners.

Choosing Toys That Are Appropriate for Your Toddler

The following chapters are filled with ideas about toddler toys (and games you can play with them), and you'll find suggestions that will help you choose appropriate playthings. But we remind you again, every toddler is an individual. All toddlers develop at different rates and have different skills and interests. So always ask yourself the following questions before you buy a new toy for your toddler.

1. Is the toy one your toddler will most likely enjoy playing with? To decide this, you have to heed your toddler's cues. Pay attention to the types of toys she plays with when visiting other toddlers. If she attends a play group or day-care center, ask staff members which toys tend to be her favorites.

2. Does the toy match your child's particular level of skill? Again, look, to your toddler for the answer. If she continually climbs up step stools or the cross braces between chair legs, she may be ready for an outdoor climbing frame.

3. Will you be comfortable letting your toddler play with the toy as she pleases? Avoid toys that are too noisy or delicate. For example, drums and pounding benches are good toys for the toddler age-group—if you can stand the noise. If you're going to say "shhh" every time your child starts banging away, leave these toys out of her collection. If you're going to say, "Be very careful," every time she plays with that exquisite expensive stuffed animal, don't buy it.

4. Does the plaything promote an experience or type of learning that *you* admire? The types of toys you do and don't provide can help pass along to your child some of your personal values and beliefs. For example, if you dislike fighting and violence, avoid giving her any kinds of toy weapons. If you want to help your toddler break out of stereotyped sex roles, give your son some typically "girl" toys (dolls and doll furniture, housecleaning sets) and your daughter some "boy" toys (play vehicles, a fireman's hat). And choose nonsexist children's books to read to your child. If you want to help your toddler learn about different races of people, be sure to supply figures (be they dolls, puppets, or play people) that represent a variety of ethnic origins.

YOUR TODDLER'S PLAYROOM

Even though your toddler doesn't limit her play to a single space, it makes sense to design one primary playroom. Every child should have at least one place predominantly suited to her interests and needs: an environment she can safely explore without hearing "No, no" and "Don't touch," a place where the furniture is scaled to her size and the objects around her are open invitations for experimentation and play. In addition, you'd probably appreciate having a central place to store most play materials, and a place where the inevitable messiness resulting from play can be hidden at a moment's notice. Your toddler's room is a logical place to consider. But remember: your child will usually want company when she plays, so this room should be comfortable for you as well.

The Playroom Walls

Walls are part of the play space, and the things you hang on them are more than mere decorations. Pictures and posters are open books for you to talk about; family photographs are occasions for learning about people and personal relationships; mirrors are vehicles for learning about the self and parts of the body. Other wall hangings serve to brighten rooms and make them more cheerful. So think of your toddler's walls as giant display spaces, not just as room enclosures.

Some things to consider hanging include:

1. *Pictures and posters.* You can use these for teaching the names of objects, for talking about colors and shapes, and for telling simple stories—just as you use the pictures in books. Most toddlers seem to like bright, colorful pictures of fairly uncomplicated, recognizable scenes and objects. Landscapes, animals, toys, and faces (even cartoony ones) are all good choices. You needn't limit yourself to juvenile pictures, however. Try hanging some posters from museums, especially reproductions of famous paintings. Still lifes, portraits, and even modern paintings lend themselves to exciting discussions. Just think of all the stories you could make up about the *Mona Lisa.* Besides, if you hang reproductions of great paintings on the nursery walls, your child may develop an early appreciation of serious art.

For a personal touch, you might put up some homemade paintings, collages, wall hangings, and such. When your toddler begins experimenting with artsy materials —especially finger and poster paints—hang some of her creations. And if your older child likes painting and drawing, be sure to ask for a number of his signed originals to hang on the toddler's walls. This tactic might help allay any jealous antagonism between the two, especially when you show your older child how much you and your toddler enjoy his work.

Hang some pictures and posters at your eye level. This will be a comfortable height for you when you hold your toddler and point to and talk about the various objects they depict. For safety's sake, you should make sure that any framed or mounted pictures that hang on hooks are placed well above your toddler's reach. In addition, though, make a point of placing some flat pictures low enough on the wall so your toddler can explore them by herself when she's playing alone. To protect these from rips, tape them to the wall around all four edges.

2. *Photographs.* Photographs of familiar people offer endless opportunities for learning: people's names ("Here's a picture of Grandma"), the names of parts of the face and body, the names of articles of clothing, and the meaning of certain facial expressions ("Here's Daddy smiling because he's so happy. Why is he so happy? Because he just loves you so!"). You can also use photographs as illustrations for stories you make up. Your child will probably enjoy looking at photographs of any size; however, for a really dramatic presentation, you might have a favorite picture of your family (maybe including grandparents and pets) blown up to poster size at a camera store or photography studio.

Hanging snapshots and photographs at your toddler's eye level presents a slight problem. Because photos are fairly fragile, they need protection from your toddler's clutching fingers; yet you want to be able to frequently replace photos with new ones. Here's a possible solution.

THE WALL PHOTO ALBUM

You need

> a piece of 1″ x 6″ pine, 4′ long
> a piece of heavy-gauge clear vinyl, 10″ x 54″ (it's sold in fabric stores)

1. Working on a flat surface, lay the board on top of the vinyl, making sure the top edges are flush.

2. Staple or tape (with very strong tape) the side and bottom edges of the vinyl to the back of the board.

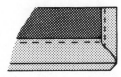

3. Turn the board over, and *voilà*, you have a giant clear pocket. Mount the board on the wall with nails or screws, and it's ready to hold a changing display of photographs.

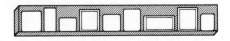

3. *Mirrors.* Since you've undoubtedly watched your toddler play with mirrors, we don't need to convince you of their appeal. A large wall mirror hung at toddler height would be an excellent addition to her playroom, *except* for safety problems. Regular plate-glass mirrors can be too easily broken by a misguided tricycle, a tossed toy, or an enthusiastic game of pounding with a hammerlike object. So if you decide to include a mirror in your child's room, take one of these precautions.

A. Hang the mirror high on the wall. Of course, if you do this your toddler won't be able to use the mirror when she's alone, but now and then you can hold her up to show her her reflection and play naming games about parts of the face and body. You might want to hang a mirror over your child's dresser, so she'll have a place to sit or stand when the two of you use the mirror together.

B. Make a safe, unbreakable mirror out of metallized polyester film. This is a flexible, plasticlike material coated with a highly reflective substance; in fact, it looks like a cross between aluminum foil and very heavy plastic wrap. It comes in rolls and can be purchased by the yard, like fabric. Metallized polyester film is usually available through art-supply stores, interior-design studios, and companies that handle display materials for department stores. Check the Yellow Pages under "Display Fixtures and Materials." Just buy a yard of the material and tape it to the wall with wide tape. Be sure

to put tape around all four sides; otherwise your curious toddler might grasp an edge and pull the "mirror" down. This wouldn't be dangerous, but metallized polyester film does crease, and the smooth mirrorlike surface could be damaged.

You can also enliven the nursery walls with any number of familiar decorations: giant decals of cartoon characters, large wooden letters that spell your toddler's name, or a full-wall hand-painted mural. For a very personal wall item, try this:

THE 3-D SCRAPBOOK

The 3-D Scrapbook is a time line containing pictures and articles that tell your toddler's life story.

You need

> a long piece of clothesline
> a number of pinch-type clothespins
> two hooks for attaching the line to the wall

1. Thread a number of clothespins on the line.

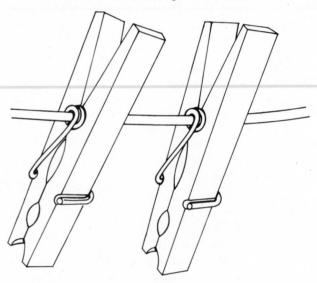

2. Then tie loops at each end of the clotheslines, and hang the line on hooks screwed into the wall.

3. Now use the clothespins to hang photographs that represent, in order, some important events in your toddler's life.

the pregnant mother
your child's birth
her first smile
the first time she's held by an older sibling
her first attempt to eat solid foods
her first steps
a visit to grandparents or other family members
first Christmas or Hanukah
birthday celebrations
your toddler and her newborn brother or sister

Interspersed among these photographs can also be articles of clothing that help your toddler understand how she is growing bigger over time, such as her first T-shirt (she'll be tickled to see how small she was), first shoes, and so forth. You might also include favorite toys of the first year, such as a rattle or teether. And, of course, add new objects as new milestones pass.

A time line like this is more than a collection of objects to catch your toddler's eye. It's also a way to help her gain a better understanding of herself and how she changes over time; it will give her a sense of the order in her development. In fact, if you have saved mementos from your own early childhood, you might construct a parallel line that tells your story, too. This can serve as a great illustration for stories about what it was like in the good old days, and how things have changed.

Storage for Toys and Other Materials

Providing adequate toy storage is a big part of designing for play. After all, even if you give your child the best toys in the world, they're just a nuisance if they're left scattered all over the floor for someone to trip over. Besides, it's a lot easier to tidy up a room if everything has a place to go.

The amount and type of storage space you'll need depends on the playthings your toddler owns. Using a few deep toy chests might seem like an easy solution at first, but actually this type of storage is quite impractical for a toddler. Small things drift out of sight in such bins, things get mixed up, the one item a child most wants is invariably at the bottom, and the constant unpacking and resorting can get very frustrating. For these reasons, we recommend toy-storage systems that offer your toddler easy access to her playthings. That way she can choose what she wants to play with, and, when she gets older, help you put things away when playtime is over. The following suggestions should help you beat the toy-storage blues.

1. *Bookcases.* Ready-made bookcases, equally suitable for holding toys, are available at department, furniture, and hardware stores. Or maybe you can pick them up secondhand—you'll save a lot of money. If the beat-up condition of a recycled bookcase offends you, mask it with a fresh coat of nontoxic paint. Choose units no more than three feet tall; anything higher will put the top shelves out of your toddler's reach. And because your toddler might try climbing on her bookcases, tall units are potentially hazardous.

Long, open shelves are impossible to keep neat. Large toys have a way of sliding around, and small things get scattered all about, eventually to end up on the floor or hidden in secret places. So if you use shelving, it's a good idea also to provide small bins that can hold things

---

A Safety Reminder: If your toddler's bookcases seem unsteady, attach them to the wall with L brackets. You may need a spacer block of wood between the bracket and the wall if baseboards prevent a flush fit.

like beads, miniature cars, blocks, rubber and plastic animals, and so forth. Fortunately, such storage containers can be found everywhere.

In the housewares section of a department or variety store, for instance, you'll find hundreds of containers designed for the kitchen which can be just as useful in the nursery. Silverware sorters, plastic cartons for storing leftover food, plastic freezer boxes, small dishpans, inexpensive wooden or plastic canisters—there are scores of possibilities. Your own kitchen is another gold mine. Just save all those empty coffee cans, mar-

garine tubs, oatmeal boxes, plastic ice-cream tubs, and the like; or cut the tops off of plastic milk jugs. Make sure any metal containers (like coffee cans) are free from sharp edges.

2. *Toy Baskets.* Bushel baskets and laundry baskets are terrific toy storers. These are light enough to carry around the room for easy cleanups, or to use for transporting toys from room to room. They're also useful as toy containers when you travel by car.

Cardboard cartons, though less attractive, can serve a similar purpose. If their bland color conflicts with your idea of a cheery toddler room, you can paint them or cover them with exuberantly patterned contact paper, or even wrap them in gift-wrap paper.

3. *Stuffed Toy Parade.* It's hard to store large stuffed animals and dolls without mashing them into dismal shapes. But here's an idea one mother gave us that solves this problem and creates beautiful wall decorations at the same time.

1. Buy some large metal rings at a fabric store. These are usually sold for hanging cafe curtains, or as belt loops for homemade cloth belts.
2. Sew a ring on the back of each toy with strong thread.
3. Hang the toys on wall hooks.

This arrangement has its drawbacks; chances are, your toddler won't be able to handle the hook-ring relationship by herself and you'll have to remove the stuffed toys from the wall whenever she wants to play with them. But if the idea appeals to you, try it. This mother reported it worked wonderfully for her.

4. *Hanging Toy Bag.* A clear-plastic hanging shoe bag with several pockets can hold and display a number of small toys within your toddler's reach. Be sure to attach this to a wall or door with strong nails.

5. *Toy Dresser.* Dresser drawers are like shelves except that they're open at the top rather than at the side. If your toddler is able to open drawers, why not store some toys in her dresser? You won't be able to see what's inside the drawers when they are closed, of course, so on the front of each drawer you might paste pictures of toys that correspond with its contents. You could draw these, cut them out of magazine advertisements, or (best yet!) cut them off the boxes the toys came in.

Playroom Storage Items You Can Make

PLYWOOD CUBES

This modular system is made from any number of 15″ plywood cubes, each open on one side. The system is fairly easy to construct because it uses simple shapes and fasteners; and since all the plywood can be cut to your specifications at a lumberyard, you don't even need a saw. A modular system is very flexible; you can make as many boxes as you need and arrange them however you see fit.

To make a basic cube you need

three pieces of plywood, each 15″ x 15″ and ½″ thick
two pieces of plywood, each 15″ x 14″ and ½″ thick
a hammer
plenty of 1½″ nails (also called four-penny nails)
sandpaper for smoothing rough edges

1. Make an open box from four pieces of plywood in the following pattern:

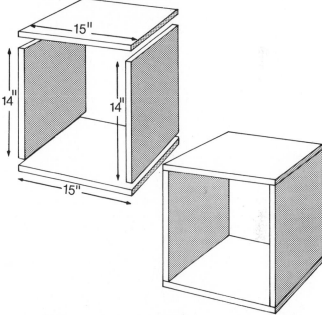

2. Turn the box so an open side rests on the ground and nail the remaining 15″-square piece on top. And that makes your basic cube! Be sure to sand all the rough edges to prevent splinters.

3. Now build as many cubes as you need and arrange them as you like. Here is one possibility:

To avoid any climbing and falling hazard, we recommend stacking no more than two cubes high. The cubes can be attached with iron plates on the back. Be sure to attach the iron plates along the outer edges, and secure them with nails or screws.

LIQUOR-BOX STORAGE

For a cheap no-lumber alternative to the plywood cubes, use wine and liquor cartons as modules.

1. Beg a number of same-size cartons from your local liquor store. Use the ones with four compartments (designed to hold half-gallon or gallon bottles). Smaller compartments aren't nearly as useful.
2. Tape the cartons together with 3″ duct tape, which is available at hardware and building-supply centers.
3. Cover the finished system with a jolly-patterned contact paper; or paint it with nontoxic paints.

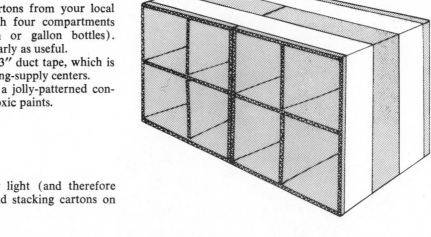

Because this system is very light (and therefore unsteady), we don't recommend stacking cartons on top of each other.

SHELVES IN CLOSET

Chances are your toddler doesn't need all her closet space for clothes. So if toy-storage space in her room is tight, use some of the closet for toy shelves.

High shelf to hold rarely worn clothing, bedding, etc.

Open space for hanging clothes. Toy shelves should be no higher than 3 feet.

Lower shelves for toys.

If the closet is long and narrow, and you don't want shelves all the way across, support the open end with a piece of lumber.

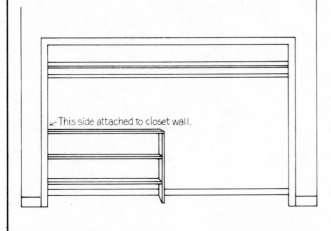

← This side attached to closet wall.

Toy Train

Here's a variation on laundry-basket toy-storage that is a terrific plaything in itself.

1. Make a series of 15″ plywood cubes as described earlier.
2. Attach four casters to the bottom of each cube.
3. Screw an eyebolt into any two opposing sides. Or, if you'd like, cut or drill holes in the plywood.

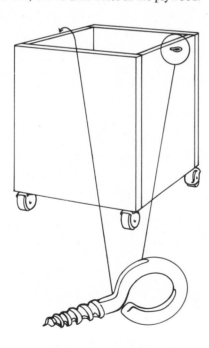

4. Tie a short piece of rope into one eyebolt on each cube. This can serve as a handle for pulling a cube along the floor, or as a hitch for tying two or more cubes together.

Wall Pockets

This item is perfect for storing a variety of small toys within your toddler's easy reach.

1. Take a 3′ x 4′ piece of heavy cotton or canvas, fold the top and bottom edges over about 2″, and stitch to make sleeves.

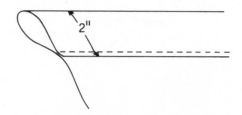

2. Sew some fabric pockets onto this canvas backing.
3. Insert a ½″ wooden dowel into each sleeve.
4. Then attach a piece of string to both ends of the top dowel and you're ready to hang the Wall Pockets on a nail or picture hook.

Playroom Furniture

An older toddler might like to sit at a low play table when she's working on puzzles, fingerpainting, experimenting with play dough, rolling cars, eating lunch, or doing a host of other fun things. You can buy a table and chair set at a juvenile furniture store. If you do so, the tabletop should be about eighteen inches from the floor and the chair seats about nine inches from the floor. Or you can make a set yourself.

HOMEMADE TABLE
You need

four pieces of 4″ x 4″ lumber, each 17″ long, for the legs
eight L brackets or angle irons with screws for attaching the legs
a tabletop. Use a piece of 1″ thick plywood, about 2′ x 3′, or larger if you have the space.

1. Attach two L brackets to the top of each leg as shown in this diagram:

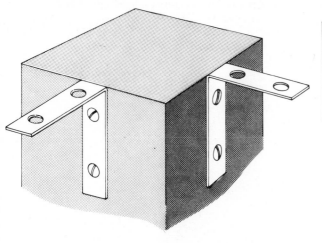

2. Lay the table top face down on the floor.

3. Position a leg in each corner and attach with screws.

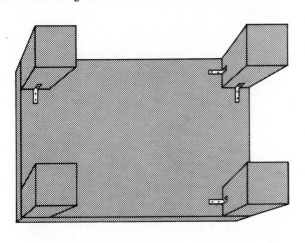

4. Coat the tabletop with clear sealer or a few applications of very glossy, oil-based white enamel so that crayons, glue, and paint won't penetrate. And the table's done.

This basic table can be adapted to whatever materials you have on hand. For example, the entire thing can be made from plywood, with solid sides instead of open legs. Or if you use a large tabletop, you might build some plywood cubes for "legs." These are handy for storing pads of paper and other large materials. Or design your own table. Just remember: the top should be about eighteen inches off the floor.

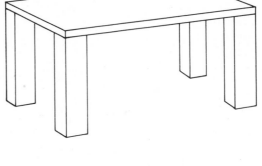

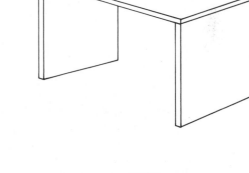

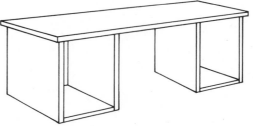

Chairs

Here are some ideas for chairs to go with your table.

THE PLAY-CUBE CHAIR

A simple, cubelike chair can be made from ¾" plywood. In addition to providing seating, a set of these cubes can be used as small tables, private desks, giant blocks, steps, and so forth.

For each cube you need

> three pieces of plywood, each 15" square
> one piece of plywood, 14" x 15" (for the seat)
> several 1½" nails (also called four-penny nails)
> sandpaper (a must when working with cut plywood)

1. Following this diagram, make a three-sided box out of the 15"-square pieces:

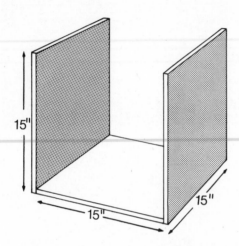

2. Attach the remaining piece about 9" off the floor to create a seat.

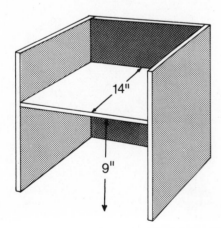

3. Sand the rough corners, and that's it. You can leave the cube-chair plain or paint it with nontoxic enamel or a sealer.

BOX SEATS

You can also make simple chairs out of low cardboard boxes. Use liquor-carton dividers as inserts to provide support, and cover the box with paint or contact paper.

SUPER STOOLS

Screw four ready-made 8" legs (available at hardware and home-improvement stores) into a 12" square of wood to make a simple super stool.

DOWN-SIZE CHAIRS

Old wooden kitchen chairs can usually be found at garage sales and flea markets. Just saw off part of the legs to make such a chair the right height for your toddler.

Playroom Furniture for Adults

Since your toddler will usually want company, include a comfortable chair for yourself in her playroom. You can use it for reading (alone and to your toddler), for sharing bedtime stories, for resting in when you need a catnap, and of course for occasional nursing if your toddler drinks from bottle or breast. You might also want to furnish the playroom with some large cushions for sitting or lounging on when you play on the floor. Whatever you introduce into your toddler's playroom will most likely be given a lot of wear and tear, so don't include any cherished pieces.

Designing a family room or den that can meet both your own needs and your toddler's is particularly tough—and particularly important. Since other family members use this room frequently, your toddler will, too. You want the room to be safe and suitable for her, of course, yet you want it to reflect your adult life-style as well. Meeting both these goals calls for some compromise and ingenuity.

One matter on which you should never compromise is safety. We've listed safety precautions earlier, and now would like to add one more. Beware of glass-top coffee tables. Unless the glass is recessed into the table frame, this type of coffee table can be very dangerous. Its sharp corners might cut your child badly, or injure her eye, if she should fall against one of them. Ideally, you should simply avoid using a glass-top coffee table during the toddler years. But if you own one already, and like having it in the family room, try padding the corners with adhesive-backed foam weatherstripping, which you can find at hardware stores. Or just tape some foam rubber over the corners until your toddler is very steady on her feet.

Toy Storage in the Family Room

It makes good sense to provide some toy storage in the family room. Your toddler will want to play with toys there, and since this is also an adult room, you'll probably want to keep the floor neat, so you'll need places where you can put things away quickly and easily. Again, your toddler should be able to reach her toys unassisted. Some of the storage ideas mentioned for playrooms work just as well in a family room, too, but many parents prefer something a little less visible. After all, open toy displays create a certain atmosphere which may not be the one you'd like your family room to project. So here are some toy-storage alternatives:

Behind the sofa. Unless your sofa sits against a wall, you can place some toy storage bins behind it: plastic laundry baskets, dishpans, the Toy Train suggested a few pages ago, even cardboard boxes. These can be carried around the room for easy after-play cleanups.

Under large chairs. Chairs with slipcovers that reach the floor are terrific storage places. But don't just shove toys underneath: they'll be too hard to retrieve again. Instead, put toys in large, fairly flat boxes that fit the space. These can act as drawers and slide in and out. If you want to be really fancy, you can use real drawers from an old dresser, or make a few drawers yourself out of plywood and pine. If you put casters on the bottom of these (as in the Toy Train), they'll slide more easily. And your toddler will be able to use them as pull toys.

In low drawers. Keep a few toys in the bottom drawers of chests and cabinets.

In the family bookcase. A bottom shelf or two of the family bookcase might be given over to toys. Store the playthings in large, attractive containers that fill the space neatly (and hide the contents from sight). In fact, it's a particularly good idea to give your toddler a shelf of the family bookcase for her books. If you teach her that her books are on this shelf and this shelf

only, and that the other books are yours (meaning do not touch), she might be less interested in destroying your collection. We said *might*—this is no guarantee.

Or . . . the best idea yet: Play Space. If you have the room and inclination and talent, create a separate play space in your den.

This sort of storage system does two things at once: it hides toys from sight, and it also defines a special play area within the family room. You might even carpet this area, or put a few pillows on the floor for sitting or resting on.

Such a play space has a number of benefits. For one thing, it can help a toddler learn which part of the room is hers, and so keep her from messing up the whole room. In addition, it enables her to see you and be close

PLAY SPACE

1. Build three, four, or more 15″ cubes as described earlier.
2. Attach these together at the top and bottom, rather than at the back, to make a long, low storage unit.
3. Decorate the back of the cubes with paint that matches the wall paint, or carpet that matches the room carpet, or wallpaper that matches the room wallpaper, or fabric that matches the curtains or slipcovers in

your family room. This matching will give the unit a built-in look.
4. Place the unit perpendicular to a wall, about three feet from a corner, with its open side facing the back wall of the room. The unit thus becomes a low room divider.
5. If you want, cover the top of the unit with a long cushion or pillows that suit the room design. Then you can use this surface as a bench. To keep the cushions from sliding around, attach them to the top of the unit with double-faced carpet tape.

to you when she plays alone. And since many toddlers like the security of small, private spaces in an adult-sized world, a special space like this might become her favorite playhouse.

Toddler Furniture in the Family Room

For an older toddler, you might add a special toddler-size chair to the family room to make it easier for her to sit with the big folks—to read, watch TV, or just enjoy chatty get-togethers. One mother we know also added a soft, furry sheepskin throw rug for her toddler to lounge on. And remember: some sit-on toddler toys can double as "furniture."

You may have one other piece of juvenile "furniture" that your toddler has basically outgrown: a playpen. Though a playpen can be quite useful for babies and their parents during the first year of life, it is usually too confining for active toddlers. On the whole, we recommend that when you need to quarter your toddler in a safe place for a short time—when you take a shower, for instance—you put her in her playroom (perhaps keeping her there with a safety gate across the doorway) rather than in a pen. But before you put the playpen away for good, consider this: some toddlers we know do enjoy them. Playpens are familiar and offer a sense of security at times. So if your toddler is content with occasional sessions in the playpen, you might continue using it for a few more months. It could be a very convenient piece of family-room furniture.

Wall Space for Your Toddler

If you have the wall space—and don't mind a possible clashing with your decor—hang a few of your toddler's artistic creations on the family-room walls. The two of you can admire these together, or share them with visiting friends. Toddlers also like photographs. And as you did in her bedroom, you might hang a few toddler-type wall decorations close to the family-room floor.

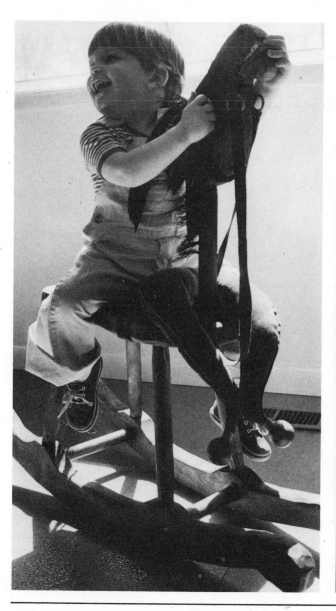

OTHER AREAS OF THE HOUSE

Your Living Room

Living rooms usually come in two types: the type the whole family frequently uses—in other words, the type that doubles as a den or family room—and the type reserved for company, adults, or just less boisterous activity. If yours is the second type, and you'd rather keep it an adults-only space, that's perfectly understandable. You don't even need to toddlerproof or otherwise change the room. Just keep a safety gate across the doorway to prevent your toddler from wandering in.

Your Kitchen

The kitchen is a terrific play area and, fortunately, requires very little redesigning to suit a toddler's needs and interests. It already contains plenty of safe, fascinating objects for your toddler to play with and plenty of storage areas. But you do need to keep an eye out for potential dangers here; be especially mindful of the safety suggestions listed earlier in this chapter. By taking the additional steps described below, you can make your kitchen an even better toddler playroom.

1. *Rearrange Cabinets.* Put heavy or breakable items in overhead cabinets and use lower ones for safe objects toddlers like to play with: pots and pans, cookie sheets, molds, plastic containers, mixing bowls, strainers, and so forth. If you don't have enough overhead space for all the hands-off items, set aside at least one low cabinet for the safe playables. Then put childproof latches on the other cabinets. Over time, your toddler will learn she's allowed to explore this one safe cabinet and that the others are off-limits. For your sake, make sure this safe cabinet is away from both the sink and the stove. Much time in kitchens is spent preparing meals and cleaning up after them, so you need free access to these areas. If your toddler's cabinet is away from these work areas, there's less chance she'll be underfoot. Of course, all household cleansers must be stored overhead; they're poisonous.

2. *Rearrange Food-Storage Areas.* Whether you store food in cabinets or in a separate pantry, try some rearranging. Heavy canned goods, things in bottles, open sacks and boxes, and other untouchables should be placed out of your toddler's reach. Use lower areas for small canned goods (like soup), unopened boxes, indestructible foods like potatoes and onions, and other objects your toddler can safely handle.

Some parents consider the food-storage area off-limits for play. After all, it can be pretty annoying to have the shelves messed up all the time. And in a home with limited storage space, where all the untouchables simply can't be put out of reach, these shelves can even be dangerous for a toddler to explore. If you want your toddler to stay clear of your food-storage shelves, tell her clearly what the rule is, and then be firm about it. Whenever she goes for the pantry, remind her that it's for adults only and distract her with other kitchen-play opportunities. If necessary, you can put a latch on the door.

3. *Rearrange Drawers.* Put safe kitchen utensils in lower drawers and install safety latches on drawers that contain anything dangerous. Here you have a slight problem: what is a dangerous cooking utensil? Obviously, scissors, knives, barbecue skewers, meat thermometers, and other sharp or pointed objects are unsafe. But what about egg beaters, cooking spoons with long handles, lemon squeezers, wire whisks, potato mashers, and so forth? These are all fascinating objects for a toddler to investigate, but they have either thin handles that might get stuck in a child's mouth, or corners where exploring fingers might get pinched. So if you decide to let your child play with utensils such as these, you should stay close enough to supervise.

If your kitchen has enough space, you might furnish it with a small table and chair set for your older toddler. She can use this both for art activities in the kitchen and as a place for sharing lunch or snacks with a visiting toddler friend.

The Bathroom
As we said before, the bathroom is not a suitable play space for an unsupervised toddler. Keep the door closed and, if possible, locked from the outside.

For when you can play *with* your toddler in the bathroom, keep a supply of empty plastic bottles and other bathtub toys on hand. You can store these in a plastic bucket on the floor, or hang them from the shower head in a mesh bag. You might also get an across-the-tub tray for bathtub fun. Your toddler can use this for holding some toys while playing with others, and also for filling-and-dumping bathtub games.

Your Yard
The great outdoors. If you're lucky enough to have a yard, your toddler will probably want to play there every day. But there's a catch. A child who is less than eighteen months old must always be closely supervised when playing in the yard. Because she's still at the everything-in-the-mouth stage, she might try to eat some of the enticing small objects she finds on the ground (including bits of the ground itself). And it's impossible to keep all these untouchables out of a yard. Of course, you should clear the ground of rocks, branches, bricks, and other debris that would hurt your toddler if she fell on them. But that's not precaution enough, so be sure to keep an eye on her at all times. If you must answer the phone or doorbell, take your toddler with you.

When your toddler passes the tasting-everything stage, usually at around eighteen or twenty months, you can relax more outdoors. She won't require such close supervision. In fact, to really give yourself a break, why not fence in part of your yard to make an outdoor play area? Then you can keep an eye on your toddler from the window if you have to go indoors for a few minutes. When friends stop by for a chat, you can give them some attention and still supervise outdoor play. A fence will also keep your toddler from wandering off—or running off—and keep strange beasts from wandering in. Just make sure your fenced-in area contains some outdoor toys and equipment, and is free from potential hazards.

That about wraps it up on designing for play. Now your home is safe and full of play potential, just waiting for your inquisitive toddler to explore to her heart's content. Since the stage has been set, let's move on to the many play activities your toddler and you might enjoy.

3
Adventure Play and Exercise

Adventure play involves what developmental psychologists like to call the gross motor skills: large-muscle development of the arms and legs, locomotion, and whole-body coordination. In other words, adventure play is what parents call crawling, walking, running, jumping, climbing, kicking, throwing, catching and rolling a ball, riding a kiddie car, rocking on a horse, sliding down a slide, and any play that involves really moving around. We adults tend to consider this exercise. Toddlers consider it fun. Unlike some of us, our toddlers need very little encouragement to exercise!

Your toddler will, however, greatly benefit from your contributions to adventure play. He needs you to provide appropriate spaces and safe equipment for his independent play. He often needs encouragement and help to try a new task, such as taking a first step or sliding down a sliding board the first few times. He likes your excited approval when he accomplishes something new, like walking a balance beam or maneuvering through an obstacle course. And he enjoys your enthusiastic participation in some social games. This chapter suggests ways you can contribute to your toddler's adventure play—and have fun with him at the same time.

MOSTLY FOR THE LEGS

From All-Fours to Two Legs

Walking is one of the major accomplishments and delights of early childhood. In fact, young children who've just begun to walk often neglect most other interests to practice this exciting new skill. Then, as coordination grows, they begin experimenting with new activities that are outgrowths of walking: pulling things, pushing things, carrying things in their hands, walking a plank, running, and so forth. Yes, walking opens a whole new world of adventure play.

FIRSTEPS

Naturally, the first step toward walking is taking those first few steps. Some babies do this at around ten months; others wait until well into the second year. If yours falls into the latter group, help him begin with some of these "Firsteps" games.

1. Walk with him while holding one of his hands.
2. Stand him on the floor beside the couch, and show

him how to use it as a support. Then encourage him to walk from one end of the couch to the other, sliding his hand along as he goes.
3. Stand him up on the floor; when he has his balance, back up a few steps and call to him with outstretched arms.

THE GO-BETWEEN

Early steps are even more fun when both parents get into the act. In this game, mother and father sit on the floor, a few feet apart, and send their toddler back and forth between them, rewarding each crossing with hugs of approval.

WORLDLY STROLLS

Outdoor walks are a welcome change. After rugs and tiles and wooden floors, it can be fun for a toddler to walk on a sidewalk, dirt, or grass; a gently sloping lawn offers quite a different challenge than a flat floor. And the constantly changing scenery outdoors can be counted on to fascinate almost any toddler. So try to make outdoor strolls a part of your day together.

CHASE

As soon as your toddler begins walking with some skill, he'll delight in chasing you. Get down on all fours and hobble away, across the floor and behind the sofa, with your toddler in hot pursuit. Be sure to let him catch up! And when he does, turn and grasp him so both of you can roll on the floor, shrieking with laughter.

In the early months of the second year, most toddlers are still only chasers. They have not learned to run away when you chase them. This is an important point, according to play specialist Dr. Brian Sutton-Smith.

It seems to show that when we learn to behave socially, we first learn just one side of the relationship. Later we learn the other side. Then still later we put them both together. So here children learn the social relationship of chasing and escaping, first by chasing, next by escaping, then with both together.

At eighteen months or so, your toddler will understand the reversal of roles and will thrill to being chased by you. And since children this age can walk very well, he'll be skillful enough to make a chasing game more interesting. You'll be able to cover several rooms, or even chase each other up the stairs.

PULL POWER

As we mentioned earlier, the experienced walker enjoys new challenges. So give your toddler a pull toy to drag around when he walks. Choose one that makes sounds when it's pulled, so he can be sure it's still there without having to turn around to look.

MESSENGER SERVICE

Toddlers also love to carry an object when walking, so occasionally you might ask your toddler to be your special messenger. He'll probably be delighted to fetch something (unbreakable!) from the coffee table, to get a toy or book from a shelf at your request, to help you carry the laundry, or to bear a gift from one parent to the other.

CROSSING THE BAR

Now that your toddler is a rather skillful walker, he may enjoy the challenge of walking across a raised plank, commonly called a balance beam. Rest the ends of a table leaf or broad board on small cartons, thus raising the plank a few inches off the ground. In a pinch you can use the crossbars between the legs of two chairs as supports. Hold your toddler's hand for the first few crossings.

Some toddlers are rather uncertain about walking a plank. They prefer to crawl, or to avoid the balance beam altogether. If your toddler balks repeatedly, respect his hesitation and put the plank away for future play. There's no hurry.

PUSH POWER

When your toddler is very steady on his feet, usually at about eighteen to twenty months, he'll probably enjoy push toys with rigid handles. Play lawn mowers and vacuum cleaners are favorites, since they have built-in imitation appeal. Toys that make noises and move in interesting ways also rank high. A very popular newcomer on the scene is a miniature shopping cart, which a toddler can also use for transporting toys and giving rides to dolls and stuffed animals. In fact, a toy shopping cart can become a portable storage bin for some of his favorite playthings.

Toddler Olympics

Walking leads to running, which toddlers really get a kick out of. Naturally, most parents prefer limiting this activity to the outdoors, where things are less breakable, but not all toddlers are so accommodating. And the weather isn't always suitable. As an agreeable compromise, some parents we know have designated indoor "tracks" where running is allowable. A track can be around the dining-room table, or all through the downstairs if your house is basically square and all rooms open onto each other, or around the perimeter of the basement, especially if you do laundry there. Teach your toddler that he is allowed to run in this specific area. You might join him in running some laps when time allows. Or use the track for playing games of "Chase." Giving your toddler a safe, acceptable indoor space to run off energy will help save the rest of your house from destruction.

Slipping Away

We can't claim this idea really helps your toddler practice walking, but it's terrific fun and gives great exercise. And it's a super antidote to the hot afternoon blahs.

Spread a heavy plastic tarpaulin or dropcloth (from the paint store) over a patch of grass or dirt—not a hard surface—and then station a lawn sprinkler beside the tarpaulin and turn on the water. When the plastic is completely wet, it becomes a super slide, for slipping on, flopping on, rolling on, anything. It's so much fun you'll probably want to put on a bathing suit yourself. Keep the sprinkler running as long as you play, and be sure to move the slide to another location every half hour so the grass underneath doesn't get cooked by the sun.

Ice Follies

A mother who lives up north told us that her sixteen-month-old loves to try walking on ice when the family goes ice skating. Like the hot-weather sliding described above, slipping and sliding on ice can be great fun. Just bundle your toddler well so he doesn't hurt himself when he falls.

Jumping Play

When your toddler is a fairly experienced walker, he'll test out a new form of movement: jumping. Jumping requires a different sort of coordination than walking, since in a jump both feet must move at once. For your toddler, it's rather thrilling to stand on air for a split second before coming safely back to earth.

Around the house, your toddler will practice jumps off the bottom step in your staircase, a low box set on the floor, his balance beam, or any other suitable platform. Help him get started by holding his hands the first several times, to give him confidence. You can also give him a chance now and then to do continuous jumping, a terrific leg exerciser. When you're cleaning your bedroom, let him jump around on the middle of your bed before you make it. Just be sure you stay nearby to prevent accidental spills. Or if you have the space, put a jumping pad in his bedroom. Then he can jump anytime the spirit moves him.

JUMPING PAD

A jumping pad provides a safe place to jump, fall, roll, tumble, and practice walking on a rather strange surface. And it's simple to make. Just put an old mattress on the floor. Used mattresses are always available at garage sales, Goodwill-type stores, or through want ads. As a good substitute, you can buy a cot-size piece of thick foam rubber. To make your mattress or foam rubber more attractive, cover it with a patterned fitted sheet, or make this special cover:

FEET FUNNIES

Decorate a white fitted sheet with colored footprints. You can draw these with permanent felt-tipped markers, paint them with acrylic paints (which withstand machine washing beautifully), or cut them out of iron-on patch material. Covering the sheet with feet is a way of spelling out the intended purpose of the jumping pad; and if this bit of symbolism goes over your toddler's head, at least it will help you explain to guests why there's an old mattress in the middle of your floor. You might include your toddler's name on the cover to make it more personal.

Next time you're at a gym, try letting your toddler jump around on a real trampoline. This exercise is a good beginning for acrobatics!

Riding Away

This is the age of kiddie cars and wheeled riding toys, and the array of different types, shapes, and styles from which to choose is mind boggling. Before you decide which riding toys are best for your toddler, consider the following points.

1. It's important to choose riding toys that your toddler can mount by himself, and that are low enough for him to propel by himself. If he always needs your help to climb onto the toy or to get it going, he'll be extremely frustrated when you're not right there. Which

will be often. Most toddlers are big enough to handle small riding toys at around sixteen or eighteen months.

2. Plastic ride-on animals with wheels have proved extraordinarily popular with the toddlers we've studied. Horses, giraffes, worms, elephants—take your pick. The ones that make noises when ridden are especially favored.

3. Unlike most vehicles for this age, kiddie cars have handlebar steering. So they tend to be less stable than other riding toys. To test for stability, turn the handlebars all the way to the side and give a tug forward. If the car tips over easily, look for one that's better balanced. Otherwise your toddler is likely to fall when he tries to go around corners.

4. Take your toddler with you when you choose a riding toy. Then you can see whether he likes the particular toy you've chosen, and whether it fits him. Let him take a test ride to make sure the wheels turn easily and that he can handle the steering mechanism without much difficulty. After all, *you* wouldn't buy a car without taking a test drive.

MOSTLY FOR THE ARMS

Hammering Fun

Most toddlers enjoy pounding: on a pot with a cooking spoon, on a drum with a drumstick, on a xylophone with a bonger. To you the result may be noise, but to a toddler it's music. So, if you can stand the "music," give your toddler some appropriate pounding toys.

A toy cobbler's bench for pounding goes these musical instruments one better. The colored pegs sticking up through the holes in the bench itself are small enough to be fairly hard to hit. So pounding the small pegs, rather than a large pot, helps your toddler develop more precise eye-hand coordination. In addition, making the pegs "disappear" through repeated hammerings gives a child a sense of accomplishment.

Pulling Punches

Remember how much your infant enjoyed swatting toys you hung over his crib? An interest in hitting things persists through the toddler years and beyond, so add a punching bag to your child's collection of toys. Punching is a great way to exercise arms, and a fine way for an angry toddler to work off some frustration.

PUNCH BALL

To make a simple punching bag, slip a beach ball or another large ball into a laundry bag or pillow case. Then hang the bag in an open doorway from a picture hook or a nail driven into the doorframe.

A heavier, more substantial punching bag can be made from an old pair of blue jeans.

BLUE-JEAN PUNCH

1. Cut off one leg, turn it inside out, and sew the bottom closed.

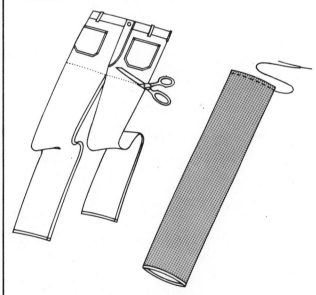

2. Turn the leg right side out again, and stuff it with tightly crumpled newspaper until it's about three-fourths full.

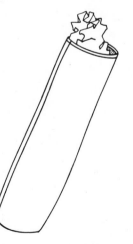

3. Tie the open end closed with a four-foot length of rope. Make this knot tight, since the rope is used for hanging the bag.

4. Hang the finished bag in an open doorway from a large hook or a nail driven into the doorframe. The bottom of the bag should be about a foot or two off the floor.

As a matter of fact, you might want to stuff both legs. The second could be used for rolling over on the floor, or for swinging like a giant bat, or even as a pillow. (And save the top part of those blue jeans, too; it can be made into a tote bag, as described on page 276).

MOSTLY FOR THE WHOLE BODY

Climbing His Way to the Top

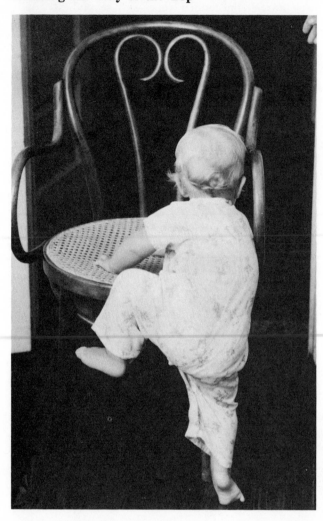

Climbing is another adventurous activity for toddlers, and one that often begins before walking. Climbing allows your toddler to use a number of large muscles at once and thus helps improve his coordination. So give your toddler plenty of opportunities to climb.

STAIRWAY TO PARADISE

There will probably come a point in your toddler's life when your staircase becomes his favorite toy. This interest is basically to the good. A child can have a lot of fun, and get some healthy exercise, climbing up and down stairs. But a staircase is potentially dangerous. Be sure you oversee all stair-climbing expeditions until your toddler learns how to come down safely (creeping backward or sliding on his fanny). And when you're not free to supervise, keep your stairs guarded with safety gates at both top and bottom.

BEAN-BAG MOUNTAIN

Bean bag chairs or large pillows in a corner make a terrific mountain for climbing on.

PAPER-BAG PLATEAU

Out of ordinary grocery bags, you can make terrific giant blocks for climbing on. Just follow these simple steps.

1. Lay a closed grocery bag flat on a table, fold the top over about eight inches, and crease well.

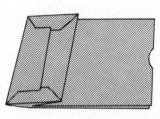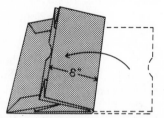

2. Open the bag and fill it with crumpled newspaper. You'll need about fourteen double-page sheets in all.
3. Fold the top over on the crease and seal with masking tape.

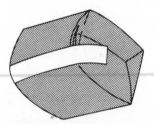

Make a number of blocks, so you can build all sorts of interesting plateaus for your toddler to scramble up and over. When the bags begin to rip, you can repair them with more tape, or toss them out and make new ones.

CLIMBING FRAME

A simple, fairly low outdoor climbing frame (also called a climbing tower or jungle gym) is a good investment for an older toddler. At sixteen months or so he'll practice simple climbing and cruising around the lower rungs. But as his skills increase over the years, his climbing frame will become an exercise gym, a fantasy house, a castle, a pirate-ship rigging, or anything else his mind can conjure up. Put the frame where it will get lots of sun and still be in view of the house—you'll need to keep an eye on your toddler when you have to go indoors for a few minutes. Also, place the frame over grass or dirt rather than pavement. Falls are rare, but are obviously more likely to be serious on a hard surface.

A Safety Reminder: A really zealous climber may try to practice on some unsuitable equipment: coffee tables, bookcases, and the like. Bookcases can present a real danger, because once on them a child can climb very high. If your toddler is a particularly enterprising and determined climber, you may have to shield the lower bookshelves with screens or some type of temporary fencing material. Or else be sure to keep an eye on your toddler when he's around your bookcases.

Down the Slide

Sliding down a slide—at first with help, then unaided—ranks high on almost every toddler's list of fun things to do. Safe, sturdy indoor slides are available at better toy stores. The popular wooden type is fairly expensive, but parents we know have found it well worth the investment. This slide will last for years, through a number of children. The steps are good for climbing, the box support is fun to crawl through and hide in, and the slide itself is practically a whole gym. Once your child has mastered simple sliding—either sitting down or sliding feet-first on his back—he'll probably try sliding headfirst, crawling or walking up the slide, bumping down the steps on his seat, rolling cars down the slide to chase after, and other such tricks. So by all means, buy one of these slides if you can. (If a new one seems too dear, try to find a secondhand slide at garage sales or flea markets. Or if you're handy with power tools, try making one at home.)

The best time to get your toddler an indoor sliding board depends on a number of factors. Some toddlers enjoy sliding at twelve months; others not until they're considerably older. Some parents we've talked to prefer waiting until the child is closer to eighteen months, regardless of his interest. At this later age the toddler is skilled and confident enough to both climb and slide without a lot of assistance and supervision. If you provide a slide for a younger toddler, you may find yourself having to deal with requests for help all day long.

In the meantime, here are some simple temporary slides that you can construct easily. Because, like any slide, they might be dangerous for an inexperienced climber and slider, you should always supervise your toddler's play with these.

1. Open a large cardboard box to form a long "runway" and place it over some pillow supports.

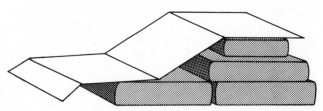

2. Lay a long, broad plank over the bottom few steps of your staircase, with one side against the wall. Your toddler can use the stairs for climbing back up to slide again. If this temporary board tends to slip, put some rubber doorstops under the bottom end.

Many toddlers also enjoy sliding down the real sliding boards found in public playgrounds. You can slide down with your toddler, cradling him in your lap, or hold his hands as he slides down alone; or if the slide isn't too high, have one parent put the toddler on at the top while the other stays at the bottom to catch him.

A Safety Reminder: Climbing on playground jungle gyms and sliding on playground sliding boards are fun, but these pieces of equipment can be dangerous! Even when your toddler becomes experienced, he might try to do more than he's ready for. Remember: he is a relatively poor judge of potential dangers. So always be on the lookout when he plays around large pieces of play equipment.

Rocking and Bouncing
Rocking horses are winners, and most toddlers love them. Choose one that's hard to tip over; it'll get some active rocking. And to save yourself a lot of running to and fro, find a horse low enough for your toddler to mount and dismount unaided.

Hobby horses on springs appeal to many toddlers, although others seem to think they rock and bounce too hard. If your toddler is the zesty sort and you think he'd enjoy one, keep these points in mind.

1. The horse should be low enough for easy mount and dismount.

2. There should be stout handles rather than thin reins for the child to hold while riding.

3. The base should extend beyond the horse in all directions, so the horse can't tip over no matter how vigorously your toddler rides.

Exercise Classes
Because toddlers are so active by nature, they really don't need the exercise routines often recommended for infants. As you know, your toddler gives both himself and you a rousing workout nearly every day! Even so, you may want to know about the exercise classes that various national and local organizations, like the YWCA, hold for parents and toddlers. These classes offer many benefits besides an exercise program: a chance for you to meet other parents, a chance for your toddler to make new friends, and an opportunity for both of you to use facilities and equipment you may not have access to elsewhere, such as a real swimming pool. So if you have the time to attend, consider looking into toddler-exercise programs in your area. Parents we've talked to recommend them highly.

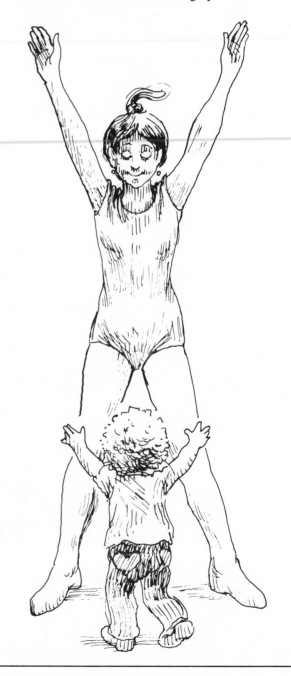

The Obstacle Course

Here's an activity that invites your toddler to practice a number of different adventure-play skills. A temporary indoor obstacle course can be set up in a matter of minutes. Include things such as—

a pile of pillows to climb over.
an indoor slide to go up and down.
a balance beam to walk across.

a dining room chair to crawl under.
a tunnel to crawl through. Cut tunnel-shape openings on two sides of a large cardboard box, or throw a blanket over a card table.

For special fun—and to give your toddler the idea of how an obstacle course is used—you can lead the way yourself on your hands and knees. Or else walk beside while he goes through his maneuvers.

A permanent outdoor obstacle course is a welcome part of any adventure playground. Each different "obstacle" can be a single plaything in itself. Some good things to include are—

a few old automobile tires for crawling over, jumping on, and stepping in and out of.
a small sliding board.
a permanent tunnel. Cut the bottom off a huge cardboard barrel and hold it in place with blocks of wood or ropes. Or cut the bottom out of a large plastic trash can and use that.
a climbing frame.
a balance beam attached to the climbing frame.
sections of tree trunk, set upright, for climbing on, jumping off, and sitting on.
an empty wading pool. Even empty, a wading pool can be a lot of fun for toddlers. It's like a low-walled playpen or playhouse. And it's fun to climb into and out of.

All-Around Roughhousing

General roughhousing is without question the most enjoyable kind of adventure play—for parents and toddlers alike, according to our parent group. And it's no wonder. Toddlers find this sort of play exciting, parents find it invigorating, and through the close physical contact of roughhouse sport, everybody gains a wonderful feeling of intimacy. There are lots of ways to have fun roughhousing, and every family has its own special variety. You can roll around on the floor together, tickle and hug each other, butt heads like dueling moose, toss your toddler in the air, swing him around, and just do whatever the moment suggests to you. This type of play is so popular and instinctive we don't need to give you long lists of suggested techniques. Don't think, though, that our brevity here means we underestimate the importance or benefits of roughhousing. It's really terrific.

The Parental Amusement Park

Nearly everyone loves the rides at amusement parks. Of course, your toddler is too young to enjoy most of the roller coaster–bumper car scene, but he's not too young to enjoy rides you can give him. So become your toddler's own amusement park at home. Most toddlers' favorite rides include horseback rides (with you on all fours), piggyback rides, and shoulder rides, as well as rides on wheeled toys and rides in safe, child-seat swings at the playground. Add variety with these:

BEACH BLANKET BINGO

This ride was popularized by the teenage sand-and-water movies of the 1960s. Put your toddler in the middle of a large blanket and drag him around the floor or yard. If both parents are present, you can each hold two corners and swing the blanket back and forth as if it were a hammock. For an exciting finale, toss your toddler gently into the air a few times.

BOX CAR BONANZAS

Push your toddler around the floor in a cardboard box. You can push him in a contraption like this faster than you can on a riding toy, because the box will protect him from spills.

THE ORIENT EXPRESS

If you have a toy box with wheels or casters, use it to give your toddler train rides. A rope tied on one end will allow you to pull rather than push the box. Or try giving him a ride in a child-size wagon.

JUNIOR BIRDMAN

If both parents are available, you can seat your toddler in a plastic laundry basket, then each take a handle, and swing the basket in great seagull-like swoops through the air.

PLAY BALL!

We give ball play a special section because the many different kinds of ball games involve so many different kinds of adventure play. There are games mostly for the arms, games mostly for the legs, and games for the whole body; there are games toddlers play alone, and games everyone can share in. All in all, balls are about the most indispensable toys for your toddler's adventure play and learning. So collect a variety. Some balls work better than others for certain types of play.

Ball Play from About Twelve Months

THE ROLL AWAY

Roll a fairly large ball and encourage your toddler to chase after it. Depending on what stage of locomotion he's currently at, he can crawl, creep, walk, or, later in the year, run to catch up with it. Then *you* catch up with him and roll the ball again.

ERSATZ CATCH

Since your toddler isn't likely to be able to catch a tossed ball until he's older, try this simpler version of catch for the early months. With your child sitting on the floor, legs spread apart, roll a large ball into his lap. Then invite him to roll it back. His rolls won't be terribly accurate, but he'll enjoy exchanging something back and forth with you.

BASKETBALL DROP

Give your toddler a basket or cardboard box and some balls to drop into and dump out of it again. Find balls that are small enough to be held in one hand; these will be the easiest for him to pick up and release. You could try tennis balls, balls made of crumpled typing paper, pairs of socks rolled into tight balls, or beanbags. Beanbags work especially well because they're so easy to grasp and hold—and drop.

To make two beanbags:

1. Cut the foot sections off a pair of socks.

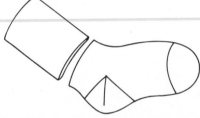

2. Fill these almost to the top with dried beans.
3. Securely sew the socks closed. Make a double or triple row of stitches to ensure that the bean bags won't reopen. Dried beans are small, of course, so they could pose a hazard should your toddler rip a bag open.

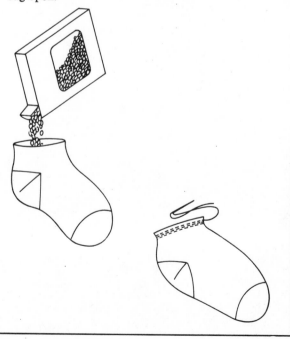

THROW THE BALL

Give your toddler a small ball and ask him to throw it to you. He'll probably throw it wildly—even behind him. But this game lets him practice releasing an object at will, and gives him the fun of sharing his play with you. Retrieve the ball from wherever he's thrown it—

or ask him to—and try the game again. You might also try this game with beanbags, which are easy to grasp and throw. They won't roll away—and as the retriever in this game you may see several advantages in this feature. Or try using a pair of rolled-up socks as a ball.

BEACH-BALL FUN

Large inflated beach balls provide special joy. They look huge to a toddler, and therefore look heavy, but are really light enough for him to carry. This difference between how heavy they look and how heavy they really are makes your toddler feel very strong and proud of himself when he lifts a beach ball. Beach balls are also fun for rolling back and forth, for chasing after, for flopping across, and for having bounced on his head. Later they'll be used for kicking games.

BATTING BALLOONS

Balloons are magical sorts of balls. They're large but light, and move in unpredictable ways when propelled. Sit on the floor with your toddler and bat a balloon back and forth between you. Or demonstrate how you can keep a balloon afloat by hitting it up, and then give your toddler a try. Or drop a balloon for him to catch. Or play dodge ball. No matter how hard you throw a balloon at your toddler, it can't hurt. In fact, it will hardly ever reach him, which is part of the surprise.

A Safety Reminder: Your toddler shouldn't play with balloons without your supervision. A balloon is pretty fragile, and if it popped your toddler might put the limp rubber in his mouth and choke on it. You should also be around to console him if a balloon bursts and frightens him.

PAPER-PLATE BALL

Here's a large, light ball that shares some of the characteristics of balloons and beach balls. But it has flaps, so your toddler can easily grasp and throw it with one hand.

You need:

> eight 9″ paper plates
> twelve thin rubber bands, each about 2″ long. Have plenty of spares on hand in case some break.
> paper hole punch
> ballpoint pen
> ruler

1. Flatten the plates as best you can.
2. On each plate, draw a triangle. Each side of the triangle should be about 8″ long, and the corners should be at the plate's edge. Press down fairly hard, since these are your folding lines.

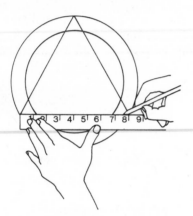

3. With the paper hole punch, make a ¾″ round notch at each point of the triangle.

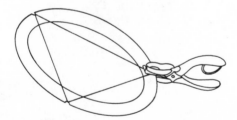

4. Fold along each on the scored lines. The flaps should be folded backward toward the underside of the plate.
5. To form a ball:
   a. Take any two plates and place a flap from one beside a flap from another. Stretch a rubber band around the flaps, making sure it hooks in the notches on each end.

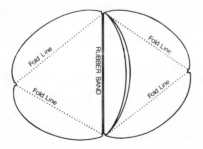

b. Continuing this process, make a four-sided pyramid out of four plates.

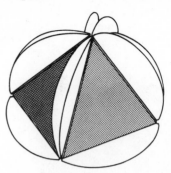

c. Make another pyramid from the remaining four plates.
d. Attach the two pyramids together to form a ball.

A Safety Reminder: Some toddlers will try to take this ball apart; they may even chew the rubber bands if left to their own devices. So always supervise Paper-Plate Ball play.

Adding More Ball Games at About Twenty-one Months

REAL CATCH

Now that your toddler is better coordinated, he may be able to catch a large ball you lightly toss to him. He'll still have a little difficulty throwing it back, but he'll try.

KICKBALL

Show your toddler how to kick a large ball, then let him try while you hold his hand. Kicking is hard at first, because it requires balancing on one foot while kicking with the other, so don't expect your toddler to master this skill right away. He might just prefer walking into the ball, which is another form of "kicking."

TARGET PRACTICE

Throwing a ball to you is one thing; throwing at a target is quite another. If you teach your toddler this game, he can play it when you're tired of being a catcher.

Draw or paint a large bull's eye on a piece of poster board, tape the target to the wall, and place a shallow box underneath. Then stand with your toddler a few feet away and show him how to throw small balls or beanbags at the target. The box will keep his ammunition from rolling too far away.

Really throwing a ball at a target is not an easy feat. It requires not only pretty good coordination but also an understanding of what the game's all about—that is, that the point is to hit the target with the ball. Your toddler may just dump the balls in the box, or with the ball still in his hand, touch the target and then drop the ball. It really doesn't matter how he plays, as long as he has fun. With time and practice, he'll begin throwing at the target from a few feet away.

EGG ON YOUR FACE

Here's a variation on the previous game. Instead of a target, paint a large clown's face, with open mouth, on the poster board. Again tape the poster up, or lean it against the wall, and put a box underneath. For balls, give your toddler the egg-shaped containers pantyhose come in. These are especially fun to throw, because sometimes on impact they break open like real eggs.

BEGINNER'S BOWLING

For a target game using a large ball—and promising more dramatic results—set up a miniature bowling alley. Line up any number of large, empty tin cans, and demonstrate how to roll the ball to knock these over. Then set the cans up again and let your toddler be the bowler while you play pinboy. Like the target games described above, this game requires a high level of skill and understanding, so don't expect immediate success. Your toddler might prefer to knock the cans down while still holding the ball, or he might not roll the ball hard enough to knock anything over. Let him practice in his own way. He'll get better over time.

4
Playthings That Stack, Roll, Twist, Turn, Fit Together, and Come Apart

Your toddler loves to handle things: not only to find out how they feel, but also to discover how they move, how they fit together, and, especially, what she can do with them. Can I put this inside here? Will that top fit on this pot? What happens when I flip this switch? What happens when I push this car? All day long you see her experimenting with toys and other objects around your house. These explorations do more than improve her ability to handle things. They also help her learn how objects behave and how she can influence the world. This chapter offers ideas for toys and games that are designed to challenge your toddler's growing manipulative and cognitive skills.

MOSTLY FOR A YOUNGER TODDLER

Stacking/Nesting Toys
Fitting things on top of and inside other things is a favorite activity, and there are many objects around your house suitable for this play; likely candidates are small cardboard boxes, plastic salad bowls, kitchen scoops, measuring cups, pots and pans, and canisters. Many commercial stacking/nesting cup sets are also available. They're cheap and have lots of uses besides stacking and nesting: they're good for water and sand play and for hiding toys under, and your toddler can also use them as dishes when she wants to feed herself and her dolls. You'll find that nesting things is more common than stacking at this age, but you might try demonstrating the latter principle a few times.

SMASHING TOWERS
Make a tower for your toddler to knock over. The higher it gets, the more dramatic the results. But you'll have to be quick. Your toddler will probably smash your structures with great glee as fast as you can build them.

You might also give your toddler a stacking-rings set. If she is less than eighteen months old, she certainly won't stack all the rings in correct sequence, but she probably will be able to stack a few in random order, especially if you first show her how to fit the rings over the spindle a few times. She'll also try to put the rings on her fingers, throw them, teethe on them, turn the base upside down to watch the rings slide off—and

probably come up with a slew of other uses for this toy that the manufacturer didn't foresee.

Activity Boards
There are several commercially made activity boards that consist of an assortment of parts that move in interesting ways; dials and wheels and cranks that turn, doors that open, and objects that slide on a rack are all attached to a rigid plastic "board" designed to hang in a crib or play pen. Chances are you have one of these toys left over from the infant years. If not, you might get one. Many parents we talked to listed this as the younger toddler's single favorite toy.

Form Boards
This is a simple puzzle with three shapes—circle, square, triangle—that fit into pre-cut holes on a base. A form board is naturally self-correcting; since each piece fits only into its own hole, your toddler has to keep trying until she places each piece right. Surprisingly, a form board doesn't lose its appeal as quickly as you might expect. Mastering this challenge is usually so satisfying (especially when you praise your toddler's early success) that most children are motivated to relive their successes again and again.

Fitting Toys
Fitting toys consist of any number of objects that fit into holes on a base. Like form boards, these are essentially simple puzzles. Most common types have round person-like figures that fit into cars or boats.

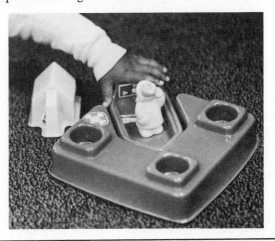

Fill-and-Dump Toys

COFFEE CAN BANK

Playing with this homemade toy helps your child practice more precise hand skills than regular filling-and-dumping games. Make a large slot in the plastic top of an empty coffee can, and help your toddler drop jar lids through the hole. When all the lids have been inserted, remove the top, dump everything out, and play again. Let her continue alone if she wants. To prevent possible cuts from this homemade toy, be sure the cut edge around the open end of the coffee can has been hammered smooth.

CARD DROP

A variation on coffee-can bank. Cut a fairly large slit in the top of a shoebox and show your toddler how to drop playing cards through the hole.

All your toddler needs is a container, like a mixing bowl or large coffee can, and a number of small items: blocks, balls, snap beads, large wooden beads, coasters, clothespins, jar lids, whatever. She drops things in, dumps them out again, and keeps going.

PACK RAT RACE

For social filling-and-dumping games on a grander scale, use a big box or basket and a large assortment of small objects. You put the toys in one by one; your toddler throws them out again. It's an exciting race to see who achieves the end of filling or emptying first.

CLOTHESPIN CAPERS

Clip colored plastic clothespins around the top of an empty coffee can. You and your toddler can then take turns pulling these off and dropping them inside.

If your toddler likes these pinch-type clothespins, try clipping them on things all over the house: your sleeve, a blanket, even her clothes. As she works to pull them all off, she'll get very good at using her thumb and fingers.

STAND-UP FILLING

Encourage your toddler to put large objects into even larger containers. She'll have to do this standing up, so her entire body will be involved in the game. Try having her put balls in baskets, and large toys in cardboard boxes. (This is a great game to play when it's time for cleanup.)

Rolling Toys

Your toddler will enjoy rolling miniature cars and trucks around on the floor, tabletop, or any flat surface. You can add interest to her vehicle play by introducing the following games:

DOWN THE HILL

Make a ramp for your toddler to roll toys down. Prop up one end of a large, flat cardboard box or piece of lumber on a chair cushion or similar support. For more drama, make a large slide out of a table leaf, or encourage your toddler to roll things down her own sliding board. Toddling over to retrieve the escaping toy aids walking skills.

MAILING TUBE TUNNEL

To make a magical disappearing-reappearing slide, cut the ends off a long mailing tube. Then hold or prop up one side, and show your toddler how to roll cars through it. She'll love watching things go in one end and come out the other.

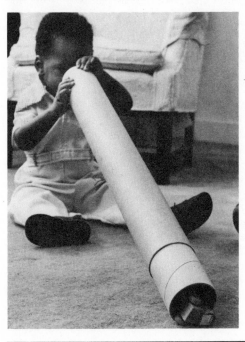

ADDING MORE PLAY AT TWENTY-ONE MONTHS

Screw-Type Toys

Containers with easy screw-on lids give toddlers an opportunity to practice new wrist and hand movements. Any plastic containers with screw lids, like freezer jars or condiments containers, work fine. You can add fun to the exercise by introducing a game like this:

CAPTURE THE RAISINS

Put some raisins or another favorite finger food in a small screw-top container. Your toddler will enjoy this reward.

Magnetic Toys

We can't claim these really develop any specific manipulative skills, but toddlers absolutely love them. Parents tell us that their toddlers spend extended periods of time arranging and rearranging brightly colored magnetic letters and numbers on their refrigerator doors. This is quite understandable. Magnets seem a bit magical for all ages, and something that sticks without apparent reason, pulls off easily, and sticks again has a special appeal. You can also get plastic shapes and animals that have magnets—they're just as much fun.

Here we'd like to add a cautionary note. In many magnetic letter or shape sets, the magnets can pop out rather easily. Since they're small, your toddler could put one in her mouth and try to eat or swallow it. So you might want to limit this type of play to times when you can supervise your toddler.

Shape-Sorting Toys

A shape-sorting toy offers a variety of interesting challenges and rewards. It satisfies your toddler's continuing interest in handling small objects, in filling-and-dumping activities, in making things disappear and reappear, and in fitting things together. In addition, a shape sorter will give your child practice in discriminating between different shapes and in learning the relationship between blocks and holes.

The first few times you give your toddler a shape-sorting toy, she'll probably need some help playing with it. Pick up a block, talk about it, then put it in the correct hole. Now retrieve the block and hand it to your toddler so she can copy you. You might need to guide her hand a few times. And even after she becomes familiar with her toy, it'll help if you hand her the pieces for inserting one at a time.

If you buy a toy with many shapes, your toddler may be overwhelmed by the variety, so at first introduce her to the circle, square, and triangle. After these have been well mastered you might add additional shapes: the oval, the semicircle, the rectangle, and the star. It's best to avoid complicated shapes like a seven-sided star or trapezoid altogether until your child is older.

Puzzles

Stacking and nesting toys, form boards, fitting toys, and shape sorters are all early puzzles, and your toddler's practice with them has helped strengthen her coordination and cognitive skills. Now's the time to introduce some inset and jigsaw puzzles of two to six pieces.

Simple inset puzzles are a good bridge between shape sorters and regular jigsaw-type puzzles. An inset puzzle has a few whole objects—animals, pieces of fruit, familiar vehicles—that fit into matching pre-cut spaces on a board. This type of puzzle is self-teaching. Simply hand a puzzle to your toddler, help her assemble it once or twice, then sit back and "kibbitz." She'll soon be working it with ease.

When you introduce a jigsaw puzzle you'll have to show your toddler how to assemble it very slowly. Do this with lots of explaining about what you're doing and why the pieces fit where they do. For example: "See this piece I have in my hand? It looks like a foot. Maybe it fits into this part of the puzzle. Think so? Yes, it does! It fits right here." Then let her have a hand. Help her if necessary, and give some verbal cues: "The head goes on top of the body." "I think that piece fits somewhere over here." Or hand her one piece at a time, as you did with the shapes for her shape sorter. Once your toddler has mastered a puzzle, and felt the wonderful satisfaction of her accomplishment, she'll want to repeat the experience many times.

When you go puzzle shopping you'll be dazzled by the variety available. We can't predict which ones your toddler will most enjoy, so you're on your own. However, our parent group has offered some observations that we'd like to pass along.

1. Toddlers like wooden puzzles with small knobs or handles on each piece. Handles make it easier for them to remove the pieces from the tray one at a time.

2. Look for puzzles in which each piece is identifiable when the puzzle is apart. A toddler will have a much easier time working a person puzzle if each leg piece looks like a leg rather than a misshapen blob.

3. Choose puzzles of familiar animals, familiar scenes, or people doing familiar things. Then you can also use the completed puzzles for storytelling and naming games, as you might use pictures in a book.

FACE PUZZLES

Have a photograph of your toddler's face (or other family members) blown up to 8″ x 10″ size. Glue the picture to cardboard, cover it with clear contact paper to protect it from smudges, and cut it into pieces.

MAKE A PUZZLE

Take any large, simple picture, paste or glue it to a sheet of cardboard, and cut it out with scissors or a utility knife. Homemade puzzles are a little harder to assemble than their wooden commercial counterparts because there's no pre-cut tray. So cut the picture into a few big pieces at first. When your toddler has learned to work this puzzle with ease, you can cut the large pieces into smaller ones.

BODY PUZZLES

Help your toddler learn about body parts and their relation to each other. Snap a picture of your toddler standing against a blank wall. To keep it simple, have her diaper-clad or naked. Have the picture blown up, mount it on cardboard, cover it with clear contact paper, and cut it into three main sections: head, body above the waist, and body below the waist. Later you can cut out the arms and legs.

5
Games of Hiding and Finding

By their first birthdays, babies are beginning to understand that objects which disappear aren't gone forever. This is when they begin searching for hidden toys. You probably played many games based on this principle last year: for example, hiding a toy under a blanket or slipping it into your pocketbook for your baby to recover. Well, hiding-and-finding games remain very popular during the toddler years. And now that your child is more active, you can introduce some exciting variations.

Finding the Hidden Toy

To refresh your memory—and resharpen your toddler's seeking skills—we'll start with some simple versions of hide and seek with toys.

SIMPLE SEARCHES

Hold a tantalizing toy in front of your toddler: "Oh, Craig, look at this!" When Craig reaches to take the toy, put it on the floor and cover it quickly with a towel. Say something like "Where did it go? Can you find it?" If he has trouble, remove the towel and start over, this time leaving a bit of the toy exposed as a clue. When Craig finally makes the discovery, you should exclaim over his success, of course. Next round, cover the toy completely.

When you and your toddler are sitting on the floor, show him a toy and then hide it behind your back. He'll have to crawl or walk around you to find it again.

Hide a small toy under a coffee can or other container and urge your toddler to retrieve it.

Now your toddler is ready to move on to bigger challenges. The following versions require your toddler to use coordinated handling skills to retrieve the hidden object.

PHONY BIRTHDAYS

This delightful game is offered by Brian and Shirley Sutton-Smith in their book *How to Play with Your Children (and When Not To).*

Wrap up [your child's] toys in paper and tie them lightly with string. "Here's a present." But he should see the whole process since this is a game of unwrapping, not an economical way of getting through Christmas. Mock exaggeration of gift giving is in order, as is the singing of "Happy Birthday" with pretended surprise and pleasure at the gift.

For variations on this theme, put a toy inside a large mailing envelope, or hide a toy in the toe of a large sock.

These next games involve more than one "hiding" place so they require your toddler to make decisions.

OUT OF THE FRYING PAN

Place a toy in a large, shallow frying pan and cover them both with a towel. Now tilt the pan and slide the toy onto the floor, keeping the toy hidden under the towel. Show your toddler the empty pan with "Where did your toy go? Can you find it?" If he has trouble, reveal the toy under the towel and start over.

WHICH POT?

Take two pots of different sizes with lids and, with your toddler watching, hide a toy in one of them. "Can you find it?" Chances are, this'll be pretty easy for the veteran searcher. But now make the job more difficult. Hide a toy and shuffle the pots around, as in a pea-under-the-shell game. Now can he find the toy? If he tries the wrong pan, say something like "It's not in there. Try the other one." And reward successes with "That's the right place. You found it!"

When he's good, try adding another pot of still a different size.

The "Which pot?" game uses size as a clue to the hiding place. You can also try using color.

THE TWO TOWELS

Using two towels of different colors, hide the toy under one of them. Can your toddler find it? Make the game harder by using three towels.

Peekaboo

Peekaboo games—where one participant hides his face, or even his entire body, and then reappears while saying "Peekaboo!"—are games of hiding, even though they don't include active "finding." Since most parents begin playing peekaboo during their babies' first year, you're probably quite familiar with this game by now. We mention it here just to remind you that toddlers love peekaboo, too.

Why is this game so popular with babies and toddlers alike? Many behavioral scientists believe that its popularity has some connection with separation anxiety. Both toddlers and babies go through periods in their development when they become quite anxious about being separated from their parents, even for short periods of time. As we've discussed earlier in this guide, this fear is a natural expression of the child's love for his parents and his temporary feelings of insecurity when separated from them. Perhaps acting out separation and reunion in nonthreatening peekaboo play helps babies and toddlers deal with this anxiety.

Hide and Seek

Hide-and-seek games combine the features of both "peekaboo" and finding the hidden toy. Someone is disappearing and reappearing, and someone is searching for a hidden object. And since *you* are probably your toddler's favorite object to find, these games are especially fun.

THE SECRET INTRUDER

While your toddler is amusing himself on the living room floor, sneak in and hide behind the couch or a chair. Then call out, "Oh, Jason, I'm hiding from you. I bet you can't find me." Pause a few seconds so he has a chance to look. If you remain undetected, peek out to see what's wrong. Jason may be avoiding you, or tricking you—or maybe he just doesn't want to play. But perhaps he's having a little trouble understanding the game. Duck back and call out again. And as in all hiding games, you should reward his successful search with squeals of delight and approval. "Oh, you clever child, you found me!"

CLOSET CASE

This game requires a bit more skill, because your toddler has to remove a barrier to get to you. In the bedroom (or wherever you happen to be playing) hide in a closet and partially shut the door. Then call out to your toddler, asking him to find you again. If he stalls, keep calling, or rap on the door. It may be pretty hard for your toddler to figure out where you are hiding. When he opens the door—he wins! Clever sleuth!

DOUBLE DETECTIVES

Have one parent go into another room and hide. Then while he or she calls to be sought, you and your toddler join forces to discover the hiding place. We recommend this sort of double-detective work in the beginning, while your toddler is still learning the techniques of search. When these have been well mastered, try letting him seek alone.

THE MISSING CHUMS

Another family game, but this time the toddler and one parent hide together for the other parent to find. Try hiding behind an open door, or maybe under the bed, or behind a tree if you're outdoors. It's better for two to hide together, because your toddler might be a bit apprehensive about hiding alone, especially if the secret spot is dark. Enhance this game with lots of giggling and whispering and "Daddy will *never* find us here, will he?"

ROLE REVERSAL

Once your toddler is good at these games, he may like to "hide" alone. He'll initiate the game by ducking from your sight. But he usually won't even wait to be sought. As soon as you call, "Where's John?" he'll probably come running back with a delighted grin on his face. This game isn't really hide and seek, because there's no seeking. It's more a game of entrances, like appearing on a stage. But even so, this version is lots of fun for toddlers—and parents, too.

6
Play with Water, Sand, and Artsy Materials

The beauty of "raw" materials—water, sand, mud, dough, and art supplies—lies in their versatility. There's no wrong way to play with them (except, maybe, eating or throwing them), and no single right way, either. Anything goes. So raw materials offer a nice counterbalance to the more structural commercial toys. And they have terrific play and learning value. They engage a toddler's imagination, and, with all their different consistencies and colors and textures and potential uses, they involve her with the world.

Sand is hard and grainy when dry, crumbly feeling when damp. Fingerpaints and mud are deliciously slimy. Different papers have different weights and surfaces. Water feels like—well, water. Scooping and pouring water, digging in sand and dirt, squishing play dough, crumpling paper, smearing fingerpaints, scribbling with a crayon—these and other explorations all help a child coordinate arm-hand-finger skills. And playing with these unstructured, responsive materials also helps a feisty toddler work off some energy and aggression.

Free play with these materials is also important in another way. Many toddlers love to mess. But all too often they choose substances their parents don't approve of. How many times have you said, "Please keep your fingers out of the applesauce," or "I wish you'd leave that tissue box alone," or "Don't play with your dirty diaper!" Play with water, sand, mud, and art supplies can help satisfy your toddler's natural urge to slop.

Exploring the Basics
Almost every toddler we know really loves playing with natural materials. Your job is to set up play opportunities, provide the props, offer occasional encouragement, and join in when you can.

WATER PLAY

Few activities can equal the value of water play. It provides opportunities for—

    practicing arm and hand skills: scooping, splashing, filling and dumping.
    strengthening eye-hand coordination: pouring from one container to another, catching falling water, grasping objects as they bobble and float.

    learning scientific concepts: what floats? what sinks? what happens when you pour water over a paddle-wheel? when you pour water over sand?
    learning new words (when parents participate): *empty, full, hot, cold, wet, dry,* and so forth.
    imitating things that parents do: washing dishes or a doll baby.

That's the news for parents. From your toddler's point of view, water play is *fun!*

Water Play Outdoors
Playing in a wading pool on a warm day is bliss, so by all means try to get one. The molded plastic ones are usually more durable than the inflatable ones, which inevitably sprout leaks. If you don't have a wading pool, use a large washtub. (And for safety's sake, be sure you empty the pool or tub after each play session.)

Fill the pool with a few inches of water, give your toddler some appropriate toys, and stay close by to make sure everything is O.K. Toys you might provide include tea strainers, empty squeeze bottles, plastic cups, a piece of rubber hose (if your toddler knows the difference between blowing and sipping), boats, funnels, balls, commercial floating toys, and (a special favorite) a plant sprayer. In short, almost anything that water can't ruin. Or for a special treat, give your toddler some water toys you've made yourself. (You might also try these in the bathtub.)

ICEBERGS

Fill large freezer containers or empty milk cartons with water, add some food coloring (so the bergs will be visible when floating in the pool), and freeze. Remove the icebergs by running hot water over the containers.

ICEBALLS

Put about ten drops of food coloring into an empty balloon. Then fill the balloon with water and place it in your freezer, in a pan (in case it bursts while freezing). When the water is frozen, puncture the ballon and peel it off. Iceballs are especially nice because they look like big balls—but are heavy and so c-o-o-l to the touch!

TUBULAR BOAT

Inflate an inner tube (either a real one or a plastic beach type) and wedge a large rubber dishpan into the hole. This makes a terrific little boat for your toddler to ride in, to push around, or to fill with other toys.

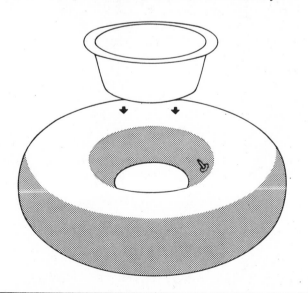

Outdoor water play needn't be confined to pools and tubs. For a different kind of fun, let your toddler run around in the sprinkler, play with a hose, or help you wash the car.

Water Play Indoors

Bathtime is an excellent opportunity for water play. When your toddler loses interest in her regular water toys, give her a dolly to wash. Or maybe a terry-cloth hand puppet, which she can use for washing herself (if you'll soap it up for her) as well as for playing with. Keep these and your toddler's other favorite bath toys in a mesh drawstring bag, which you can hang over the shower head. It will always be within your easy reach but out of the way, and the toys will be able to drip-dry between playtimes. Or if you don't have a bag, keep a plastic wastebasket for toys in the bathroom.

If your toddler loves playing in the bathtub, you don't need to limit this to bathtime. Let her enjoy some tub play anytime you have to be in the bathroom for more than a few minutes: to dry and set your hair, clean bathroom fixtures, or wash delicate clothes in the sink.

When it's too chilly for your toddler to actually sit in water, you can always give her a container of water and some toys. This sort of play is less convenient for parents than many other indoor activities because it can get messy, and you have to provide close supervision. But water play is so much fun, and so rewarding, it's worth the extra trouble. You can minimize the hassles by planning water-play sessions around your own activities and preparing for the mess. For example:

When you clean the bathroom, sit your toddler in a dry tub or shower stall with a pan of water and appropriate toys. A rubber dishpan or her old baby bath will work fine. And her inevitable splashings will be well confined.

When you take a bath, let your toddler play with a pan of water and some toys on the bathroom floor. You can keep a close eye on her, and you'll feel less annoyed about mopping up afterward, since your own post-bath drippings will have contributed to the mess.

Since you spend lots of time in the kitchen, the kitchen floor is another good place for water play. Spread newspaper under the pan of water to absorb most spills; any far-flung puddles can be mopped up easily.

Most toddlers we know love water play in the kitchen sink. It's very adult: parents do it. But it can be unsafe. Your toddler might slip off the chair she's standing on, or turn on the hot water. So save this kind of play for times when you're going to be stationed at a nearby counter or standing at the sink right beside your child, washing food or dishes. Or if you have the time, join in.

Here's a special type of sink play most toddlers we know absolutely love: run a few inches of water in the sink, add a squirt of dishwashing soap, and show your toddler how to whip up bubbles with an eggbeater. If she knows the difference between sipping and blowing, you can also give her a piece of rubber tubing or a long straw to blow bubbles with in the sink.

A Safety Reminder: Always, and we mean always, stay close when your toddler plays in or around water. The chance of drowning is very real.

SAND PLAY

Sand is just bursting with play opportunities. Like water, it can be scooped and poured. But it's also different. When dribbled, it makes interesting patterns. It's good for digging in, drawing in, and hiding toys in. When damp, it becomes doughlike and holds its shape. A magical substance, actually: a solid that's not really solid, a wet material that's not really liquid.

Good sand toys include cups for scooping and pouring, a serving spoon or plastic shovel for digging, a toy drumstick or cooking spoon for drawing, a funnel, a strainer, a sifter, a bucket, and (for an older toddler) a play vehicle like a dump truck.

If you live near a beach or a sandbox-equipped playground, you're lucky. If, like most of us, you're not so conveniently located, consider a backyard sandbox. Any fairly large, shallow container, with holes in the bottom for water drainage, works fine. Buy one ready-made, build one out of lumber, or use a molded plastic wading pool. Fill your box with builder's sand, which is available at hardware and building-supply stores.

Sandboxes pose a cleanliness problem. Ideally, a sandbox should be covered when it's not in use, since an open pit is likely to be used by neighborhood cats as a litter box. You'll be hard pressed to keep a public sandbox covered, so if you take your toddler to one of these, try to sift through the sand before she plays in it. If you have a backyard sandbox, be sure to make a cover for it. This can be as simple as an old plastic tablecloth, weighted on the corners, or as sturdy as a plywood lid. Or for a rather intriguing play set that solves the cover problem, make a "Giant Surf 'N Turf Play Clam."

THE GIANT SURF 'N' TURF PLAY CLAM

The Play Clam is essentially two identical plastic wading pools attached together. One is used as a sand-box, the other as a wading pool. When the pool is empty, it doubles as a sandbox cover.

You need

two identical plastic wading pools
two old cloth belts with double-loop fasteners. (You can make these yourself with materials from a fabric store)
a sharp knife
a drill, or a hammer and a very large nail

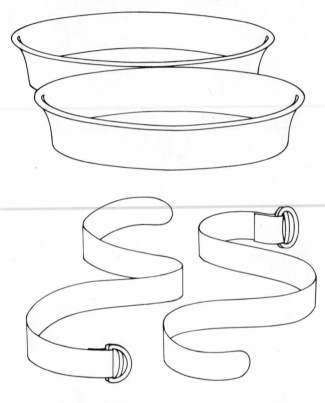

1. Drill about five small drainage holes in the bottom of one pool (the sandbox).
2. In the lip of each pool, cut a slit large enough to accommodate a belt.

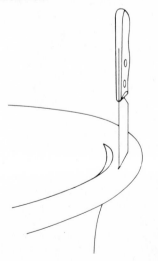

3. Strap the two pools together with one of the belts.

4. Then turn one pool on top of the other and cut additional slits (for the second belt) on the side opposite the first two. By belting both sides, you'll be able to keep the clam tightly closed when it's not being used.

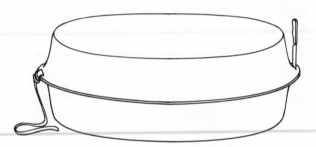

5. Open the clam, and fill one side with sand permanently. This is the Turf. When your toddler wants to play in the Surf as well, fill the other side with water.

We recommend using belt straps rather than rope because they're easier to remove when you open the clam. Also, an adjustable belt strap can be easily loosened when you want to empty the pool.

A Safety Reminder: Like water play, sand play has some inherent hazards. Always supervise sand play for a child under eighteen months old. She could choke from eating it. And teach your toddler not to throw sand. It could get in her eyes or yours or, in a public playground, in another child's.

DIRT AND MUD PLAY

Just plain old dirt is another natural material most toddlers enjoy. You can surely find a patch of bare dirt somewhere. A spoon or plastic shovel for digging, and maybe a sticklike object for drawing, are probably all your toddler will need.

Of course, wet dirt makes mud, which is a delightful material for toddlers who love to mess. That is, if you can stand the mess. Give your toddler a spoon and a few scoops or cups, and let her go to it. For easy cleanups on warm days, you can wash your toddler outside under a hose, or splash water over her from a bucket.

Play "Clay"

Play "clay" goes mud two better. It's cleaner (a plus for you), and it holds a shape until your toddler changes it. Change it she will, too: by squishing, rolling, pounding, kneading, and squeezing it between her fingers. To keep these play sessions fairly neat, cover the floor or

table with a plastic cloth or newspaper and, if possible, provide a wooden board for working on.

Here's a recipe for homemade "clay." It's edible (though not very tasty), clean, and keeps for weeks in the refrigerator when stored in a plastic bag.

You need

    2 cups flour
    ¾ to 1 cup salt
    1 tablespoon salad or cooking oil
    ½ cup water
    Food coloring

Mix water and oil in a cup; mix flour and salt together in a bowl. Slowly add liquid to solid, working the mixture with your hands until it's smooth. Add a little more water if necessary. And color with food coloring.

Play "clay," unlike mud (unless you like sitting in mud pits), is something *you* can have fun playing with, too. Your toddler will love having you involved.

PAPER PLAY

Paper is cheap, easily available, fairly neat, and very exciting to toddlers. Squeeze it and it makes noise (and different kinds make different noises). Crumple it and it retains a shape (a ball, a snake). Toss it and it sails away (without breaking anything). So keep on hand an assortment of scrap papers, all different sizes and textures and weights:

    pages from old magazines
    discarded telephone books
    waxed paper
    newspaper
    tissue from clothing boxes
    mail advertisements
    old catalogues
    grocery bags
    wrapping paper

Toddlers enjoy paper play almost anytime, but especially when it fits in with something you are doing. For example, when you must sit at your desk to sort mail or pay bills, give your toddler your junk mail to play with on the floor. When you're working in the kitchen, give her paper towels or waxed paper or grocery bags. When you're reading the newspaper in the evening, give your toddler sections you've finished. Newspaper play can get messy, though, since the ink rubs off, so when you do this be prepared for after-play cleanups.

Paper play, like most kinds of play, is more fun for your toddler when you join in. The two of you can talk about the different colors, crumple paper together, throw paper balls at each other. You might even show your toddler how to stuff envelopes. For really spirited play, make a Newspaper Wallow. (Hint: plan this as a prebath game.)

THE NEWSPAPER WALLOW

Crumple up a sheet of newspaper, toss it at your toddler, crumple another, toss it, and keep crumpling and tossing until your toddler's surrounded by a veritable sea of paper boulders. Then let her wallow away. When she tires, scoop her up for a washing spree.

A Safety Reminder: Since paper is easily torn, and some toddlers try to eat it, be sure to supervise your toddler's paper play.

ARTSY PLAY

Artistic activities for toddlers aren't quite as grandiose as the name might imply. Frankly, toddlers aren't skillful enough, artistic enough, or really mature enough to consciously produce works of art. They're far more concerned with the process, not the final product; with the scribbling and painting, not the resulting picture. But that's not to say artistic activities are worthless. As long as you don't look for masterpieces, and don't give your child the idea that you expect her to produce something specific, like a picture of a flower, artistic activities can be a lot of fun.

Because most artsy play requires a certain amount of concentration and an understanding of basic rules if things are to be kept reasonably neat, we recommend that you not introduce these activities before your child is about eighteen months old. Even when you're sure your child is old enough, it's a good idea to keep art supplies handy and easy to use, so playing with them doesn't have to be a big deal for either you or your toddler. It isn't likely that any art project will keep her enthralled for long. She'll probably just enjoy dabbling with paint or crayons before going off to play with some other toys. So be casual about this type of play.

Getting Started

Artsy activities usually go best when your toddler is comfortably seated. Have your toddler sit on the floor, or use

- a toddler-size table and chair set
- a high chair with tray attached
- a high chair (with tray removed), which has been pulled up to the kitchen or dining table

These last two options have the advantage of keeping your toddler somewhat confined. Not that you want to force her to sit still; that never works. But many toddlers need a little help concentrating, and being confined in a familiar place can work wonders. Naturally, your toddler should be allowed to get down when she signals that artsy time is over, no matter how soon after starting this may be.

Protect the tabletop with an old tablecloth, preferably

plastic. Toddlers aren't known for neatness. In fact, when bringing out the paints, you might want to protect the surrounding floor as well, and even protect your toddler's clothes. You can make a fine smock by buttoning your child backward into one of your old short-sleeve shirts.

The first few times you bring out a material, help attract your toddler's interest by taking part yourself. For example, when introducing crayons, draw a scribble and then ask, "Can you do that, too?" When you have the time, sit down beside your toddler and draw something yourself while she experiments. Or paint alongside with your own brush when she paints. And keep up a lively conversation about what you're both doing.

Crayons
The toddler needs jumbo crayons, about a half inch in diameter, because she grasps them in her fist like a drumstick. Look for the nonrolling type—they're more likely to remain in reach. Any large pad or sheets of paper will do. To keep single sheets of paper stationary, you can tape them to the high-chair tray or table covering.

Toddlers often do more with crayons than scribble: they slide them in and out of the box, peel them, drop them on the floor, try to taste them, and no doubt break them in half. Be sure you supply only nontoxic crayons, and start immediately teaching your child not to eat them. Just remove the crayon each time she puts it in her mouth and say, "Crayons are for drawing with, not for eating." After a few warnings she'll get the idea.

When crayons become a regular fact of life, your toddler will often draw quite happily alone while you go about your business. Just stay nearby to make sure she's not inspired to redecorate your walls. When you have time to color with your child, though, she'll have even more fun. Many parents in our group reported that their toddlers loved watching them draw things, even if the parent wasn't terribly talented. One mother would draw an object and ask her toddler to guess what it was. Another mother took her cues from the child, and drew his requests. Sometimes these toddlers enjoyed "coloring in" the drawn figures as if they were pages in a coloring book. And along the way, the children learned a number of new words.

Pencils and Pads
Pencils are like crayons, but more convenient to carry about and less likely to mar inappropriate surfaces. Keep a pad and pencils in your purse for emergency writing fests in the doctor's office, train station, or wherever you might have to wait with your toddler. Because pencils are sharp, this play must be closely supervised.

Chalk
A nice, clean, easily removed scribbling medium. A small blackboard slate with colored chalks can keep a child occupied for a long time.

Felt-Tipped Markers
These have it all over crayons and pencils: they're easier to manipulate and make far more brilliant scribbles. On the negative side, they stain. When you provide felt-tipped markers, also provide large, large sheets of paper taped over a protective table covering. And in case accidents happen, be sure you choose water colors rather than permanent markers. You should probably avoid felt-tipped markers altogether if your toddler tends to chew her art supplies (unless you fancy colored lips).

Fingerpaints

These are traditional first paints, because they feel so delightful and are so direct. No tool comes between the substance and the hands—or more correctly, the hands, fingers, wrists, and forearms; your toddler will use them all when fingerpainting. Fingerpainting is messy, so you might prefer saving it for outdoors. Or protect your indoor table well. Or have your toddler fingerpaint in a dry bathtub.

Before rushing out to buy fingerpaints at a store, why not make sure your toddler enjoys fingerpainting? Let her start with some homemade fakes.

FAKE FINGERPAINTS

Here are four "recipes" to choose from. The first two are easy to wipe up, the third is edible, and the fourth requires no preparation. Have your toddler do her fake fingerpainting on the high-chair tray or tabletop itself, a cookie sheet, a plastic tablecloth, or any surface that rinses or sponges clean.

1. Beat some soap flakes (not powdered detergent) with a little water until the mixture becomes thick and gooey. If you like, add some food coloring.
2. Mix 1 cup flour, 4 tablespoons salt, ⅞ cup cold water, and a little food coloring. This mixture makes a nice gloppy paste.
3. Mix a package of instant pudding according to package directions.
4. Give your toddler a few globs of aerosol shaving cream.

If your toddler enjoys messing with any or all of these ersatz paints, chances are she's ready for the real thing. Real fingerpaint pictures can be hung around the house as decorations when dry. And some of your toddler's productions will be quite beautiful.

REAL FINGERPAINTS

Fingerpaints are usually sold in toy and hobby stores, or you can make your own. Be sure fingerpaints you buy are marked "nontoxic"; and for an extra safety measure—as well as to prevent accidental redecoration of your walls and floors—be sure you always supervise your toddler's fingerpainting sessions. Here's a recipe for a homemade version:

> In a heavy pan, combine 2 heaping tablespoons of cornstarch with ½ cup of cold water, and stir the mixture until it's smooth. Then add another 2 cups of cold water, and bring everything to a boil, stirring frequently. Now beat in 1 tablespoon of soap flakes. When the mixture has cooled, add food coloring.

Any glossy type of paper is good for fingerpainting: shiny shelf paper, gift wrap, or special fingerpaint paper sold in stores. Dampen the paper with a wet sponge, add a glop of paint, and show your toddler how to smear it around. Who knows? You might enjoy fingerpainting, too.

Paints

Fingerpainting is wonderfully sloppy and allows a toddler to practice many arm and hand skills, but it's limited in scope. Around twenty-four months or so, your child may be ready for a new challenge: painting with a brush. The best paints are poster paints and powdered tempera. These come in exciting colors and are very easy to spread. Supply brushes with thick handles and bristles about an inch across. And try to have one brush for each color of paint, to prevent messy mixing in the jars.

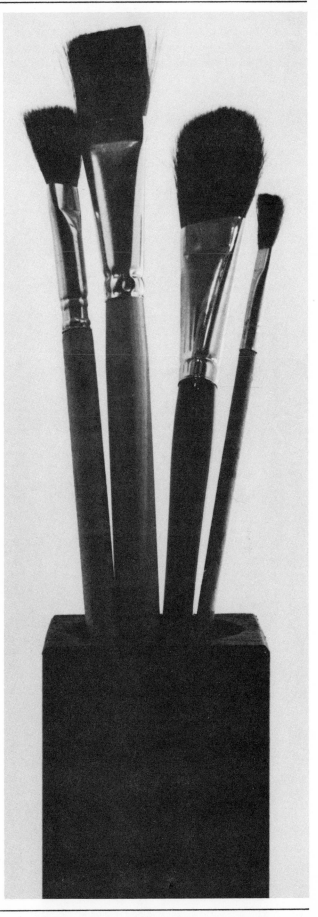

Brush painting can be done on a table or floor, but the ideal place is an easel. Set this up over a large drop cloth (to protect the floor) or outdoors on a warm day. Then hang a large piece of newsprint (or even newspaper, in a pinch), cloak your toddler in a smock, and help her get started. Make the first lines yourself, and talk about the color you use or the shape you make. This will probably pique her interest. Don't expect more from her than splotches and scribbles. She's just experimenting with color and arm movements. In a year or two these early experiments will take recognizable shapes.

A final note about poster paints: Many older toddlers love painting with brushes but others couldn't be bothered. If you've eagerly assembled all the painting paraphernalia and your toddler ignores it, just put it away for a while. For that matter, many parents don't enjoy this activity, either. It's so messy! Can you stand the possible spills and splatters? If you *do* mind, hold off until your toddler's older and better coordinated. Painting won't be much fun for her if you're constantly saying, "Be very careful," or "Make sure you don't drip anything." Your toddler will have plenty of opportunities to experiment with poster paints when she goes to a play group or nursery school.

Some Unusual Artsy Activities

If your toddler seems to enjoy quiet artsy play, and you both have a taste for experiment, try adding some new experiences to your regular art projects.

1. *Squeeze Bag Art.* A novel art medium in its own right, and a terrific alternative to fingerpainting for the finicky toddler who hates to get her hands dirty. Take a clear food-storage bag (the self-locking kind is especially good) and put a few tablespoons of fingerpaint inside. Smooth the bag evenly with your fingers until the paint covers the inside with a solid film. If necessary, use more paint. Then gently press most of the air out of the bag, and lock it closed with cellophane tape. You might also reinforce the other three edges with a layer of tape. Lay the finished squeeze bag on a flat surface and show your toddler how to draw on it with her finger. Or let her squeeze it in her hands to make interesting patterns. To smooth the paint for renewed drawing, place the bag on a flat surface and lightly rub your hand across it.

2. *Sponge Painting.* Instead of a brush, give your toddler a small piece of sponge to use with her paints. Make sure she doesn't chew it!

3. *House Painting.* A good activity for hot days. Give your toddler a big paintbrush and a bucket of water, and get her started "painting" your house or porch or driveway.

6. *Deodorant Bottle Pens.* Pry the top off a roll-on-type deodorant bottle and rinse both parts thoroughly. Then fill the jar with thinned fingerpaint or poster paint and replace the top. The result? A giant colorful ball-point pen for rolling over paper!

4. *Simple Collage.* Most toddlers aren't into cutting and pasting. But they do like to stick things on paper. Good things to stick include: wildlife stickers and Christmas seals that come in the mail (teach your toddler how to lick these or dampen them on a wet sponge), bits of colored tape, self-adhesive dots and labels from the stationery store.

5. *Paint-with-Water books.* These are special coloring-type books, sold in most drug and toy stores, which have paint printed directly into dots on the page. When your toddler brushes a picture with water, the paint magically appears. It's mysterious! And so easy.

7
Explorations with the Five Senses

From the time you're born, you use your senses—seeing, hearing, smelling, tasting, and touching—to learn about the qualities of different objects. Through your senses you learn that objects come in different shapes and sizes and colors; that objects are hard or soft, smooth or scratchy or rubbery; that objects have different smells and tastes and make different sounds. Our senses help us learn more about each thing we encounter, and to distinguish among all the different things; thus they help us learn about our world.

The games in this chapter concentrate on exploring with the five senses. Actually, your toddler is exploring with his senses every waking moment. He sees and hears and touches things all day long; he tastes things right and left (sometimes you wish he wouldn't); and he's always surrounded by odors. But often these sensory experiences escape his notice because they're part of larger schemes. Take eating. Eating involves more than smelling and tasting foods. If you're a toddler, it probably involves sitting in a special chair, sharing time with your parents, maybe holding a spoon, trying to guide a spoonful of food toward your mouth, and finally getting a bit of tasty stuff inside your lips. There are so many sensory experiences going on at once! The activities we present here will help your toddler become more aware of each sense separately, and how each sense helps him learn different things about objects. And then, more alert to all the impressions his senses receive, he can become more fully responsive to the richness of the world around him.

Look at That!
We rely primarily on our sense of sight, because visually we can explore things far beyond our reach. And there's always so much to see! The main point of this seeing game is to cut down on visual alternatives—not by removing distractions but by directing your toddler's attention to specific objects. Because this game requires little more than your attention to detail and your willingness to talk, it's great to play anywhere.

Wherever you and your toddler happen to be, talk about the things that surround you. Give more than just names; talk about the shapes and colors and sizes. This is a time to flex your own brain and sling around adjectives. The more you embellish an object with words, the more importance it takes on.

For example:

You and your toddler are sitting together on the living-room sofa, fresh from a game of hide and seek and resting to catch your breath. What are some things you can talk about? Things on the coffee table. "Look, Jeremy, see all those things on the coffee table. What do you see? I see a silver bowl. See that? A silver bowl and it's round on the top and filled with dozens of beautiful seashells. It's right there in the middle. And look what's next to it; that's a book. It's square and has a very pretty picture of a princess on it, and some words that tell us the book's name. The words say 'Italian Fairy Tales,' and it's one of my favorite books. And see over in that corner? That's a picture of you, taken when you were just a few hours old. I love that picture, and I love that gorgeous gold frame around it, and one reason I love it is because it's a picture of you, and I love you."

Or look around the room. There are pictures on the walls, and maybe a fly, a tiny fly walking along the ceiling, and pieces of furniture, each with a different shape and color, and doors that lead to other rooms. Talk about these, and ask your toddler to point to things as you describe them, and maybe to repeat names after you say them.

A favorite place to look is out the window. Suppose you live in an urban high rise. As you look out the window with your toddler, talk about the smokestacks and church spires and other verticals that pierce the sky. In a suburban neighborhood talk about the cars you can see, or animals, or flowers on the lawn across the street, or people you see walking by.

Wherever you're stuck waiting with your toddler—a doctor's office, for instance—talk about things you see. This game might interest your toddler enough to keep him from fussing. And you don't have to be sitting in one place to play. Carry your toddler around so he can see things up close. When you're riding in the car, talk about the scenery you pass. You'll not only sharpen your toddler's awareness, you'll also help him learn more names of things.

Paying Attention to Sounds

We're constantly surrounded by sounds—so many, in fact, that we often take them for granted and tune out all but the most prominent. So whenever you have the time, draw your toddler's attention to sounds. In your home, you can probably hear appliances, clocks, the television or radio in the next room, and maybe footsteps in the apartment above. Outdoors there are the sounds of traffic, airplanes (a favorite), dogs barking, other people talking—just listen. You'll hear all kinds of things. The following games will give you some more specific pointers.

LISTEN TO THIS

Help your toddler distinguish among the different sounds different objects make by holding sound-making objects up to his ear. You might use a ticking watch, a small music box, a transistor radio turned low, a large seashell at the ocean, a piece of paper when you squeeze it. Or let him press his ear against your chest or stomach to hear body noises (a source of great fascination). Talk about each object and the noise it makes. "This is a watch, and it goes tick, tick, tick, tick. Can you hear my heart beat? It goes something like lub-dub, lub-dub."

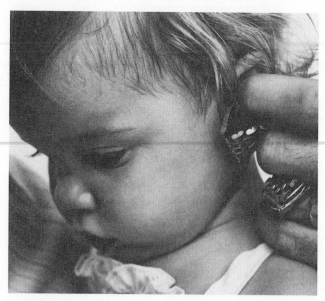

WHAT ARE WE LISTENING TO?

Here's a good game to play when you want to sit quietly for a few minutes. Be very still, shut your eyes (and ask your toddler to shut his), and just listen. Periodically break the silence to talk about the things you hear. Start with the easy things. "Shhhhh. Be very quiet. What can you hear? Hear that? That was an airplane going overhead. (If you like, ask your child to repeat the name of the object after you say it.) Now what do you hear? I hear a truck rumbling by. Anything else? I think I hear a bird singing to us. Now I hear a dog barking."

If your toddler seems to enjoy this game, add some less familiar sounds to your listening play: the humming of the refrigerator, the air conditioner going on and off, the television blaring in the next apartment, the tiny sounds of voices from the street. Just listen, and you'll discover many sounds you probably haven't noticed before.

SOUND TOURS

When your toddler is too restless to sit still, try sound tours of your house. Pick any room, and make familiar sounds for him to listen to. In the bathroom, turn on the tap or a hairdrier or flush the toilet. In the kitchen switch on the mixer, open a drawer, or drop a spoon. In other rooms flick on a light switch or turn on the vacuum cleaner. An older, more talkative toddler might like to try shutting his eyes and guessing the source of the sound, but don't press this. The purpose of this game is to make your child aware of the sounds, not really to figure out what makes them.

For a variation on this game, pick one room for a sound tour and instead of having your older toddler shut his eyes, let him wear a blindfold. Then make a familiar sound, pause so he can distinctly hear it without distraction, and go on to another. But a note of caution. Blindfolds are fun for some older toddlers, but frightening to others. If this game appeals to you, try it, but give up easily if your child balks.

The World of Odors
Give your toddler's nose an education. Whenever you're in a garden, help him smell the flowers, or crush some fragrant herbs or leaves in your palm and let him smell these. At the market, lift him up so he can sniff the fresh fruits and vegetables. When you're preparing a recipe, pause to let your toddler smell spices like vanilla and bay leaves, or ingredients like mustard. If he likes to join you in your morning washup, introduce him to the smells of soap and colognes and after-shaves and other body anointments. For added adventure, you might like to counterbalance all these wonderful smells with some less pleasant: garlic, onion, smelly cheeses, and the like. Surprisingly, though, your young toddler may not react negatively (as you might) to these more pungent odors. There is growing evidence that many children under the age of two don't respond negatively to noxious smells, and that these reactions begin with toilet training.

One word of caution: you should avoid having your toddler sniff jars of crushed spices unless you're very careful. He might accidentally inhale some of the fine particles.

INDOOR SNIFF-IT GAME

Here's a safe way to introduce your toddler to many different smells at one sitting. Take a number of cotton balls, sprinkle each with a different aromatic liquid, and hold them under his nose one at a time while you talk about odors. Good liquids to use are: vanilla and lemon extracts, onion juice, different colognes, vinegar, lime juice, and other fruit juices. Just make sure your toddler doesn't *eat* these yummy smelling puffs.

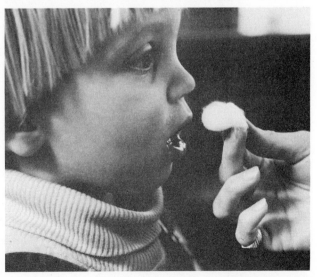

Games of Good Taste

As we mentioned in the introduction to this chapter, your toddler will try to taste almost anything. There are probably lots of times when you have to discourage his tasting explorations because they involve unsuitable substances. Here we recommend that you encourage your toddler to explore the world of tastes, by giving him a variety of interesting and appropriate foodstuffs.

SMORGASBORD LUNCH

This tasting game is probably the most fun of all sensory activities. And it's a good way to introduce your toddler to different foods. You can use this game in lieu of your toddler's regular lunch some day when you feel like a change and have enough time to talk to him about the different foods he will be eating.

Prepare a plate of small portions of four or five different foods and set this on your child's feeding tray. Include such things as:

> a bit of applesauce seasoned with cinnamon
> slices of raw vegetables (try new ones like broccoli, zucchini, and radishes)
> a slice of lemon
> a dab of peanut butter
> a hunk of banana
> some new kinds of crackers
> cottage cheese
> any teeny bits of leftovers

As your toddler eats each food, talk about the different tastes (sweet? hot? salty?) and textures (crunchy? creamy? squishy?) he's encountering.

If your toddler drinks well from a cup, and you feel like being extra creative, you can add a variety of different drinks to this smorgasbord.

Games of Touching

As you well know, your toddler loves to touch things. In fact, at times it's almost impossible to stop him! You can help him become more aware of his sense of touch by drawing his attention to the textures of things he handles. You needn't do this in a formal way. Rather, sometimes when the two of you are sitting and your toddler's exploring your body, talk about the softness and dampness of your lips, the scratchiness of your beard, the hardness of your teeth, the sharpness of your fingernails. When he's playing in the kitchen while you cook or wash or whatever, talk about the objects he's handling, or hand him new ones with interesting textures, like a pot scrubber or a melon rind. Make him more aware of the things he touches by using detailed descriptions to focus his attention on their specific characteristics.

TOUCH TOUR

You can also take your toddler on touch tours, both of your home and of the outside world. Carry him around the house, stopping frequently to let him handle things normally out of reach: carvings on the banister post, wall hangings, knicknacks on shelves and dressers, and so forth. Because you're with him, you can let him touch even delicate and breakable things that he would never get a chance to feel otherwise. Outside, lift him up to reach leaves, the doorbell, brickwork on buildings.

blank book from pieces of thick paper (staple these together, or punch holes in one margin and fasten the pages with yarn), and glue different-textured materials onto the pages.

Include:

> fabric swatches (from the ragbag or remnant store):
> cotton, burlap, corduroy, velvet, dotted swiss, denim, wool, terrycloth
> pieces of sandpaper
> cotton balls
> wooden popsicle sticks
> wallpaper samples
> old greeting cards with embossed surfaces or glitter

FEELIE BOX

This activity differs from other touching games because in this one your toddler can't see what he touches. He explores with his fingers alone.

Cut a round hole, big enough for your toddler's hand to fit through easily, in the end of a shoe box. Then drop two or three small textured objects inside and ask your child to reach in the hole, feel an object, and pull it out. Use things like a piece of sponge, a rubber ball, a small doll or toy animal. When your toddler pulls something out, tell him what it is and talk about how it feels. Use your imagination; there are lots of things that could fit inside, and lots of ways to describe them.

When your child nears the end of his toddlerhood, he might be able to guess what an object is just from feeling it. So try using things with which he's very familiar, and ask him to name the object before pulling it out. You'll probably find, as we did, that this Feelie Box gets a lot of use. In addition to reaching inside to touch things and pull them out through the hole, your toddler will most likely stuff things back inside, remove the lid to play fill-and-dump games with the contents, and even use the holes as tunnels to push small cars through.

Or don't bother to carry him. Walk with him, and invite him to trail his fingers along tree trunks, sign posts, step railings, even the pavement. Pause to touch the same things and tell him what you feel.

TOUCH-ME BOOK

To introduce your toddler to a variety of textures in one place, make a "Touch-Me Book." Make a regular

8
Pictures, Books, and Stories

Almost all toddlers love books. They love to hold them, riffle through pages, look at pictures, point to familiar objects, try to say names, imitate the sounds of pictured animals, and, yes, some even enjoy listening to stories. There are two kinds of book play with toddlers: active games, and quiet listening. Each has a special place in your toddler's world.

Books and Active Play
Active play with books means playing games with pictures, so choose books with large, colorful illustrations and little or no text. Simple pictures showing just a few familiar objects—toys, eating utensils like cups and spoons, clothing, vehicles, and animals—rank high for younger toddlers; slightly more complicated pictures depicting scenes tend to interest older ones.

Before we suggest some appropriate active games, we'd like to add a word of advice that comes from our research with parents. Book play, these parents caution, is like most other types of play: your toddler pays attention for a few minutes, then toddles off in search of some new interest. So don't pressure her to sit and look at picture books with you any longer than she feels like it. If your toddler's not in a receptive mood, she won't get anything out of the activities anyway.

Toddlers often initiate active book play. They choose the appropriate times—by bringing a book to you—and start many of the games. So keep your toddler's books within her reach, and do try to enter in when she requests playtime with you if you're not horribly busy. Chances are it'll only last for a few minutes anyway, and then, satisfied, she'll leave you alone for a while.

Picture Talks
Talking about pictures is the most commonly enjoyed kind of active book play. It helps your toddler to concentrate on something for a moment and also helps her learn to connect words with objects. When you talk about a pictured object, you should point to it, even tap on it. Trace its outline as you repeat the name in a number of sentences. For example: "Look, Jill, here's a cat. Do you see the cat? He's a big, white cat. He's like our cat, Hercules. See? The cat has whiskers" (*point*) "and a tail" (*point*) "and do you know what the cat says? The cat says 'Meow.' Can you point to the cat? Can you 'meow' like a cat? That's right! Ter-

rific!" If Jill's interest is still high, make up a brief tale about the cat: what he likes to eat, what he's doing in the picture, or whatever.

Sometimes your toddler will be the first to point. Pick up on her cues and supply information as before. You should also be alert to your toddler's other cues. For example, suppose she waves at a person in the book. Step in and say something like "Are you waving bye-bye to the man? Is the man going bye-bye?" You can also encourage your toddler to repeat the name of the pictured object. "Can you say 'cat'?" Older toddlers are especially good at this.

SILLY SOUNDS
When you look at animal picture books with your toddler, make the appropriate sounds as you point to a picture. Ask your toddler, "Can you be a cow, too?" Once your toddler knows the sounds pretty well, you can skip your part. Just point to an animal and say, "What does a dog say?" This game can also be played with pictures of vehicles. Cars and trucks have rumbling sounds, a train *toots* or *choo-choos,* and an airplane *whooshes.*

From Page to Page

Take a story that has a recurring character, especially an animal. Then on every page, ask your toddler to find this character. Don't even bother with the other parts of the picture, just seek the hero. This is a good game for older toddlers.

Hidden Pictures

This is a good game to play with familiar books that show more than one object per page. Open to any page (your toddler may already have done this) and say, "I see a mouse" (or whatever) "on this page." Then, with great drama, walk your fingers around the page until they land upon the mouse and say, "Here it is!" Remove your hand and start over, only this time let your toddler find the hidden picture. With very familiar books, you can eliminate the finger exercise and encourage your toddler to search for an object right away.

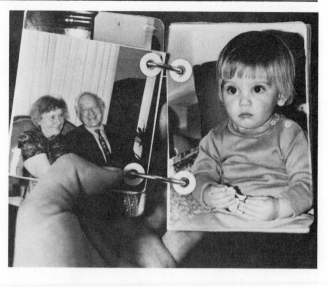

Homemade Action Books

Good picture books are hard to find, and building up a collection of them can run into some cash. So add to your toddler's commercial library with homemade books.

Books are easy to make: remember, they're only separate pages of pictures bound along one margin. For the pages, use thick paper or sheets of shirt cardboard onto which you can glue pictures cut from magazines. When you're ready for binding, punch holes in the margins and "sew" your pages together with yarn. Or use metal rings (available at stationery stores) to hold the pages together. Or use a blank photograph album as your basic book and fill the pages with photos, drawings, postcards, and pictures cut from magazines. You might want to organize your picture book around some of the following themes:

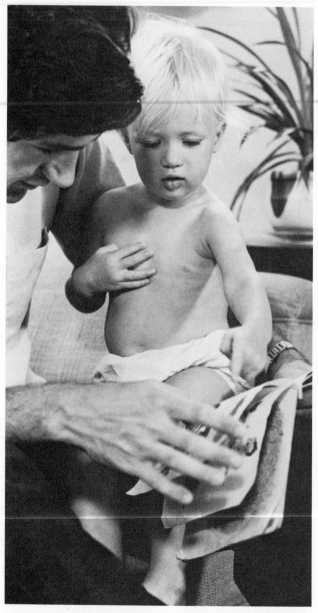

My Favorite Things

Make a book with pictures of your toddler's favorite things: toys, eating utensils, favorite foods, articles of clothing, pictures of your family and pet, a picture of your house. Let your toddler help you choose which pictures she wants to include.

Greeting-Card Book

Make a book of old Christmas and greeting cards. These have lots of colorful pictures, plus extras like glitter, embossed fronts, cut-out holes, feathers, and other eye-catchers. And best of all, your toddler can open each card and look inside it before moving on to explore others. A mother who made greeting-card books for each of her children told us they were far and away the favorite toddler books in her house.

Shopping Book

Many toddlers can recognize packages of their favorite foods in the supermarket. Why not make a book of package labels? Not only will your toddler enjoy looking at pictures of these familiar "objects," but you can also use this book for games that involve matching

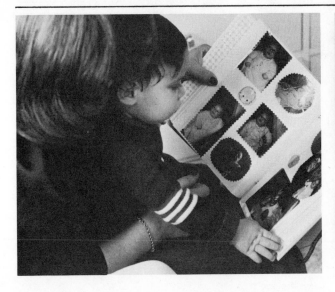

real objects to their pictured counterparts. To make this book, either cut pictures of packages from magazine advertisements, or cut the fronts off empty packages.

ALL-ABOUT-ME BOOK

You can also make a book all about your toddler. Choose some favorite snapshots that tell a very simple story about an aspect of her life: a typical day, a visit to Grandma's, her favorite facial expressions, or anything else. Paste the photos to pages, and then cover the pages with clear contact paper to prevent smudges on the pictures.

ZOO CREATURES

Take a camera along on your next zoo visit and make a book about the animals you see. A book like this is good for sound games, and a fun way to extend your zoo visit, too.

ANYTHING BOOK

Look through some old magazine or catalogues with your toddler. Whenever she finds a picture she really likes, cut it out and paste it on a page for her. This way she'll have the satisfaction of being the "author" of her own book.

To play action games with pictures you don't have to limit yourself to children's books. Suppose you're reclining on the couch with a favorite magazine and your toddler sidles up to join you. You can talk about the pictures of things you see in the advertisements. Use your imagination. In the background of that picture of a pretty model and her washing machine there's probably a lot of detail to point out.

Reading Stories

This is the other side of book play, when your toddler is content to listen quietly to a story. Such times will usually be right before a nap, when everyone else is drowsy in the late afternoon, at bedtime, or when your toddler first awakens in the morning. The content of a story isn't really important, because it's the quiet rhythm of your voice that she's paying attention to. But you might as well use this time to introduce her to children's stories. Pictures are helpful, because they give your toddler something to look at. But don't bother to play picture games now unless you want to. In fact, many parents have told us that when they read aloud, they try to discourage any activity except listening and looking. After all, the main purpose of this play is to give you and your toddler quiet time together, and (sometimes) to lull your toddler off to sleep.

Telling Stories

Many toddlers who won't sit still long enough for you to read them stories—except possibly at nap and bedtimes—love to watch you tell action stories. Use dolls or stuffed animals as your characters, and have them act out the plot. After all, that's how the *Winnie the Pooh* stories came into being: they were based on stuffed animals owned by the author's son. Stories can be as long or short as your toddler wants, and as fanciful as your imagination allows.

9
Music and Nursery-Rhyme Play

We don't need to convince you that your toddler likes music and rhythm. Chances are that, as a baby, he was soothed to sleep with lullabies, shook rattles, bounced and swayed to records, banged on cooking pots with spoons, and took great delight in nursery rhymes. This enjoyment of music and rhythm will continue through the toddler years—and, if your child is lucky, straight through adulthood.

Music play offers more than just enjoyment. Language development, body coordination, sound discrimination, and a sense of timing are a few of the other benefits of early exposure to music play and songs. Games involving music and rhymes can also save the day sometimes when your toddler is bored and irritable and a crisis looms ahead. Suppose your toddler starts getting fidgety on the bus. Just nimble up those fingers and launch into "Eentsy Weentsy Spider." Or say your toddler is squirming in his car seat and you know your destination is still far away. Try breaking out with some choruses from "Old MacDonald." Musical games are a wonderful way to share happily in one another's company wherever you may be.

Listening and Dancing
Almost every toddler we know loves listening and dancing to music. You don't need any fancy preparation. Just turn on the radio or stereo and let your toddler dance when and how he pleases. If you have a yen (and the time) to participate, hold your toddler in your arms so the two of you can dance together. Or let him stand on the floor, take his hands in yours, and waltz around with him. Try your best to follow his lead. If the song has a marching beat, march in a parade around the living room. Or if you're near a full-length mirror, dance together in front of it. Most toddlers love watching their own moving reflections.

What kind of music and when? You won't need to provide special children's records. Your toddler is too active, and his attention span too short for him to listen attentively to *anything* for long periods of time. He'll listen (and probably dance) for a few minutes, go on to another sort of activity, pause to listen again, become engrossed in a new task, listen attentively for a few more minutes, then proceed with something else. Any records you enjoy will most likely please your toddler also.

Many parents we've interviewed like to coordinate listening and dancing play for their toddlers with their own adult activities. For example, one mother turns on rhythmic music when she cleans the house. She says it makes her feel more sprightly about her work and gives her toddler something to do when he becomes bored with other tasks. Another parent switches on dancing music when preparing dinner. And since he's standing at the sink or counter anyway, he turns around periodically to join his toddler in dance. This musical background makes them both happy.

Recorded music isn't the only source of listening and dancing fun. You can make your own music with an instrument. You don't have to be an accomplished musician, either. One mother we know beats a pot with a spoon for her twenty-three-month-old to march to. She finds the simple beat of her makeshift drum is much easier for him to follow than the more complex rhythms of recorded music.

Music can be helpful in other ways. Remember: it "hath charms to soothe the savage breast." Mellow jazz or quiet symphonic music can help a rambunctious toddler calm down when you don't feel up to dealing with his boisterousness.

Making His Own Music

Toddlers like to make their own music, so simple musical instruments are wonderful toys for this age group. The sounds they make may not sound like music to you, but what accounts for taste? Here are several homemade instruments toddlers enjoy experimenting with.

Clappers: Two big wooden blocks with cabinet handles attached.

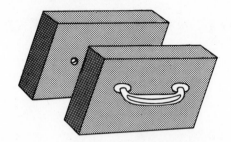

Two pieces of broom handle or wooden dowel to clack together.

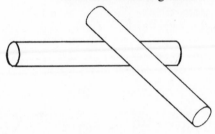

Pie-plate cymbals. Nail a small wooden block onto the bottom of each aluminum pie-plate for handles.

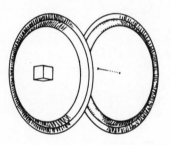

Shakers: Baby rattles.

A metal spice shaker with screw-on top filled with uncooked rice.

Jinglers: A regular schoolhouse-type bell.

Scrapers: Two clapper blocks covered with sand-paper (staple or glue it on).

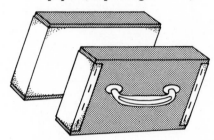

Scraper stick. Saw notches in a wooden dowel or a piece of broom stick. Then show your toddler how to scrape a wooden spoon over the notched stick.

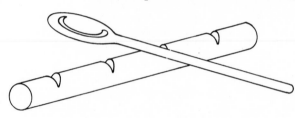

Bangers: Drums. These can be pots turned over, or empty coffee cans, or small cardboard boxes. Use spoons for drumsticks.

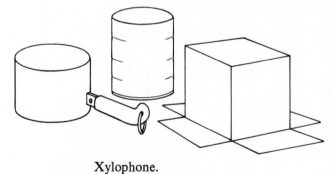

Xylophone.

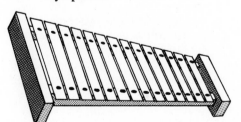

And, of course, it's nice to let your toddler experiment with *real* musical instruments if he has the interest.

Nursery Rhymes

For simple musical play together, toddlers of all ages love nursery rhymes with actions that parallel the words. "Pat-a-cake," "This Little Piggy," "Row, Row, Row Your Boat," and other standards from the infant years continue to be enjoyed. But unless you have a lot of experience with children, or a good memory from your own childhood, you may be stumped for new ones. So here's a compendium of nursery-rhyme games that toddlers we know usually relish. They can be chanted or sung.

Singing to Your Toddler

Your toddler will love hearing you sing even when you're not playing musical games together. You might be washing the dishes while he's playing on the floor. Or you might be working side by side with him in the garden, or folding laundry, or making beds. There's something special about singing that communicates real emotional involvement in life. And nearly everyone enjoys being surrounded by musical sounds.

Sometimes when you're singing, especially if the song is lively, your toddler will pause in his activity to watch your face, dance or sway, and even warble a few notes of his own. These little musical interludes are signs of his happy involvement with you even when you are both busy with separate tasks.

Your singing can also be a very pleasant part of your toddler's bedtime routine, especially if you gently rock him in your arms as you sing. The combination of soothing sounds and warm, intimate contact is a lovely way for you to end your day together.

At some point, your toddler may take an active interest in really singing songs with you. Of course, he won't be able to remember an entire song, but he can join in on the choruses, or croon along with familiar, repetitive lines. So when you both feel like spending some quiet time together encourage him to join your songfests. You don't necessarily have to stick with children's songs. Sing pop songs from the radio, or drag out standards like "Clementine," "Yankee Doodle," "Down by the Old Mill Stream," and "Baby Face." Anything you sing often enough will become familiar, and familiarity often breeds attempt.

As far as children's songs are concerned, most toddlers like ones that give them an excuse to make weird noises. In "Old MacDonald," for example, your child can join you in making the animal sounds. In "Pop Goes the Weasel" he can help provide the explosive POP. Encourage your toddler to join you on loud "Toot Toots!" after each line of "I've Been Working on the Railroad."

Eentsy Weentsy Spider

The eentsy weentsy spider climbed up the water spout.
Down came the rain and washed the spider out.
Out came the sun and dried up all the rain,
And the eentsy weentsy spider went up the spout again.

A younger toddler will delight in just watching you mime the spider's climb and fall. Later he may try to imitate your hand movements.

Where Is Thumbkin?

(Sing this to the tune of "Frère Jacques," or "Are You Sleeping?")

Where is thumbkin? Where is thumbkin?
Here I am, Here I am.
How are you today, sir? Very well, I thank you.
Run away. Run away.

Repeat with:
Where is pointer?
Where is tall man?
Where is ring man?
Where is pinky?

Two Little Blackbirds

Two little blackbirds sitting on a hill,
One named Jack and the other named Jill.
Fly away, Jack. Fly away, Jill.
Come back, Jack. Come back, Jill.

See Saw, Margery Daw

See saw, Margery Daw,
Jack shall have a new master.
He shall have but a penny a day,
Because he can't work any faster.

(As you sing or chant this one, rock your toddler back and forth on your knees or in a rocking chair.)

For more active body involvement, try these:

Ring Around the Rosy

(Join hands and walk around in a circle, falling down on the last word.)

Ring around the rosy
A pocket full of posies,
Ashes, ashes,
We all fall DOWN!

Here We Go 'Round the Mulberry Bush

(Follow each other around a chair or small table while singing.)

Here we go 'round the mulberry bush,
The mulberry bush, the mulberry bush,
Here we go 'round the mulberry bush,
So early in the morning.

The Mulberry Bush ditty lends itself to other applications. For example, you can substitute daily activities for the mulberry bush part, and pantomime them for your older toddler to imitate.

Here's the way we wash our face.
Here's the way we drink our milk.
Here's the way we eat with a spoon.

Or use this rhyme to teach your toddler simple actions that involve the names of body parts (again, act them out while singing):

Here's the way we clap our hands.
Here's the way we stomp our feet.
Here's the way we touch our nose.

Jack Be Nimble

(Tie an old necktie or piece of colored cloth between two chairs, low enough so it nearly touches the floor. Chant this rhyme as you step back and forth over the cloth, and encourage your toddler to copy you.)

Jack be nimble, Jack be quick,
Jack jump over the candlestick.

Those got you started; now go out and get some nursery-rhyme books so you can increase your repertoire.

If your toddler likes to sing along, you might start investing in some sing-along children's records. Then he'll be able to enjoy sing-along fun even when you're not available. You can also use these records for group sings, or for learning more songs that the two of you can sing when out for a walk, or riding in the car, or visiting someplace where there isn't a record player.

Good children's records are often hard to find, since most music shops emphasize the top pops over all else. Here are a few companies that ship children's records by mail. You can write them for free catalogues.

Children's Book and Music Center
5373 West Pico Boulevard
Los Angeles, California 90019

Folkways Records and Service Corporation
43 West Sixty-first Street
New York, New York 10023

Caedmon
2700 North Richardt Avenue
Indianapolis, Indiana 46219

10
Imitation Play and the Beginnings of Fantasy

Your toddler takes a keen interest in imitating things that you do. Such an interest isn't new. Even as a baby she imitated simple facial expressions (sticking out her tongue), gestures (waving bye-bye), sounds (babbling to your babbles), and actions (playing pat-a-cake, giving a kiss). Copying others is one way a child learns acceptable—and even unacceptable—social behavior.

During the second year your toddler tries to imitate more complex adult activities, and she'll try to participate in things you do that she feels are important. Her ability to walk and handle objects with skill enables her to try to copy lots of your chores: making beds, washing dishes, wiping floors, dusting, and sweeping. Naturally her interest in all of these jobs puts a burden on you: she's probably often underfoot, and what's more, many of the things she attempts are dangerous. Still, imitation is a good way for her to learn and practice new skills, so try not to discourage all her intrusions. Some of the suggestions given in the chapter titled "A Special Play Reference" will help you meet both your needs and hers.

Your toddler also engages in other forms of imitative play, the most common of which involves caretaking procedures and "self-help" skills. She "drinks" from an empty cup, "feeds" herself with an empty spoon, "washes" her face with a cloth, and tries to comb her hair. The difference between this kind of imitative play and her imitation of your work is that she performs these actions even when *you* aren't doing them.

And between eighteen and twenty-one months of age, this play undergoes an important shift: your toddler will probably begin to perform such activities on dolls and stuffed animals as well as on herself. She'll give a dolly a bath, put it to bed, try to undress it, brush its hair, "feed" it, hug it—in short, do for the doll all sorts of things that you usually do for her. This is the real beginning of fantasy play. In the coming years these scenarios will grow to include far more complex plots and other children.

Near the end of the second year, some toddlers also begin fantasy play involving vehicles. Rather than rolling a miniature car for the sake of rolling, they push it along an ill-defined track, making car noises, stopping and going as in a real car. If there's room, they might put dolls or miniature people inside the car for the ride. Some imaginative toddlers also pretend that their kiddie cars are real, and make "beep beep" noises while traveling the backyard highways. Or they sit in cardboard boxes, pretending to steer.

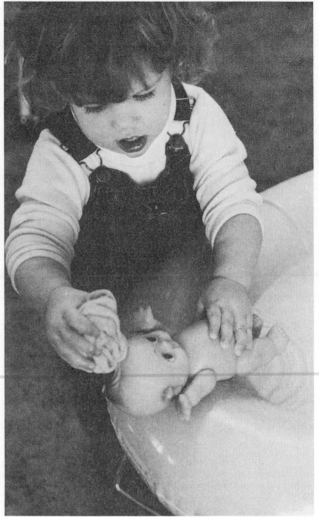

The Value of Fantasy Play

Many specialists have studied fantasy play, and many theories have evolved concerning its contribution to development. In fact, as is so often the case when lots of experts deal with a subject, there are so many theories that some seem to contradict others. There are two conclusions on which the specialists generally agree, however, and we think parents might like to know these.

1. Fantasy play is linked to creativity. Studies by Sara Smilansky and others have shown that children with very active fantasies tend to have personality traits that contribute to creativity: originality, spontaneity, verbal fluency, and a high degree of flexibility in adapting to new situations. Now, we can't be sure whether fantasy play causes this creativity, or whether the creativity inspires the fantasy. But there is a definite correlation between the two.

2. Children who fantasize a lot also have unusually good inner resources for amusing themselves. One study found that highly imaginative children are able and willing to sit still for longer periods of time than less imaginative children.

How You Can Help

You can't actually teach your toddler to make believe, just as you can't teach her to be imaginative. But you can encourage her natural gift for fantasy. According to Dorothy and Jerome Singer, in their book *Partners in Play: A Step-by-Step Guide to Imaginative Play in Children:* "While the capacity for fantasy or pretending is inherent in all reasonably normal human beings, the degree to which it is used by children depends to a large degree on whether parents or other adults have fostered it."

You can help foster fantasy play by—

providing materials that lend themselves to fantasy play.
making occasional suggestions and encouraging your toddler to try new ideas when she plays alone.
playing pretending games with your toddler.

Good Fantasy Toys

Dolls

Dolls are among the most popular fantasy toys throughout early childhood. The mainstay of your toddler's collection should be a simple rubber doll with molded hair and a painted face. Simplicity is important because the doll will be dunked in water, dragged through mud, stepped on, chewed, banged against the floor, and otherwise used and abused. Rag dolls are also favorites. They will receive rough treatment too, so make sure they're fully washable.

Doll-care Set

A collection of caretaking articles for her dolls will enable your older toddler to practice self-help skills as she plays with her dolls or stuffed animals. Take a small drawstring bag or shoebox and fill it with things like a brush and comb, a washcloth, a small cup, a play nursing bottle, and a doll-size blanket.

Doll Furniture

An older toddler might like some doll furniture, such as a doll bed and a play stroller. But don't buy anything exquisite; it'll just be destroyed. Of course, you can fashion some simple doll furniture from boxes and pieces of fabric. For example, a folded hand towel in a shoebox makes a terrific doll bed.

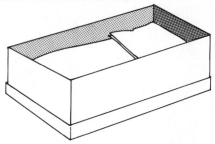

Stuffed Animals
Like dolls, stuffed animals are very popular; and like dolls, they'll get lots of use, so be sure they're washable.

Housecleaning Sets
A set of toddler-size housecleaning props will enable your toddler to participate when you go about your domestic chores. You can make a toddler broom and a toddler mop by just cutting your old broom and mop handles down to toddler size. And a homemade cleaning kit may be just the thing to keep your toddler occupied when you have to drag out your own cleaning supplies. Fill a small plastic bucket with real and imitation cleaning supplies: dust rags, a small scrub brush, empty plastic bottles (to take the place of your cleansers), maybe a small kerchief to wear on her head if you wear one. Remember: most real cleansers are poisonous, so your toddler shouldn't play with them. This kit will offer her a safe alternative.

Dress-up Clothes
Because of her fascination with the way adults look as well as with the things they do, your toddler might like experimenting with grown-up clothes. Take a box and fill it with your old accessories: scarves, gloves, shoes, and the like (real clothing is too hard to put on). Hats are special favorites, so collect a variety.

Some toddlers like wearing "disguises," so include a few of these: old sunglasses, eyeglass frames without lenses, and, if you can, wigs. A novel slip-on wig can be made from an old pair of pantyhose. Cut off the feet, cut each leg into three strips, and braid these to form pigtails.

Shoulder Bag

A shoulder bag like the ones parents often wear—for carrying wallets, cameras, books, or toddler necessities—can inspire a good bit of imitative play. Your child can use one of these for dragging her own things around in, too. Just give her a small tote bag with handles long enough to wear as shoulder straps, or let her have an old pocketbook you no longer use. Or make her a *special* shoulder bag all her own:

MAKE A SUPERBAG

This really is a superbag: it has a roomy compartment in the middle, and plenty of outside pockets for hiding and stuffing things in. (Hint: it's also great for adults to use.)

1. Cut the legs off an old pair of blue jeans.

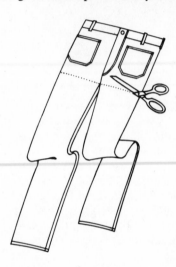

2. Turn what's left of the pants inside out and sew the leg openings closed.

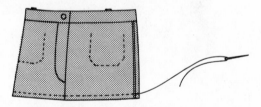

3. Turn the pants right side out again. Take an old scarf or a piece of rope about a foot longer than the waist, thread it through the belt loops, and tie the ends together. Pull up the excess rope on two opposing sides of the bag to make two shoulder straps.

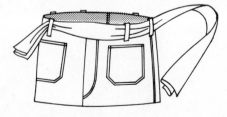

Play Vehicles

Cars, trucks, airplanes, and other play vehicles are indispensable toys throughout childhood, and now's the time to start building your child's collection. You might as well look for sturdy metal, wooden, and rubber ones, rather than cheap plastic, because your toddler will play with these for years to come. Small cars and trucks will fit conveniently into your purse for play on outings. And at home you might also provide a small empty box with one side cut off for your toddler to use as a garage.

You may recall that we mentioned wheeled toys earlier in this "Play and Playthings" section. We mention them again here as props for fantasy play because an older toddler does far more than simply roll her cars and trucks around. Just as she acts out real-life caretaking scenes with her dolls, she acts out real-life street scenes with her play vehicles. You can help inspire this type of fantasy activity by taking an active part in your toddler's play with vehicles. You might encourage her to drive her cars into a shoebox garage, or up the mountain slope of her sliding board.

Steering Wheel

In one child-care center we visited, many of the toddlers were fascinated by a toddler-size steering wheel attached to a wooden support at about chest height. This particular steering wheel had come from a store, but you can make your own version.

MAKE A STEERING WHEEL
You need

> a large wheel off an old wagon or doll buggy
> a block of wood, about 12″ square and 1″ thick
> a hammer
> long nail for attaching wheel
> two screw eyes
> two nails for hanging toy on wall

1. Attach the wheel in the center of the block of wood. Be sure you don't hammer the nail in so far that the wheel can't be turned.

2. Screw the eyes into the top of the block of wood. Then hammer the nails into your toddler's wall at an appropriate height and suspend the steering-wheel block from the nails.

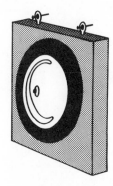

If you can't find a wheel, make one by taping a stack of eight or ten paper plates together around the edge.

Giving Words of Encouragement

Suggestions and encouragement from you can go far to increase your toddler's enjoyment of a fantasy scenario. By encouragement, we don't mean formal structuring.

A toddler is too young to follow detailed instructions. Rather, we mean elaborating on things you see your toddler doing, and suggesting ways she might extend the play. There's no formula to follow, because what you say really depends on the situation. You'll have to use your own—aha—imagination. You shouldn't be directly involved at all times, either. Just drop some hints as you go about your own tasks.

Here are some examples of encouragement, taken from our own observations of toddler play in homes:

One mother was washing dishes while her eighteen-month-old son, Shane, played with a large pot and spoon on the floor nearby. After he had stirred the empty pot for a while she said, "Are you making some soup, Shane?" She sniffed the air exaggeratedly. "It sure smells good. Can I have a taste of your soup?" Shane carried his pot to her and offered her the spoon. "Mmmmmmm, it's so good! What kind is it? I bet it's stone soup." He nodded proudly and went on stirring.

A minute later she asked, "Can you make another kind of soup, Shane? How about some teddy-bear soup. I'd love some teddy-bear soup." While she continued washing dishes Shane went into the living room, to appear a few minutes later with his stuffed teddy bear in the pot. "Bear soup," he said, again offering his mother a taste. "Yum, yum," she said, "that's even better. I love teddy-bear soup. How about making another kind. Can you make another kind of soup?" Again, Shane disappeared to return a few minutes later, this time with Raggedy Ann peeking out of the pot. "Ann soup."

A fairly simple five-minute exercise, but what happened here? The toddler "made" three kinds of soup, practiced saying some words, engaged in the social game of giving something to his mother—and all the while his mother got her own work done with minimal interruption.

We were photographing a mother bathing her six-month-old infant when her twenty-four-month-old

daughter, Jessica, came into the room. Realizing this was not a good time for a toddler interruption, the mother said, "Jessica, why don't you give your baby doll a bath like I'm giving your brother. She's over there on the floor, and she looks so lonely and dirty." Jessica got her doll and proceeded to wash it in the infant's tub, with her mother occasionally saying things like "Why don't you wash her hair?" and "Did you get her face all clean?" and "I think it's time to dry your dolly off."

Pretend Games to Play Together

TELEPHONE TALKS

Toddlers—and, for that matter, children of all ages—are fascinated by telephones. They're practically magic! Pretend someone is calling your toddler. Pick up the receiver on a toy phone (or a real one that's unplugged) and say something like "Just a minute, I'll see if she's home. . . . There's a phone call for you, Donna." Then hand Donna the receiver. A younger toddler will probably just listen for a few seconds and then hand the receiver back for you to continue the conversation: "Donna's just too busy to talk now. Can I take a message?" Then on with: "Oh, the phone's ringing again. . . . Here's another call. . . . It's for you again, Donna. I think it's Speckles (your dog)." When Donna's a bit older she'll probably jabber away when handed the receiver.

Give your toddler opportunities to talk on the real phone, too. Put her on when Mommy or Daddy calls from work; and especially when you talk to her grandparents.

Hold a make-believe conversation. Hand your toddler a toy phone while you take a real one (or another toy if you have it), and then stand across the room from her and "talk." If you shout loud enough, you can also talk from another room. These conversations will most likely be short and confusing, but fun.

For an older toddler, try adding a theme to the phone conversations. For example, call from another room and ask your toddler if she'd like you to bring home groceries, or maybe dinner. Then deliver a pretend pizza or something. If she likes this game, she might begin ordering things herself.

PLAY BEASTS

Get down on your hands and knees and pretend to be an animal. For example: "I'm a dog like Percival [the family pet]. I say, 'Woof, woof.' " Nuzzle your toddler gently with your head. "I just love to be petted. Can you pet me?" Then: "Woof! Woof! Woof! That means I love you to pet me." If your child likes this, go on to different animals.

An older toddler might like being a beast herself, so invite her to play along. "Can you be a dog (or cat or cow) like me? What does a dog say? He says, 'Woof, woof.' Can you say, 'Woof, woof,' like a dog?" Pet your toddler saying, "Nice doggie. Good doggie."

FEEDING THE ANIMALS

Set your toddler's stuffed animals on the floor and pretend to feed them. Dry cereals or even pictures of food can be used.

Playing family is a good way to elaborate on your older toddler's mimicry with dolls. Just keep it simple. For example, "You're the mommy and I'm the daddy [or Granny or Aunt Brunhilda or Uncle Rumplestiltskin] and your doll is the baby. This box can be her bed, and see this towel—this is your baby's blanket. I think it's time for baby to go to bed. Can you put her in bed? That's right. And can you tuck her in so she won't get cold? Now kiss your baby good night."

TAXI PLEASE

Push two chairs together to form a make-believe car. Let your toddler be the driver, and ask her to take you to the store, playground, or some other favorite place. If you have hung a play steering wheel on the wall, put the chairs in front of this.

ALL ABOARD

Two chairs, arranged one behind the other, form a fun play train. Seat your toddler in the first chair, as the engineer, and then you sit behind her, as the passenger, doubling as the sound effects. Encourage your toddler to join in making train noises.

LUNCH PALS

If your toddler has her lunch at a small table, invite her favorite doll or stuffed animal to sit in a low chair (or in a stroller) and join her. She might like feeding her pal some food with a spoon, so make sure it's a pal you can easily wash.

11
Outings

Homes are familiar and comfortable and secure and full of play-and-learning potential, but few homes can match the excitement of an outing. New places to explore! New things to do, and people to meet! New sensory experiences! Outings are little vacations to a toddler and terrific opportunities to learn new things.

This chapter is about places toddlers enjoy visiting and ways you can make these visits more rewarding. But before we go anywhere, here are some factors that should be taken into account before the start of any elaborate outing:

Your Toddler's Typical Behavior
Is he very active? Does he love running around? Then it's best to avoid places where he'll have to be confined for long periods in a stroller, backpack, or cart.

Your Toddler's Interests
What are the things he likes to see and do? If picture books are favorite toys, he might like a trip to the art museum. If he's fascinated by cars and trucks and trains, think about a transportation museum. If he likes animals, try a trip to the pet shop or zoo.

Your Toddler's Mood
Before you leave the house, think about your toddler's mood. If he's tired, he's not going to enjoy anything you do. Wait until later, or drop the excursion altogether. Once an outing is underway, it's a good idea to recheck your toddler's mood periodically. Even if he left the house chipper, he may become irritable as time goes on. Try giving him a snack if he starts to fuss: he may be hungry. Or let him rest quietly awhile. If the fussiness persists, it's best to call it a day. Otherwise you'll spend all your time trying to jolly him up (usually to no avail), and the outing will have lost its purpose, anyway.

Your Mood
Are you in a pretty good mood, equipped to handle the inevitable small hassles that will arise? No? Don't go.

The Available Time
Toddlers are dawdlers and rarely respond to "Hurry up!" So plan on having plenty of time, especially when you're taking a walk or when your outing includes errands. If you rush your toddler, be prepared for tears.

Keep Things Simple and Flexible
Don't plan an extravaganza, like zoo at 9:30, museum at 11:30, lunch in a restaurant with friends, etc. Shorter, simpler outings are more fun. For one thing, you can never predict your toddler's mood. If you've arranged something really special and he wakes up fussy, you're bound to be disappointed. Also, an overly elaborate outing may exhaust him—or you—and end up being called off halfway through on account of tears.

Bring the Experience Home
Even on outings as simple as walks, try to bring part of the experience home. For example, save a rock or leaf your toddler picks up. It can start, or add to, a collection. At the art museum, buy some postcard reproductions of paintings, and hang them on the wall at home or use them to make a book of your museum visit. You and your toddler can share this book many times, both to recall the outing and for general book play. If he especially enjoyed that last visit to the public gardens, you might buy a flowering plant or make a flower garden in the yard.

Toddlers' Favorite Places to Go

Parents in our group listed the following as their toddlers' favorite outings.

Neighborhood Walks

Far and away the favorite—in fact, most parents we know make walks a part of the daily routine. Walks can be long or short, goal-directed or aimless wanderings. Be sure to budget a lot of time because you'll stop frequently: to talk to passersby, feed and pet neighborhood animals, smell flowers, toss stones, examine cracks in the sidewalk, feel the textures of trees and buildings, look down sewer grates, and enjoy other such diversions. As you walk, talk about the things you see. Familiar landmarks are favorites. So are passing vehicles. Tell your toddler their names, talk about their colors and shapes, and try to imitate the sounds they make. He may join you in doing this. On walks with specific goals, talk about what you'll do when you reach your destination: "We're going to the store to pick up a gallon of milk, then off to buy you some new shoes since Rover ate your left sneaker." If you pass a mailbox, lift your toddler so he can shout into it. The echoing noise is terrific. If he shows particular interest in a found object, you might take it home with you, and use it to start a collection or scrapbook.

Most parents think of walks on nice days; but you shouldn't dismiss rainy or snowy walks. As long as both you and your toddler are well protected from the weather, excursions on sloppy days can be delightful.

Walks are more than enjoyable play and learning trips. They're also excellent for working off a little toddler energy. Parents of feisty toddlers know how necessary this can be!

The Supermarket

This is one of the best or one of the worst places for an outing, depending on your tolerance and your toddler's behavior. The parents we talked to had some quite contradictory feelings about supermarket outings.

On the positive side: a trip to the supermarket can be a terrific play-and-learning experience for a toddler. There are people to see and talk to, lots of activities to watch, and hundreds of fascinating objects for a toddler to look at, smell, touch, and, if you don't mind, taste. As you shop, you can talk about the products you select: what's inside a package, who eats it, why you like that brand, what you're going to do with it when you get home, or whatever. These are good language-

minutes. Once your attention is directed elsewhere, you can kiss your groceries good-bye."

"We put Justin in the seat and push the cart backwards. That way he can see where he's going rather than looking at our stomachs."

"When Angela tires of looking around and holding things, she gets a banana, which takes so much time to peel and eat that my shopping trip is almost finished by the time she's done with it. If by some chance she downs it too quickly, it's followed by a small box of raisins. Taking them out and stuffing them in her mouth takes Angela all the way up through bagging and loading the car."

learning experiences. Let your toddler handle some unbreakable items and, if he's able, drop them into the cart. The checkout counter is a good place for talking about money and, if this has been an expensive jaunt, the rising cost of living.

On the negative side: supermarkets can also mean smashed bottles, crushed fruit, ripped packages, screamingly bored toddlers, and frazzled parents. No matter how much play-and-learning potential a supermarket may have, the potential is useless if you can't shop and pay necessary attention to your toddler at the same time. If you constantly have trouble, try to leave your toddler with his other parent or a baby-sitter when you shop. Or else plan to shop for food when both parents can be present. Then one can play and teach while the other concentrates on really buying the food. If your toddler and the supermarket don't mix well but you have to take him with you unassisted anyway, try these parent-supplied hints for beating the supermarket blues.

"Stay away from large displays, keep the cart in the middle of the aisle, be careful what you put in the cart that's within your toddler's reach, and don't turn your back for a second!"

"Shop early in the day. The store is less crowded then, and you have less of a chance of running into someone you know. Why is this important? Well, you'll be less tempted to stop and chat for a few

Parks

Parks, playgrounds, gardens, and other public green spaces are perfect places for learning more about nature, or just for letting off steam through adventure play.

These sites also attract other families with children, so they're good places for making new friends. You might like to take along some books or other quiet playtime materials. And when you have the time and inclination, you might also include a picnic meal.

Zoos

Most toddlers love animals, and zoos offer a wide range of the more exotic ones. Beasts are not only fun to look at, they make wonderfully weird sounds. So zoos are excellent places for listening games. Visit the bird house. Some cries are shrill, some melodic, and some harsh. The great cats speak in throaty roars or high snarls.

You might like to prepare for a zoo visit by first looking at animal picture books. And expand the experience with more book play that evening. As you talk about each animal, try to make its sound.

Museums

Art museums are recommended for toddlers who like picture and painting books—and who have a better-than-average attention span. Talk about the colors, shapes, and familiar objects you see in the paintings. Many toddlers especially like portraits and landscapes.

Remember: art museums are only one of several different kinds of museums. You might also try visiting museums of natural history, science museums, transportation museums, toy museums, and so on.

Stores

Stores and shopping malls can be wonderful places to explore when you're there to look, not to buy. Then you can give your toddler all your attention. Use stores as you might a museum: talk about the different things to be seen in them. Favorite shops include pet stores, department stores (the escalators are magic stairs, the elevators fantastic time machines), and toy stores. You might take home a small reminder.

Libraries

For a toddler who enjoys books, library visits are special treats. Let your toddler look through any number of books, and check out some of his favorites for reading again at home. Try to find a library that has a special children's section. These usually have good book selections, carpeted floors, and toddler-size furniture. And the staff in these sections is apt to be understanding about a little noise.

YOUR Favorite Places

One reason why people go places in twosomes, threesomes, and moresomes is because it's so much fun to share new experiences with friends and loved ones. Well, your toddler is a friend and loved one, so share with him some of YOUR favorite places to go on outings. When you have a terrific time, chances are your enthusiasm will be infectious.

12
A Special Play Reference

So far we've talked about play and learning in what seem to be close to ideal situations: your toddler's in a pretty good mood, you're relaxed, your family is sharing pleasant experiences together, your toddler plays contentedly alone while you're busy elsewhere, or you have plenty of time to play with her in all sorts of creative ways that you both enjoy. So day after day, your child develops new skills and discovers more and more about herself, her parents, her playmates, and the world around her through satisfying play. That's the best part of the play picture. Here comes the flipside.

Of course, life with a toddler isn't always so blissful, despite what television likes to pretend. So here we present some survival tactics for frazzled parents, all of which have been tested and found helpful if not downright enjoyable with real toddlers in real families.

A COMPENDIUM OF FAVORITE GAMES

The following games, selected from this "Play and Playthings" section, were most often listed as favorites by our parent group. These are basics which nearly every toddler enjoys and which require little or no preparation. Keep this section in mind for those times when your child is eager for play and companionship, but you're too harried to think of some fascinating new activity.

When both of you are feeling energetic:

1. *Hide and Seek.* All forms and variations. You hide (around the corner, in the closet, behind the sofa, in another room, under a blanket) and call for your toddler to find you. Or reverse the roles. When you add a lot of variety, this game can go on indefinitely.
2. *Chase.* Chase your toddler around the house: behind furniture, up the stairs, into the kitchen: GOTCHA!
3. *Racing.* Run off some of your toddler's excess energy with races around the dining-room table, the outside of your home, the perimeter of your basement, or any other appropriate track. One. Two. Three. GO!
4. *Dancing.* Turn on the stereo or radio, sweep your toddler into your arms, and dance away. Or dance separately so she can watch and try to imitate you.

Or encourage her to dance alone while you watch. Dancing is a good game to share with your toddler when you have to be standing up anyway, say to wash dishes or sweep the floor. Then you can entertain your toddler and get your job done at the same time.

5. *Roughhousing.* Almost any form of exciting body contact will please your toddler. Swing her in the air, tickle her, butt heads with her, roll around on the floor with her, fling her gently onto your bed, give her airplane rides, lie down on the floor so she can crawl over you.

When you'd rather be a little quieter:

1. *Peekaboo.* Like hide and seek, this game never seems to lose its appeal for toddlers.
2. *Knee Rides and Nursery Rhymes.* When you both feel like sitting on the couch or in a chair for a few minutes, try some nursery-rhyme play. "Pat-a-cake," "This little Piggy," "Row Your Boat," "Eentsy Weentsy Spider," and "Where Is Thumbkin?" seem to be perennial favorites.
3. *Books.* Our parents ranked book play the number-one favorite. And we personally feel that books can never be overused, provided your toddler enjoys them.
4. *Handing Objects Back and Forth.* Handing things back and forth is a game many parents and toddlers enjoy. The objects used (snap beads, blocks, kitchen utensils, miniature cars, or whatever) can also be used in other types of play, but don't forget that giving and receiving is a fun game in its own right.
5. *Mirror Play.* Most toddlers love looking at themselves in a mirror. With a hand mirror, you can talk about parts of the face and the meaning of different facial expressions when you and your toddler are sitting together. If you use a wall mirror, you can also help her learn about other parts of the body.
6. *Looking Out.* For a quiet respite, look out a window or open door with your toddler, and talk about all the things you see.
7. *Naming games.* When you sit together, help your toddler learn the names for parts of her body. Or if she's not in the mood to sit quietly, carry her

around your house and name the things you see on walls, dresser tops, tables, desks, counter tops, in bookcases, and so forth.

8. *Catherine's Quiet Game.* One mother reported that her favorite game, and one of her daughter's, is "How Long Can Catherine Be Quiet and What Can She Hear When She Is?" This is a good game to play when you want your toddler to relax and be a little less vigorous. You might want to play it in the late afternoon when *you* need a little peace.

Here's how our mother describes the game:

"Catherine and I lie on her bedroom floor together and quietly listen. I usually talk about all the different sounds we hear, or ask her to identify them. I say things like 'I hear an airplane; do you hear it?' Or 'What do you hear now? Is that a dog barking? That's right; that's a dog barking. I hear the air conditioner going on again. Do you hear other children outside, laughing?' This game is really soothing for both of us."

PLAY TIPS FOR TOUGH TIMES AT HOME

As every busy parent soon discovers, sometimes your need to concentrate on an "adult" matter collides with your toddler's demands for attention. Here are some situations when such conflicts commonly arise, and suggestions for helping you deal with them.

Daily Household Activities

How do you get your housework done when your toddler wants company? Here are some of the hints our parent group supplied when asked this question.

1. Plan ahead!

"I do everything possible to avoid conflicts, and one of the best things I've done is to divide my household tasks into two lists: things I can do when Daniel is awake, such as laundry and dishes; and things I absolutely can't do: iron (because he might get burned), clean the bathroom, take a shower. These things I save for naptime."

2. Involve your toddler whenever possible. He usually loves doing what you're doing, and household chores are no exception. Participating in them makes him feel very grown-up. Besides, when he works alongside of you, he gets to practice lots of useful skills while you still get your work done—though admittedly not as quickly as you probably would without help.

"When I have to get work done, I get Alex involved in the activity as much as possible. Like, when doing the wash, I let him help carry the clothes to the basement and load the machine. Later he helps load the drier, and still later he helps me sort the clothes. When I make the beds he helps tuck in the sheets and hands me the pillows. When I clean the living room, I give him a rag to dust the furniture, or let him play with the vacuum-cleaner attachments. In the kitchen he helps me sort the silverware."

"If I'm watering the flowers, I give Amanda an empty watering can. If I'm working with tools, I let her handle one of them, or ask her to hand me things as they're needed."

3. When your toddler wants to help, but the task is too difficult or dangerous for him, start him on a similar task.

"One thing I need to concentrate on when I do it is sorting and answering mail. This is when I throw junk mail, empty envelopes, color catalogues, and other stuff on the floor next to my desk. Daniel plays with them so I can get the bills paid. This works extremely well."

"When I take a shower, I give him a pan of water and some water toys to play with on the bathroom floor."

"If I'm in a hurry to get dinner ready, I let Shane watch me from his high chair, and tell him what I'm doing. Or else I give him some unbreakable things to play with that let him feel he's involved: placemats, plastic cups, pots and pans, things like that."

4. When your toddler doesn't want to help, but does demand your attention (and you're just too busy to cooperate), take a minute to get him involved in something new and different.

In the kitchen, open up the pots-and-pans cabinet for him to explore. Or give him plastic containers with smaller utensils to play fill-and-dump with. Or drop some dried macaroni into a covered container for rattle play. Or let him stand on a chair at the sink and play with the water (be sure to stay close by). Or sit him in his high chair and put out some novel toys: a deck of cards, a crayon and paper (tape the paper to the tray), magnetic letters (if the tray is metal), a bit of dough (if you're baking), even just a few ice cubes.

In your toddler's bedroom, let him empty out his bureau drawers. Sure, you'll have to rearrange things later, but cleaning up is part of being the parent of a toddler. Or copy the strategy of this parent: "I have some shelves in Sam's closet with toys on them. This is usually kept shut, so when I open the door these toys keep him occupied a while."

In your bedroom, let your toddler empty low bureau drawers, or pull the shoes out of your closet. Place your pillows on the floor for him to jump and fall on. In the bathroom, give him some empty shampoo bottles to play with. Or if you're going to be in there for more than a few minutes, put him in the tub for a water-play session. Just be sure you keep an eye on him.

Or try some of these general tips.

"I block off an entire room, like the den, with a gate or playpen and let him explore at will."

"Sometimes I open the front door and put a safety gate across the space. She stands and looks out for really long periods of time."

"I turn on a record for Linda to dance to."

"When I know I'm going to be busy for a while, I try to give him a large selection of toys to play with."

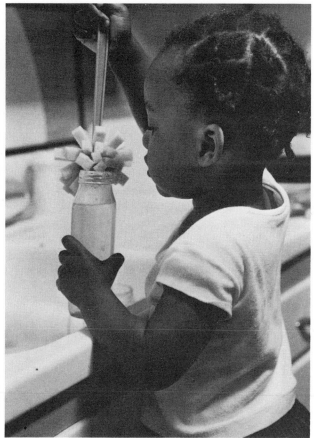

"I put her in a room with her older brother and ask him to be Mommy's helper. This keeps them both occupied."

"If I'm really desperate, I give him a snack, like a cup of raisins. He eats them one by one, so it takes a long time for him to finish." (One mother added a twist to this: she puts raisins or Cheerios in a small plastic jar with an easily-opened screw top.)

When all else fails, you can still try the direct approach, like this mother:

"When I'm really too busy to play and Catherine demands my attention, I tell her I am busy, I just can't play with her at the moment, she has to find something else to do, that's that and she just has to accept that fact of life. And you know, she usually does accept it."

Talking on the Telephone

It seems that every time the telephone rings, your toddler materializes out of thin air, like a genie summoned by rubbing a magic lamp. And because phone calls are usually unexpected, you don't have time to plan a task that will keep him occupied while you talk. So keep these hints in mind; they may reduce his interruptions to a tolerable minimum.

1. Ask your child to go get his play phone, so he can imitate your conversation. Or if you're foresighted enough, keep his play phone near your real one.

2. Instead of a play phone, give him a real phone that's unplugged.
3. Keep a jar of soap bubbles near the phone, and blow bubbles for him to watch and catch.
4. In the kitchen, hand your toddler a damp sponge and ask him to clean the floor.
5. Keep a roll of masking tape near the phone. While you talk, tear off a few strips and give them to your toddler to stick all over himself. Adhesive bandages, although more expensive, serve the same purpose.
6. Send your toddler on a simple errand: to fetch a toy or a pair of socks or something unbreakable from the coffee table.
7. If there's a ball within easy reach, roll it back and forth with your toddler or play "Go Fetch."
8. If the conversation just keeps going on, grab a newspaper or old magazine, crumple the pages into balls, and toss these to your toddler. He'll find all kinds of things to do with them.
9. If cuddling is what your toddler really wants, no

distraction is going to work. Hold him on your lap.
10. If all else fails, wind up the conversation as quickly as possible. You won't really be able to talk anyway.

Unexpected Visitors at the Door

You and your toddler are quite happily playing together when the doorbell rings. It's the termite exterminator, a girl scout selling cookies, the plumber coming to give an estimate on that backed-up toilet, or a neighbor with some news that "will just take a second to tell you." How do you switch from social play with your child to giving this unexpected intruder your attention?

1. Try the tips listed under "Talking on the Telephone."
2. Try some of the tips listed under "Daily Household Activities."
3. Give your toddler a snack if it's near snack time (healthy food, please!)
4. If time isn't of the essence, use your visitor as an occasion for a lesson. "See, Jordan, this man is a plumber. Can you say *plumber*? That's right, plumber. He fixes leaky faucets and broken pipes and stuffed-up toilets. Remember last night, when you flushed your boat down the toilet, and water ran all over the floor? He's the man who fixes things like that. He has a lot of tools in his box. Can you say *box*? Good." Your visitor might fidget a little while you educate Jordan this way, but you can deal with him later.

He fixes leaky faucets and broken pipes, and stuffed toilets... remember?

the evening. Otherwise, no one (you, your toddler, or your company) will be happy.

PLAY WHEN YOU'RE STUCK IN ONE PLACE

There are always special occasions when you and your toddler are confined to one place: when you're traveling by plane, train, or bus; when you're meeting someone at a station or airport; or when you're just waiting your turn at the doctor's office or children's shoe store or supermarket checkout counter. Sure enough, after a few minutes your toddler gets bored and fidgety, and then fussy. Because these are public areas, you especially want to keep her cheery. Here are a few hints for keeping peace with yourself, your toddler, and your fellow citizens.

A surprise bag, filled with intriguing toys and reserved for these special occasions, might help save the day. So prepare one beforehand. Take any simple drawstring bag that's easy for you to carry and drop in some appropriate travel toys. Choose things that your toddler can explore alone and that you can play with together. For instance, you might include—

an old toy that used to be her favorite. If she hasn't played with it for a while, it'll seem new again.

small cars and toy animals.

playing cards. These are messy, but often worth it. She'll use them for play dealing, sorting, bending, smacking together, and handing back and forth to you.

a few favorite books.

a cloth diaper or small towel for playing peekaboo.

a set of old keys you no longer need. These probably accumulate around the house. Put them on a special ring for your toddler.

Keep this bag in a handy place at home—maybe in the front closet by your toddler's coat. And right before you leave to go out, stick in a favorite comfort toy (teddy bear, blanket) and a snack (small container of raisins or dry cereal; bits of cheese and raw vegetables; banana; bottle of water or juice). If your toddler likes this special bag, take it with you when you visit grandparents or friends who don't have children. They rarely have appropriate toddler toys lying around.

If you're stuck somewhere without your toddler's special bag (because she *doesn't* like it, or there were unforeseen circumstances, or you forgot it), your purse is an excellent substitute—from your toddler's point of view if not your own. As one mother put it:

"When I'm strapped, I let Ellie play with things I ordinarily never let her play with. Like bandages. She loves unwrapping them and sticking them all over herself. I let her play with my wallet, my keys, my credit cards, even my change. Usually I never let her play with something so small as a penny, but if she's so supervised, sitting in my lap, there's really no danger."

Company Comes

As the past two situations suggest, a toddler can usually sense when a parent's attention is divided between him and another person. And most toddlers don't like this one bit. Even if your child was off happily playing by himself, the presence of another person—on the phone or in your home—often draws him to your side. Fortunately, phone calls and unexpected visitors don't generally claim your attention for more than a few minutes at a time. Your toddler is soon reassured that he hasn't lost you, and things return to normal. When one of your friends drops over for a lengthy chat, however, it's a completely different story. In the face of such a threat as this many a Little Mary Sunshine has turned into a Genghis Khan; a jealous toddler can thoroughly ruin a friendly visit between two adults. If this ever happens in your house, keep these suggestions in mind.

1. Try any or all appropriate tips listed in the previous sections.

2. After you've introduced your company to your toddler and settled down for a visit, bring out one favorite, fairly complicated toy and set it on the floor close to you. With luck, this will keep your toddler content for a while.

3. If your friend has a child, ask her to bring the child along. The two children *might* keep each other company.

4. Resign yourself to the fact that your attention will be divided. This isn't necessarily the most pleasant compromise, but it's often workable. And if your friend has children, she'll certainly understand.

5. If your toddler is almost always a terror around company, limit visiting hours to his naptime or in

Just exploring these fascinating objects probably won't keep your toddler occupied as long as you might wish. So join in her play. Use her toys for as many different games as you can invent. Or add some other games, not so dependent on props. Things like peekaboo, naming body parts, nursery rhymes, and lap games. If you're waiting in an office or store, carry her around and talk about all the things you see. On a bus, talk about what you see out the window. On a train, take a long walk through all the cars, stopping to explore the bathrooms, the diner or snack bar, and the water fountain, or to chat with other passengers.

Many active toddlers simply cannot tolerate confined spaces for more than a few minutes. If your child is one of these, take a tip from another mother:

"I've found the best thing to do is avoid confinement as much as possible. If we have to wait in the doctor's office, I ask how long it will be and then take Susan for a walk. And after our last trip, we've decided to swear off travel until she gets a little older."

Unavoidable airplane trips have been a special problem for many parents we've talked to. Flying and active toddlers just don't mix well, mostly because during a flight your toddler is confined to such a small space. Unless the plane is enormous and the flight perfectly smooth, you're not allowed to roam up and down the aisles to work off your toddler's excess energy. If a plane trip with your active toddler is in the offing, we

can add only a sympathetic pat on the back and these few suggestions.

1. Take along your toddler's special bag of tricks.
2. Try any and every game that comes to mind.
3. Have things to eat and drink handy. And be sure to let your toddler suck on a bottle of water (or milk or juice) during takeoff and landing. This will help relieve the pressure in his ears.
4. When the inevitable tears do start to flow, stay calm and grin and bear them. Your toddler's behavior is not your fault, and you're doing the best you can to cope. And take heart. Unless you're flying cross-country or across the ocean, the trip will last only a few hours at most. Besides, the hum of the engines helps to reduce the noise for other passengers: your toddler's cries won't seem as loud and obnoxious to them as they do to you.
5. Of course, you can always pretend you don't know that child sitting on your lap. But chances are you won't fool anyone.

THE DREADED LATE-AFTERNOON EDGIES

Late afternoon is usually the hardest time of the day. Parent and child are often tired and cranky; patience has dwindled to a minimum; other family members are arriving home, adding to the disorganization; dinner has to be prepared for everyone; and all-out war looms over the household. Here's how some families we talked to make it through. Some of these ideas might work anytime you and your toddler feel out of sorts.

Again, plan ahead. Your attention to meal preparation, rather than to your toddler, is often the culprit. So try to prepare the bulk of dinner during his afternoon nap, or even the night before if both parents work. Later, let him help as much as possible: breaking up lettuce for the salad, washing fresh vegetables in the sink, carrying napkins, taking things out of the pantry for you, and so on.

Hunger is another big cause of toddler edgies, so a snack might be in order:

"I let her eat things as I cook them. Like if I'm making a casserole, I give Zoe a few cooked noodles. Or I give her a slice of raw onion—she loves it. Or maybe a few raw vegetables before I steam them."

Try to have everyone rested and in a good mood whenever possible. You might try this ounce of prevention, suggested by a mother of two young children:

"I avoid late-afternoon hassles by preparing early. Around 4:30 or so, both kids are up from their naps but are sort of groggy and short-tempered, and I'm usually exhausted. So before Barry [her husband] gets home we all curl up and play on the floor or my bed, laughing, talking, and cuddling. I let Catherine [twenty-four months] play with Matthew [six months], or I read to them if they want a story; quiet stuff like that. After this brief vacation we all seem ready to take on the rest of the day."

THE DREADED LATE-AFTERNOON EDGIES

Fresh reinforcements are a big help in honing the edgies.

"When things get hassled and fussy before dinner, luckily my husband is usually home to take care of the kids. They go down to the playroom or outside to play."

"I send all the kids to a neighbor's house. All her kids have grown up, so she welcomes their visits. And, boy, so do I!"

"We have a set baby-sitter, a teenage girl, who stops by to play with Jason on her way home from school. It's a little expensive, but it's sure worth it to me. Plus they're great friends."

If you don't need both hands for cooking, try carrying your toddler around on your hip, and talk about chores while doing them.

Sometimes the fussiness is so bad you're just going to have to stop your tasks for a few minutes and spend time with your toddler. Cuddle on the couch, read a story, sing a song, look out the window, or enjoy any quiet shared activity. Or try this tip:

"When both Bryn and I are hassled and frustrated, the only thing that works is to change environments. We go from the inside to the outside, from one room to another, or from a noisy place to a quiet one, and vice versa. Change of scene, change of environment often leads to change of behavior—for both of us."

COPING WITH RAINY-DAY DOLDRUMS

It's rained and rained, and by the third or fourth day you've hit the play pits. We would love to be able to say, "Here's that perfect antidote to rainy-day doldrums!" But, alas, we have no fail-safe solution. Rainy days, like some unpleasant relatives and odors, are a fact of life and must be endured. But that doesn't mean you have to throw in the towel and spend the day gnashing your teeth. If all your energy hasn't been sapped by the weather, here are a few tricks to drag out.

1. A simple, but rarely-thought-of solution, is to trade parenting duties with another homebound parent. "If you'll take Todd this morning, I'll take Timmy after lunch." Chances are, the toddlers will have some fun playing together, and at least this way each parent gains a little solitary rest time.

2. Resign yourself to the fact that this is a wasted day, and enjoy something you might normally feel guilty about. Forget the household chores. Instead, let your toddler help bake a whole bunch of cookies. Save some for dessert, and wrap up the rest to give away as presents—if you keep them around, they'll all be gone by tomorrow. Lie in bed with your toddler and watch game shows and soap operas and tenth reruns of old comedies. Luxuriate in your leisure.

3. Try a special lunch. Fix something a little different from your usual noontime fare, then have lunch together with your toddler in an exotic place. Under the dining room table, perhaps, or on your bed, or on the balcony, or in a tent made from sheets draped over furniture, or on the stairs, or sitting on top of a large table so you can both look out the window.

4. Introduce your toddler and yourself to a new activity. Surely there are some games in this "Play and Playthings" section that you haven't tried yet. Maybe introduce some art activities you've always felt were too

advanced for your toddler. She might be ready. Or bake a loaf of bread from scratch. Your toddler can help mix the dry ingredients, knead the dough, and form the loaves.

5. Get out of the house. Take a walk in the rain. If you're both bundled up and waterproofed, you'll be o.k. Place newspapers or an old throw rug by the front door before you leave in order to save drippy cleanups later. Or visit a museum, shopping center, or similar public place where other families in a like plight may take refuge. After all, misery loves company.

6. If you're stuck at home and things get intolerable, ask a friend to come over and help you out. Maybe you and your toddler both need a little company to break the one-on-one monotony.

PLAYING IN THE CAR

Although some of us wish it were otherwise, the automobile is a ubiquitous fact of life. Most toddlers spend a lot of time in cars, and luckily, most toddlers enjoy car rides, at least for short trips around town. So playing in the car for brief periods of time usually presents few problems. When your toddler tires of looking out the window in silence, try to occupy him in these ways:

1. Talk about the things you pass. Embellish these narratives with descriptive words: talk about the colors of vehicles and buildings, the height of the trees, the noises animals make.

2. Sing along with the radio, and encourage your toddler to join in.

3. Ask your toddler to point to things: parts of his body, landmarks you pass, the traffic light, and so forth. Of course, you won't be able to tell if he's pointing correctly, but many toddlers like this game anyway.

4. If your toddler gets bored, hand him a small toy next time you stop at a light.

Longer automobile trips present more problems, because toddlers inevitably become restless after sitting still for more than an hour or so. So for these trips, you should make an extra effort.

1. Take your toddler's special bag of toys.
2. Keep snacks handy.
3. Sing.
4. If both parents are along, one of you can oc-

casionally sit in the back with your toddler and read stories, play peekaboo, or engage in any favorite games.

5. Talk about what you see along the road and at gas stations where you stop.

6. Special Hint: for short car trips, about three or four hours long, plan your departure to coincide with your toddler's regular nap or bedtime. If he's sleeping, he won't be fussing.

FORMING AN INFORMAL PARENT AND TODDLER PLAY GROUP

As part of our research for this "Play and Playthings" section, we spent many hours observing toddlers, both at home and in groups. Our objective was to learn about toddler play behavior in real settings, but we learned many more things. And one of the most important is that parents and toddlers benefit enormously from participating in play groups.

Many books stress what group play can offer toddlers: new friends, new play environments, new play materials, and new ways of playing, made possible by exposure both to other children and to different adults, each with his or her personal style. Less often discussed, but just as important, is what play groups can offer parents.

Now let's be honest. Raising a toddler is often a tough and somewhat frustrating job. You're bound to have periodic doubts and questions about your parenting abilities, especially if this is your first child. Am I handling problems correctly? Am I doing the best for my child? Am I doing things right? Am I a good parent? Chances are, yes. There are no absolutely "right" or "wrong" ways to raise a child. Each parent has a per-

sonal style. Groups give you a chance to discuss these personal styles, and to see that each parent does things a little differently.

Groups also give you a chance to talk about some of your problems, to listen to the problems of others, and to discuss how these might best be resolved. Groups offer you a chance to swap anecdotes about the trials and tribulations of parenthood, and to see that *every* parent has them. Such informal discussions can go a long way toward building up your confidence. And groups can give you a warm, friendly pat on the back for a job well done. No book, however well intentioned, can give you that!

On a more practical side, groups are a great place to exchange information: advice about where to buy toys and how to find baby-sitters; suggestions for new games; tips on handling rainy-day hassles; and household hints, like the best way to remove peanut butter from your upholstered sofa. Groups can also help you better understand your toddler's unique pattern of growth and development. If you watch the same toddlers play week after week, you'll quickly see how different each child is.

One more thing. Raising a toddler can get lonely. Nearly every parent likes some company, and looks forward to a little adult conversation. So do yourself a favor and organize a play group.

Play groups come in all sizes and styles. Unless you have a lot of experience, trying to start a full-size play group with equipment and rented space takes a lot of planning, time, and money. So we suggest you keep your play group small and informal to start with. The following guidelines will help get you started.

1. Find an interested group of friends. This is probably simple, because most parents are just waiting to be asked.

2. Decide on group size. Between three and five toddlers is a good size to start with.

3. Decide on location. Small, informal groups can take turns meeting in each other's homes. Be sure all houses have been toddlerproofed!

4. Discuss frequency and length of meetings. Work out a schedule that suits everyone's needs. You may want to meet once or twice a week, or even every day. One play group told us that they meet in the morning rather than the afternoon, because toddlers are perkier in the morning, and that two-hour sessions seemed to suit everyone.

5. Discuss your goals and philosophies. Certain de-

cisions should be made beforehand if the group is to run smoothly. For example: what are your goals for the toddlers? The basic goals of most play groups are that the children should enjoy themselves and be safe from physical harm. But you may want to add some more specific goals of your own. One group we know decided they wanted to include some structured activities as well, so for each group meeting, one or another parent prepared an informal curriculum centered around improving certain skills. One parent was in charge of music play. Another was in charge of exercises and body-coordination games. Another was responsible for art activities such as painting, drawing, and collage making.

You should also decide on your goals for the parents. Is this to be a parent-support group or just a play group–cum–baby-sitting service, where parents aren't expected to stay and participate? If you envision your play group as parent-support group, make sure everyone understands he or she is supposed to take an active part at all meetings. Clarifying your expectations at the outset will spare ill feelings later. You should also discuss each parent's philosophy of discipline. Questions about how to handle disciplinary problems like fights among the toddlers should be worked out in advance. You'll never get full agreement, since everyone has personal feelings about these things, but you can work out acceptable compromises.

6. Discuss the daily "schedule" for parents and toddlers alike. Will there be totally free play, or will there be planned activities? If all parents stay, how many (and which ones) will be responsible for supervising the toddlers while the rest talk? Or will the arrangement be more informal, with adults meeting in or near the playroom and drifting in and out as needed? There are no right or wrong ways, so try to find a way everyone is comfortable with. Planning ahead will spare some potential short-staffing problems.

7. Snacks. Make sure someone is responsible for a snack at each meeting. It might be the parent in whose house the group is being held that day. And decide on what type of snack—for toddlers and parents alike.

8. Keep the play group informal. This is most important. The formal-sounding guidelines listed above are just to help you get your play group started without some of the hassles brand-new groups sometimes encounter. When you actually have the group together, you should approach each session in a relaxed, informal way. We've found that too formal a situation tends to destroy the toddlers' spontaneity and harmony in free play and to turn the parents into rigid rulers. Remember: you're all there to have *fun,* to play and to learn, singly and as a group. So keep your meetings simple and enjoyable, and success is almost assured.

Bibliography

We suggest the following books for your further reading because we feel that each one can make a contribution toward better understanding both your child and your role as parents.

Health and Physical Care

Baby and Child Care, by Benjamin Spock, M.D. New York: Pocket Books, 1974.

Feed Your Kids Right, by Lendon Smith, M.D. Boston: McGraw-Hill, 1979.

A Sigh of Relief, by Martin H. Green. New York: Bantam Books, 1977.

Toilet Learning, by Alison Mack. New York: Little, Brown, 1978.

Your Baby and Child: From Birth to Age Five, by Penelope Leach, Ph.D. New York: Alfred A. Knopf, 1978.

General Parenting

The First Three Years of Life, by Burton White, Ph.D. Englewood Cliffs, N. J.: Prentice-Hall, 1975.

Kids: Day In and Day Out, edited by Elisabeth Scharlatt. New York: Fireside Books, 1979.

The Magic Years: Understanding and Handling the Problems of Early Childhood, by Selma Fraiberg. New York: Charles Scribner's Sons, 1959.

The Mother's Almanac, by Marguerite Kelly and Elia Parsons. Garden City, New York: Doubleday, 1975.

The Natural Way to Raise a Healthy Child, by Hiag Akmakjian. New York: Praeger, 1975.

New Ways in Discipline, by Dorothy Baruch. New York: McGraw-Hill, 1949.

The Roots of Love: Helping Your Child Learn to Love in the First Three Years of Life, by Helene S. Arnstein. New York: Bantam Books, 1977.

Supertot, by Jean Marzollo. New York: Harper and Row, 1977.

Toddlers and Parents, by T. Berry Brazelton, M.D. New York: Delacorte, 1974.

Special Problems

The Courage to Divorce, by Susan Gettleman and Janet Markowitz. New York: Ballantine Books: 1974.

The Half-Parent, by Brenda Maddox. New York: Signet Books, 1975.

How to Live with Other People's Children, by June and William Noble. New York: Hawthorne Books, 1977.

Part-Time Father, by Edith Adkin and Estelle Rubin. New York: Vanguard Press, 1976.

The Single Parent Experience, by Carole Klein. New York: Avon, 1973.

Talking About Divorce: A Dialogue Between Parent and Child, by Earl Grollman. Boston: Beacon Press, 1975.

Illness and Death

A Hospital Story, by Sara Bonnett Stein. New York: Walker and Co., 1974.

On Death and Dying, by Elisabeth Kübler-Ross, M.D. New York: Macmillan, 1969.

Talking About Death: A Dialogue Between Parent and Child, by Earl Grollman. Boston: Beacon Press, 1976.

Index

Maddox, Brenda, 171
Magnetic toys, 237
Manners, at mealtime, 36
Markers, felt-tipped, 251
Markowitz, Janet, 171
Meals (mealtime):
    manners at, 36
    See also Eating; Feeding; Food
Medicines, 196–97
Mehrabian, Albert, 54–55
Messes, from eating, 35–36
Milk, 32, 38
Minerals, 30
Mirrors, 204, 289
Modular system, 207–208
Moving to a new home, 171–73
Mud and dirt play, 249
Muscular Dystrophy Associations, Inc., 180
Museums, 287
Music play, 267–71
Musical instruments, 268–69

Naps, 46–47
National Association for Hearing and Speech Action, 180
National Association for Retarded Citizens, 180
National Association for Visually Handicapped, 180
National Child Development Study, 166
National Council on Family Relations, 170
National Easter Seal Society for Crippled Children and
    Adults, The, 180
National Foundation–March of Dimes, 179
National Hemophilia Foundation, The, Inc., 180
National Kidney Foundation, 180
Neighborhood walks, 284
Nelson, Katherine, 52, 56
New baby, 147–51
Newborns, personality differences in, 23, 26
Nightmares, 45
Nighttime wandering, 44–45
Noble, June, 171
Noble, William, 171
Nonverbal communication, 54, 57
Nursery-rhyme books, 58
Nursery rhymes, 269–71, 289
Nutrition, 30–32
    See also Food

Obesity, 32
Obstacle course, 227
Odors, 259
Office of Child Development, 177
Outings, 283–87
    rainy-day, 296
    libraries, 287
    museums, 287
    neighborhood walks, 284
    parks, 285–86
    stores and shopping malls, 287
    supermarket, 284–85
    zoos, 286

Pacifiers, 123–25
Pads and pencils, 251
Paints, 252–55
Paper play, 249–50
Parallel play, 138
Parents Anonymous, 170
Parents Without Partners, 170
Parks, 285–86
Peekaboo games, 242, 289
Peers, 135–43
    aggression toward, 141–42
    arranging for your child to meet, 136–37
    exploring, 138–39
    greetings between, 138
    parallel play with, 138
    sharing among, 139–40
    timidity toward, 137–38
Pencils and pads, 251
Personality differences, 23, 25–27
Photographs, for playroom, 203–205
Phrases, 52, 54
Picture talks, 263–64
Pictures, for playroom, 203
Plastic bags, 196
Play:
    adventure. *See* Adventure play
    artsy, 250–55
    benefits from, 185
    books and, 263
    in cars, 297
    when company comes, 293
    in confined spaces, 293–94
    cooperative, 142–43, 146
    definition of, 185
    designing your home for. *See* Designing your home
        for play
    dirt and mud, 249
    disabilities and, 178
    fantasy. *See* Fantasy play
    with fathers, 132
    friendship and, 135–36
    housework and, 290
    imitation, 273, 276
    late-afternoon edgies and, 294–95
    music, 267–71
    paper, 249–50
    parallel, 138
    parents' role in, 185–91
    for rainy days, 295–97
    sand, 247–48
    with siblings, 136
    social environment for, 186–91
    talking on the telephone and, 279, 291–92
    unexpected visitors and, 292
    water, 245–47
    See also Games; Peers; Roughhousing; Toys
Play groups, 137, 159, 297–99
Playpens, 215
Playroom, 203–12
    furniture, 211–12